Transport Economics

This book takes an interdisciplinary, institutional, and historically informed approach to the economics of transport, providing a more nuanced and complete understanding of human transport choices, individually and collectively, and the related choice of location, including the formation of cities.

The first principles of standard economic theory – referred to here as the core model – are systematically analysed, with a particular focus on the strengths and weaknesses of the simplifying assumptions used. The economic dynamics of modern transport systems are explored in light of theory and practice, covering such topics as the role of incentives, technological change and economic growth, and the enabling role that transport plays in productivity. Many historical and present-day examples are provided to explore the real-world nuance and subtlety that crops up repeatedly in transport activity, using additional disciplinary lenses such as planning, engineering, psychology, and sociology. Overall, the book examines the implications of the unique particularities of human beings, including the quirks of their psychologies and physical bodies, for transport planning, development, and implementation. A focus is kept on the "real world" policy complications that arise so frequently in the transport arena.

The book, while aimed at university students, will also appeal with its holistic, thoughtful approach to researchers interested in transport, urban planning, and its effective delivery. Policy-makers and practitioners seeking a broad overview of the field beyond their specialisations will also enjoy this book.

Cameron Elliott Gordon is Adjunct Associate Professor (Australian National University) and has been on the faculties of the City University of New York and University of Southern California; served on Transportation Research Board (TRB) programme committees; and worked in the US federal, and New York City governments.

Transport Economics

An Institutional, Policy, and Human Factors Approach

Cameron Elliott Gordon

Routledge
Taylor & Francis Group
LONDON AND NEW YORK

Designed cover image: Getty Images

First published 2026
by Routledge
4 Park Square, Milton Park, Abingdon, Oxon, OX14 4RN

and by Routledge
605 Third Avenue, New York, NY 10158

Routledge is an imprint of the Taylor & Francis Group, an informa business

British Library Cataloguing-in-Publication Data
A catalogue record for this book is available from the British Library

Library of Congress Cataloging-in-Publication Data
Names: Gordon, Cameron Elliott, author.
Title: Transport economics : an institutional, policy and human factors approach / Cameron Elliott Gordon.
Description: Abingdon, Oxon ; New York, NY : Routledge, 2026.
Identifiers: LCCN 2025007353 (print) | LCCN 2025007354 (ebook) | ISBN 9781032396811 (hbk) | ISBN 9781032396804 (pbk) | ISBN 9781003350866 (ebk)
Subjects: LCSH: Economics.
Classification: LCC HB171.5 .G638 2026 (print) | LCC HB171.5 (ebook) | DDC 330–dc23/eng/20250305
LC record available at https://lccn.loc.gov/2025007353
LC ebook record available at https://lccn.loc.gov/2025007354

ISBN: **9781032396811** (hbk)
ISBN: **9781032396804** (pbk)
ISBN: **9781003350866** (ebk)

DOI: 10.4324/9781003350866

Typeset in Sabon
by Newgen Publishing UK

Dedicated to the many transport colleagues who have guided me and collaborated with me over these many years. I couldn't have written this book without you. I express gratitude to you all. And, as always, I am very glad to have my wife, Josephine, the love of my life, by my side in all my endeavours, professional, and otherwise.

CONTENTS

BOXES

ACKNOWLEDGEMENTS

I am very grateful to colleagues who reviewed draft chapters of the book before publication and offered very valuable insights and guidance, most of which have been incorporated in the version you are reading now. These are, in alphabetical order: Corinne Mulley, Doug Hecox, Benoit Ladouceur, Yasen Markov, Robert ("Buz") Paaswell, Peter Rimmer, Roger Rooney, José Manuel Vassallo, and Glen Weisbrod. Special thanks to Glen Weisbrod who actually reviewed and provided extensive feedback on most of the manuscript. I also received valuable feedback from several anonymous reviewers. This book is a much better product than it would have been without the generosity of these individuals. Of course the responsibility for any errors, etc., is all mine.

ACRONYMS AND ABBREVIATIONS

AC	average cost
AFC	average fixed cost
AI	artificial intelligence
AR	average revenue
AVC	average variable costs
BCA	benefit–cost analysis
BCE	Before Common Era
BE	behavioural economics
BEV	battery electric vehicle
BRT	bus rapid transit
BT	behavioural transport
CBA	cost–benefit analysis
CBD	central business district
CE	common Era
CEA	cost-effectiveness analysis
CRS	constant returns to scale
CS	consumer surplus
DRS	decreasing returns to scale
DWT	deadweight tonnes
EU	European Union
EV	electric vehicle
FC	fixed cost
FCEV	fuel-cell electric vehicles
GDP	gross domestic product
GHG	greenhouse gases
GO	general obligation
GRT	Gross Registered Tonnes
GVW	gross vehicle weight
HIA	health impact analysis
HR	human resources

HSR High Speed Rail
IE impact analysis
IPE international political economy
IRS increasing returns to scale
ITS intelligent transportation systems
JIT just-in-time
JTW Journey to Work
km kilometres
KPH kilometres per hour
LOS level of service
LRT light rail transit
m metres
M&E monitoring and evaluation
MaaS Mobility as a Service
MC marginal cost
MCA multi-criteria analysis
MR marginal revenue
NEG new economic geography
NPV net present value
P Price
P&O Peninsular and Oriental Steam Navigation Company
P&R park and ride
PKM passenger kilometres
PPP public–private partnership
PS producer surplus
PV present value
Q quantity
RADR risk-adjusted discount rate
Ro-Ro Roll–on–roll–off
ROW right-of-way
RTS returns to scale
SCM supply chain management
SHEL software, hardware, environment, and liveware

SOE	state-owned enterprise
SWF	social welfare function
TAZ	travel activity zone
TBL	triple bottom line
TC	total cost
TCE	transactions costs economics
TEU	twenty-foot equivalent unit
TfL	transport for London
TFP	total factor productivity
TKM	tonne-kilometres
TOD	transit-oriented development
TR	total revenue
UK	United Kingdom
UPT	urban public transit
US	United States
VC	variable cost
VKT	vehicle kilometres travelled
VMT	vehicle miles travelled
VOTT	value of travel time
VTTS	value of travel time saved
WEB	wider economic benefits
WTP	willingness to pay

GLOSSARY OF MAIN TRANSPORT AND ECONOMICS TERMS

Accessibility: The potential ease of reaching, from a given location, desired or necessary activities and services, given the transport system available.

Active transport: Refers to any means of transport that does not require an energy source external to human power; essentially walking and cycling.

Agent, economic: The individual decision-maker and actor of economic theory, assumed to be rational, maximising, self-interested, atomistic, and disembodied.

Agglomerations: In an economic sense, any dense spatial concentration of economic activity such as production, consumption or residences and employers.

Agglomeration economies: A situation in which agglomerations yield economic returns directly because of the spatial densities they give rise to. Examples of such occurrences are labour market pooling, knowledge spillovers, and EOS in input markets.

Bypass effect (tunnel effect): A location's loss of accessibility in a network when changes in network infrastructure or other conditions (such as the building of a new arterial road that bypasses local roads) place it significantly outside higher speed links.

Car culture: A sociological term that refers to the entire bundle of human desires which include aesthetic, emotional, and sensory responses that incorporate the often intimate relationships people and groups have with their cars. More generally one can refer to mobility cultures.

Ceteris parabus: A Latin term that translates roughly as "all other things being equal", meaning that only one factor is changed in a before–after comparison, with every other operative parameter being held constant.

Circular flow: The conception of an economy as a constant cycle where consumers provide inputs to producers (mainly in the form of providing their labour) to enable production of outputs by producers which are then sold back to consumers, the cycle feeding upon itself over and over.

Comparative statics: The setting up of a theoretical scenario in which analysis is done by altering a single factor to see how a scenario changes and comparing the net change between the scenario with and without the alteration. This technique is widely used in economics. To work the method must be applied *ceteris parabus*.

Complement: A pattern in which the consumption of one good (e.g. petrol) is positively related to the consumption of another (e.g. car driving).

Consumer sovereignty: An assumption of economic theory that consumer preferences are independent of the larger economic environment, including production choices. The term also can refer to an implicit ethical standard of economic theory that consumer preferences and their maximisation should be considered as sacrosanct.

Core model: The term used in this book to refer to neoclassical economics with all its standard simplifying assumptions in place.

Cost allocation: The process of tracing and attributing costs to specific activities.

Cost function: An obverse side of a production function which maps out the relationship between production costs and inputs, technology and production levels.

Cost, common: A situation in which the production costs of two different outputs have a degree of separability that is not total and hence are partially common to both. An example is a plane that provides both cargo and passenger service on each round trip. The round trip cost of the flight delivering these two services is common, but there is some ability to adjust the cargo and passenger carriage and hence the costs of each segment.

Cost, external (cost, social): Any cost that is not internalised by market agents, e.g. pollution from one agent's production activities imposing costs on other producers and/or consumers but which are not borne by the polluter, and hence not included in the polluter's decision making.

Cost, fixed (cost, sunk): A cost that has to be taken as given and cannot be adjusted – fixed – within a given time-frame, usually the short or intermediate run. Fixed costs do not vary with the level of activity undertaken (e.g. overhead expenses).

Cost, generalised: The cost of travel consisting of its direct monetary expense (such as cost of petrol for a car) and the "welfare" costs to each individual taken up by the time it takes to travel, which is represented by lost satisfaction (disutility) due to opportunity cost.

Cost, joint: A situation in which the production of one output necessarily results in the production of another output, and thus, the cost incurred in producing the first output necessarily leads to the cost incurred in the second. A classic transport example is a cargo ship that carries goods to a port and then must eventually return home. The return trip is a necessary and inevitable outcome of the outbound trip. The only way to escape a joint cost such as this is to avoid the activity entirely.

Cost, opportunity: The cost entailed by a choice of one option over the next best alternative forgone.

Cost, specific: Costs that are fully identifiable and attributable to a specific activity of a production process. The wages paid to stevedores unloading a ship are an example of a specific cost, completely identifiable as an input cost separate from any other expenses.

Cost, transactions: A cost necessarily incurred in undertaking economic trades and bargaining in internal and external markets that do not contribute directly to production or consumption but which are required to allow production or consumption to occur.

Cost, variable: Costs that can be varied – and hence variable – within a given time-frame, usually the short-run. Variable costs vary with the level of activity undertaken (e.g. wages).

Demand: Total amount of a product or service desired by consumers in a particular market.

Demand curve: A graph of how much of a product or service is demanded by consumers at various prices at a given time. The curve can be for consumers either individually or in aggregate.

Demand, latent: Consumption that would occur if supply were available but which remains unrealised until supply is provided.

Density economies: A pattern of declining costs when output increases while the network extent (e.g. total number of kilometres) is held constant.

Derived demand: The assertion by economic theory that travel is seldom consumed for its own sake but is a means towards more desired ends and that the demand for travel depends on the characteristics of those ends, generally consumption and/or production activities.

Economic geography: The branch of economics that focuses on the three elements of market activity – production, consumption, and exchange – with the dimensions of physical space, time and embodiment incorporated into each one.

Economics of strategy: A field of economics consisting of the moving parts: (1) decision-makers, (2) goals, (3) choices, and (4) relationship between choices and outcomes. Much transport is bound up with business decisions of various sorts. The economics of strategy focuses in on the critical issues: (a) the boundaries of the firm, (b) a market or competitive analysis, (c) firm positioning and dynamics, and (d) internal organisation.

Economies of scale (EOS): A broader concept that includes RTS but also the effects of factors such as market prices and managerial capacity on net revenues obtained from sales as the scale of production increases.

Positive EOS refers to increasing unit net income from a given unit of input. Constant or negative EOS, respectively, refers to constant or decreasing unit net income as scale of production increases.

Efficiency: In a narrow technical sense, a condition in which maximum unit output is produced from a minimum unit input. In a broad sense, a condition in which economic processes maximise well-being across all consumers and producers.

Elasticity: The percentage change in one quantity (X) divided by the percentage change in another quantity (Y) – *ceteris parabus*; i.e. (% change in quantity X) ÷ (% change in quantity Y).

Elasticity, cross-price: The change in quantity of X demanded or supplied by an agent in response to a change in the price of some other good Y.

Elasticity, income: The change in quantity of X demanded or supplied as the income of the agent doing the demanding or supplying changes.

Elasticity, output: The change in an agent's output in response to a change in a given amount of input.

Elasticity (price): The change in quantity of X demanded or supplied in response to a change in the price of X.

Equilibrium (market): A balance point in which the price set for the good/service "clears" the market by exactly balancing supply and demand. Equilibrium can be partial, referring to balance in a single market; or general, referring to balance across a number of interrelated markets.

Equity: Fairness in distribution of resources and/or accomplishment of socially desired values and ethical/moral standards.

Externality: A cost or benefit that affects parties other than those involved in consumption or production transacted between those parties, and which is not reflected in market prices.

Financing: The form in which funding is delivered, e.g. debt versus paying out of current income.

Funding: Obtaining and committing scarce resources to a particular purpose.

Gross domestic product (GDP): A measure of national output generally calculated as the total product of an economy valued at current market prices.

Household production: A term that refers to all goods and services produced within the household but outside the market, such as home cooking, cleaning, and childcare.

Intermediate good: An input in a value-add process that is added between the raw material and final output stages to complete production. Transport is typically considered as an intermediate good.

Intermediate run: A period of time between short-run and long-run.

Long-run: A period of time long enough for all factors of production to be adjusted, including technology.

Macroeconomics: The branch of economics that considers the behaviour of the economy from the point of view of the economy as a whole and looks at the parts from that vantage point, not automatically assuming equivalence between additive sum and totality.

Marginal cost pricing: The condition in the core model in which, in a perfectly competitive market, the price (P) of any good will ultimately be equalised to the marginal cost (MC) of producing it and hence delivering efficiency in both production and consumption. The term also refers to any pricing scheme that sets the price of a service (like transport) equal to MC if the market is not doing so.

Market: The place, actual or conceptual, where goods and services are traded between buyers and sellers.

Market, thick versus thin. Thick markets are those with many buyers, sellers, and transactions. Thin markets are those with few buyers, sellers, and transactions. Thick markets tend to be more economically efficient than thin ones (*ceteris parabus*) because of the greater competition and information that comes with many trades rather than fewer ones.

Market structure: A term referring to how consumers and producers – demand and supply – are differentiated based, respectively, on the types of goods they buy or sell and how their operations are affected by competitors. Examples of market structure include perfect competition and pure monopoly.

Methodology, economic: The practices and procedures used by those working in the professional discipline of economic theory and analysis.

Microeconomics: The branch of economics that considers the behaviour of the economy from the point of view of its parts (such as supply and demand). When considering an entire economy, the whole is assumed to be equal to the sum of those parts.

Mobility: The basic meaning of the term refers to the ability of an agent to move across space. When considering relative transport advantages across different groups, the term refers to an individual or group's relative physical ability to move around and to take trips to activities outside the home.

Mode: Technical term for a means of transport. Modes are typically broken down according to medium (surface, water, air), vehicle (such as walking, car, or bicycle), and purpose (freight versus passenger).

Mode choice: Refers to the traveller's calculations of the choice of means to get to where they desire to go (e.g. car versus bicycle).

Monocentric model: A model of a city in which economic activity is located within one single spatial centre.

Neoclassical economics: A theory positing that for all economies, the following conditions hold: there is a total "endowment" of basic resources in a given economy (such as raw materials and labour effort); "commodities" are created out of these endowments in the form of composites from the basic resources of which they consist (e.g. wheat is grown from seed, soil, water, and human planting and harvesting); there are economic agents who consume these commodities and/or produce them (i.e. create them out of the resource endowments and application of labour, capital investment, and technical processes); consumers and producers trade with one another in some of exchange process; perfectly competitive markets deliver "optimal" outcomes in terms of economic efficiency.

Polycentric model: A model of a city in which economic activity is located within multiple spatial centres.

Price discrimination: A use of market power by producers to charge different prices to different classes of consumers rather than one marginal price for all consumers.

Price war: A market in which one firm cuts prices in the hope of trying to strike a knock-out blow to its competitors and become the dominant or only supplier. If rival firms then respond with price cuts of their own, this "war" of pricing can result in a cycle that drives prices sometimes down below production cost until a new economically sustainable equilibrium price is reached.

Production function: A conceptualisation of the production process of transforming inputs using technology to produce new (higher value) outputs. An archetypal generic model is $Y = f(K,L)$, where Y refers to total output, f refers to technology, and K, L refer to the inputs of capital and labour, respectively.

Productivity: A measure of the relative efficiency of an economy, typically expressed as units of output produced by given units of input.

Pure public good: A technical term that refers to goods (or services) that are non-rival in consumption (i.e. if one agent acquires a unit, other agents will, by definition, have access to it); and nonexcludable in consumption (i.e. one agent cannot keep others from consuming that same unit).

Pure private good: A technical term that refers to goods (or services) that are rival in consumption (i.e. if one agent acquires a unit, the other agents will, by definition, not have access to it); and excludable in consumption (i.e. one agent can keep others from consuming that same unit).

Quasi-public good: A technical term that refers to goods that are hybrids of pure public and pure private goods. Roads are an example, referred to as "club goods" because they are excludable in consumption but only partly rival since the use of the road by some drivers affects all other drivers in the form of congestion.

Rent, economic: Any unearned return garnered not because of any value-add by the owner but simply due to the mere fact of ownership itself. Land is a classic example of an asset that generates rents.

Rent gradient: The relationship between land rents and centrality of location within a particular city or local economic region.

Returns to scale (RTS): A technological relationship between input and output which determines the amount of output feasibly produced from a given amount of inputs with a given technology as the scale of production increases. Constant returns to scale (CRS) refer to a unit proportionality (one to one) between output and input as production scale increases (i.e. the average amount of unit output yielded from a unit of input is constant regardless of scale). Increasing returns to scale (IRS) refer to an increasing proportionality (unit output increases per unit of input as scale increases). Decreasing returns to scale (DRS) refer to a diminishing proportionality (unit output decreases per unit of input as scale increases).

Satisficing: A decision-making process in which one makes a "good enough" choice rather than the "best" one to economise on decision processing time and effort.

Short-run: A period of time short enough so that only some factors of production can be changed and/or changed to only a limited degree.

Substitute: A pattern in which the consumption of one good (e.g. petrol) is inversely related to the consumption of another (e.g. diesel).

Supply: Total amount of a product or service offered by producers to a particular market.

Supply curve: A graph of how much of a product or service is supplied by producers at various prices at a given time. The curve can be for producers either individually or in aggregate.

Taxation: The governmental power to compel private individuals and entities to surrender a portion of their resources to the public treasury.

Tax wedge: The difference between the pre-tax price and the after-tax price and the efficiency loss (deadweight loss) this engenders.

Time budget: The total amount of time an individual has available for all activities, including travel. There is a universal limit of 24 hours per day available to each individual.

Time–space convergence: The lowering of travel times via improvements in transport and other technologies and the building of new infrastructure which yields increased overall accessibility and lower transport costs across an area. This is contrasted with time–space divergence in which a deterioration of transport flow decreases accessibility and increases transport costs.

Transit-oriented Development (TOD): A policy of redesigning transit nodes to encourage and shape economic concentrations in ways desirable to consumers, producers, and residents, while also encouraging transit use.

Transport economics: An application of economic theory used to analytically model the choice to engage in transport, and the closely related choice of where to locate activity.

Trip chain: A series of linked trips, e.g. a journey from home to work that also involves dropping off children along the way.

Trip hierarchy: The idea that demand for travel consists of a hierarchy of linked choices, with decisions about where to work and where to reside at the top and these then dictating travel choices between sets of origin–destination pairs.

Utility: An economics term referring to the subjective satisfaction that economic agents get from consumption of goods, services, and activities given their individual preferences.

Value capture: The leveraging of some portion of future property value uplift caused by a transport investment and committing it towards funding facility building in the present.

Value of travel time (VOTT): A metric used to monetarily value the generalised cost of travel for travellers. This value varies widely by group, time-of-day travelled, and trip purpose (e.g. business versus leisure travel).

Value of travel time saved (VTTS): The standard benefit measure of any transport investment which comprises the total amount of travel time reduction delivered by a project valued at the appropriate opportunity cost.

Value uplift: Refers to the increase in land values caused by a transport investment, such as a new rail line. This is the basis for the amount of potential value capture possible in financing.

Value-add: The increase in value that each producer contributes to a product or service value across stages of production, from raw materials to goods-in-process, all the way through to final product.

Welfare (economic): Economic well-being as captured by total net consumer utility and total net producer surplus.

Yield management. The maximisation of revenue yields to a producer through the use of price discrimination for the service or product being offered.

USEFUL WEBSITES AND FURTHER READING

Below is a list of further reading, mostly contained in easily accessible websites or free e-books. All links are current as of time of publication. Links change frequently, and if these do not work, a search engine should uncover the latest web addresses. Many of these links go directly to transport-related sections of larger websites that often contain useful information in other areas. A look at the relevant home pages is always suggested.

Macroeconomics and microeconomics
Econ CORE (Curriculum Open-access Resources in Economics).

> Econ's vision is that a radically transformed economics education can contribute to a more just, sustainable, and democratic world in which future citizens are empowered by a new economics to understand and debate how best to address pressing societal problems.

Many free open-source textbooks are available across microeconomics and macroeconomics: www.core-econ.org/

Mathematical methods for economic analysis
A free basic text on mathematical analysis: https://mjo.osborne.economics.utoronto.ca/index.php/tutorial/index/1/toc

Transport economics theory
Transportation Economics Wikibooks: https://en.wikibooks.org/wiki/Transportation_Economics/Introduction. Authored by Levinson et al. 2016.

Course H 111 Verkeerskunde Basis, Basics of Transport Economics. A short introduction to fundamental concepts, prepared in February 2004 (updated August 2007) by L.H. Immers and J.E. Stada, for the Department of Civil Engineering at the Katholieke Universiteit of Leuven (Belgium). www.mech.kuleuven.be/cib/verkeer/dwn/H111part4.pdf

Economic geography
The World Bank, formally known as the International Bank for Reconstruction and Development, is a multilateral financial institution providing loans and grants to low- and middle-income country governments for pursuing capital projects. The *World Development Report 2009: Reshaping Economic*

Geography is a useful applied overview of the topic: https://openknowledge.worldbank.org/entities/publication/58557d74-baf0-5f97-a255-004829098l0a

The Geography of Transport Systems. 6th edition. Jean-Paul Rodrigue (2024), New York: Routledge. Official access to the online version of the book is provided here (along with other supporting resources): https://transportgeography.org/

Transport demand: users, modes, and cost

The Victoria Transport Policy Institute (VTPI) is an independent research organisation based in Victoria, Canada, dedicated to more sustainable transport, especially in the use of active modes like cycling, walking, and transit. A variety of resources are available free at: https://vtpi.org/

The International Association of Public Transport (UITP) is a global network of public transport stakeholders. Various resources are referred to on its webpage, although many of these are available in full to members only: www.uitp.org/. Headline data can be gleaned by mode by non-members here: www.uitp.org/data/#

Transport demand: health and the human body

The World Health Organization (WHO) is a specialised agency of the UN responsible for international public health. Basic statistics can be found in World Health Statistics 2023: www.who.int/publications/i/item/9789240074323

Transport supply: finance and funding

The US Transportation Research Board Committee on Revenue and Finance was part of the US National Academy of Sciences. The committee maintains an archived site containing information about transport finance, focusing on PPPs and distance-based charges.

https://sites.google.com/site/trbcommitteeabe10/#h.p_KnN8Ru3xu36q

The World Bank (see above) maintains a transport portal connecting the many useful resources: www.worldbank.org/en/topic/transport/overview

The Asian Development Bank (ADB) is multilateral regional development bank, headquartered in the Philippines that provides loans and grants to development projects in the region. Its transport research and data can be found at: www.adb.org/what-we-do/topics/transport. Research reports across a variety of topics are provided through the ADB Institute (ADBI). www.adb.org/adbi/main

Transport supply: Planning, managing, governance, policy, and political economy

The Organisation for Economic Co-operation and Development (OECD). The OECD is an intergovernmental organisation of 38 member countries, founded in 1961 to stimulate economic progress and world trade amongst high income nations. The OECD iLibrary is a collection of policy and research reports on all topics: www.oecd-ilibrary.org/. (Transport reports can be found by searching by "theme".)

The International Transport Forum (ITF) at the OECD is an intergovernmental organisation with 69 member countries that serves as a think tank and high-level policy coordinator for transport policy-makers, covering all modes and much of the developed world. It is administratively integrated within the OECD, yet politically autonomous. A wide range of studies and data can be accessed at: www.itf-oecd.org/. ITF data are available at: https://itf-oecd.org/transport-data-and-statistics

World Bank transport blog. A blog highlighting current World Bank transport research projects and programmes in the developing world. https://blogs.worldbank.org/en/transport

Transport markets: equity and fairness

Equitable Access to Transportation Systems: Getting Started. A website of the National Transportation Library of the US Bureau of Transportation Statistics of the US Department of Transportation. Contains many links to research, concepts, and American policies in the area.

https://transportation.libguides.com/Transportation-Equity

Transport markets: Economic evaluation methods

The UK Department of Transport maintains Transport Analysis Guidance (TAG), an overview of how the transport appraisal process supports the development of investment decisions to support a business case. www.gov.uk/government/publications/webtag-tag-overview

US Transportation Research Board Committee on Economics and Finance (TRB Committee AJE50) cost–benefit analysis website. Part of the US National Academy of Sciences, this site provides a guidebook to the principles and practices of transport CBA:

https://sites.google.com/site/benefitcostanalysis/

Transport markets: Logistics, freight, and value chain

World Bank Development Report on Global Value Chains (2020): www.worldbank.org/en/publication/wdr2020

United Nations Conference on Trade and Development (UNCTAD). UNCTAD is an intergovernmental organisation within the UN that examines issues of world trade in developing countries. Its Review of Maritime Transport (Biannual) 2023 edition is here: https://unctad.org/publication/review-maritime-transport-2023

Its transport, logistics, and trade facilitation page is here: https://unctad.org/topic/transport-and-trade-logistics

OECD freight portal. www.oecd.org/en/data/indicators/freight-transport.html

Transport markets: Resilience, sustainability, climate change, and the energy transition

The most current assessment of the current status of global climate change can be found at the International Panel on Climate Change (IPCC), 2023 Sixth Assessment Report: www.ipcc.ch/report/sixth-assessment-report-cycle/United Nations (UN)

– Act Now: website devoted to sustainability metrics among many areas, including transport.

www.un.org/en/actnow/facts-and-figures

– UN-Habitat. The United Nations Human Settlements Programme (UN-Habitat) is mandated by the UN General Assembly to promote socially and environmentally sustainable towns and cities. UN-Habitat is the focal point for all urbanisation and human settlement matters within the UN system. Its mobility and transport page is here: https://unhabitat.org/topic/mobility-and-transport

International Energy Agency (IEA). The International Energy Agency (IEA) is a Paris-based autonomous intergovernmental organisation providing policy analysis and data on the global energy sector. IEA transport data, some of it freely available here, can be found here: www.iea.org/energy-system/transport

Transport markets: Human factors

The Human Factors and Ergonomics Society (HFES) website. The Society "advances the science and practice of designing for people in systems through knowledge exchange, collaboration and advocacy": www.hfes.org/

World Health Organisation (WHO) Road Injuries Fact Sheet: www.who.int/news-room/fact-sheets/detail/road-traffic-injuries

Transport data sites

Our World in Data: Transport. A collaborative online publication that presents and maps empirical research and data showing how living conditions around the world are changing. The site covers a wide range of topics. The page dedicated to transport can be found here: https://ourworldindata.org/transport

OECD data portal. A portal to access searchable data and data analysis on a whole range of reports. www.oecd.org/en/data.html

UN Big Data. A collaboration between international agencies led by the United Nations Statistics Division (UNSD) and the International Civil Aviation Organization (ICAO) to provide policy-relevant high-frequency indicators for international trade, air travel, and maritime transport. This is an experimental venture generally not using official statistics, with estimates and methods in process. Its Dashboards on Trade, Travel and Transport are here: https://unstats.un.org/bigdata/task-teams/ttt-dashboards/index.cshtml

UN Statistics Division. Links to national statistical agencies for participating member countries. These statistical agency websites can then be queried for relevant transport data as well as a wide variety of other national data. https://unstats.un.org/home/nso_sites/

European Commission (EC). The EC is the primary executive arm of the European Union. Its research, policy, and data on transport can be found at its webpage devoted to "Mobility and Transport": https://transport.ec.europa.eu/index_en

Statista. Statista is a private firm that collates and analyses a wide variety of data across all sectors. Its webpage dedicated to transport and logistics can be found at: www.statista.com/markets/419/transportation-logistics/. Most of the information requires a subscription but some snippets and headline information can be gleaned from site pages.

SECTION 1

Transport economics basics

CHAPTER 1

Introduction

BOX 1.1 OPENING CASE STUDY: THE ECONOMICS OF THE NATURAL ICE TRADE

Before the invention of artificial refrigeration, naturally formed ice from mountains and lakes during the winter months was all that was available for use in cooling and preservation during warmer times and in warmer climes. While there was plenty of this renewable resource, transporting it from source to final use was largely impossible. There is a record of cut ice being shipped from the European Alps down to towns on the hot shores of the Mediterranean in the 1500s and a similar trade in some parts of the South American Andes (XV). (Discussion and page references in this section are from Weightman (2001).)

But it was industrialisation and global integration in the 19th century that transformed a localised niche activity into a complex economic process of major scale, scope, and impact. The New England region of the relatively new country of the US, with its cold winters and many pristine freshwater lakes, ponds, and rivers, naturally produced a huge stock of natural ice. And it was Frederic Tudor, a Massachusetts entrepreneur, who saw the potential of this stock with his plans in 1805 to export ice to Havana and Martinique in the tropical region then known as the West Indies (1).

How could one ship a literally melting asset for weeks from a very cold location to a very hot one? This was the key question in an era before refrigeration. Tudor was one of those classic figures, not entirely likeable or always admirable personally, who refused to let common sense or the contempt of his business peers put him off. Harvesting ice was relatively simple, since at the time no one owned lake ice, and there was abundant cheap labour during

DOI: 10.4324/9781003350866-2

the agricultural off-season of New England to literally chip away at the frozen surface into irregularly sized chunks (26–27).

Shipping was much harder. There was knowledge about how to insulate ice to keep it from melting too fast, but only for local preservation, not long journeys to very hot climates. Tudor bought his own ship for a maiden voyage to Martinique, stacking it with wooden boards, wood known to be a good insulator. A saleable amount survived to the destination, after which other shippers were ready to hire out their vessels to Tudor, allowing him to expand his operations (15). Ice was also a perfect ballast material, melting slowly if properly insulated, and, unlike rocks, not having to be expensively dug up at the origin only to be discarded at journey's end (29–30).

Once the ice was delivered, it had to be stored and brought to the customer's home, where added meltage could destroy further profitability. Indeed, this was a big problem in the Martinique business (20–22). Tudor solved it in his next market of Havana where, through trial and error, he perfected a wooden ice house design using nested timber chambers insulated with peat and sawdust which kept melting down to an economical minimum. These methods would be improved over time (44–45).

Tudor also attended to stimulating demand. Ice-creams preserved by on-board ice were an instant hit in all locations, but sales were insufficient to cover costs. Fruit similarly shipped, and thus nicely preserved, offered some profit, but not enough by Tudor's lights. So Tudor decided to initially give ice to bartenders for free, allowing them to serve cold drinks at the same price as warm ones for a limited period. This and other initiatives had the desired effect of creating a demand for cold beverages in hot climes, and, of course, the ice that made this possible. Once the Havana and Martinique markets became established, Tudor expanded to selling ice in the American southern states and British India (65–66).

As demand grew, ice harvesting techniques needed to be refined beyond early crude techniques. A man named Nathaniel Wyeth pioneered a method for scoring lake ice with a form of scythe pulled by horses or teams of men repeatedly until they became easily stackable blocks, minimising the amount of ice left behind in the lake, maximising the use of a ship's capacity and also, incidentally, further reducing the melting that occurred within the air gaps between rough cubes of ice. Wyeth soon became Tudor's employee (74–76).

The ice market continued to expand. Tudor added Baltimore and Washington, DC to his existing southern US markets, including the sizeable one of New Orleans. But relatively cold weather markets like Boston, New York, and Philadelphia became important too, as northern Americans, already acclimated to cold drinks in winter, wanted them in warm months as well, with intensified urbanisation and population growth steadily increasing consumer numbers, along with demand for ice by food producers to preserve meats, fish, and poultry (113–114).

By the 1840s, ice harvesting and shipping was a big market. Ice now had a value, even in frigid New England, and with increasing competition for supply, there was a need to establish property rights over it. Lake ice ownership was now determined by property frontage along the lake (118). Another previously "worthless" material, sawdust, also became a tradable commodity, given its superior insulation qualities for storing and carrying ice (129).

Once railways had arrived in New England, lake ice owners, including Tudor, lobbied for lines to be extended to them. A boom in ice house building followed to store ever-growing amounts of ice, both along the lakes where the ice was harvested and at rail terminals and ship ports where ice sat before being further distributed. This long-haul system was supplemented by an essential short-haul distribution system (*drayage* as logisticians refer to it) from storage terminals to final consumers (119–129).

In 1847, 52,000 tonnes of American ice were shipped down the east coast of the US to 28 different locations, carried in 258 vessels, with 23,000 more tonnes carried by 95 more vessels to foreign ports, including Calcutta, Madras, Bombay, various West Indian islands, Hong Kong, Whampoa, Rio de Janeiro, Batavia (now Jakarta), three ports in Cuba, and Liverpool (128–129). By 1855, this trade had more than doubled to 110,000 tonnes within the American domestic market and 48,422 tonnes to foreign markets. The only market that the US ice industry shipped less to was England, which now sourced its ice from Norway (157–158). A contemporary source estimated that $US6–$US7 million was invested in the "frozen water" sector (160), roughly $US212–$US247 million in 2024 dollars.

New England, where Tudor had originated the market (and who had largely retired from the business by mid-century), began to lose its dominance as an ice supplier, even within the US. Demand was growing across the country and local markets looked to source ice closer to home, with Midwestern urban centres using their frozen local lakes and the Hudson Valley towns of New York, such as Poughkeepsie, drawing from the often frozen-over Hudson River (164). Ice houses and fleets expanded in their turn, with the railways becoming an increasingly integral part of the distribution network, critically assisting with "last mile" distribution by the local "ice man".

Industrial customers had meanwhile become very important by the 1880s. Fresh food producers had long been fresh ice customers but now had much larger and diversified operations. The brewing industry, centred in Milwaukee, used ice to make lager all year long (previously it was only brewable in the winter). The Chicago meat-packing industry, notably the Swift and Armour companies, specialised in making and running ice-cooled rail wagons to keep and ship their product across the country. Specialist harvester-shipper concerns combined the two stages of production, while some producers, meat-packers included, bought their own ice supplies and harvesting operations (169–170).

Boom and bust in ice markets became a norm, with ice "bonanzas" being driven by times of especially cold weather in one area with particularly warm weather in another. When weather was warm everywhere, "ice droughts" were the result, leading to shortages, but bumper profits for those who had supply (175). The 1870s and 1880s were considered by some to be an "ice rush" in the US, enough so that the US Census finally began efforts to tabulate its activities. Previously ice harvesting had fallen between "mining" and "agriculture" and thus had been ignored by official statisticians. Now, in a special 1883 report, the US Census estimated that over 5 million tonnes of ice had been consumed in the US during the 1879–80 census year, with 8–10 million tonnes harvested, much of it sitting in ice houses (178–179).

At this point, though, stresses were beginning to appear. Increasing urbanisation was degrading and polluting some ice sources, with some local health authorities banning the cutting of ice near populated areas (178–179). Corruption and monopoly was also emerging, as it was through the rest of the US economy. A trust was formed in the 1890s to dominate Northeastern

FIGURE 1.1
Men delivering ice in the Netherlands in the 1930s, before refrigerators.

Source: National Archives of the Netherlands (Nationaal Archief). Spaarnestad Photo, SFA001020080. www.spaarnestadphoto.nl/ No known copyright restrictions.

cutting and distribution, squeezing supply into New York City, with the connivance of the municipal government which owned the entry ports. It was soon found that the Mayor was an important shareholder in the trust (184–185).

This proved to be the high water mark of the natural ice trade. Pollution was becoming an ever greater threat, and the widespread use of rail, with its regular occurrences of sparks, had emerged as a significant risk factor to wooden ice houses, exemplified by a disastrous 1910 fire in Maine, amongst many smaller incidents. Unstable market conditions created volatile supply and demand. All this was before artificial refrigeration emerged, ending the industry as a large-scale enterprise, though some rural US towns, and many European villages, still used ice boxes and ice men as late as the 1950s (188–189) (see Figure 1.1).

1.1 INTRODUCTION: A MORE FULL-BODIED APPROACH TO TRANSPORT ECONOMICS

Box 1.1 illustrates the importance of transport in the shaping of the modern economy, as well as the interplay between transport, urbanisation, industrialisation, and globalisation. A number of economic dynamics and concepts are present as well: the power of incentives; the centrality of the goal of profit (and other) maximisation; the role of technological change and economic growth; the enabling role that transport plays in productivity; and many other themes explored throughout the book.

But this historical example also indicates the real-world nuances and subtleties that occur repeatedly in the history of transport systems and economic change that do not always conform well to purely abstract conceptions. In the ice trade, transport was not just an "input" into the "output" of ice production, but a core part of the product itself, creating two different products in a sense, namely ice in a cold climate (or season) and ice in warm one. Transport considerations shaped organisational form constantly, especially as the form of transport changed from sail to steam to rail, affecting stages of production of harvesting, storage, shipping, and distribution along the way.

Supply and demand were also intimately related to one another, the boundaries between the two being changeable over time. Ice production and marketing was not simply a passive meeting of a consumer demand but played a role in stimulating, creating, and shaping that demand, which further shaped supply. While standard economic theory emphasises rationality on the part of all actors, consumer taste is often non-rational (e.g. emotional), as is, arguably, the motivation of rugged entrepreneurs like Tudor who carried on against major odds and often without clear reason for continuing on.

1.2 APPROACH OF THE BOOK

This book thus takes a broader approach to transport economics. As the opening case indicates, interdisciplinary and historical context can provide a more nuanced and complete understanding of the economics of transport, and the related choices of location of economic activity, including the formation of cities. Human development is a process and the path of the past is embedded in what we see today in myriad ways. So history is used here as illustrative, but also to bore down into how human transport evolved and what the nature of that evolution actually is. Institutions and their role in transport are given special attention. This term refers to organisations and other human entities, such as "rules of the game", that often serve as key mechanisms of cause and effect.

At the same time, the "first principles", premises, and basic dynamics of what is referred to here as the "core" theory of economics will be elaborated in some detail. Unlike many transport economics books that focus on higher-order applications of theory while taking the structure of that theory for granted, this one will elaborate the theoretical foundations to start with, in order to understand just what these foundations consist of, especially the assumptions that underlie them. This allows for a greater understanding economic theory's strengths, limits, applicability, and inapplicability as applied to transport in the "real world". To paraphrase Shakespeare, this is not to bury theory, but to praise and critique it in appropriate ways, and thus be better able to apply it in proper context in practice.

One particular framework that will be drawn on is the economics of strategy. Besanko et al. (2013, 6–7) define this as a field of economics consisting of the moving parts of (a) decision-makers, (b) goals, (c) choices, and (d) relationship between choices and outcomes (2). Much transport is bound up with business decisions of various sorts. The economics of strategy thus focuses on; (a) the boundaries of the firm; (b) competitive analysis of the market; (c) firm positioning and dynamics; and (d) internal organisation. The field is based in the "core" model referred to above. But it hones in more on the way actual marketplace institutions, especially firms, deal with economic problems and opportunities. In this book the focus will be, of course, on applications to transport.

While the book aims to be grounded solidly in economics, it is interdisciplinary in a genuine and fundamental sense as well. Economics is the base because it is so widely used and has penetrated deeply into even "independent" disciplines such as planning and political theory. Therefore, it must be mastered for that reason alone, as well as for the analytical power it does bring to many issues. But there are other perspectives that must be considered to gain a true understanding of the transport world as it is, and this must be done as more than mere adornment.

This book also takes a human focus, explicitly grappling with the undeniable fact that human beings are always involved in some way in transport decisions, plans, impacts, and consequences. The implications of the unique particularities of humans, such as the quirks of the human form, are largely unexplored in most treatments. This book will fill such gaps, both in specific chapters (such as Chapter 8 which looks at transport and the human body), and more generally throughout the book where relevant.

Finally, transport policy is, obviously, a widely discussed topic in most transport economics books. But this book will approach this theme in a more extensive manner in two ways. First, the various pertinent sub-fields of economics (e.g. fiscal federalism, public choice, and political economy) will be delineated and applied explicitly to applicable topics; second, the "ground truth" policy complications that arise so frequently in the transport arena will be a regular feature of the discussion. This includes issues arising in areas such as transport planning, engineering, financing, and operations and maintenance, among many others.

REFERENCES

Besanko, D., Dranove, D., Shanley, M., & Schaefer, S. (2013). *Economics of strategy* (6th edition). John Wiley & Sons.

Weightman, G. (2001). *The Frozen Water Trade: how ice from New England lakes kept the world cool.* HarperCollins.

CHAPTER 2

Basic elements

2.1 INTRODUCTION: TRANSPORT ECONOMICS AND THE "CORE" MODEL OF NEOCLASSICAL ECONOMIC THEORY

The data and history are clear: economic, population, and transport activity growth have all risen dramatically since 1800. But why? A much more elaborated theory is required to describe and attempt to explain the dynamics of transport and economic change, both historically and in the present day and beyond (Box 2.1).

Transport economics in its most widely applied form is drawn from an elaborated system of theory known as neoclassical economics which models the choice to engage in transport or not, and the closely related choice of where to locate activity. The basic structure and logic of neoclassical economics is referred to here as the "core" model, to distinguish it from various theoretical outgrowths that will also be discussed as relevant.

Because this model is so central, the first three chapters spell out its architecture in some detail, beginning with the underlying assumptions of the theory, most of which deviate greatly from observed reality. This unreality does not necessarily invalidate the model itself. But, as with any theory, there is a trade-off between the analytical powers of simplification it offers and the distortions it necessarily introduces.

DOI: 10.4324/9781003350866-3

BOX 2.1 INTRODUCTORY DISCUSSION: TRANSPORT AND THE SHIFT INTO ECONOMIC MODERNITY

Around 1750, a dramatic urban and economic turn got underway, primarily in Europe, in which the world grew more economically productive and urbanised with the start of the First Industrial Revolution. This turn had roots going back to the 1400s when a Commercial Revolution in trade and finance was well underway, dramatically transforming cities, trade and transport, and the European economy and society more generally. But this rise in economic activity dramatically accelerated with the dawn of the 19th century (see Table 2.1).

Between 1800 and 2000, global population more than sextupled, itself a dramatic break from the past prior to 1800, in which there was a significant expansion of the world population but one gradually unfolding over millennia. The first billion people were the product of tens of thousands of years. But it took only two centuries to add another 5 billion.

Urbanisation, which broadly refers to the proportion of the total population living in dense agglomerations, also intensified, with an almost 22-fold increase in the population living in cities during this period. This urbanisation has been enabled by a vastly increased ability to generate output from a given set of economic inputs, measured by Gross Domestic Product (GDP), which, on a global scale, increased by almost 84 times between 1800 and 2000.

All this output growth was based on an intensification of the extraction and usage of an ever more extensive range of resources, especially energy, which saw a roughly 22-fold increase in primary energy use over the 200-year span. This shows how much more resource-intensive modern economies have become; but also how much more efficient, since that proportionate increase in energy use supported an output increase almost four times larger.

Transport of people and things across the world has been a critical part of this process of economic and demographic change. In a raw sense, the sheer movements of people and things really exploded after 1950, along with almost everything else. In 1963, there was an estimated total global stock of around 177 million motorised vehicles, almost 97% of which were owned and operated within the rich Organisation of Economic Cooperation and Development (OECD) nations. By 2009, there were 1.2 billion such vehicles, with the OECD countries still accounting for a majority share but only around 56% of the total. During the same period, the sum of fixed landlines in 1963 was roughly 100 million, again almost entirely within the OECD. By 2009, the sum of landlines and mobile phones was 5.85 billion, almost 70% of these to be found within non-OECD (i.e. lower income) countries. Meanwhile, between 1965 and 2009, international airline

TABLE 2.1

Changes in selected socioeconomic and earth system trends 1800–2000

Socioeconomic trends	Year 1800	1900	2000	Units of measurement	Total increase 1800-2000 (factor of X)
Population	0.96	1.66	6.12	Billions people	6.375
Real Gross Domestic Product	0.47	1.89	39.33	2005 US dollars (trillions) (1820 data for 1800)	83.68
Urban population	0.08	0.27	2.86	Billions people	35.75
Primary energy use	20.0	49.4	434.4	Exajoule (EJ)	21.72

Source: IGBP (2015), selected measures and years extracted by author.

arrivals had boomed from 112.9 million to 882.1 million in 2009 (breakdowns between OECD and other countries are not readily available) (IGBP 2015).

More localised figures show these trends to be continuing but plateauing in various places. A detailed study of 25 mostly developed countries showed that travel as measured by vehicle-kilometres per person per year rose from a bit over 6,000 in 1963 to just less than 16,000 by 2010, in a steady growth pattern, despite some large changes in causal variables such as petrol prices and taxes (BITRE 2012, Figure 2.1, 12). However, this global metric had actually peaked around 2008, earlier in some countries, though not yet in others.

2.2 BASELINE CONDITIONS

Neoclassical economic theory starts by positing that for all economies, the following baseline conditions hold:

- There is a total "endowment" of basic resources in a given economy (such as raw materials and labour effort).
- "Commodities" are created out of these endowments in the form of composites made from the basic resources of which they consist (e.g. wheat is grown from seed, soil, water, and human labour).
- There are economic agents who consume these commodities and/or produce them.

- Consumers and producers trade with one another in some of the exchange process.

To summarise, commodities are made by producing agents from a given stock of resources available at a point in time and traded with consumers.

Three further sets of basic assumptions are added, with one focusing on the principal actor in the model, referred to as an economic agent; another focusing on the nature of material reality and the general environment in which the agent moves and makes decisions; and a third which sits over the first two which describes economic processes and structures in particular.

2.3 CORE MODEL ASSUMPTIONS ABOUT ECONOMIC AGENTS

The economic agent is an individual who is said to be:

- Rational (having consistent personal preferences and a logical and orderly cognitive approach to the world)
- Maximising (with limitless desires – more is always better than less)
- Self-interested (seeking to further one's own interests in the first instance)
- Atomistic (there is no inherent social connection or bonds between agents. All interaction is inherently transactional)
- Disembodied (agents have no physical embodied form)

2.4 CORE MODEL ASSUMPTIONS ABOUT GENERAL ENVIRONMENT

Agents work within a general environment in which the following conditions are present:

- Scarcity (there are not enough resources to satisfy all agent wants and needs)
- Costless transactions (interactions between agents, e.g. negotiations, entail no additional sacrifice of resources)
- Perfect and costless information (everything that can be known is known by all agents and there is no extra sacrifice required to obtain such information. There is also no cost entailed in processing and analysing available information, including using mental effort)
- Perfect certainty (all possible outcomes and their probabilities are known. There is risk regarding actual outcomes that eventuate – one can predict wrongly – but the distribution of possible outcomes is known with certainty)

- Timelessness (all actions take place and play out instantaneously; there is sequential action and prior cause and subsequent effect, but these take no time to unfold)
- Spacelessness (there is no physical space)

2.5 CORE MODEL ASSUMPTIONS ABOUT ECONOMIC PROCESSES

Additional characteristics are posited for economic activity in particular. There are some boundary issues between economic and non-economic spheres that are not spelt out explicitly. But if the activity is economic, one assumes the following conditions hold:

- An organised structure for exchange transactions exists, referred to as the market mechanism (Interestingly this mechanism does not arise organically out of the theory but must be postulated first)
- Markets are perfectly competitive (no agent has the power to individually affect a market price, nor any possibility for effectively colluding with others to do so)
- Markets always can potentially "clear" (whatever is brought to market for exchange will be exchanged at the right price. To put it another way, there is a price that exists at which those bringing something to market will always find buyers for it)
- Prices are completely flexible and markets always clear (the former being a means to achieving the latter since there is always a price that will clear the market)
- Perfect and fully specified property rights exist (each agent has a clear and enforceable legal right to whatever it is that they are buying and selling and that right will always be enforced. Given the assumption of costless transactions above, there is no sacrifice entailed in the acquisition or enforcement of rights)
- Constant Returns to Scale (CRS) in production (the scale of production does not affect the unit cost of production, i.e. the unit cost of production will always be the same regardless of how much is being produced)

2.6 CORE MODEL ASSUMPTIONS – OTHER "TECHNICAL" SPECIFICATIONS

Finally, it must be noted that there are assumptions of a very technical nature that are required to solidify some of the inferences made from the core model. CRS could be considered to be one of those, but it is enumerated above because it has significant implications for transport economics, as discussed later. Other assumptions consist of things such as restrictions to functional forms, spelled out in more fully operationalised models. To label these simplifications as technical is not to say that they are unimportant or uncontroversial. Some of the strongest predictions of neoclassical theory rely on them, and amongst economic methodologists in particular there is an understanding that these technical restrictions make models more tractable but sometimes more implausible as well. They are mentioned here for that reason, but consideration of them is beyond the scope of this book (see Neck 2022 for a more detailed discussion).

2.7 THE SUPPLY AND DEMAND PARADIGM

With economic agents posited to be rational, selfish, maximising, and atomistic, and with the other supporting assumptions laid out above, it is notionally possible to derive consistent and coherent schedules of consumption by consumers and production by producers; and, even more importantly, add up all these individual schedules up into aggregate consumption and demand schedules for each market. Economists refer broadly to consumption as "demand" and production as "supply", and the graph of consumption and production schedules as supply and demand "curves". Figure 2.1 presents a standard diagram of them. (For simplicity the supply and demand curves are depicted here as linear functions, though often they will be nonlinear.)

The initial demand curve here (labelled D_1) shows how much of the commodity being traded is demanded at various prices at a given time within a particular market. The supply curve (labelled S_1) shows how much of the commodity is being supplied at the same array of prices at a given time. In this case an equilibrium between supply and demand is found at a price of P_1 and a quantity of Q_1.

The strong assumptions outlined already allow for some correspondingly strong predictions to be made about the behaviour of these curves and their underlying functions. First, there always exist stable functions and curves. For example, irrational demanders and suppliers would likely be inconsistent about their pairings of prices and quantities, possibly precluding capturing their preferences in functions and curves at all. Adding the conditions that they are rational, and also self-interested, maximising and atomistic allows for the curves to be stable and for strong predictions to be made about their behaviour.

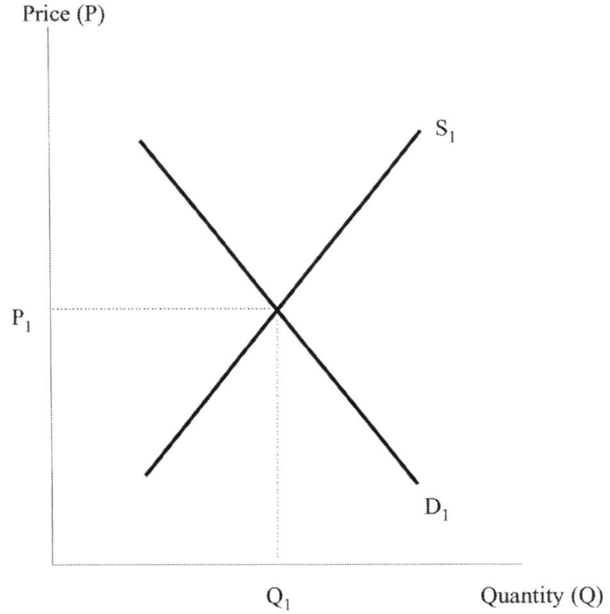

FIGURE 2.1
A supply and demand diagram.

The demand curve slopes downward from left to right, meaning that at high prices relatively little of the commodity is demanded while at low prices relatively more of it is sought. The supply curve, by contrast, slopes upward from left to right. Thus, at low prices, relatively little of the commodity is offered by the supplier while at high prices, relatively more is provided. These patterns are held to be so consistent as to be referred to as the law of demand and the law of supply respectively. Rational agents can be said to have some logical structure to their actions (they do not move about wildly or randomly); maximising implies that an agent will always prefer more to less, and hence demand (supply) more (less) as price decreases (increases); selfish atomism means that agents will form preferences independently of one another and be primarily concerned with their own advancement, so things like social relations and forces can be safely ignored.

Figure 2.2 illustrates that curves can shift, with demand in this case moving from D_1 to D_2 and supply moving from S_1 to S_2. The relationship between price and quantity for a supplying or demanding agent is indicated by a movement along the supply or demand curve. A given curve simply shows demand and supply changes as price changes, at given states of agent preference, income, and other background variables at a particular time. A shift is caused by a change in these background variables. For example, if

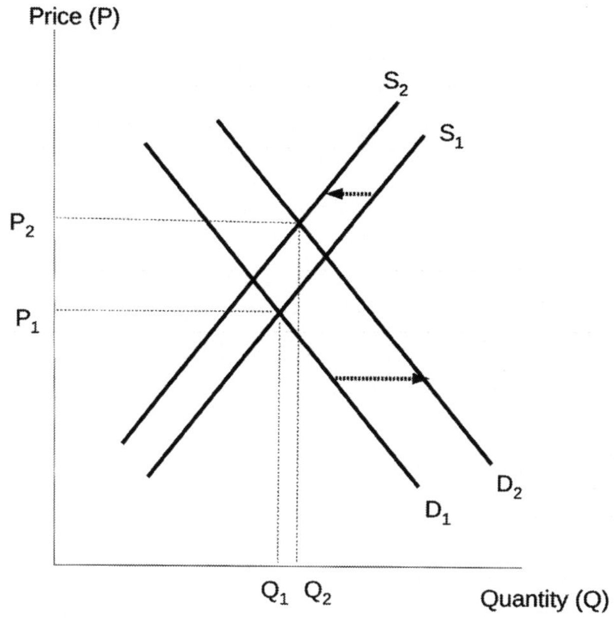

FIGURE 2.2
Shifts in supply and demand curves.

an agent's income suddenly increases, the demand curve will shift outward, as depicted here (all other things being equal, as economists like to say). A reduction in profitability of production of a commodity will similarly cause the supply cause to shift inwards, also as depicted here. The combination of shifts depicted here leads to a new equilibrium at a higher price of P_2 and a higher quantity of Q_2. There are many other scenarios that cause shifts both inwards and outwards with many differing equilibria resulting.

2.8 ELASTICITY OF SUPPLY AND DEMAND

The shapes of the curves indicate the responsiveness of supply and demand to various factors. A flatter curve indicates a greater change in quantity relative to a change in price. A steeper curve indicates the opposite, i.e. less change in quantity relative to a change in price. This responsiveness is summarised in the concept of elasticity. An elasticity is equal to the percentage change in one quantity divided by the percentage change in another quantity.

For supply and demand, one typically wants to know the price elasticity, which equals the change in the quantity of X demanded or supplied in response to a change in the price of X, calculated as: (% change in the quantity of a good supplied or demanded) ÷ (% change in the price of that good). By convention, for demand only, this division has a minus sign before it denoting that price and quantity are related inversely, as opposed to supply which has a positive relationship.

A few other key elasticities are:

Income elasticity: The change in the quantity of X demanded or supplied as income of the demanding or supplying agent changes

Cross-price elasticity: The change in the quantity of X demanded or supplied by an agent in response to a change in the price of some other good Y.

Elasticity of Output: The change in a producer's output in response to a change in the price of a given input.

To say that supply or demand is "elastic" refers to price elasticity, unless otherwise noted. Elastic demand means that the quantity demanded changes proportionately more than the change in price. Inelastic demand means that the quantity demanded changes proportionately less than the price change. The value of price elasticity will vary between 0 and infinity. If the demand elasticity is greater than 1 (i.e. more than –1 as per the convention above) then demand is said to be elastic. If the demand elasticity is less than 1 (less than –1) demand is said to be inelastic. When price and quantity demanded change in equal proportion – an unusual case – demand is said to be unit elastic. An example of the measurement of transport demand elasticities and their implications for policy is presented in Chapter 3.

2.9 LOCATION AND TRANSPORT IN THE CORE MODEL

In the core model, there are neither cities nor transport since space does not exist and agents are disembodied. There also is, as mentioned, no time. The relaxation of the spacelessness, timelessness, and disembodiment assumptions are the first steps towards applying the core theory to transport across physical space and the spatial agglomerations, such as cities, that occur. Production, consumption, and exchange are still assumed to be conducted by rational, self-interested, and atomistic agents, but now in embodied forms moving across a physical area.

Since overcoming friction is costly, economic agents, whether they are producers or consumers, set about minimising the costs associated with that friction. The two most obvious ways to minimise those costs are either to minimise the friction itself, i.e. locate so as to limit the distances which must be travelled; or minimise the costs associated with overcoming that friction, such as lowering transport costs through faster, cheaper travel as might be obtained through transport innovation or improved transport networks. These two strategies are interdependent. Concentration in space lowers transport costs (holding all other factors constant) while lowered transport costs allow for less concentration, with economic agents minimising their overall costs and maximising their overall returns through trading off between the two. These issues will be covered in more detail in Chapter 4.

2.10 "DERIVED DEMAND" AND UTILITY MAXIMISATION

Agents in the core model do not demand transport as an end in and of itself. These are rational, maximising agents, and transport is a cost that must be taken out of resources that they would rather devote to other ends. This makes transport a very unique "commodity" in that agents actually want as little of it as possible rather than more. Economists thus refer to transport as a derived demand, i.e. derived from the quest to satisfy more fundamental objectives, with the aim of minimising transport costs in doing so.

Economists argue that agents maximise their subjective satisfaction from the consumption of goods, services, products, experiences, etc., given their individual preferences. The technical term for this satisfaction is utility and economic agents are said to have a utility function which converts raw consumption inputs (e.g. attendance at a concert and eating a nice meal) into personal individual utility. The inverted twist for transport is that its consumption actually reduces agent satisfaction (a disutility in economics parlance). Agents will minimise the amount of transport they "consume" required to attain their desired commodities because of the disutility it entails. This is a very common view amongst transport economists, though it has been challenged (see Box 2.2).

2.11 TRANSPORT SUPPLY AND DEMAND IN EQUILIBRIUM

Formally speaking supply and demand in a transport market equilibrium consists of a constrained optimisation problem for agents individually and collectively. That is, agents are seeking to minimise transport costs but are constrained by the supply of transport, and, implicitly, by the interactions between one agent's demand and that of others. But even in the pure theory world, there is much more to this story.

On the supply side, if an agent chooses to walk, then, in effect, transport supply is provided by the transport demander, which obviously collapses the supply and demand curves into one. Many trips do require agents to use

BOX 2.2 TRANSPORT FOR TRANSPORT'S SAKE

Mokhtarian et al. (2001) argue that, far from being purely utilitarian in nature, transport often represents an intrinsic need for a movement that is deeply bound up with personal freedom and an innate desire for variety in life. They quote a variety of scholars across many disciplines who note that travel is both psychologically desirable and physically necessary for fitness, the two interacting with each other to allow a healthy balance between body and mind. Transport, they thus argue, should be considered as consisting of both intrinsic and extrinsic components. Travel can deliver "positive utility" in the form of the sensation of speed, exposure to different environments, a sense of mastery and control, enjoyment of beauty along a route, adventure-seeking, escape, and curiosity. This can be true of undirected travel, which is done for its own sake, and hence definitely intrinsic. But it also exists in many cases for directed travel in which people may choose to take the longer and slower way to their destination. It is therefore arguably more realistic to see the travel choice as being an interactive trade-off between the positive features of travel itself and the negative costs of travel sacrificed to obtain the desired ends at the destinations being reached (356).

There is, to be sure, a distribution of travel satisfaction preferences across the population. Many people, perhaps the majority, are primarily utilitarian in their travel choices, especially for daily routines like commuting. But there are others who cannot get enough travel, and even the average "typical" traveller undertaking mundane movements will sometimes meander just for enjoyment. This derives partly from human beings being territorial animals, with a travel instinct that goes beyond purely rational calculation (357).

Seeing travel as always or primarily a travel cost-minimisation exercise is thus likely too simplistic, at least in some settings. "Excess travel" beyond pure transport economising requirements is often found in examination of real-world choices, suggesting that transport is more like other goods, having both positive and negative characteristics which people weigh against each other to make a final decision about whether to travel or not. The standard assumption of transport being a derived demand may be good enough in many circumstances but not necessarily all (377).

means of transport beyond their own body, such as an automobile, in which case supply and demand curves apply once more. But travel of any sort usually requires infrastructure systems to support them, such as passable roads for automobiles and landing fields and air traffic control for aeroplanes. All of this constitutes transport supply but is not usually provided by a single supplier or in a single market. The provision of infrastructure in particular is not a seamless or automatic process generated purely by market dynamics as implied here. A collective decision-making and provision process for transport system investment is generally needed, and this typically requires organisations that are created and run outside, or at least alongside, markets, in most cases with some sort of government involved – an institution that the careful reader will have noticed has not yet been posited.

Also the form of the market for transport itself is not obvious. The core model assumes a market that is "perfectly competitive". But while it is easy to imagine, say, an open-air space for sellers hawking used goods along these lines, it is not obvious how a competitive market for automobile travel would look, with the sellers of automobiles, roads, energy stations, and parking spots all interacting with drivers and non-drivers with different kinds of preferences and transport needs. Much more elaboration is required to flesh out the workings of a transport market in practice (see Box 2.3).

2.12 "MACRO" VERSUS "MICRO"

The core model of transport economics is drawn from microeconomics and is the main focus of this book. Microeconomics considers the behaviour of the economy from the point of view of its parts (such as supply and demand). When considering an entire economy, the whole is assumed to be equal to the sum of those parts. Macroeconomics by contrast considers the behaviour of the economy from the point of view of the economy as a whole, and looks at the parts from that vantage point, not automatically assuming equivalence between additive sum and totality.

The "macro" view is most relevant to transport economics when considering productivity and economic growth over time. In this case transport is often viewed as an industry and/or an input into other industries, and how such linkages might increase or decrease measures such as Gross Domestic Product (GDP) per capita (GDP is a measure of an economy's total market output at market prices during a given interval of time). A basic construct for the "macro" economy is the circular flow model (see Figure 2.3).

In this very simplified construct, two sorts of economic activities take place: consumption and production. Consumption refers to the use of current resources to obtain some immediate end (such as eating or drinking). Production refers to the transformation of one set of resources to create a new "value-added" resource (e.g. bringing together wood, nails, a saw, and labour to produce a table).

BOX 2.3 IS TRANSPORT PLANNING NEEDED IN A PERFECT WORLD?

Transport economics is obviously only one of a number of transport disciplines, such as transport design, engineering, finance, and planning. The core model focuses on the economic aspects of the transport system only. So the omission of explicit consideration of things like how to build a structurally sound bridge, or how to raise money for a new road is understandable. These are important activities, to be sure, but are ancillary to the primary economic decisions and impacts that neoclassical theory focuses on.

Also, in the core model, all transport requirements essentially take care of themselves. Economic agents interact and compete with one another through markets and their autonomous processes yield all the transport outcomes needed, ranging from design, construction, and other sundry matters, including large system decisions such as where to locate cities and what infrastructure to construct.

But transport planning exists, as well as the related areas of urban and development planning, playing quite central roles, often outside market transactions. Economic theory suggests that this is because not everything important can be achieved through markets so intervention and coordination outside the market must occur in such instances. This can be for many reasons, to be discussed later, such as market imperfections or "failures", e.g. pollution caused by transport activity that the market will not take care of; or social values that markets are indifferent to, such as social justice. To this way of thinking planning is needed in cases where the simplifying assumptions of the model do not hold in the real world or where non-economic considerations are collectively judged to outweigh economic ones. In all other cases, the outcomes of well-functioning markets are to be preferred. Some economists have referred to "planning-versus markets" to capture this dichotomy.

However, there is also a significant ideological component here, in terms of beliefs about the world and appropriate ethical standards. The planning/markets dichotomy was actually coined during the Cold War, when there was a competition between centrally planned societies led by the Soviet Union, and market economies, led by the United States, with a notional contest between two visions (Banerjee 1993).

The demise of the Socialist bloc and the end of the Cold War threw central planning out as a desirable policy option for most societies. But planning more generally also became somewhat devalued with that turn. Planning, however, is especially important in transport and urban arenas, amongst others, and not necessarily just as an option to be used when markets "fail". It is no longer self-evident that markets always deliver an optimum, even economically, just as it has been long evident that planning can fail spectacularly at times, but can succeed in others. In this context "planning versus markets" can point to legitimate debates about approaches, without prejudging the choice, especially in a world of uncertainty and contested values.

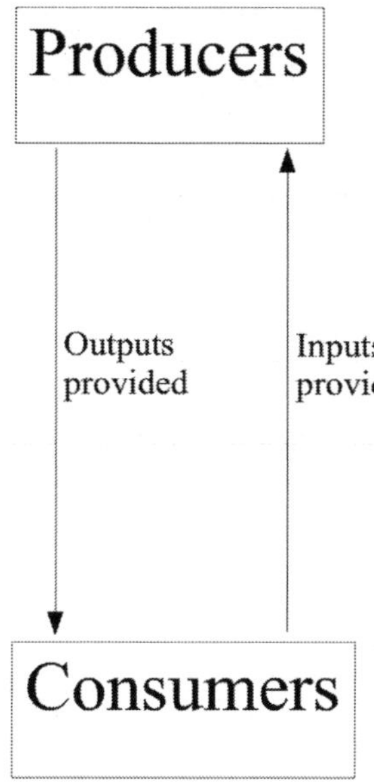

FIGURE 2.3
A circular flow diagram of an economy – real resource flows only (see text).

One might notice that this looks a bit like a circulatory system, and that is exactly the idea. The economy can be seen as a cycle where consumers provide inputs to producers (e.g. providing their labour) to help enable the production of outputs by producers sold back to consumers in an on-going feedback loop. There is a symmetry here with one agent's outflows being another's inflows. So consumers receive resource inflows from producers for their inputs, which represents outflows for producers. Conversely, consumers have an outflow of resources when they buy products from producers, which is an inflow for producers. (As an aside, the diagram presented here depicts only real resource flows, such as labour hours and product. Money flows and values will be added to this diagram in a later chapter. This is also a "closed" economy rather than one open to foreign trade, and there is no government sector. These will be considered later.)

A key macro question is the role that transport plays in total production and consumption. More efficient transport allows consumers to keep more of their income and time to devote to desired activities because improved modes of travel take less time and cost less money. Producers meanwhile will be able to lower the portion of their income that they have to devote to moving things around within their production processes. Resources within a circular flow are freed up to be devoted to new consumption activities and new business investments. The net result will be to increase the overall level of economic output within given resource constraints.

2.13 ECONOMIC METHODOLOGY

Methodology generally refers to the practices and procedures used by those working in a professional discipline. (The term also refers to the academic study of such practices and procedures but that will be not a primary focus here.) The methodology has already been implicitly touched on with respect to the simplifying assumptions that economists use within the core theory. But standard economic analysis is structured in other unique ways.

The first is a tendency in economics to focus on comparative statics. This refers to the setting up of a theoretical scenario and then altering a single factor within it to see how that scenario changes. Economists assume that the alteration is *ceteris parabus*, a Latin term that translates roughly as "all other things being equal", which means that only one factor is changed in the before-after comparison, with every other operative parameter being held constant.

The classic example is the supply and demand graphic already shown in Figures 2.1 and 2.2. The economist might ask what happens if income for all consumers increases by 10%, with every other parameter held fixed. This holding constant of all but one variable allows for the relatively confident prediction that total consumer demand will increase since, with more income, rational maximising consumers will spend more overall. This will likely shift the demand curve outward and increase the price of the goods being exchanged in the market (assuming, among other things, "normal" goods, which are discussed in Chapter 3). The changes that result between the initial state before the alteration and after it are then assessed to determine pre- and post-cause and effect due to the changed variable. If other factors, such as tastes, were allowed to vary as well, the likely outcome would not be so clear.

This method of analysis – the comparison itself and the fixing of all parameters except one – is highly restrictive – which is why the overall method is referred to as comparative statics: two "snapshots" in time are being compared, the actual paths in between largely inferred from end results. In practice, economists do employ methods other than these also, including dynamic analysis. But much economic theory is done statically, and much empirical analysis conforms to it as well. There is a lot of analytical power to such a method, but it obviously does have its limits since it suggests straightforward cause-and-effect between factors, which is not always the case in actual fact.

Two other implicit axioms aid this approach as well. One is the assumption that markets tend towards stable equilibrium and that such equilibria are ultimately optimal because agents are rational and maximising and, in a competitive process, will only be satisfied with optimum results. Once more, this is very clear with supply and demand analysis. If markets were unstable, did not tend towards equilibrium and/or these equilibria were not optimal, then comparative static analysis would either be largely impossible; or it would not be that useful in cases where movement was from one undesirable state to another, or where any optimum reached was very temporary.

There is still much more theoretical elaboration required to have a fuller working economic model of the economics of transport. More model development is needed and is presented in the next chapters.

REFERENCES

Banerjee, T. (1993). Market planning, market Planners, and planned markets. *Journal of the American Planning Association*, *59*(3), 353–360.

Bureau of Infrastructure, Transport and Regional Economics (BITRE). (2012). Traffic growth: Modelling a global phenomenon, Report 128, Canberra ACT.

IGBP (2015). *Great Acceleration*. International Geosphere-Biosphere Program. http://igbp.net/globalchange/greatacceleration.4.1b8ae20512db692f2a680001630.html

Mokhtarian, P. L., Salomon, I., & Redmond, L. S. (2001). Understanding the demand for travel: It's not purely "derived". *Innovation: The European Journal of Social Science Research*, *14*(4), 355–380.

Neck, R. (2022). Neoclassical economics: origins, evolution, and critique. In *The Palgrave Handbook of the History of Human Sciences* (pp. 1501–1540). Singapore: Springer Nature Singapore.

CHAPTER 3

Markets

3.1 INTRODUCTION: MARKETS AND EXCHANGE

Chapter 2 outlined the basics of transport supply and demand. This chapter bores down on the market, the place, actual or conceptual, where goods and services are traded between buyers and sellers in a series of transactions in which each transactor is seeking to close a deal where they are left better off than before the exchange. If there is no mutual gain possible, then no exchange will take place because everyone is assumed to be a rational maximiser and if one party finds no gain or, worse, a loss, they will not bother to participate (though in pure models of economics a transaction that leaves a party the same as before would say that person would be "indifferent", i.e. they could take or leave that transaction and might decide on it using a notional flip of a coin). Transactions in modern markets are conducted with money, and the market prices arrived at through exchange are said to be critical indications of true underlying resource cost and benefit (Box 3.1).

3.2 TRANSPORT MARKETS FROM A "MACRO" VANTAGE POINT

At the level of a national economy, economic activity is subdivided into broad categories. One approach is to look at aggregate components of total expenditure in a given period, usually a year. This relationship is captured in the formula:

$$Y = C + I + G + NX$$

DOI: 10.4324/9781003350866-4

BOX 3.1 INTRODUCTORY CASE: THE VALUE OF NONMARKET PRODUCTION

Although economic theory posits markets as centrally important to economic activity, there are many activities that take place completely outside of them, such as taking children to and from school, or cooking home meals. Economists refer to these activities as household production and consumption. Indeed, the Gross Domestic Product (GDP) metric, which measures the value of a nation's market output, significantly underestimates the actual value of production because it excludes goods and services produced by the unpaid labour of household members.

Economists have tried to measure the extent and value of these nonmarket activities. A seminal work is Chadeau (1992) who estimated that unpaid housework in the US, France, German, Australia, and Norway, using various years in the 1970s and 1980s, was equal to, or up to 20% greater than, the value of similar work done for payment in the market. A more recent estimate for Australia is that the market value of unpaid work, including volunteering, was equivalent to between 40% and 60% of Australian GDP in 2006, depending on how value and activity was estimated (PC 2017, Box 2, page 5).

Trends indicate that there is likely a relative decrease in the proportion of unpaid to paid work as busy people in wealthy countries increasingly "outsource" more of those activities to paid providers. Much transport activity, however, such as going to the store to buy groceries, is however still done outside formal markets and not captured in GDP. Official market data on the transport sector is overall reasonably good but does not give a full economic picture.

Many economists argue that even where formal markets do not exist, market dynamics may occur if there are self-interested parties bargaining with one another to arrive at self-advancing outcomes. For example, there are instances, such as parents paying children for chores or providing rewards for academic performance, where there are economic incentives in play. In this case the core model may still be applicable.

where Y refers to the market value of total output (e.g. GDP) consisting of

C = consumption
I = investment
G = government spending
NX = Net Exports

In practice, these are all very subtle and fluid categories. For simplicity, C refers to spending for goods and services in the short-run (usually within less than a year), while I refers to spending devoted to generating returns for the longer-term (a year or more). It is assumed that all funds not consumed in the short-run are saved and recycled into investment through the financial system or directly by those running businesses and reinvesting their profits (as discussed in Chapter 10).

The circular flow model discussed in Chapter 2 was simplified in at least two respects. There was no explicit government sector and associated expenditure (G), and there was a "closed economy" (i.e. one that does not trade with other economies outside itself). Sales of domestic goods and services to foreign countries are referred to as exports (X being the typical symbol), purchases from the outside world are imports (M being the typical symbol), and NX (Net Exports) is equal to X-M. The equation above thus captures all the major components of real-world circular flow.

Transport affects all of these. Rodrigue (2020) asserts that transport spending typically accounts for between 6% and 12% of the GDP of most high-income nations. GDP is a measure of income flows over a given period. When one considers wealth, i.e. the value of assets accumulated out of these income flows, the value of all transport assets, both infrastructure and vehicles, can equal close to 50% GDP for an advanced economy.

These gross numbers do not give a complete picture of how economically important transport services are. Transport is part of most producer and consumer activities and the core of freight distribution systems. Wealthy economy household expenditure on transport amount to around 10%–15% of household expenditures, on average. For manufacturing costs in high-income countries, the average is only around 4%, though this varies across business line and some service businesses, such as delivery companies, are focused almost exclusively on providing transport (Rodrigue 2020, Section 3.1).

Transport thus plays a vital role in the circular flow between producers and consumers. Most market activity cannot take place without transport of some kind and defects in transport can degrade the level and growth of a national economy and its sub-units. These impacts can be (a) direct, with transport directly entering into economic activity (e.g. commuting to work or delivering product to market); (b) indirect, with transport affecting non-transport activity (e.g. when the cost of commuting goes up sufficiently to make a particular area less attractive to investment and thus reduces business activity there); and/or (c) induced, which refers to flow-on effects from transport usage in one sector flowing to another (e.g. a reduction in transport costs for inputs into steel production then lowering the cost of steel and thus boosting production of industrial machinery) (Rodrigue 2020, Sections 3.1.1, 3.1.5).

GDP can also be broken down according to its distribution across consumers and producers. The total value of national output (GDP) will be the same as that derived from the expenditure framework, but the components of the total are calculated and measured differently. Conceptually the economy is treated like a big machine with a production function transforming inputs, via technology, to produce new (hopefully higher value) outputs. The archetypal generic model is

$$Y = f(K,L)$$

where

Y = technology (typically measured by GDP for an entire economy)
f = "technology" (which refers to any process that transforms and "adds value" to inputs)
K = capital (which refers to any physical asset devoted to production, such as machines)
L = labour (which refers to labour effort, as indicated, for example, by work-hours put into production by workers)

In this model transport is embedded within K, L, and f. But the model could be extended to explicitly include T – Transport – as an input into production, as well as energy (E) and materials (M):

$$Y = f(K,L,T,E,M)$$

T itself has a production function, which can be specified as follows:

$$T = g(K, L, E, M).$$

T can enter production directly (e.g. when raw materials are shipped from mines and farms to upstream processing points). But T also enters indirectly through L (as with commuters getting to and from their places of work) or K (as with machine parts assembled at different locations being transported between them). T also plays a role in "f" – technology – with many production processes transformed by transport inventions, such as the steam engine, the automobile, and the jet plane. The various measures of T (e.g. passenger-kilometres) can be considered as both inputs and outputs, depending on the context.

A final approach to looking at a total economy is by value-add components. Here economic output is broken down into its stages of production, from raw

TABLE 3.1

Simplified stages-of-production and net value-add for a milk producer

Stage of Production	Cost of materials ('000 $)	Value of sales ('000 $)	Net value added ('000 $)
Farm (raw materials)	100	200	100
Milk pasteurisation and packaging plant	100	250	150
Carriage of milk to retailers	250	400	150
Retailer	400	500	100
Totals	850	1350	500

materials to goods-in-process, all the way through to final product. Value added is the increase in value that each producer contributes to a product or service's value along the way. Table 3.1 provides a highly simplified template for a hypothetical milk producer. A farm produces the milk and sells it on to a milk pasteurisation and packaging plant for a net profit of $100,000. The value-add of this stage of production is $100,000. The plant purifies and packages the milk adding an additional $150,000 of net value. This plant then sells these packaged goods to a carrier to bring the milk to retailers. This is the "T" net value-add, which amounts to another $150,000. Finally, the retailer marks-up the final product it receives for a final net $100,000, with a total value-add across the chain of production of $500,000.

This is obviously a very primitive example applied to a single firm. But value-adds can be tallied up across an entire economy. Transport activity does add significant value by providing services to move things (and people) from one point to another. T is always an intermediate service, however (except for companies whose business is providing T). Because T is a service, it is not storable. It is usually delivered to consumers across networks, but is unlike many other network products, such as electricity, because unused network capacity available now cannot be sold later (Levinson et al. 2016, 125–126).

3.3 TRANSPORT AND PRODUCTIVITY

Productivity is a measure of the relative efficiency of an economy. Conceptually the term refers to the amount of output one gets from a given unit of input. For example, if there are two car manufacturers and one takes 100 labour hours and 10 hours of machine time to make one car valued at $30,000 and the other takes 50 labour hours and 5 hours of machine time to produce the same value, then one can say that this second manufacturer is twice as productive as the first because it uses half as many inputs to produce the same value of car. A broad measure of such productivity for an economy is referred to as total factor productivity (TFP) which measures the amount of general output produced by a given general set of inputs (also called factors).

Transport plays a key role in productivity. Efficient transport can deliver efficient access to raw materials, lowering production costs as a result, and increasing output per unit of input. Efficient transport also improves access of firms to labour generally and skilled workers in particular. These issues are considered in more detail later.

3.4 TRANSPORT MARKETS FROM A "MICRO" PERSPECTIVE

From a microeconomic theory perspective, the transport market consists of suppliers of transport services and users of these services. Transport supply refers to infrastructure, vehicles, and providers within a geographic area and period of time. The maximum traffic that can be handled by available supply is termed as capacity, while the geographic extent of the network is summarised under the term coverage. One can also consider the frequency of service. Transport can be provided on "own account", i.e. by the travellers themselves, using a vehicle (e.g. a car trip) or not (e.g. walking). Transport demand refers to the travel needs of agents, with a distinction made between consumptive and productive transport needs. In market equilibrium, as per the core model, the total amount of transport supplied will meet the total demanded and will do so efficiently since the price is set by market dynamics (Rodrigue 2020, Section 3.4.1).

Since transport is a derived demand, its level and characteristics are driven by underlying economic and social activity patterns. Transport demand can be stable and recurrent, as, for example, with many commuting patterns. Other times, transport demand is more unstable, e.g. during emergencies or crises or planned but one-off events such as a large concert.

Transport supply in the core model is assumed to follow transport demand. This is because demand in a sense cannot be realised without sufficient supply in the form of infrastructure, vehicles, and so on (walking being something an exception though even here trails must be available, though these may be naturally arising in many environments). But transport supply can exist without any immediate corresponding transport demand, and indeed often has to, especially for large systems such as highway or rail networks providing capacity even during slack periods, or, when newly built, before existent demand, which may or may not come to pass or may develop along a different than expected time-frame or form (Rodrigue 2020, Sections 3.4.2, 3.4.3).

Economic theory assumes that there only pure private goods, a technical term that refers to goods (or services) that are rival in consumption (i.e. with a fixed supply of goods and multiple agents, if one agent acquires a unit out of that supply, the other remaining agents will, by definition, have one less), and excludable in consumption (i.e. one agent can keep others from consuming that same unit). Private goods can be easily traded and priced, thus allowing for viable market transactions. But it turns out that not all goods (and services) are private in this sense, often the case with transport services. If some "publicness" of goods and services arises, then markets malfunction in various ways. These issues are discussed in detail in Chapter 13.

3.5 EQUILIBRIUM: GENERAL VERSUS PARTIAL

Equilibrium of supply and demand was depicted in Figures 2.1 and 2.2, showing the demand for the good and the supply of the good matching up at a single point in the middle. This point is at a price that "clears" the market by exactly balancing supply and demand. At prices lower than the equilibrium, demand for the good will exceed supply and at prices higher than that supply will exceed demand.

This equilibrium is a final result. This point is reached through feedback loops that are not explicitly specified in the core model. A negative feedback loop is an inverse relationship where an increase (decrease) in factor A causes a decrease (increase) in factor B. For example, if A refers to congestion on particular road and B refers to demand for travel on that road, then increased congestion reduces demand. A positive feedback loop, by contrast, is where an increase (decrease) in A leads to an increase (decrease) in B – a direct relationship. An example of this is where A is road capacity and B is travel demand, with an increase in capacity leading to an increase in demand for travel on that road (Levinson et al. 2016, 11).

These feedback loops are assumed in theory to tend towards equilibrium and to an economic optimum in a sort of see-saw dynamic where the oscillations diminish until there is stability in the notional middle, but of course, these loops can also lead to disequilibrium and/or a sub-optimum. Thus, if an increase in traffic causes new roads to be built, this, in turn, could lead to added travel demand to fill the new capacity. This could optimally equilibrate over time, but could also cause overshooting of demand beyond capacity, followed by undershooting, in a cycle that may take a long time to equilibrate, if it ever does (Levinson et al. 2016, 11). Still, in the core model, the system is posited to adjust over some time-frame in the end, with market price being the flywheel, so to speak.

Thus, far the focus is on a single market in isolation, something referred to as partial equilibrium. But there are typically many markets in an economy interrelated with one another, with equilibrium in one market, or lack thereof, causing equilibrium, or lack thereof, in one or more of the other markets. The presence of equilibrium in all related markets is known as general equilibrium, as depicted in Figure 3.1. (If markets are unrelated to one another, there is no meaningful general equilibrium since the status of one market has no bearing on any other one.)

An example of general equilibrium in a particular transport market would be the supply and demand for (a) steel; (b) plastics; (c) glass; and (d) automobiles. It is easy to see that the equilibrium of demand and supply in the market for automobiles will affect the equilibrium in the other markets and that equilibrium in the other markets will affect the equilibrium in the market for automobiles. This comes about in this case because the first three markets represent inputs into the output of automobiles. Thus, the amount of cars that a society creates will have a major impact on the amount of steel, plastics, and glass that will be created and vice-versa.

Although general equilibrium conceivably can encompass all markets for an economy, this is a sum-of-the-parts analysis. Microeconomic theory assumes that all individual markets can in fact be added up to get a total impression because the behaviour of the whole will act exactly as the sum of the parts would. This may not always be the case and is the main reason that the field of macroeconomics exists in the first place, i.e. that there

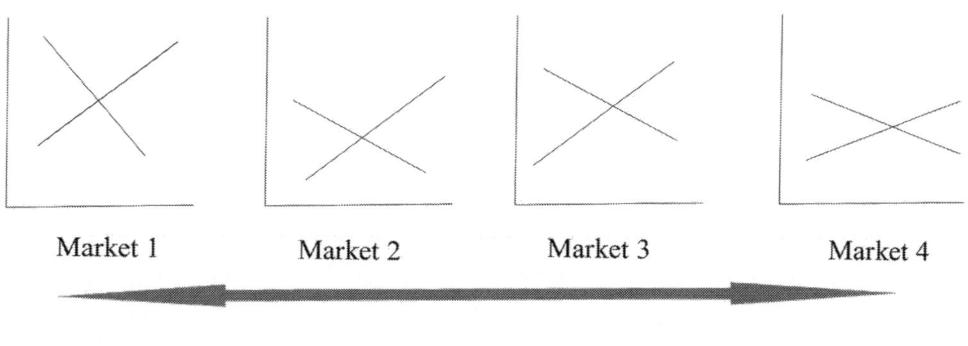

FIGURE 3.1

A simplified diagram of interrelated markets and general equilibrium.

may be a fallacy of composition in which the whole might not necessarily be equivalent to the sum. In the case of transport markets, individual travellers may behave one way in isolation but another when acting in a social or more aggregated context. These issues are considered at various points later.

3.6 INTERRELATED MARKETS: SUBSTITUTES AND COMPLEMENTS

Markets are not only related by the fact that one market provides inputs to a production process relevant to another, as with the automobiles example. Markets are also related to one another by patterns in consumption.

Consider three transport goods: cars, bicycles, and petrol. Purchase of petrol is related to the purchase (and use) of cars because the services the car provides require petrol purchases. Thus, petrol is a complement to car usage, with one good being consumed along with the other. But cars and bicycles are substitutes, with one used in lieu of the other. These three markets are related by consumption with changes in one market flowing on to other related markets. Figure 3.2 graphs this out, showing an increase in petrol supply, from S_1 to S_2 lowering the petrol price from P_1 to P_2 (as depicted in the left panel).This price fall leads to an increase in the use and purchase of cars since it lowers the cost of operating them, as shown by the outward shift in car demand from D_1 to D_2 (as depicted in the middle panel). This increase in car usage leads to a fall in cycle usage and purchases because cycling is a substitute for driving and there is an inward shift in cycle demand from D_1 to D_2 (shown in the last panel).

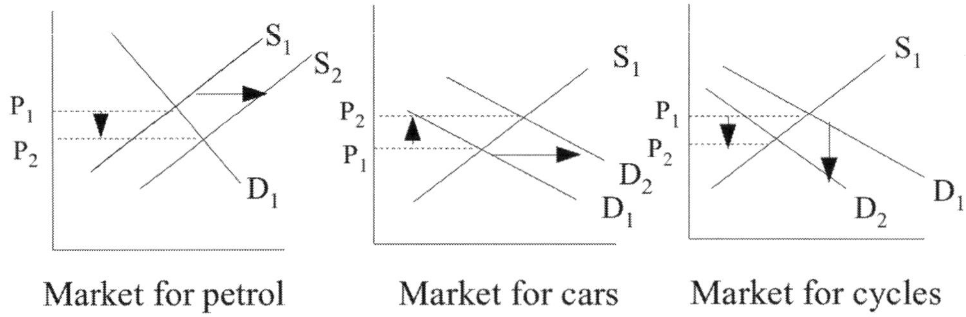

FIGURE 3.2
How a change in supply in the petrol market affects demand in the car and cycle markets (see text).

BOX 3.2 ELASTICITIES AND NEW YORK CITY BRIDGES AND TUNNELS

New York City is composed of five boroughs, the borough of Manhattan being an island surrounded by water (see Figure 3.3). Many vehicles from the "outer" boroughs must get into and out of Manhattan via bridge or tunnel. The same is true for connections between some of the other boroughs as well. Not all these crossings are tolled, and those that are have differing toll amounts.

Prima facie one might think that the price elasticity of demand for these crossings might be similar, especially those going into and out of Manhattan where much employment and activity of New York City is concentrated. (Elasticities are covered in Chapter 2.) It turns out, however, that the estimated demand price elasticities of these bridges differ considerably. Available data as of 2008 showed that

FIGURE 3.3
Manhattan and surrounds – with transport system features. Created from Openstreetmap.org. Licenced under a creative commons licence. https://creativecommons.org/licenses/by-sa/2.0/

average demand was quite inelastic overall, typically between –0.1 and –0.19. That is, a 10% increase in toll would elicit on average only a 1%–1.9% reduction in bridge or tunnel usage. But a few facilities stand out as having price elasticities two or three or more times as large. These include the Triborough Bridge (–0.21), the Henry Hudson Bridge (–0.289), and the Brooklyn-Battery Tunnel (–0.358). Drivers using one of these facilities are much more sensitive to price than when using other facilities (such as the Marine Parkway Bridge, the least elastic at –0.1).

What might account for these differences? A common element is that the crossings with the highest price elasticities (technically referred to as highest own-price elasticity of demand) are all within 1 mi or less of a free (i.e. untolled) alternative crossing. This means that some people are choosing to avoid a tolled crossing for an untolled alternative and hence more able to adjust their "consumption" of the bridge or tunnel as desired. Where such nearby alternatives do not exist, own-price elasticities are obviously lower because users cannot so easily adjust their use of the bridge by using free alternatives. Put another way, some of these crossings are greater substitutes for one another than others. Where there are strong substitutes, price elasticity of demand is greater than where there are weak substitutes (Peters & Gordon 2009).

All this shifting is assumed to be *ceteris parabus*, holding all other factors constant. The depicted flow-ons are driven by the posited consumption relationships of substitutes and complements. Other factors obviously enter in but these are held fixed to simplify the analysis. Moreover, this is assumed to be a first round of feedback. Over time there will be further price alterations leading to new shifts in demand and supply of the other goods. These shifts are not shown here but ultimately will result in new supply/demand configurations with new price/quantity equilibria across all three markets.

Box 3.2 provides a real-world example of substitute/complement relationships inferred from price elasticities of different New York City bridges and tunnels.

3.7 NORMAL AND INFERIOR GOODS

Consumption of goods and services is also affected by changes in agent income. A normal good is one whose consumption relative to income increases as income increases. An inferior good is one whose consumption relative to income falls as income rises. For example, the richer one gets, the less one is likely to take transit (it is an inferior good) and the more likely they are to take a taxi (it is a normal good), *ceteris parabus*, of course.

An interesting facet of modern transport is that it seems to be very strongly a normal good when considering the economy overall, but an inferior good for individual households. As global GDP increases, the amount spent on transport overall, especially as part of production, tends to increase as well. But with household budgets, transport tends to stay at around 8%–9% of the total budget even with big increases in income (Zahavi & Talvitie 1980).

There is no contradiction here. Modern industrial economies have increasingly fragmented and sophisticated supply chains which rely more and more on value-adding across multiple producers and processors (see Chapter 16). This structure is usually more cost-effective, replacing some internal production activity with transport, raising the overall level of movement of goods and services while also (hopefully) increasing productivity. Meanwhile, on the consumer distribution side, more and more product is delivered by a carrier of some sort. There is some countervailing reduction in travel by consumers to a physical store because of this, but not, at least so far, enough to outweigh the increase in delivery activity. As the economy grows in size, the use of transport generally rises as well.

At the household level, however, to the extent that transport is a derived demand, it makes sense that consumers will want to minimise the overall amount of time and money that they spend on moving themselves and their things around. Some movement is necessary, whatever one's income level. But as the above statistics show, the proportion of income devoted to transport plateaus at a certain point. Even here there are distinctions to be made. Basic travel done by basic means is likely an inferior good. But more discretionary travel, done by more commodious means (such as a luxury cruise), is probably a normal good to a degree. As people get richer their basic travel needs do not necessarily change much, but their travel spend may still proportionately increase with more discretionary travel via better quality means, though at a certain point transport needs and desires are fully satisfied.

3.8 COMPLICATIONS: MARKET STRUCTURE AND IMPERFECT COMPETITION

Market structure refers to how consumers and producers – demand and supply – are differentiated based on the types of goods they buy or sell and how their operations are affected by competitors. The core model assumes a baseline of perfect competition. This refers to a market where there are many firms and many consumers; homogeneous products; firms and consumers that act autonomously and do not collude; free "exit and entry" into

TABLE 3.2

Selected types of market structure

Perfect Competition: Many firms, many consumers, homogenous products, firms, and consumers act autonomously and do not collude, free "exit and entry" (i.e. firms can move into and out of the market at will), firms and consumers are "price-takers", i.e. do not have market power sufficient to influence price by themselves

Pure Monopoly: Only one firm, restricted exit and entry, firm has market power to set price

Discriminating Monopoly: Same as monopoly but firm can charge different classes of consumers different prices for same good

Oligopoly: Few firms, may or may not collude, firms have market power constrained by actions of competitors

Duopoly: Special case of oligopoly with only two firms

Monopsony: Only one buyer

Bilateral Monopoly: Monopsonist trading with a monopolist (i.e. one buyer dominating the market buying from one seller dominating the market)

Monopolistic Competition: Same as perfect competition except products are differentiated in some way to allow for differential pricing.

the market (i.e. firms can move into and out of the market at will); and "price-taking" by firms and consumers (i.e. a single firm or consumer does not have market power sufficient to influence price by themselves, and being atomistic, rational, maximising self-seekers are disinclined to form alliances with each other to bring a collective influence to bear on price). In aggregate one gets the supply-demand "cross" that over some time period – how long is not well-defined – is subject to competitive pressures between firms and consumers that will lead to an efficient equilibrium in which all resources are allocated in such a way that there is maximum well-being and output from available resources.

In practice, actual markets generally deviate substantially from perfect competition, and this is often the case with transport markets. These potential deviations from perfect competition are all classified as conditions of imperfect competition. Most markets fall somewhere along a continuum of degrees of competition. Table 3.2 provides a brief typology.

One prediction of economic theory is that sellers of goods and services will attempt to use any market power they do have to extract as much as possible from the buyer. The most extreme example is monopoly, where a single producer controls supply and price. A more common type of imperfectly competitive market structure in transport is oligopoly in which a few large firms dominate. This is often the case especially in large international shipping markets, where a few large shipping firms control much of the trade.

Oligopoly tends to be less efficient because there is less competition. However, the outcomes of oligopoly can be difficult to predict because firms are often large enough to have some independence of action, yet not dominant enough to have the consistent freedom to squeeze consumers like a monopolist. There are examples of episodes of sharp competition in oligopoly markets where one firm tries to strike a knock-out blow to its competitors in the hope of becoming the dominant or only supplier. If the rival firms respond with price cuts of their own, sometimes a price war can result. For example, in 1992, Peter Pan Bus Lines, a regional coach company serving points north of New York City in the New England region of the US, entered the market to provide bus service between New York City and Washington, DC., competing against the dominant firm on that route, the national carrier Greyhound Bus. Peter Pan tried to break into the market by providing an initial one-way fare of \$9.95 as against a prevailing fare of \$25. The result was a price war between the two carriers in which the Greyhound fare fell to \$5 at one point, less than what Greyhound had charged 40 years before. Peter Pan matched the fare and for a while both firms were operating below their costs. This situation obviously could not last, and fares went back up to prior levels after a time. In this case prices arguably fell more than they might have under perfect competition, but the result was very temporary. The entry of Megabus, a large multinational firm, into the UK and German markets in the early 2000s was not quite as disruptive but also temporarily lowered existing coach ticket prices substantially as the firm sought to establish a competitive market position (Krämer et al. 2016). Box 3.3 provides an example of an historical long-term transport oligopoly that resulted instead in collaboration between firms in the form of a cartel.

3.9 PRICE DISCRIMINATION AND YIELD MANAGEMENT

Transport markets are rife with the use of market power by firms to impose price discrimination and yield management on consumers. Under perfect competition, the equilibrium price established by the interaction of supply and demand equals the price the consumer is willing to pay for the marginal unit. But as the demand curve in Figure 3.4 shows, there are a whole series of consumers willing to pay more than that price. Suppose the market price in competitive equilibrium is P_3 and the quantity supplied is Q_3. The firm would obtain revenue equal to the rectangle $P_3T_3Q_30$ and would have to leave it at that. Inframarginal consumers (i.e. consumers with a willingness to pay for some units above the competitive equilibrium price) have a pure gain that suppliers would prefer to capture for themselves but in this case are not able

BOX 3.3 THE US RAILROAD EXPRESS CARTEL (1851–1913)

Between 1851 and 1913 five firms operated a cartel that controlled parcel post service in the US. The US Railroad Express Cartel set prices, territories, and governance procedures over the only established way of transmitting a parcel in that country at the time. This enterprise maintained stability within the industry and all five firms managed to earn annual profits in almost every year of the cartel, even during periods of national economic depression, of which there were several.

Parcel services in the US were unique in that, unlike Europe and other parts of the world, it was a private industry, not a government service, and it was virtually unregulated. American parcel post service started in 1839, and by 1850, two large regional firms dominated the trade. (Over time three other firms joined to make up a cartel of five.) Having previously conducted price warfare against outside competitors, these two firms signed their first cartel agreement in 1851, setting out their respective territories and setting up a system to facilitate transshipments and express payments for parcels going from one territory to another. This initial cartel succeeded in providing stability in traffic and consistency in operations, the simplification of transshipment proving especially appealing to customers.

But the arrangement also proved to be an effective barrier to entry by new competitors since they had to not only compete on parcel shipping price but also effectively build a competing delivery network to compete at all. Thus, viable competitors either had to join the network (if invited) or face large start-up costs with uncertain returns in attempting to build an alternative.

At transfer points between cartel member territories, packages were transferred in bulk with expeditious inter-firm payments at costs far lower than posted rates. Thus, the network provided real benefits to its member firms, in addition to its function as an anti-competition device. The cartel members used outside railroads for much of their carriage rather than doing it themselves. But the railroad companies were given a good margin for their services, with a good profit left over for the cartel. This kept the railways bought in enough to not consider setting up their own rival network, which would any case involve considerable cost if carried out.

The network also provided substantial incentives to keep cartel members from cheating or undercutting each other. Good and stable profits were attained by playing by the rules. Any game-playing by a single firm carried the threat of being expelled from the network, thus being locked out of the business entirely, unless it could establish a rival network. In this way the typical problem of cartel instability due to the rival interests of members was effectively solved.

The cartel also provided good and relatively low-cost service to customers – though with lower quantities and higher prices than likely would have occurred under perfect competition – while yielding good and steady profits for members. It also proved for a long time to be beyond the reach of government regulators, refusing, until 1890, to even provide basic business information to the US Census Bureau.

However, all things must come to an end, and in 1906 the Interstate Commerce Commission (ICC) was established by the US federal government to regulate this, and other, cartels, and in 1909 a public rate structure was imposed on the arrangement. In 1913 Congress created a government parcel post service, effectively ending the cartel's operations.

Details above taken from Grossman (1996)

FIGURE 3.4
Price discrimination (yield management) along the demand curve (see text).

to because if they did try to raise their prices for these consumers, they would be rapidly undercut by a competitor.

A transport provider with market power, however, can try to use it to charge different prices to different consumers and capture their inframarginal gain. Figure 3.4 shows how this might work, depicting a series of three differential tariffs for different classes of customer, along with their corresponding revenue yields as shown by the corresponding rectangles. In this case three prices are shown (P_1, P_2, and P_3) at 3 different tariff points (T_1, T_2, and T_3)

with revenues raised in the three tranches indicated by the rectangles $P_1T_1Q_10$, $P_2T_2Q_20$, and $P_3T_3Q_30$. The last rectangle represents the revenue obtained by the perfectly competitive firm. But here the firm uses market power to obtain additional revenues equal to $P_2T_2AP_3$ and $P_1T_1BP_2$. In the extreme, a monopoly provider with the right technology would seek to impose as many differential prices as there are inframarginal consumers, maximising their revenues by expropriating the entire triangle of CT_3P_3. The practice of maximising of firm revenue through the use of price discrimination is referred to as yield management and is widely used in transport pricing.

3.10 COMPLICATIONS: INCREASING RETURNS TO SCALE

Returns to scale (RTS) is a technological relationship between input and output which determines the amount of output feasibly produced from a given amount of input with a given technology as the scale of production increases. Constant returns to scale (CRS) refer to a unit proportionality (one-to-one) between output and input as production scale increases (i.e. the average amount of output from a unit of input is constant regardless of scale). Increasing returns to scale (IRS) refer to an increasing proportionality (output increases per unit input as scale increases). Decreasing returns to scale (DRS) refer to a diminishing proportionality (unit output decreases per unit input as scale increases). As noted in Chapter 2, economists assume CRS in production by default. Box 3.4 provides an example.

RTS is a technological relationship between input and output. Economies of scale (EOS) is a broader concept that includes the effects of factors such as market prices and managerial capacity. For example, automobile production typically exhibits IRS. Does that mean that ultimately only one big firm will dominate? Not necessarily, because a large firm is also subject to management control limitations: if it gets too big, it can get inefficient due to the difficulty of controlling a large enterprise. Also high levels of production may drive up prices of inputs such as labour, and this cost increase may partially or fully counteract the cost savings from IRS. EOS thus generally rests on RTS, but also on many other factors, just one being technology. Box 3.5 provides an historical example of this.

3.11 COMPETITION AND SCALE IN TRANSPORT MARKETS

How competitive are transport markets and what RTS exist within them? Generalisations must be tentative since "transport" encompasses many

BOX 3.4 THREE SIMPLE PRODUCTION FUNCTIONS AND RTS

Imagine three competing firms in the same market but employing different technologies (with "Y" = firm output and "X" equal to a unit of input, both measured in units standardised across all firms)

(PF1) Y = X

(PF2) Y = 1/X

(PF3) Y = 2X

PF1 has constant returns to scale (CRS), i.e. if the input X is doubled, say from 1 to 2, output Y also doubles from 1 to 2.

PF2 has decreasing returns to scale (DRS), i.e. if X is doubled from 1 to 2, Y increases proportionately less than that, from 1 to 0.5 (and this is an unusual case where returns are actually negative). Decreasing returns exist when output increases proportionately less than input.

Finally, PF3 has increasing returns to scale (IRS), i.e. if X is raised from 1 to 2, Y increases proportionately more than that, from 1 to 4.

With only 1 unit of input, the firms all start out equally, producing 1 Y for 1 X. But at 2 units, PF3 produces 4 units of Y, outpacing PF1 with 2, and poor pitiful PF2 with ½. *Ceteris parabus*, the firm with PF3 has a strong chance of driving out its competitors, possibly even becoming a monopolist. (Note, though, that technologies may also have different RTS over different scales, e.g. increasing returns at low levels, constant returns at medium levels, and decreasing returns at high levels of output.)

different means (modes) of travel (e.g. railways versus airlines), many different spatial extents (e.g. a single city versus a global region) and a wide variety of technologies and providers (e.g. e-scooters versus normal bikes). In general, increasing RTS militates against perfect competition, *in extremis*, producing a pure monopoly. Many of the new industries of the Second Industrial Revolution, such as electricity and railways, quickly became monopolies or oligopolies because of RTS. And some, like railways, acted as monopolists within their geographical areas of service, due both to their increasing scale economies and their locational advantage. So widespread was this phenomenon that a theory of natural monopoly arose, arguing that industries with large positive technical RTS would become pure monopolies unless some external force, such as government, came in and regulated. Some of these issues are considered in Chapter 13.

Certainly, there are generally potentially large degrees of spatial market power since transport takes place in unique configurations of space and local conditions that affect the user's choice of a route and whether to make a trip at all, change the destination, or delay travel (Levinson et al. 2016, 16). But

BOX 3.5 HENRY FORD AND THE $5 DOLLAR DAY

On January 5, 1914, Henry Ford announced that his flagship Highland Park auto plant would operate on 8-hour rather than 9-hour shifts and that all workers would be paid 5 dollars a day for their work, a more than doubling of their wages. On an annual basis this was more than two-and-a-half times the pay of the average American manufacturing worker of the time, roughly double what the average railroad worker took home, and about a third greater than that earned by the relatively privileged US federal government employee. The new policy was estimated to cost $10 million a year, $2.5 million greater than the 1913 net profit of General Motors (GM), Ford's largest competitor.

Ford's bold gamble was motivated by frequent labour turnover, which in 1912 averaged around 48% monthly. Other auto manufacturers had large absentee problems, but Ford had implemented his famous assembly line method of production, which had not yet been adopted by the rest of the industry. The assembly line was very efficient, but involved hard, unattractive rote work and most workers disliked it intensely. Ford did cut worker turnover substantially with some equalisation in pay and work allocations, but realisation of the full-scale economies of mass production required a more cooperative and stable workforce.

Ford's business model was already solidly based on technological RTS. He first hit upon model standardisation as a way of lowering unit production costs, creating the Model T in 1907 (see Figure 3.5). That car was already much cheaper than any other available touring car with a price of $850

FIGURE 3.5
A 1910 Ford Model T. picture from US national archives. https://catalog.archives.gov/id/234118055. Unrestricted use.

as it went into production in 1908, largely because of assembly line efficiencies. In 1909 Ford announced that the Model T would be the company's only model with several body styles offered on a common chassis, allowing him to cut per unit costs even further. No other competitor produced this way, and the move was successful because the Model T was so cheap relative to other cars of similar quality. In 1910 Ford opened his Highland Park plant on a 60-acre plot outside Detroit, Michigan, in which assembly-line mass production was run on an unprecedented scale, with moving conveyor belts pushing a car chassis part past worker's stations at a steady 6 ft per minute, with one Model T leaving the plant every 24 seconds by 1914.

Ford had gambled on scale and efficiency and won on both the supply and demand side. Labour force retention and stability was just another facet of this overall strategy. After the 1914 wage increase, 500,000 cars came off the assembly line in 1915 as compared with 300,000 a year earlier. But while car production increased 67%, the number of workers increased only 46% with turnover rates far lower than other manufacturers. The wage increase, estimated to cost $10 million, ended up only costing $5.8 million in 1914, the year that it was fully instituted, due to lower labour turnover and attraction of highly qualified and productive workers from competing manufacturers.

Ford also saw his workers as potential customers and figured that he would get back much of his higher wage outlay in the form of new purchases of Model T's. The company's low prices generated such expanded demand that in 1917 it stopped national advertising altogether, not to resume it until 1923.

All this led the Ford Motor Company to be in a strong oligopoly position in 1914 when it instituted its wage increase. Its estimated $10 million cost was still only 35% of the company's profits that year. GM had only made $7.5 million in profits in 1913, while Ford had earned $27 million then. Ford was in a dominant market position which allowed it to take gambles that its competitors could not.

Furthermore, Ford had long employed a corporate philosophy of paying few dividends to shareholders, and its steady profitability allowed the firm to finance all its initiatives out of internal earnings growth. This meant that there were no outside parties, especially banks, to which the firm was financially beholden. This could spell trouble for some firms since it meant a firm's owner could not be restrained from making foolish bets. But Ford proved to be a strategic genius with the right timing and, in this case, the lack of external restraint was a good thing.

Interestingly, Ford was generally quite anti-union. His generous pay policy was motivated purely by profit considerations. As the auto industry collapsed during the Great Depression of the 1930s, and labour strife and union organising increased, Ford's anti-unionism did not serve him so well, although all car companies suffered at this time. When the industry matured into essentially a three-firm oligopoly with one or two secondary domestic competitors in the 1940s and 1950s in a highly unionised environment, mere wage increases were not sufficient, a solid labour relations policy also being required for success. The company's performance slipped significantly during this time.

But during his heyday Henry Ford was a natural in developing and exploiting RTS and EOS in labour and production as well as marketing and distribution, to say nothing of managing consumer demand to fit his supply side plans. (Basic information for this discussion taken from Raff & Summers 1987; Sears 1997.)

BOX 3.6 BUNCHING AND OTHER COMPETITIVE STRATEGIES IN COACH MARKETS

Most every coach (bus in American usage) rider is familiar with the phenomenon of bunching, in which, on high-frequency routes, coaches tend to come in close succession followed by long gaps, rather than at the scheduled intervals. This is an example of a positive feedback loop in which the leading coach picks up the most passengers, increasing its number of stops and the length of time spent at each one, slowing down its average speed over the route. By contrast, the follower coaches move faster as there are fewer and fewer passengers waiting, since the previous coach has already picked them up. Eventually this dynamic will cause coaches to bunch together as the follower coaches catch up with the leading coach.

This phenomenon is sometimes deliberately exploited in coach markets where there are competing operators on the same route. In many markets regulations require operators to publish schedule changes in advance, typically with around six weeks lead time. In this situation, competing operators have an incentive to engage in "route jockeying" or "head running" to run immediately ahead of competitors and take away their customers. This practice works because passengers are generally indifferent to service operator so long as they get to their destination and are paying a similar or identical fare. Operators subject to this will often retaliate by running service so frequently as to prevent competitors from attracting sufficient patronage to survive, a practice known as "route swamping".

Where there are "thick" markets with a very high level of demand and transactions, head running is not much of a problem since there is enough traffic to keep everyone profitable. In "thin" markets with relatively little demand, however, the problems caused by such interloping are more problematic. In this case, the "anchor" of a scheduled service may be "dissolved" by competing operators essentially wrecking it through what game theorists refer to as "strategic behaviour", i.e. gaming of the system. The policy answer here is not straightforward. The obvious move of providing exclusive rights to one firm to operate a particular route introduces the corresponding problem of monopoly power. But what the "optimal" answer is not clear and varies according to context.

(Discussion above from Levinson et al. 2016, 44–45)

the ability of suppliers to take advantage of this varies considerably. In a particular market, there will often be varying degrees of RTS and EOS even within a single type of mode. Thus, there appear to be essentially CRS in providing local coach (bus) services in a many urban markets, but IRS for rail services in that same market. Yet some large coach firms have sometimes been able to limit competition through price wars or other means (see Box 3.6). And rail, having a high fixed cost and a slow ability to change their networks in response to changing travel demand patterns, may not always be able to effectively squeeze riders in terms of price, especially if there is viable competing coach service (Levinson et al. 2016, 44).

3.12 TRANSPORT REGULATION AND "CONTESTABLE MARKETS" THEORY

Because of the widespread presence of imperfect competition in transport markets, a variety of regulatory policies have been devised over the years to deal with the inefficiencies and other issues such imperfection entails. (These are discussed further in Chapters 11, 13, and 18.)

However, an economic theory known as contestable markets became quite influential in the 1970s through the 1990s. The argument was made that markets with only a small number of firms, or even just one, might nonetheless behave as if they were perfectly competitive, achieving efficient outcomes in the absence of regulation (Spence 1983). The idea is that the threat of competition can be effective in keeping incumbent firms with significant market power in line, especially if there is relatively easy market exit and entry.

This theory was used to justify a broad wave of transport deregulation in developed economies in the last decades of the 20th century. One of many examples was in the European Union, and its air service deregulation wave starting from 1997. This led to the rise of the low-cost airline sector there, Ryanair and EasyJet being the most iconic carriers. There was a parallel rise of budget airlines in the US during its own sector deregulation in the 1970s, though in that case the low-cost operators tended to be more regionally focused, like Southwest Airlines. This experience lent some credence to contestable markets since base fares were lowered on many services, though with a concomitant elimination of service frills such as free meals, and often added extra charges for things like checked baggage that legacy carriers gave away as part of the whole ticket price (Knowles 2006, 420–421). In this case deregulation did help unlock a large latent demand for air travel that was not met under regulation.

Nevertheless, the medium-term legacy of airline deregulation has been more chequered, lowering average travel times and costs across some routes, while depleting service to others, leading to what Knowles (2006) refers to as "a mis-shapen world in travel time" (422). After some initial periods of hot competition, there has been a re-emergence of oligopoly, and in some cases, monopoly at many airports, especially in the US, and fares have since risen overall on average (though with a great deal of volatility), especially as yield management and the unbundling of fees from fares (most everything being an "extra" now, even carry-on bags for the lowest classes of service) have taken hold. After a transitional period of competitive "shake-out", it seems that the market power of airlines have reasserted themselves, calling into question the general applicability of contestable markets doctrine (Kim 2016). While contestable markets theory suggests that many low-competition markets will equilibrate at or near competitively efficient levels in many cases if there is strong potential for market entry by competitors, in fact this potential does not really exist in many cases; and even if it does, the dynamics are not as simple as the theory suggests. That outcomes in many deregulated non-transport markets, such as electricity, have also not performed anywhere near as predicted has led to the contestable market paradigm being more contested than it once was.

REFERENCES

Chadeau, A. (1992). What is nonmarket production worth? *OECD Economic Studies*, 18(Spring), 86–105.

Grossman, P. Z. (1996). The dynamics of a stable cartel: The railroad express 1851-1913. *Economic Inquiry*, 34(April), 220–236.

Kim, D. (2016). The effects of airline deregulation: A comparative analysis. *Asian Journal of Business Environment*, 6(3), 5–10.

Knowles, R. D. (2006). Transport shaping space: Differential collapse in time–space. *Journal of Transport Geography*, 14, 407–425.

Krämer, A., Jung, M., & Burgartz, T. (2016). A small step from price competition to price war: Understanding causes, effects and possible countermeasures. *International Business Research*, 9, 1–13.

Levinson, D., Gillen, D., et al. (2016). Transportation economics. en.wikibooks.org July 9, 2016. Page references from print (pdf) version.

PC (2017). Shifting the dial: 5 year productivity review, supporting paper no. 2, non-market productivity sector. *Australian Government Productivity Commission*.

Peters, J. R., & Gordon, C. (2009). Results not guaranteed: A tale of road pricing in New York and London. *Journal of Urban Technology*, 16(1), 113–131.

Raff, D. M., & Summers, L. H. (1987). Did Henry Ford pay efficiency wages?

Journal of Labor Economics, 5(4, Part 2), S57–S86.
Rodrigue, J.-P. (2020). *The geography of transport systems* (6th edition). Routledge.
Sears, S. W. (1997). The $5 Day. *Audacity*, (Summer), 11–19.
Spence, M. (1983). Contestable markets and the theory of industry structure: A review article. *Journal of Economic Literature*, 21(3), 981–990.
Zahavi, Y., & Talvitie, A. (1980). Regularities in travel time and money expenditures. *Transportation Research Record*, 750, 3–19.

CHAPTER 4

Geography

4.1 INTRODUCTION: THE ECONOMIC SHAPE-SHIFTING OF GEOGRAPHY

Economic geography studies the way in which physical geography affects economic activity. This became increasingly complex, with the rise of both Europe and the Islamic world during the Renaissance making ocean shipping much more efficient and cost-effective than the combined land and coastal/inland waterway routes of the Silk Road and its counterparts. Economies had become sophisticated enough that location near natural waterways and fertile soil was not as essential as it once was, and some of these locations now became economically peripheral (Sachs & McCord 2008).

By 1500, Europe already had a clear urban hierarchy tied into international trade, first in the Mediterranean – Florence, Venice, Genoa, Milan, and Cádiz being the major entrepôts – shifting, in the 1600s, to the Low Countries, especially Bruges, Ghent, and Amsterdam, which had populations of between 50,000 and 100,000. This was increasingly the age of European colonisation ("discovery", as the Europeans called it) via the ocean. Increasing prowess in trade, urban growth, seagoing ventures, and accumulation of overseas territories, along with increasingly sophisticated finance, was beginning to transform international production, consumption, and distribution, marginalising some once central economic locations in China, the Middle East, and India, and creating entirely new colonial cities and centres of economic activity in Africa and "Latin" America (Watson 1993) (Figure 4.2).

With the coming of industrialisation, these processes rapidly intensified and expanded. Economies of scale (EOS) in production were unleashed by the

DOI: 10.4324/9781003350866-5

BOX 4.1 INTRODUCTORY CASE: THE RISE OF CITIES, TRADE, AND LONG-DISTANCE TRANSPORT

The first city is believed to have arisen around 3200 BCE, between the Tigris and Euphrates Rivers. Other cities and civilisations that followed were also generally and independently located in fertile river valleys, i.e. the Nile, Indus, Yellow, and Yangtze Rivers (the Mesoamerican Mayan and Incan empires being partial exceptions). These areas had the critical resources required by ancient economies, namely water and good soil, which provided the ability to raise and accumulate agricultural surpluses (Sachs & McCord 2008). Domesticated agriculture, developed during the Neolithic Revolution around 5,000 years earlier in the same "Fertile Crescent" of the Middle East, is asserted to have allowed for the sustained production of surplus food that could support a significant non-agricultural population in fixed locations for long periods of time (see Figure 4.1). This, in turn, provided for divisions of labour between specialised groupings of people now engaged in secondary (manufacturing) and tertiary (services) economic activities, in addition to the primary activity of farming and basic mineral extraction. Such specialisation fed further requirements for surplus, which in turn gave impetus to more extensive and intensive cultivation of land (i.e. drawing additional but less productive land into agriculture while working productive lands more constantly). Innovations such as irrigation made this process more productive (Fox & Goodfellow 2022).

These developments were not sophisticated in modern economic terms, but they were big advances from pre-Neolithic societies. Relatively permanent settlements were not new. Anthropologists have found traces of very ancient small villages from the Baltic to India. The human impulse to stay close to other "like" people (family, clan, ceremonial group, etc.) is instinctual. And while some people do this while staying on the move as nomads (e.g. many Australian aboriginals), many others stay put for various reasons. But prior to proper agriculture, these settlements were small, autarkic, and came nowhere near to constituting cities (Watson 1993).

Once cities arose, the formation of states followed, and the first sizeable urban areas were administrative capitals, agglomerated to allow for better defence behind fortifications and, probably, greater and more efficient control by governing cliques over competing interest groups and government bureaucrats. The earliest cities were typically independent city-states of one sort or another, with perhaps 15 existing by 3000 BCE, some with populations of around 25,000 serving and being served by rural hinterlands of around 500,000 people. With the rise of empires, such as Egypt and Babylon, these cities grew, and some estimate that ancient Babylon had some 200,000 in residence. The peak of ancient empires and cities came with the Romans, with Rome peaking at a populace of 800,000 and perhaps even 1 million by the turn

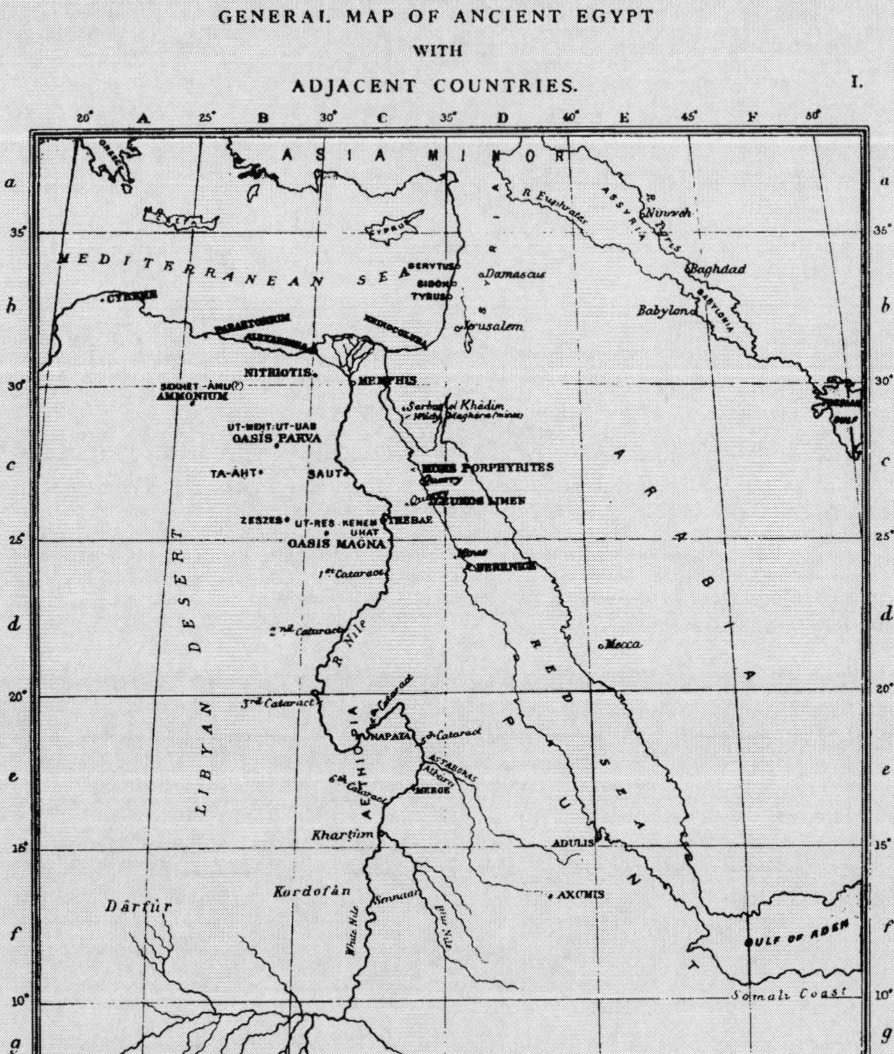

FIGURE 4.1

Ancient Greece, Egypt, and Fertile Crescent, circa 1450 BCE.

Source: Egypt Exploration Fund (1894); book and image are in the public domain.

of the first millennium CE. Empires required a great deal of political, social, economic, and military oversight, and this encouraged urban centralisation of various sorts, both in the central capital and various sub-capitals. As politico-economies became more complex, other types of cities emerged, such as the Phoenician coastal trading settlements and the Greek city-states, Athens and Sparta being the archetypal examples. These were smaller but, in ancient terms, could still be quite large. Athens is estimated to have once been inhabited at its peak by 100,000 persons (Kim 2008).

Ancient urbanisation went hand in hand with trade and the rise of international and regional trade networks. Cities were productive because of the specialised skills of their populations. But they required many goods, few of which could be produced locally. By the beginning of the Common Era, caravan routes, such as the Silk Road, Spice Route, and Gold and Salt Route, were firmly established distribution networks between Asia, the Middle East, and the Mediterranean. These had their own specialised urban concentrations where transshipment, trade services, and other support were offered along the way. Timbuktu, for example, started as a camel stop along the Gold and Salt Route but soon developed into a major rest stop and trading city of great significance. These routes were enhanced by the major road building of the Roman Empire – 50,000 mi of paved road at its peak – which integrated Europe and the Fertile Crescent into a relatively unified market and offered an alternative trade route, mainly as a replacement for the overland route in Arabia. Even after the decline of Rome, these routes prospered well into the Middle Ages (Weisbrod 2008).

These routes were generally a positive-sum affair, enabling new forms of trade between industries and locations, enhancing travel and trade reliability while reducing unit costs, leading to economies of scale and scope in production and distribution, and encouraging innovations in transport modes and finance. Coastal shipping remained a central aspect of movement throughout, but inland movements along rivers and surface paths were also used and became more and more important (Weisbrod 2008). Indeed, partly because of the inherent uncertainties of sea travel between Asia and Europe, this sophisticated land–sea trade network was essential, linking seaports by land caravans between Asia and the Near East and using dedicated transfers to ship to and from Rome. The locations of ancient and mediaeval cities were based partly on considerations of external trade, with river and coastal locations being prime import and export points (Casson 1994).

A critical role was played by intermediaries that handled movements of people and especially of cargo. Freight agents, including shippers, consignees, and transporters, were all involved in a growing and active marine cargo transport industry that arose during ancient times and was sophisticated in ways parallel to the modern logistics and supply chains that will be discussed more in Chapter 16 (Bernstein 2008).

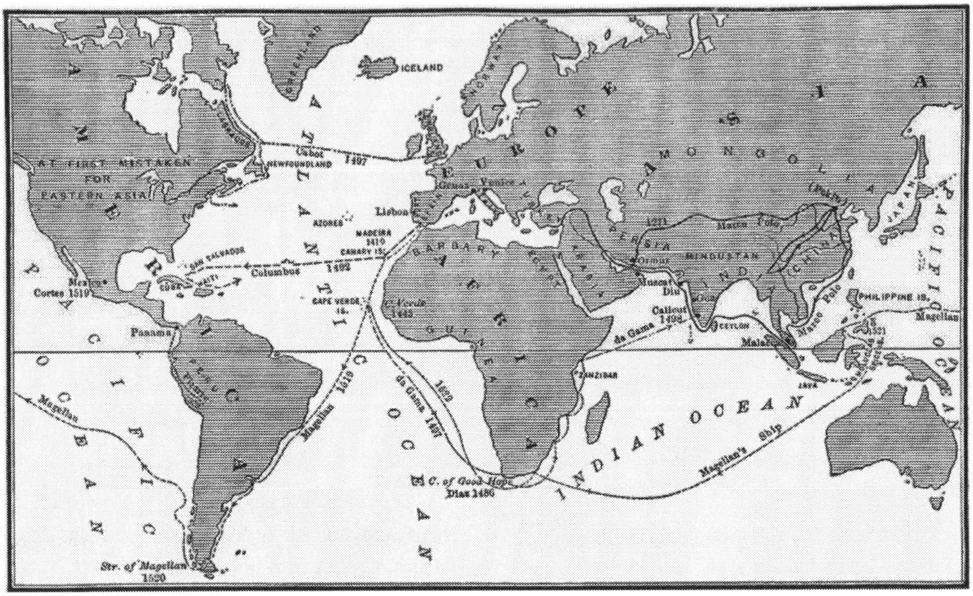

FIGURE 4.2
Selected land and sea routes and explorations during the 1400s and 1500s.

Source: Robinson (1919, 233), no known copyright restrictions.

arrival of coal as an alternative power source, allowing for the use of steam in various production and transport processes, leading to new forms of division of labour and specialisation. Factories no longer needed to be located near watercourses for sources of power and transport and, by the middle of the 19th century, could be located almost anywhere, giving rise to new cities, like Manchester and Birmingham in England, an earlier industrialiser. Factories and cities grew in size and scale as a technological Transport Revolution delivered rapid innovations, first with canals and then with the railroads and the steamship. These lowered the cost of transport, increasing demand for it. The increase in global accessibility thus fostered growing volumes and distances in trade, often involving European colonial or semi-colonial hinterlands (Kim 2008). This in turn fed urbanisation in both Europe and its "offshoots" of the US, Australia, Canada, and New Zealand. Between 1800 and 1950, Europe shifted from a 12% to a 50% urban population, and cities grew larger than ever before (Fox & Goodfellow 2022). The First and succeeding Industrial Revolutions, beginning around the middle of the 18th century, widened and deepened a system of urbanisation, transport networks, and long-distance trade that became truly global. In a real sense, a modern economic geography was born.

4.2 THE THEORY OF ECONOMIC GEOGRAPHY

The theory of economic geography (along with the related disciplines of urban economics and regional economics) focuses on the three main elements of market activity – production, consumption, and exchange – the same elements which constitute the core of traditional economics, but with the difference that the dimensions of physical space, time, and embodiment are incorporated into each one. (Note that some have tried rather paradoxically to incorporate spatial elements into the core theory without these relaxations, but these have been found analytically wanting; see Box 4.2.)

BOX 4.2 TRAVEL AND LOCATION IN THE "IDEAL" WORLD OF AN ECONOMY WITHOUT TIME, SPACE, AND BODIES

As already noted, the core theory of economics by default simplifies away the existence of physical space in the economy and hence the need to get from points A to B. Additionally, everything in the economy, ranging from agents to commodities, has no physical form or embodiment. While economic processes are referred to, there is no explicit time in the model, everything taking place inherently instantaneously.

Surely this model can have nothing to do with reality, much less the basic history already outlined. Yet some economists have nonetheless attempted to elaborate a "complete" model without any basic earthly realities and that purportedly behaves the same way as an economy with such realities necessarily present. Arrow and Debreu (1954) attempted to build such a world with the introduction of the concept of "complete contracting", in which all transactions between agents are made through contracts containing all attributes of reality. These contracts are time-stamped for all relevant periods across all time. Thus, time "exists" in this model, but only as part of a transactions contract, not as a multidimensional flow as mere mortals would experience it. Physical space is added to this contracting construct in Debreu's *Theory of Value* (1959), in which the contract adds location to the characteristics list of every commodity being traded. This means that a particular apple, say, is treated as a different good for each time and space it exists in, potentially and actually, with a single good or service moving through time and space conceptually being totally distinct commodities. While practically unwieldy, this construct does, however, yield a "complete" marketplace incorporating optimisation across time and space and without embodiment.

Unfortunately for economic theory purists, Starrett's impossibility theorem (1978) shows that, even keeping the very restrictive and artificial assumptions needed to make an Arrow–Debreu and Debreu-extended world work, this analytical "solution" only reached equilibrium under either an assumption of an infinite number of locations, consumers, and firms, or a finite number without transport costs. Neither condition can be applied to real-world situations.

Economic geography is otherwise founded on the same sorts of behavioural premises that regular economics is based on, namely rational, self-interested, and atomistic agents who busily maximise on an individual basis and whose aggregate activities are guided by the "invisible hand" of the market mechanism, to use Adam Smith's phrase. By introducing physical space, time, and embodied agents into the analysis, there is "friction" that maximisation over physical distances must grapple with. Since overcoming friction is costly, economic agents, whether they are producers or consumers, set about minimising the costs associated with that friction. The two most obvious ways to minimise those costs are either to minimise the friction itself, i.e. limit the distances which must be covered, or minimise the costs associated with overcoming that friction, such as lowering transport costs through transport innovation or building efficient transportation networks.

Economic theories of location arise from these behavioural implications since density in location is one way of economising on friction and its associated costs. This is one rationale that economic geographers give for the existence of cities themselves, namely that the concentration of consumers and producers in one place is undertaken to limit the friction of distance and its associated costs.

4.3 HOMOGENEOUS VERSUS NON-HOMOGENEOUS SPACE

The earliest formal spatial economic models were still highly restrictive in their assumptions beyond the premise that transport costs are non-zero and movement across space costs resources. In these versions, it is assumed that all space is homogeneous; or to put it another way, space consists of a "featureless plain" without barriers or contours such as mountains or rivers. In this case, the existence of positive transport costs is the sole driver in making some locations economically preferable to others because transport costs are minimised at those points. Thus, all rational, maximising, atomistic self-interested agents will aim to be as close as possible to economic activity they desire to engage in by choosing locations with the lowest possible transport costs. This is the basis of the oldest of explicit spatial theories, referred to as central place theories (von Thünen [1850] 1996).

In this model, overall equilibrium is conceptually quite simple: locate any activity, whether it be consumption or production, where the marginal benefit of market access is equal to marginal transport cost (as yielded by a given transport infrastructure and available transport technology). It turns out that the dead centre of the featureless plain will be where all economic activity concentrates, since that is the best way to minimise overall transport costs.

4.4 NON-HOMOGENEOUS SPACE AND TRADE

This basic model becomes more robust by adding an assumption of non-homogeneity in space. This could be as simple as allowing for the fact that some locations have natural geographic advantages (a port, for example) or some natural resource endowments (such as oil or coal or gold or agriculture). In this case, there will not necessarily be just one central place but potentially multiple centres with economic specialisation occurring at each.

This sort of locational difference is observed widely in actual fact and is the basis for the classic argument for free trade developed by David Ricardo, a 19th-century English economist who theorised that a country should specialise its own production in those goods and services which it produces the most efficiently relative (or comparatively) to other goods and services it could make and trade with other countries for those goods and services with other countries that specialise in the same way, a dynamic labelled comparative advantage (see Box 4.3).

Comparative advantage in its simplest form is inherently about locational advantage at the national level. As Ricardo exposited it, these are based on natural advantages in resource endowments. For example, a tropical climate brings an ability to grow pineapples, while a dry climate is better for producing wine. But these could extend to other features such as long navigable coastlines and rivers that facilitate internal and external movements. More modern theories also consider the possibility of creating a human-made comparative advantage, such as converting an unskilled workforce into a specialised skilled one. One could say thus that "Ricardian" theories of trade based on comparative advantage are basically models of spatial markets in which locations are differentiated by various "first nature" advantages (such as natural resource endowments) and then by "second nature" advantages built up through human effort.

4.5 AGGLOMERATIONS

Spatial trade theories imply that it pays, up to a point, to agglomerate in areas with comparative advantage. The existence of positive transport costs reinforces this dynamic because locations with lowered transport costs help enhance local specialisations, with transport cost differentials making some locations preferred to others at the margin in some cases.

Agglomerations have several drivers. Spatial specialisation in trade has already been mentioned. However, in the core theory, the quirks of embodiment can also play a role in leading to spatial concentrations. Koopmans and Beckmann (1957) argue that if inputs into production, such as capital and

BOX 4.3 THE THEORY OF COMPARATIVE ADVANTAGE

The most accessible explanation of comparative advantage is by example. Take the following two countries, A and B, producing goods X and Y, using only labour (L). Suppose that each country can produce one unit of X and Y with the following units of L (as shown in Table 4.1):

A requires 2 units of L to produce X and 6 to produce Y, while B can produce either X or Y with one unit of L.

Who has the comparative advantage? To produce X relative to Y, A has to devote 2 units of L versus 6 units of L, for a ratio of 2/6 (reducing to 1/3). This compares to B's input ratio for the same goods of 1/1. 2/6 (1/3) is less than 1/1, so A has a comparative advantage in X. B, on the other hand, has a comparative advantage in Y: its 1/1 ratio for that good is less than A's 6/2 (reducing to 3) ratio. (Remember to read these numbers as fractions. Thus, 1/3 – one-third – is less than 1/1, i.e. 1.)

It might seem that because B requires less L to produce either good – an absolute advantage in production – it should produce both goods on its own without trading with A at all. But Ricardo argued that A should still specialise in the production of X and B should do the same in Y, with the two trading with one another in the goods they do not produce themselves. If A produces 1 less unit of Y, that releases 6 units of L, which can be devoted to producing 3 more units of X. A's specialisation causes world output of Y to drop by 1 unit and output of X to increase by 3 units. B's specialisation, meanwhile, leads to 1 less unit of X being produced by it, but 1 more unit of Y. With both countries specialising in their respective comparative advantages, the marginal increase in production in X across the two of them is 2 units (A produces 3 new units of X, B produces 1 less), while the worldwide production of Y is marginally a wash (A produces 1 more, B produces 1 less).

TABLE 4.1

Example of comparative advantage

	... to produce one unit of X	... to produce one unit of Y
Country A: inputs of L...	2	6
Country B: inputs of L...	1	1

labour, were perfectly divisible in the sense that they could be divided infinitesimally into whatever quantities were desired (referred to by economists as a "putty-clay" property), then economic agents working with such perfectly divisible capital and labour could locate anywhere and geography would largely not matter. They demonstrated this conclusion analytically, but the intuition is that perfect divisibility would essentially allow economic agents to divide up their activity into efficient spatial chunks without having to concentrate them in any particular place. Positive transport costs would affect the choice of location and might even cause some limited concentration at certain points, but this would be temporary, dynamically altered by changes in transport costs and economic conditions.

In the real world, divisibilities are everywhere. One cannot divide a worker or a machine into fractions. So, if indivisibilities work against agglomeration, divisibilities tend to work for them. Economic agents must live with minimum scales of activity and investment even if the theoretical "indivisible" optimum is below that level. Indivisibilities can be across time as well as physical space, and indeed most facilities, production, or otherwise, are "lumpy" in both senses. However, Garretsen (2005) posits that real-world divisibilities are generally too small-scale to encourage aggregation up to units as large as modern cities, although they certainly could be sufficient for smaller scale concentrations. Other causal factors must be added into the mix.

4.6 IMPERFECT COMPETITION ACROSS PHYSICAL SPACE

Harold Hotelling's classic 1929 paper sets up a simple game theory model (though he did not use that term) in which consumers are assumed to be uniformly distributed across a bounded spatial line, rather like a boardwalk or market street, and posits two firms considering which location along that line gives each one of them a strategic, profit-maximising advantage over the other in terms of access to consumer demand. He assumed a homogeneous good with consumers each seeking one unit of the good, thus making each consumer equal – and negligible – in their individual buying power over the firms. These facts drive firms to focus on the spatial position that captures the greatest number of consumers, rather than appealing to market segments (see Figure 4.3).

Because consumers are evenly dispersed across locations on the line, and because travel is not costless, they differ in their access to a particular store. This fact gives rise to the need for both consumers and sellers to consider the interaction between transport costs and location. Firms seek a limited spatial monopoly over some consumers, with each one competing with the other in terms of its "mill price" (i.e. the posted price of the good they offer) while also calculating the travel costs that consumers must bear to go to whatever store they choose to buy from. Consumer choice of store will be based partly on

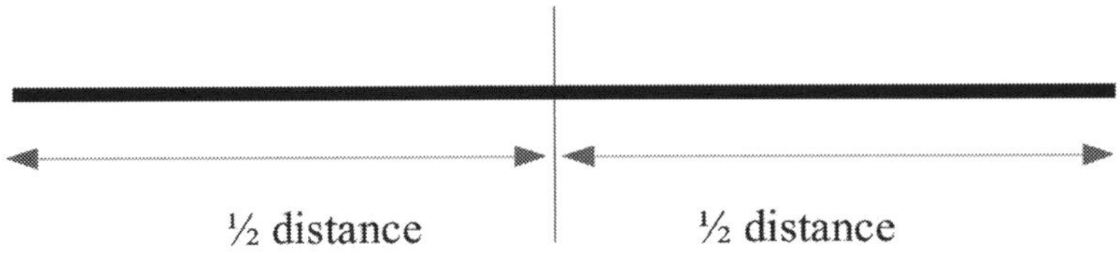

FIGURE 4.3
A Hotelling "boardwalk" (see text).

how close a particular outlet is to them, and they will trade off proximity of location with mill price in deciding where to shop (Thisse 2008). Firm choice will be to set the mill price and location choice to maximise their own profits.

Formally speaking, Hotelling's model introduces a role for imperfect competition, in this case in the form of a localised spatial monopoly, in shaping firm location and consumer travel decisions. He thought that the optimal location in the two-firm case would be to locate as close as possible to the centre of the line, thus getting a bare majority of consumers coming in. Later authors showed this to be an analytical error and that firms actually trade-off between central locations that capture a larger share of the market against peripheral locations which lessen the intensity of competition they face from other firms.

Even for this simple "game", the equilibrium solution is thus not straightforward. Things get more complicated as the number of firms is increased, something that expands overall competition but also increases the locational advantage of some positions over others in somewhat unpredictable ways. It also gets more complex if there is some slight differentiation of products introducing monopolistic competition (see Chapter 3) or if there is some cost to consumer searches for information about price and product quality offered at the different locations (Duranton 2008; Thisse 2008).

Despite the shortcomings of Hotelling's original conceptions, his work helped formalise the notion that spatial location can, all by itself, create a locational advantage for firms and some advantage for consumers who exert some power over firms by voting with their feet, so to speak. This formulation has provided one set of building blocks for considering the drivers for potential agglomerations and, conversely, dispersals of economic activity.

4.7 AGGLOMERATION ECONOMIES

Before Hotelling, the great neoclassical economist Alfred Marshall (1890) considered agglomerations from a different angle. He proposed a "trinity" of efficiencies gained from spatial concentration in industry:

1. EOS in specialised input markets, such as occur with spatial clusters of specialised manufacturers buying inputs from one another, because their spatial proximity lowers transport costs and time spent searching for suppliers. Strange (2008) provides the example of clothing manufacturers located near button manufacturers, the latter supplying the former, with minimised transport and search costs enhancing the cost-efficiency in a symbiotic way and yielding spatially based EOS.
2. "Localised skills" (or in more modern terms, "labour market pooling"), whereby clusters of specialised employers lead to thick and proximate specialised labour markets that allow firms easy access and lowered search costs to obtain the labour they require. Many examples of this exist, such as the historical concentrations of newspaper publishers on Fleet Street in London and film-makers in Hollywood, where, in both cases, firms can quickly find the skilled operatives they require and, conversely, employees can find jobs that fit them well, with little or no relocation required, and minimised search and recruitment costs.
3. "Trade secrets" (what are now referred to as "knowledge spillovers"), which arise out of unplanned interactions among specialised workers across firms resulting in productive knowledge transfer and creation outside the market system (e.g. Silicon Valley programmers from Google and Facebook interacting with one another outside their normal work hours and coming up with generalised knowledge about coding improvements). This is a market "externality", somewhat outside market exchange and processes, while (1) and (2) are largely external to the firm, though not to the market because, in the end, transactions between firms are conducted through the market. Externality is discussed in more detail in Chapter 13.

These "Marshallian" dynamics are not exclusively spatial in nature. But it is concentration in space that leads to the economic synergies identified and from which can come an economic return ascribable to agglomeration. Hence, the term "agglomeration economies", which was not a term that Marshall used, but one that is implied by his theory (Ioannides & Rossi-Hansberg 2008).

4.8 AGGLOMERATION ECONOMIES VERSUS EOS

What is the difference between EOS and agglomeration economies? EOS refers to the relationship between the scale of production and the various factors behind it and unit costs. For example, if, as an automobile manufacturer grows in size, it can produce more automobiles for a given unit cost of inputs and sell at a greater unit profit, then it can be said to be reaping increasing EOS. Here, as the scale of the enterprise grows, so too does the value of a unit of output per given unit cost of input. EOS is therefore generally considered to be "internal" to the economic organisation in question.

Agglomeration economies, by contrast, refer to economic synergies resulting from spatial concentration, even across separate producers, consumers, and/or input sources, like the aforementioned knowledge creation and lowered search costs. In this sense, agglomeration economies are "external" to an organisation, arising in the aggregate due to location proximity, not in the individual entities themselves, although these aggregate effects do ultimately ripple through these entities as well.

It is true that agglomeration economies and scale economies are closely related. Firm EOS often involve returns from localised physical concentration of plant, equipment and labour, as with Ford's Highland Park plant, described in Chapter 3. But agglomeration economies go beyond this, with concentration of separate producers, consumers, and/or input sources as the driver of economic efficiency, rather than spatial concentration arising as a by-product of increasing returns to scale (IRS) in production technology, or EOS, within a single firm (Parr 2002).

Agglomeration economies and EOS both tend to lead to specialisation in spatial location, sometimes through a spatial comparative advantage, as when a critical mass in specialised production occurs in a geographic cluster (e.g. Silicon Valley); sometimes arising from a natural comparative advantage (e.g. oil reserves giving rise to specialised extraction and refining expertise); and often a combination of both. "Ricardian" trade dynamics can arise from this as both cause and effect. Thus, one place may become a centre of high finance, and another of watch manufacturing, at first due to respective agglomeration economies, but then reinforced by comparative advantage in trade between the two.

4.9 SPATIAL DISEQUILIBRIUM AND THE NEW ECONOMIC GEOGRAPHY (NEG)

The theories considered thus far provide some rationales for the economic returns of concentrations of activity. But they are still too simplistic to be completely satisfactory, being grounded in an optimal equilibrium framework. Once optimal locations are arrived at, these theories suggest that they should be stable until some major exogenous shift is observed. However, while some concentrations of activity are quite persistent over long periods, others are constantly coming and going without obvious outside "shocks" occurring. And some of the persistent agglomerations are troubling too, seeming to outlast the obvious economic efficiencies that may have led to them in the first place.

These "exceptions" might be explained by non-economic factors. For example, Rome's predominance during the Roman Empire has been posited to be an example of what economists refer to as "rent seeking", in which resources are concentrated in dense locations at least partly because they could be more easily accessed or divvied up among the elites – the "rent seekers". In the case of Rome, these were only occasionally shared with plebeian Romans in the form of "bread and circuses" to preserve domestic peace. The example of Ancient Rome suggests that some cities exist not because they are more productive, but because they facilitate upward redistribution of existing resources by privileged groups from the masses (Strange 2008).

But to account for the "anomalies" above, older spatial economic theories needed to be adapted further. This came with the rise of so-called new economic geography (NEG) in the 1980s and 1990s (now rather ironically close to four decades old as of this writing). NEG was developed largely by Paul Krugman, who would later earn a Nobel Prize in Economics for his work (Krugman 1991, 1995; Krugman & Fujita 2004). Imperfect competition and IRS are here both taken as normal conditions, thus moving spatial theory closer to reality. In its initial formulations, homogeneous space was assumed (e.g. no physical features or natural resource concentrations) to allow focused consideration of how these two conditions might play out in location across space. But this assumption would be relaxed later.

NEG also introduced an explicit recognition that spatial concentrations and agglomerations have costs as well as benefits, such as pollution, congestion, noise, and higher operating and land acquisition costs, which must be factored into location and transport decisions. NEG additionally recognised the role of historical accident in initial location and persistent concentration. Some initial location choices by firms can be "accidental" in the sense that one location is chosen over other similar locations because of random chance or a very small advantage, such as the initial presence of a very few specialist individuals in a field, e.g. diamond-cutters. Once located, a successful firm can benefit from a first-mover advantage, and, with increasing returns and imperfect competition, persistent agglomerations can result. The presence of any deviation from perfect competition, e.g. a slight product differentiation or very slight initial IRS, can quickly cause small economic concentrations in space to gradually cumulate into big persistent ones over time. The presence of historical accident has the theoretical disadvantage of being economically unexplained. But it does accord with some historical experience whereby, indeed, locations became central for long periods based on a "chance" first-mover advantage (Sachs & McCord 2008).

Overall, spatial-economic optimisation can be seen as a balancing of negative and positive factors and not just pure optimisation in the pared-back sense of the core theory augmented by time, space, and embodiment. In that theory, equilibrium is permanent without exogenous shifts of some sort. In NEG, equilibrium is far more dynamic and, in a sense, unstable. Small advantages can lead to agglomeration, but small disadvantages can then lead to dis-agglomeration. The specific locations and the scale and configurations of specialisation where these occur will also be dynamic. In this sense, NEG is as much a spatial disequilibrium schema as it is an equilibrium one.

Transport costs play an important additional role in NEG. Krugman (1991) notes that the farther away production takes place from input markets and/or final product markets, the greater that transport costs will be as a proportion of total costs. Minimisation of transport cost will interact with internal firm EOS and the degree of "footloose" production (referring to the level of freedom that a firm has in location choice) to determine location choice. Entirely footloose firms can locate wherever they want, and footloose industries are more sensitive to location-driven costs.

Krugman (1995) thus provides a hypothetical example of two bordering countries, one larger than the other, each one having an existing positive economic agglomeration just across the border. What happens if the national border is removed (e.g. through a free trade agreement)? Traditional theory would suggest that the larger country would gain the smaller country's industry, with the big nation becoming the industrial core, while the smaller nation becomes the industrial periphery, largely due to specialisation and EOS.

But there is another possibility. There could instead be two cores, with the small nation not only retaining its centre but expanding at the expense of the larger nation because the smaller nation now has full access to the other nation's hinterland. Or not. It all depends on the amount and nature of transport costs, footloose industry and firm EOS. Depending on these factors, there may be one core, more than one core, or perhaps no core at all.

4.10 URBAN FORM AND FUNCTION

This issue of core and periphery is tied to a related area of inquiry into the urbanisation process. NEG is in fact a move beyond a traditional two-sector approach used by economists studying economic development, in which there is a rural sector and an all-purpose urban sector, with population moving from one to the other due to exogenous factors such as shifts in technology or changes in the terms of trade (measured by the ratio of export prices/import prices), the urban sector usually gaining a trade advantage at the expense of a relatively declining rural/agricultural counterpart. NEG has been characterised as a shift to a new two-sector model that swaps in a core–periphery dichotomy in place of rural–urban one (Rimmer & Dick 2010).

Theories of urban economics seek to model and explain how these shifts are manifested. In practice, there exist urban hierarchies where some cities have a wider scope and scale of production than others in a symbiotic pattern of interdependent specialisation. Some cities focus on higher value-add, and others on lower value-add, while some specialise in similar value-adds but in different product or service lines. Typically, commodities with low transport cost and high returns to scale (RTS) are provided by only a few cities, while commodities with high transport cost and low RTS are provided by most cities. (These models can also be applied across countries using international comparative advantage models as discussed earlier in the chapter.) The basic ideas are like those of NEG, involving subtle and delicate balances between forces simultaneously pushing and pulling economic agents together and apart, and indeed, NEG can also theoretically generate both cities and hierarchies (Berliant 2008).

However, urban economics as a field developed well before NEG and grew directly out of central place models while adding increasingly sophisticated assumptions and methods. The first major influential formal discourse on urban spatial structure was a monocentric city model in which any economic activity was assumed to tend towards a single economic core referred to as a central business district (CBD) (hence the term "mono" centric). This *ex ante* pattern naturally results in a "bidding up" of land prices and rents in the centre, falling the further one locates outside it. The relationship between land rent and centrality of location, here the two varying inversely, is referred to as a rent gradient (Mori 2008).

The earliest cities of the industrial era, such as London, which had a long-standing existence, and new cities like Chicago, did roughly follow this monocentric pattern with a rent gradient that fell the farther one moved out from the CBD. This pattern was driven partly by the widespread presence of increasing RTS in most industrial enterprises and agglomeration economies, such as meat-packing in Chicago and automobile manufacturing in Detroit. Monocentric models, however, imposed this historical pattern exogenously on all cities, limiting its explanatory power. The monocentric city itself later became less and less common in practice, replaced by polycentric cities (those with multiple and dispersed CBDs), suburban centres that grew bigger while

CBDs declined, and "edge cities", which are agglomerations on the fringes or larger metropolitan areas.

Urban hierarchy was also unexplained by CBD models since these focused only on cities in isolation. Given that urban density has costs as well as benefits, there must be, at least theoretically, some optimal limiting city size in which net benefits are maximised, with the optimal scale for individual cities in a network differing from their scale if considered separate, unrelated entities. Monocentric models did not explicitly consider such factors (Henderson 2008a).

The urban economics literature is too vast and complex to be fully catalogued here. But the major relevant findings thus far are as follows:

1. Whether in isolation or as part of a system, cities are posited as having an inverted "U"-shaped pattern of maximally efficient sizes where net benefits are maximised. At some point, the incremental production benefits of urban density and breadth are overtaken by the incremental costs of rising commuting and other diseconomies. This can be seen by the logical counterfactual of a world where density has only agglomeration benefits without costs, logically implying one massive city containing the entire urban population emerging within each country. This is obviously unrealistic, and the presence of costs as well as benefits suggests, at least generically, that optimal city size is in the middle of some spectrum from very small to very large, with urban hierarchies leading to a portfolio of different sized and specialised cities within each country rather than one huge one (Henderson 2008a).
2. Transport costs, combined with the size of the markets for inputs and outputs, are key shaping factors in both city size and density and the location of activity centres within cities. This follows from the inverted "U" curve dynamic above. Growing cities face rising transport costs both intensively (in the form of congested transport networks) and extensively (in terms of increasing distances to obtain inputs and sell outputs as the area of the city expands). Spatial concentrations of natural resources (like oil) and natural barriers (like mountains) will also affect specific city shapes and layouts. Still, it is assumed that city size and function are fundamentally a process of economic maximising across physical space (Henderson 2008a).
3. There is no predetermined theoretical answer to what city size or city number is optimal or what transport or other policy investments are most desirable. This is a clear implication of NEG, for reasons already discussed. The very rough empirical consensus is that doubling city size

increases productivity from between 2% and 8%, with diversity of the local urban environment being a positive contributor (Strange 2008). But causality is complex and two-way: the way in which cities develop drives the way transport networks develop and vice-versa, and these, in turn, depend upon many factors, economic and otherwise.

4.11 LAND DEVELOPMENT

A critical feature of urban development and location is land. In an embodied world, activities not only occupy physical locations; they also use land as an input into production and/or consumption. Producers, at a minimum, need to occupy land for their production activities, with agriculture using land as a direct input. Workers and other individuals, meanwhile, occupy land for housing, which is generally produced by a housing industry using land directly as an input, though in a very different way from manufacturing and agriculture.

Land, like transport, is quite distinct from most other commodities, whether as an input or an output. In some ways, it too is a derived demand, being used not generally for its own sake but to achieve other ends. The big difference between the two is that unimproved land is in fixed supply at any given moment, and thus owners of such land have a sort of monopoly power which they can exert in land markets, obtaining an excess profit in the form of rents – which in economic parlance refers to an unearned return garnered not because of any value-add by the owner but simply due to the mere fact of ownership itself. Housing, which involves improvement of land, involves what economists refer to as quasi-rents, with housing developer income garnered partly from genuine value-add (the housing itself as well as associated land improvements like landscaping) and partly from land title and all the prerogatives this confers.

Land prices and land developers are key variables in channelling the economic forces that shape cities. Land prices guide activity as the foundation of rent gradients, affecting where producers and workers locate, trading off between transport costs and location expense. Indeed, many historical changes in urban form and transport can be explained just by looking at transport costs and land price changes as affected by changes in background technology and income levels. Thus, the invention of the car and rising household incomes during the last seven decades of the 20th century lowered relative transport costs and increased consumption of housing, leading to demand for bigger houses on bigger lots on cheaper land further outside the urban core (assuming housing is a normal good as per Chapter 3). These changes account for much of what happened across much of the developed world in this period, namely suburbanisation, which in economic terms represents a flattening of the rent gradient, aided by strong population growth, itself partially driven by rising incomes (Quigley 2008).

However, this cannot be the end of the story. Strategic actions by developers play a key role as well. Housing units have traditionally been extremely durable, with useful lives of 40 or more years. Thus, while suburbanisation may be economically driven in similar ways across cities, the way this process rolls out will certainly be very different within individual cities, even if they are overall very similar in most other respects. A CBD with large amounts of sturdy but outmoded housing may remain economically dominant for many years beyond its peak economic efficiency simply because the property value and use it already has are difficult to replicate elsewhere quickly (Quigley 2008).

Earlier models employed a simplifying assumption of perfect foresight by developers, which eliminated the issue of durability since developers could plan their investments in such a way as to anticipate changes in income and activity so that housing would be reaching the end of its useful life just in time to make way for new investments in new locations (although durability does still introduce some lumpiness which makes this process not completely smooth). But, of course, the real world does have uncertainty, and this introduces the probability of mistakes in developer planning, such as developing peripheral properties too soon. Part of this planning problem is to predict consumer tastes for housing needs years into the future, a task that is often quite difficult. The core model assumes perfect consumer sovereignty in which demand preference is entirely independent of supply dynamics, with things like producer marketing campaigns having no effect on fundamental consumer preferences, an assumption that is often quite divergent from what often happens in actual housing markets. This real-world interdependence between supply and demand may potentially increase developer certainty about changes in consumer wants, though not completely (Quigley 2008).

A key point is that housing developers are not atomistic agents as per standard core theory because they exercise considerable market power and long-lived influence over urban economic geography. Some more modern models do aim to incorporate this fact. For example, to diversify risk, a developer may buy up a lot of peripheral land that would seem to be purchased prematurely based on pure profit maximisation in the present but which allows for strategic price-setting of plots by the developer over time. This may result in "leapfrogging", in which development skips over points closer to the CBD in favour of points farther away. This is one way that "Edge Cities" can be explained consistently with the dynamics of the core model (Mori 2008). It also accords with many historically observed and more recent city growth patterns.

4.12 TRANSPORT INFRASTRUCTURE AND THE SHAPING OF SPACE-TIME

Thus far the discussion has a distinctly Newtonian cast, with time and space treated as separate objective dimensions within which separate agents move and interact. But, in fact, time and space are intimately related to one another. Investments in transport infrastructure and the creation of new transport technologies can lead to what is referred to as time–space convergence, not in the literal sense of shifting physical space, but in the sense of lowering travel times between locations and increasing overall accessibility. This compression has been going on in some way since time immemorial, beginning with the invention of the wheel, which expanded the distance that could be covered in a given time frame, in some instances dramatically when compared to walking. The domestication of horses and other draught animals would be an example of a further pre-modern advance of this type.

But the modern Transport Revolution really began with the Industrial Revolution, generally conceived of as starting in 1750 or so, with the term time–space convergence coined by geographer Don Janelle (1969) to describe the spatio-temporal outcomes of innovations, such as steam railways, steamships, automobiles, and jet aircraft. Indeed, with the advent of electronic communications, Frances Cairncross went so far as to declare the "death of distance" (Knowles 2009, 442).

This triumphalism, some have argued, is in need of modification. Putting aside the fact that internet-based meetings have proven to be only a partly satisfactory replacement for face-to-face interaction, the benefits of transport innovation in terms of delivering faster and more efficient movement have arguably plateaued since the 1990s. Also, transport infrastructure investments and services have never been equally distributed across regions, and time–space convergence, while manifesting on average across the whole world, has not reached equally into every corner of it. This arguably has created a misshapen world in terms of travel time, accessibility and personal mobility (Knowles 2006, 408).

Much of this has to do with changing patterns of service across existing networks. A somewhat minor but illustrative example is the withdrawal of Concorde supersonic jet services in the 1990s, which offered an immediate time–space divergence for the relatively few privileged customers it served.

Examples of more widespread divergence are the increases in traffic congestion on strained road networks and expanded security checks at airports, both of which increase travel times and "spread out" time–space rather than compress it. Particularly pernicious has been the reduction of a range of transport services, such as cuts to urban transit and intercity rail networks and the withdrawal of airlines from peripheral locations and smaller settlements (Knowles 2009, 442).

Development patterns are also critically important. Suburbanisation has in some ways lengthened travel times for many people while "stranding" some others in economically declining locations, including CBDs. Transport infrastructure investment has often been insufficient with respect to potential demand in many places for decades now, leading to both congestion on existing facilities and other areas remain outside a good travel network entirely (Knowles 2009, 443–444).

This is not to say that convergence has completely stopped or gone into total reverse. Innovations in freight transport and management continue, and in many ways, convergence is more on-going there than on the passenger side. Intermodalism – referring to the efficiency in transferring from one mode (e.g. rail) to another (e.g. road) – has been a long-standing area of freight investment and attention with significant payoffs in terms of monetary cost and travel-time savings. The term "intermediacy" has been used to describe intermodal and other break-points between intended origins and destinations, such as airport hubs, route junctions and break-in-bulk points, which serve mainly to make movements more cost-effective for cargo carriers and other transport operators. Yet even these kinds of improvements do not necessarily result in time–space convergence that comes with them, especially when there is congestion. Airport hubs are the biggest example, the bane of most airline passengers who may be paying lower fares than on a direct point-to-point flight, and for the airlines, who are realising fleet management and other economies, but with both spending a lot more time in transit overall (Knowles 2009, 446).

REFERENCES

Arrow, K. J., & Debreu, G. (1954). Existence of an equilibrium for a competitive economy. *Econometrica*, 22, 265–290.

Berliant, M. (2008). Central place theory. In Durlauf, Steven N. and Blume, Lawrence E. (eds). *New Palgrave dictionary of economics* (2nd edition). Palgrave Macmillan, 734–736.

Bernstein, W. (2008). *A splendid exchange: How trade shaped the world.* Atlantic Books.

Casson, L. (1994). *Travel in the ancient world.* John Hopkins University Press.

Debreu, G. (1959). *Theory of value: An axiomatic analysis of economic equilibrium.* Yale University Press.

Duranton, G. (2008). Spatial economics. In Durlauf, Steven N. and Blume, Lawrence E. (eds). *The New Palgrave dictionary of economics* (2nd edition). Palgrave Macmillan, 6165–6170.

Egypt Exploration Fund (1894). *An atlas of ancient Egypt* (2nd edition rev.). Sold by Kegan Paul, Trench, Trübner & Company.

Fox, S., & Goodfellow, T. (2022). On the conditions of 'late urbanisation'. *Urban Studies*, 59(10), 1959–1980.

Garretsen, J. H. (2005). From Koopmans to Krugman: International economics and geography. In Gijsel, P. and Schenk, H. (eds), *Multidisciplinary economics in a new economics faculty in the Netherlands*. Springer, 425–436.

Henderson, J. V. (2008a). Systems of cities. In Durlauf, Steven N. and Blume, Lawrence E. (eds). *New Palgrave dictionary of economics* (2nd edition). Palgrave Macmillan, 6487–6493.

Ioannides, Y. M. & Rossi-Hansberg, E. (2008). Urban growth. In Durlauf, Steven N. and Blume, Lawrence E. (eds). *New Palgrave dictionary of economics* (2nd edition). Palgrave Macmillan, 6900–6902.

Janelle, D. (1969). Spatial reorganisation: A model and concept. *Annals of the Association of American Geographers*, 59, 348–364.

Kim, S. (2008). Urbanization. In Durlauf, Steven N. and Blume, Lawrence E. (eds). *New Palgrave dictionary of economics* (2nd edition). Palgrave Macmillan, 6917–6921.

Knowles, R. D. (2006). Transport shaping space: Differential collapse in time–space. *Journal of Transport Geography*, 14, 407–425.

Knowles R. D. (2009). Transport geography. In Kitchin, Rob. and Thrift, Nigel (eds). *International encyclopedia of human geography*. Elsevier, 441–451.

Koopmans, T. C., & Beckmann, M. (1957). Assignment problems and the location of economic activities. *Econometrica: Journal of the Econometric Society*, 25(1), 53–76.

Krugman, P. (1991). Increasing returns and economic geography. *Journal of Political Economy*, 99(3), 483–499.

Krugman, P. (1995). *Development, geography, and economic theory*. MIT Press.

Krugman, P., & Fujita, M. (2004). The new economic geography: Past, present and the future. *Papers in Regional Science*, 83, 139–164.

Marshall, A. (1890). *Principles of economics*. Macmillan.

Mori, T. (2008). Monocentric versus polycentric models in urban economics. In Durlauf, Steven N. and Blume, Lawrence E. (eds). *New Palgrave dictionary of economics* (2nd edition). Palgrave Macmillan, 4348–4350.

Parr, J. B. (2002). Agglomeration economies: Ambiguities and confusions. *Environment and Planning A*, 34(4), 717–731.

Quigley, J. M. (2008). Urban economics. In Durlauf, Steven N. and Blume, Lawrence E. (eds). *New Palgrave dictionary of economics* (2nd edition). Palgrave Macmillan, 6892–6896.

Rimmer, P. J., & Dick, H. (2010). Appropriate economic space for transnational infrastructural projects: Gateways, multimodal corridors, and special economic zones. *ADBI Working Paper* #237, Asian Development Bank Institute.

Robinson, J. H. (1919). *Medieval and modern times; an introduction to the history of western Europe form the dissolution of the Roman empire to the present time*. Ginn and Company.

Sachs, J. D., & McCord, G. C. (2008). Regional development, Geography of. In Durlauf Steven N. and Blume Lawrence E. (eds). *New Palgrave dictionary of economics* (2nd edition). Palgrave Macmillan, 5481–5484.

Shepherd, W. R. (1921). *Historical atlas* (second revised edition). Henry Holt and Company.

Starrett, D. (1978). Market allocations of location choice in a model with free mobility. *Journal of Economic Theory*, 17(1), 21–37.

Strange, W. C. (2008). Urban agglomeration. In Durlauf Steven N. and Blume Lawrence E. (eds). *New Palgrave dictionary of economics* (2nd edition). Palgrave Macmillan, 6889–6892.

Thisse, J.-F. (2008). Location theory. In Durlauf Steven N. and Blume Lawrence E. (eds). *New Palgrave dictionary of economics* (2nd edition). Palgrave Macmillan, 3773–3777.

von Thünen, J. H. ([1850]1996). *Isolated state; an English edition of Der isolierte Staat*. Translated by Carla M. Wartenberg. Edited with an introduction by Peter Hall. Pergamon Press.

Watson, C. (1993). Trends in world urbanisation. In *Proceedings of ICUP-1st International Conference on Urban Pests*.

Weisbrod, G. (2008). Models to predict the economic development impact of transportation projects: Historical experience and new applications. *The Annals of Regional Science*, 42(3), 519–543.

SECTION 2

Transport demand

CHAPTER 5

User travel choices

5.1 INTRODUCTION: TRAVEL BEHAVIOUR AND GENERALISED COSTS

The changes in travel behaviour over time and the rather extraordinary consistency of time expended on travel across time, space, history, and culture are driven by multiple factors. The core model, augmented with time, space, and embodiment dimensions, provides a basic explanation, which is that travellers make their trip choices based on a calculus of maximising their net benefit based on their preferences and the constraints they face at any particular time. The individual agent is the core unit of travel behaviour analysis (although this individual may also be making decisions on behalf of others, such as parents on behalf of dependents, or as intermediaries on behalf of clients). If one accepts transport as primarily a derived demand and agents as atomistic, rational, selfish, and maximising, then it is a natural inference to consider the individual's demand for the underlying activities that they travel to as the primary object of theorising and ask how individuals will minimise their travel costs (referred to as generalised costs) to obtain these activities given their time, resource, and spatial constraints (Banister 2008, 73) (see Box 5.1).

These "generalised costs" (G) consist of the sum of the monetary and the non-monetary costs of travel and are typically defined in the following way:

$$G = p + u(w),$$

where
p = direct monetary costs of travel
u(w) = utility costs of travel
w = some level of service of the transport network.

DOI: 10.4324/9781003350866-7

BOX 5.1 INTRODUCTORY CASE: THE EXPANDING SCOPE OF TRAVEL CHOICE

Economic modernisation and industrialisation have radically altered all phases of human economic and social life. This is no less true of human travel and movement across space. Residents in ancient and mediaeval cities moved mainly by foot. Assuming a 1-hour travel budget to go and return home, in earliest times a pedestrian's territory would have been within a radius of 2.5 km with an area of about 20 km^2 referred to as "the territorial cell of the individual on foot". Many walls of ancient cities were within 5 km in diameter (though population did sometimes spill out beyond the walls), and even activity within imperial Rome appears to have been organised within small cells. Topographic maps until about 1,800 are generally tiled with cells of about 20 km, often with a village at the centre. Although population density increased as urbanisation took hold, a 20 km^2 territorial cell, though now filled with more people, still remained the primary axis of daily movement (Ausubel & Marchetti 2001, 21–22).

Travel between cities and beyond obviously involved coverage of greater distances and took greater time. Surface travel by foot, horse, or other draught animals, or by boats and ships along rivers and sea coasts, had travel times that could be slow and unreliable, affected by variable weather, poor roads, and even brigandage. Sea travel was especially hazardous. Margócsy and Brazelton (2023) estimate that around 15% of voyagers going from Europe to the East Indies in the early modern period succumbed to disease or shipwrecks before ever reaching their destination. Many cargo shippers would commission multiple vessels or vehicles to ensure that at least one would make it (5). For this reason, there arose a sophisticated intermodal land-based transport network that carried cargo and people to supplement and support water-based movements, diversify travel options, and manage risk.

Of course technological change in the means of travel was not static over the long pre-modern period. Neolithic humans invented the wheel and domesticated draught animals, and various improvements were made to ships, carts, and other conveyances over later centuries. The Roman Empire built an extensive system of high-quality paved roads in Europe, while the Chinese built various canals to aid their irrigation and commerce. All these meant that travel time and ambit improved overall, though gradually, and generally faster on water than on the ground.

With industrialisation, change accelerated. As already noted in Chapter 3, beginning in the 19th century, urbanisation exploded, transport technology improved dramatically, and national and household income grew prodigiously, first in the rich countries of the West and then elsewhere. Households, as noted in Chapter 1, have become considerably less self-sufficient, buying most of their goods and services in the marketplace, some of which requires additional travel. The range of leisure activities has exploded with the rise of mass entertainment, culture, sport, and especially mass tourism, which made going away just for the sake of it the province of the poor as well as the rich. All of this has led to more aggregate travel in the modern era than before, driven not just by the expansion of available activities but by greater spatial dispersal of destinations, with growing congestion along with it (Banister 2011, 955).

Concomitant with this has been growth in demand for more personal living space. Household space in London grew from 32 m^2 per person in 1832, 112 m^2 per person in 1950, and 224 m^2 in 2010, a doubling in just 50 years due primarily to the spreading of the city metropolitan area and the decline in central business district (CBD) population from 1950 to 1990 (Banister 2011, 952–953). Modern cities at first grew upwards with the advent of the skyscraper and the safety elevator and then outwards with suburbanisation. The overall net effect has been to increase distances travelled.

Yet modern households also seem to converge, on average, to having fairly set and narrow limits on the amount of money and time they are willing to spend on transport. For example families across the globe spent, on average, around 12%–15% of their disposable income for mobility in 1970, unchanged in 2000, with other surveys showing similar results. The same can be said for allocation of time, which, unlike money, is definitely bounded by the length of a day. Measured travel time in the 1970s indicated that each adult travelled about 1 hour per day, measured across the year, with these results largely consistent across time periods and countries, though there are some local differences, such as Californians having a higher-than-average travel budget than the rest of the US. These estimates seem to be roughly similar to what prevailed 5,000 years ago, though sweeping statements such as these are necessarily speculative (Ausubel & Marchetti 2001, 20–21). Of course, as travel speed has increased, distances traversed in a given time period have increased too. It just seems that there are limits, however, on how much time and money people can devote to travelling.

Thus, the cost of travelling consists of direct monetary expenses (use of a car would, for example, entail expenditures on petrol, vehicle maintenance, and, if applicable, road tolls) and the disutility incurred by each individual by the time it takes to travel due to the fact that this time could be spent doing something else, such as utility-increasing leisure or remunerated work. This amount of time and lost utility will be further affected by the level of service, w, available on a network: travel time on an empty road is much higher than

BOX 5.2 SUBJECTIVE TIME AND SPACE

Newton's idea of two objective dimensions of time and space that independent actors move through is so strong that most people think of time and space in just this way. However, the differences between individual experiences of time and space vary widely, including travel. Everyone can attest to a routine car trip that dragged on for one traveller yet seemed to fly for a companion on the same trip.

Why this is so is not entirely clear. Some argue that human beings concretise time into particular metaphors which then structure perception of temporal duration and intensity. These metaphors are highly affected by internal moods such as mania, which often appears to speed things up, and depression, which tends to slow them down. Perceived and actual pleasantness and unpleasantness obviously affect this as well, as do thinking patterns and expectations. One possibility is that the mind structures our perceptual experience immediately after it occurs, giving events differing degrees of coherency in individual memory, in turn affecting estimates of duration (Glicksohn 2001). Thus, recurrent and regular trips, such as working or shopping, may seem shorter than other non-recurring trips which are more memorable. Alternatively, routine trips like daily commutes may be more memorable due to their perceived unpleasantness and hence "feel" longer: people are going to work after all, and this is not always a source of joy (Van Acker et al. 2010).

The experience of space is also highly subjective and variable across individuals. The concept of a "mental map" was developed by geographers to describe how people make sense of highly complex spatial environments by breaking them down into a series of relatively generalised features, such as paths, edges, and landmarks. As with time, these are internalised conceptual and mental reconstructions, not the thing itself, and thus have their own subjective quirks, including meanings that are ascribed to a selected number of features in the environment. It is these subjective features that become focal points of internal spatial models which then influence daily travel behaviour along with time (Van Acker et al. 2010). These presumably can be ignored in many cases, and are. But they may be very important in some settings, such as the valuation of travel time, an issue which is considered in Chapter 15.

on a congested one, and utility will be that much lower as a result (Bruzelius 1981). Note, however, that while time is treated as an objective quantity here, subjective experience of time may often be as, or more, important, for many travel decisions (see Box 5.2).

5.2 ACTIVITY MODELS, DISCRETE CHOICE, AND TIME BUDGETS

Because travel is assumed to be a derived demand, much economic theorising focuses on the underlying activities that motivate it. The activity analysis approach to travel behaviour predicates travel choices on underlying activity choices which then generate travel demand and its associated direct and indirect costs (Guiliano 2001, 15870).

The most elaborated version of this approach comes from the time geography school, which emerged in the Swedish literature in the 1970s. The individual is posited as having a set of resources (time, money, vehicles, etc.) and a set of constraints (demands on time, etc.) that define a feasible set of activities that can be achieved during a day. This set is referred to as a space–time prism, and activity-based models attempt to model the choices made within that prism. Figure 5.1 provides a schematic of this choice set.

The horizontal plane represents physical space, while the vertical axis measures time on a 24-hour scale: a "time budget", in other words. The prism maps out the possibilities individuals have for taking part in daily activities given their spatial and temporal constraints (Gutiérrez, 2009, 410, 415). The individual space–time paths trace a given individual's position in time and space, mapping out their activities and associated travel across a day. The slopes of the prism depend on travel speed, with

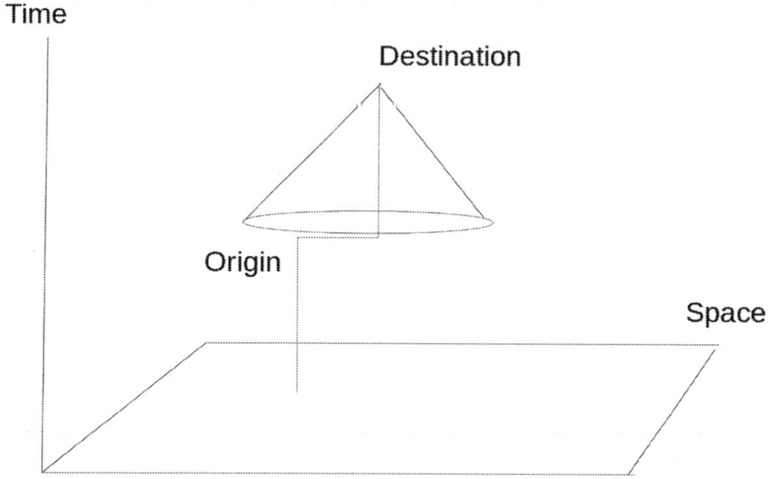

FIGURE 5.1
A basic space-time prism.

Source: Figure drawn by author, adapted from Miller (2017, Figure 2).

BOX 5.3 TIME GEOGRAPHY IN MORE DETAIL

Time geography begins with the constraints that shape the outer contours of time–space prisms. Capability constraints consist of physiological necessities of the agent such as sleeping and eating. Coupling constraints consist of temporal and spatial limits on how much an individual can interact with others. Authority constraints are those imposed externally, such as shopping hours. Taken in conjunction with an individual's activity locations and durations, time budget, and potential travel speeds, the prism is fully delineated within which the individual moves on a particular path through both space and time (Van Acker et al. 2010). Time geography is potentially meant to apply to any object, living or otherwise. But the main interest is in human motion (Dijst 2009, 266–267).

Some activities are assumed to be fixed in time and locations and thus referred to as "bases" (such as a primary residence). From these bases, actions are undertaken, such as shopping, with the bases determining the available opportunities within the constraints to be pursued within available "time windows" or "time intervals". Time–space prisms expand or shrink depending upon these and other factors. Faster transport speed increases the extent of prism area (when travel is undertaken), while slower ones shrink it. Changes in constraints also change the potential action space, as do decisions taken as the day progresses. One may run an errand on the way to work, for example, economising on time as a result and altering the remaining prism for the rest of the day afterwards (Dijst 2009, 267–268).

During a day, there are three choice possibilities: to spend the entire available time budget on travel only and no other activities; to stay in the base location without going anywhere; or to do a mix of some travel, some staying at bases, some engaging in activities at the various bases and then travelling on. This choice is summarised by the "travel time ratio", which is travel time divided by the sum of travel time and activity duration. This ratio will be somewhere between 0 and 1. Fragmentary empirical evidence suggests the average time ratio for daily commuting is 11%, for personal maintenance 45%, and for discretionary activities 25% (Dijst 2009, 269).

faster movement covering more space in less time and thus expanding prism width accordingly. Of course, some activities require no travel, like sleeping, in which case the timeline moves up the vertical axis without covering any space. "Activity behaviour", i.e. the spatial and temporal characteristics of performed activities, are studied first in order to derive travel behaviour patterns and hence the "demand" (derived) for travel (Van Acker et al. 2010) (see Box 5.3).

The time geography model clearly delineates the differences between two important transport terms used frequently throughout this book (occasionally with some contextual shift in meaning): "accessibility", which here refers to the potential ease of reaching activities from a given location by using a given transport system, whether these are travelled to or not; and "mobility", which refers to actual ability to move across space (Gutiérrez 2009, 410).

The core theory dictates that the exact path chosen by each individual boils down to a series of discrete choices that are continuously made to maximise utility, i.e. to obtain minimum travel disutility and maximum utility from desired activities. This joint determination varies by individual according to their particular preferences and the attributes of the activities themselves, the latter sometimes being invariant across individuals, e.g. an hour sleeping involving roughly similar actions across different people, but not everyone deriving the same utility from them. Utility, of course, cannot be directly observed, and a class of what are called discrete choice models assign probabilities to predict what alternatives will be chosen based on assumptions about agent preferences. There are many choices here, but the simplest is to focus on mode choice and then extend the analysis to things, such as destination, route, and vehicle ownership selections (Guiliano 2001, 15870). Mode choice will be considered more fully in Chapter 6.

The economist Gary Becker's work on household production is the basis for many models, positing that all consumption can be analysed in terms of activities which are the source of that consumption and hence agent "welfare" (i.e. total net utility). Consumers trade off time-consuming activities (including travel but also sleeping, eating, and working) for desired consumption items and, in some cases, another activity that itself generates utility, e.g. playing a sport. The consumer maximisation problem can thus be simplified down entirely to a choice of preferred activities subject to the constraints of home "technology" (such as appliances), available resources, and time, the last being fixed for everyone at 24 daily hours (Gronau 2008).

This formulation greatly simplifies the analytical requirements of travel demand analysis because it effectively treats all activities just like transport, i.e. as a means towards another end, with disutility traded off for desired consumption. Additionally, because time is finite and irreplaceable (in the sense that everybody always only has 24 hours per day over the course of life), the allocation of time is thus a fundamental and identical constraint for all agents regardless of money income or wealth – though freedom to use it as one pleases is not as equally distributed (Ironmonger 2008).

5.3 THEORETICAL ISSUES WITH ACTIVITY CHOICE MODELS

There are a number of theoretical issues that arise with activity-based approaches to travel demand. A fundamental one is regarding the definition of choice itself. Transport indirectly involves, in a fundamental sense, potentially much of one's life activity overall, such as work and home location. The travel component of this broader bundle has to be separated out, not always an easy analytical task. One also has to distinguish between continuous choices (e.g. total kilometres traversed) and discrete ones (one mode versus another) and between absolute outcomes and probabilistic ones (Levinson et al. 2016, 8).

The issue of some travel having positive utility also arises. These types of trips are potentially much harder to predict, complicating choice definition considerably. People derive pleasure from travel itself, sometimes choosing to go to more places than the pure rational choice approach predicts and/or choosing time–space inefficient routes or modes to conduct necessary travel like a work commute because they get pleasure from "going the long way round" or walking when driving would be faster. These would be left out of purely rational choice approaches (Guiliano 2001,15871).

The notion of the time budget is also not without controversy. Time is certainly finite, but the idea that people are explicitly optimising across a time budget that is absolutely fixed can, in the extreme, lead to a sort of determinism that conflicts with assumptions of rationality and utility-maximising behaviour which imply a full consumer sovereignty. Some geographers do take this tack, claiming that time budgets determine travel. The consistency of the data of travel time being around 1–1.5 hours a day and averaging around four (one-way) trips per day, observed across many times and places, actually reinforces the notion of a determinative time budget. But this doesn't sit entirely comfortably within the rational agent model (Guiliano 2001,15871). (Paradoxically, though, it can enhance the ability to predict and model aggregate behaviour, considered in a later section.)

The assumption of atomism has also been called out by some, especially social theorists, who note that time geography treats individuals as independent of their social settings in daily life, the emphasis being not on the social origins of people's activities, domains, and constraints but on individual behavioural routines instead. This is, some argue, a form of disembodiment, with the human body treated as undifferentiated, reduced to a path through time and space. A related critique is that time geography posits an infinite, unbounded, and transparent three-dimensional space that is also undifferentiated. The movement of differentiated bodies through differentiated space may add emotional content to posited objective constraints and paths, changing choice accordingly. Thus, many women may experience fears of sexual harassment in some spaces, different from many men, with the same to be said for some minority versus majority populations (Dijst 2009, 276–277). It has been realised that different gender and socioeconomic groups may adopt different activity patterns which require suitably adapted modelling approaches (Van Acker et al. 2010). This is discussed further below.

Other theorists challenge the assumption of full rationality, claiming that particular activities, such as work, act as "pegs" around which other activities are arranged, with some activities planned consciously while others are more habitual and routine. Thus, there is the possibility that the assumption of perfectly rational maximising travel behaviour is too strong. This does not invalidate the rational choice approach entirely but limits its domain, with some transport theorists distinguishing between a theory of reasoned action (TRA), where human choice is considered as being made by rational human beings, and models that incorporate social, psychological and other non-rational factors (Van Acker et al. 2010).

5.4 MODIFIED ECONOMIC AND NON-ECONOMIC APPROACHES TO TRAVEL BEHAVIOUR

For all these reasons, modified economic models of travel behaviour have arisen. Observations of the relative invariance of travel time over many different conditions of income and transport technology suggest that travel decisions may not be completely rational and/or maximising, perhaps with a significant instinctual or emotional component. The basic travel impulse of most humans may be to reside in a protected territorial base, taking the risk of movement outside of this base only for essential purposes. The relative immutability of travel time budgets perhaps may indicate that this is still operative on some level (Ausubel & Marchetti 2001, 20).

Among the large number of factors that affect travel choice, subjective assessments, personality traits, attitudes, and prior experience all can be important (Pronello & Camusso 2011). While arguably the immediate transport choice can be adequately explained by balancing cost, time, distance, and purpose against utility gain from the activity being travelled to, each individual may be reasoning from very different foundations that are not always fully rational or conscious (Smart & Klein 2018).

Habits, for example, can have a powerful influence on daily travel behaviour, as can prior experiences, both of which often have meaningful effects on present travel choices, even when their present context has altered considerably. There are many examples of this, e.g. people who grow up in transit-rich environments becoming regular, life-long users of transit, even when living in areas with much less transit later on. The converse is also observed, with those growing up in auto-dependent areas early and moving to transit-rich ones later still relying on the car even if it is no longer the most efficient travel option. Agent preferences are obviously shaped by early experiences, and thus differences in trip and mode choices can sometimes be explained through differences in preferences about travel. But perceptions are equally important and not always in accord with rational calculation. To return to the transit usage persistence example, those with long experience of using transit often perceive transit as the more available and efficient option, even when it isn't, simply because of past emotional and psychological training (Smart & Klein 2018).

The theory of repeated behaviour (TRB) assumes initial travel choice to be based on rational maximisation and cost-minimisation. But once behaviour is repeated, the possibility of habit-formation and routine arises, which, on the one hand, economises on the effort involved in rational calculation but, on the other hand, can lead to choices that are neither fully maximising nor fully reasoned out. Since much travel, such as commuting, is repetitive, habits may be more dominant in such arenas and should be considered with more subtle approaches (Van Acker et al. 2010). Sociologists, meanwhile, focus more on the non-atomistic aspects of travel choice, as discussed in Box 5.4.

5.5 AGGREGATE TRAVEL CHOICE: GRAVITY AND AGENT-BASED MODELS

The problem of analysis is quite a bit simpler if the focus is on aggregate rather than disaggregated travel behaviour. In theory, one could consider both simultaneously using game theory. In game theory, real-life situations, such as market transactions, are posited as games with rules and matrices of possible payoffs and penalties resulting from different moves and strategies by players. This framework could be theoretically applied to constructing space–time prisms for multiple persons and adding them up in an aggregate assessment. In practice, though, this is intractable, with the analytics even for small numbers of agents being problematic. For this reason, much transport modelling uses top-down aggregate analysis. In such models, individuals are either ignored, with movement of masses across a wider and given space and time studied instead; or, generalisations are made about individual agents

BOX 5.4 SOCIOLOGICAL APPROACHES TO TRAVEL BEHAVIOUR

Sociologists take a quite different approach to the study of travel behaviour than economists, seeing individuals as embedded firmly within larger social structures rather than atomistic agents acting on a basis of purely rational maximisation. Human beings can have strong emotional and social relationships with material things, being highly creative in inventing and making such things. Instead of seeing the traveller as independent of the means of transport and its context, as neoclassical economics does, travelling can be viewed as a process that has not just a utilitarian function but a social one as well, particularly in terms of providing meaning and a sense of belonging (Dant 2004, 71–75).

Much sociological attention has been paid to the driver and the automobile. Economists see the automobile as just another transport technology that has sped up travel and allowed greater minimisation of travel time (on average) with a concomitant increase in individual and collective net utility. But cars have also created entirely new social categories with important social consequences. These categories have changed the way people think about and interact with the transport system, leading to changes in that system that are not purely economic. Thus, "car consumption" is about an entire bundle of human desires which include aesthetic, emotional, and sensory responses; hence, the term "car cultures", which incorporates the often intimate relationships people and groups have with their cars (Sheller 2004, 222). Indeed, some claim these relationships are so close that there has emerged a hybrid being of "driver-car" rather than two separate entities (Merriman 2009, 142; Dant 2004).

Some would object that these concepts and ideas may be interesting but secondary and that the economic focus is properly the primary focus of travel behaviour study. But, as already seen, travel decisions are not always purely rational, with subjective factors operative, such as mental maps and habits. And they are not always atomistic. Even time geography admits social factors into the constraints that shape time–space prisms and paths. Many social theorists also note that human beings have to make considerable adaptations to the technological systems they create and that "cultural" factors, in the narrow sense of shaping the human to technical systems, are critical in shaping this adaptation in ways that go well beyond selfish rational action – of which more in Chapter 19.

to homogenise them and allow easy simulation of their interactions in large groupings.

An influential example of the simplest aggregate transport model without individual agents is the gravity model. The gravity model consists of two basic drivers of flow between places that might be potentially travelled to: (a) the travelling population of each place; and (b) the distance between places. Flows from a given origin to a given destination are driven by the potential of the origin for "generating" trips and the attractiveness of the destination (referred to as "attractors"), both of which increase the number of trips as the size of both increase. The distance between origins and destinations affects total travel negatively, i.e. as distance increases, travel falls, *ceteris parabus* (Guiliano 2001, 15870).

The basic idea is that travel across space faces impedance, i.e. a physical resistance from having to move an embodied form from one point to another. The "friction" of space discourages travel between destinations while the attractiveness of destinations and number of people desiring to get there is an impetus for movements at an aggregate level. The net result of this counterpoised set of forces between origin–destination pairs across a network determines the amount and pattern of travel across a particular space and period (Gutiérrez, (2009), 410–411). They are called "gravity" models because the presence of spatial friction to be overcome for desired ends is the primary balancing point, with flows following the paths of least (net) resistance. The new economic geography (NEG) models, discussed in Chapter 4, in many ways have at their core a similar underlying logic.

Gravity models are widely used in practice for transport planning. Many basic elements of transport modelling arise from them, including the trip generation and trip attractors already mentioned, as well as trip distribution, which refers to the allocation of trips from origins to destinations according to the relative attractiveness of destinations and distance expressed as a generalised cost (Guiliano 2001, 15870). These models often perform quite well in terms of aggregate prediction and description, especially for relatively long-standing and well-known networks and traffic patterns. They can be quite data-intensive and sophisticated but also can be scaled down to very simple levels with little loss of functionality (though at a cost of accuracy). The four-step mode trip and assignment model, considered in the next chapter, is based on this approach.

Gravity models are by definition mechanistic and do not consider individual choices at all. Since much transport planning and policy is, in fact, concerned with prediction at a large scale, averages may matter much more than what happens for individuals. And individuals are arguably highly constrained in many urban and modern economy environments where broad changes in the structure of work and economic output may have strong and direct effects on individual commuting and residential location patterns (Guiliano 2001, 15872).

But this is not always reliably the case. Agent-based models of choice are often a critical part of a hybrid approach. Here individuals are modelled as autonomous agents, interacting with one another as well as the factors affecting the overall network that gravity models capture. The basic elements of such models consist of the agents, provided with characteristics, goals, and rules of behaviour; environment, which is the "space" in which agents operate; and interaction rules that describe agent and environment interaction. These micro-level elements play off against one another in an evolutionary manner to create macro-level properties that themselves dynamically change over time (Castiglione et al. 2015).

In theory, agents could be modelled to have individually distinct personal preferences and constraints, interacting with the environment in deep and complex ways, thus potentially approximating the time geography approach. In practice, even in the world of "Big Data", mass computing power, and "Artificial Intelligence" (AI), this is still not quite achievable, especially as the modelling of agents as true individuals is a difficult analytical exercise, to say the least. However, agent-based modelling is widely applied in various settings, including exploratory analysis and smaller and specialised travel scenarios (Castiglione et al. 2015).

5.6 GROUP TRAVEL CHOICE

An intermediate level of analysis is to consider how socio-demographic attributes and other group attributes affect travel behaviour. Many aggregate and disaggregated analyses stratify their samples according to age, gender, and socioeconomic status as a way of deepening the analysis or to focus in on groups of specialised interest. A major focus has been on travel choices and behaviour by group categories of gender, race, income levels, physical ability, and age. In this context, the term mobility is defined slightly differently from its meaning in time geography: here it refers to an individual's or group's physical ability to move around and to take trips to activities outside the home (Mollenkopf 2007, 196).

As already noted, aggregate travel has been increasing since the Industrial Revolution, being especially prodigious during the second half of the 20th century. Global traffic volume has been estimated to be around 5.5 trillion person-km in 1960, rising to 23.3 trillion in 1990 (Mollenkopf 2007). But this growth has been demographically uneven. In the United Kingdom, to take one example, only one-fifth of women in the 1960s held a driving licence, as compared to half of adult men. The uptake of driving by women did grow prodigiously in England beginning in the 1970s. Still, even in 2013, four out of five English men drove, as compared to three out of five women (Gunn 2018, 21). Indeed, "gendered driving", to use the sociological term, has been a major focus of transport analysis.

Just as women were once largely disadvantaged by the lack of automobile access, many poorer, peripherally located and especially older people still suffer from this lack. The aged have been found to have particularly limited out-of-home mobility because of lack of car access, often newly created because of age-based license restrictions due to declining abilities in eyesight, reaction time, and so forth. One study found that only 14% of the trips by the European elderly went further than 10 km from home, often requiring external assistance. Similar findings apply to the US. Some of this is due to changing life patterns and preferences, such as being retired from active work and hence the need to commute. But surveys have found that, on average, older adults who are still able to drive and have access to a private automobile are typically much more satisfied with their general mobility than those without such access or who have access only as a passenger. Which is not to say that the car is king. Many European elderly walk or take transit in dense urban areas, often following long-standing patterns from youth (Mollenkopf 2007). These populations often do not experience the same levels of decline in actual or perceived mobility.

One line of research looks at individual "lifestyles" and how these might influence travel behaviour. This thread is mostly empirical rather than analytical but suggests that the lifestyle concept adds explanatory power to travel analyses. A lifestyle refers to an individual's opinions, attitudes, and tendencies towards general ways of organising their lives around themes like family, work, and leisure orientation. These are related to, but distinct from, objective socioeconomic and demographic characteristics of the individual and the household. Thus, middle-class suburban individuals might have similar attributes but very different lifestyles, with one subset organising activity around work and another organising it around leisure and cultural activity, for example. Lifestyles do appear to influence activity and travel behaviour but are outweighed by objective socioeconomic and demographic characteristics (Pronello & Camusso 2011, 1296; Van Acker et al. 2010).

Clearly travel patterns and choices change over the life-cycle, and for various reasons, this has led to the rise of "mobility biographies" that assess patterns in travel behaviour over an individual's life course. These are applied to changes such as ageing and also critical life events such as relocation of work and home. Some changes, positive and negative, correlate with particular demographic and socioeconomic groups to be addressed by policy initiatives where indicated (Van Acker et al. 2010). Chapter 14 discusses equity and transport disadvantage in more detail.

5.7 BUILT ENVIRONMENT

Although travel choice is typically assumed to be about individual utility maximisation, in fact the built environment that allows for and shapes travel is often highly limiting and thus directive of individual decisions. Gutiérrez (2009) has gone so far as to say that geographic position has in some cases become less important than position along transport networks. This is especially the case, he argues, in the case of rapid travel systems such high speed rail (HSR) lines and limited access arterial roads, where placement significantly outside such links can greatly reduce accessibility because agents are effectively excluded from the benefits of speed. Gutiérrez refers to this exclusion as the tunnel effect, since his focus is largely on HSR. But previous literature has noted an analogous bypass effect in which formerly vibrant towns withered after being bypassed by new freeways such as the Interstate Highway System in the US (Andersen et al. 1993, 410–411). Indeed, a number of "Film Noir" movies in the US during the 1940s and 1950s had this effect as a background theme, such as *The Postman Always Rings Twice* (1946) and *Ace in the Hole* (1951), which both feature characters that are owners of general stores and petrol stations facing ruin with the approaching new highway and getting into personal dark corners as a result.

Bypass and tunnel effects are one example of how the built environment interacts with transport technology to shape economic geography and, with it, travel and location choice. Thus, the automobile and the highway created an entirely new set of travel choices, expanding the set on the one hand but limiting it to those with access to a car, good roads, and the ability and capacity to drive. This development deeply changed urban and spatial form, reshaping it in many cases to focus on the car. Did people "choose" to drive more, or were macro-changes requiring them to do so?

The question certainly does not have an either/or answer. But standard modelling explicitly assumes atomistic optimisation that is constrained by the environment, rather than shaped by it. Sheller and Urry (2000) argue that urban architecture and planning shifted from a pedestrian focus in which speed was a secondary consideration to one where speed became primary and central to the definition of mobility (742–744). Travel choice is not really as simple as having an agent act on their preferences in a given environment and then choosing the optimal cost-minimising route. This can be a reasonable approximation for much modelling work, and it may even be pretty close to what happens in many actual travel choices, but it is not applicable to all cases.

However, as Van Acker et al. (2010) put it, individuals do not act within a "vacuous space". Trip decisions are made in the context of personal and community social networks, the physical and social layouts of neighbourhoods that encompass residential and workplace origins and destinations, and the infrastructure and modes available across the trips taken. Standard theory takes all this as "exogenous", i.e. given and outside the model. And except for rational maximisation, agent preferences are generally taken as exogenous as well. The key question is what is exogenous or endogenous and when? Van Acker et al. (2010) propose that travel behaviour questions in the main entail spatial, socioeconomic, and personality components. Not all of these need be included or detailed in every analysis. But they do need to be understood and considered as appropriate.

REFERENCES

Andersen, S. J., Mahmassani, H. S., Helaakoski, R., Euritt, M. A., Walton, C. M., & Harrison, R. (1993). Economic impact of highway bypasses. *Transportation Research Record*, 1395, 144–152.

Ausubel, J. H. & Marchetti, C. M. (2001). The evolution of transport. *Industrial Physicist* (April/May), 7(2), 20–24.

Banister, D. (2008). The sustainable mobility paradigm. *Transport Policy*, 15(2), 73–80.

Banister, D. (2011). The trilogy of distance, speed and time. *Journal of Transport Geography*, 19(4), 950–959.

Bruzelius, N. A. (1981). Microeconomic theory and generalised cost. *Transportation*, 10(3), 233–245.

Castiglione, J., Bradley, M., & Gliebe, J. (2015). Activity-based travel demand models: A primer. *US Strategic Highways Research Program* (No. SHRP 2 Report S2-C46-RR-1).

Dant, T. (2004). The driver-car. *Theory, Culture & Society*, 21(4–5), 61–79.

Dijst, M. (2009) Time geographic analysis. In Kitchin, Rob and Thrift, Nigel (eds). *International encyclopedia of human geography*. Elsevier, 266–278.

Glicksohn, J. (2001). Temporal cognition and the phenomenology of time: A multiplicative function for apparent duration. *Consciousness and Cognition*, 10(1), 1–25.

Gronau, R. (2008). Value of time. In Durlauf, Steven N. and Blume, Lawrence E. (eds). *New Palgrave dictionary of economics* (2nd edition). Palgrave Macmillan, 6946–6947.

Guiliano, G. (2001). Transportation geography. In Smelser, Neil J. and Baltes, Paul B. (eds). *International encyclopedia of the social & behavioral sciences*. Pergamon, 15866–15873.

Gunn, S. (2018).The history of transport systems in the UK. In *Future of mobility: Evidence review foresight*. Government Office for Science, Centre for Urban History, University of Leicester.

Gutiérrez, J. (2009). Transport and Accessibility.In Kitchin, Rob and Thrift, Nigel (eds). *International encyclopedia of human geography*. Elsevier, 410–417.

Ironmonger, D. (2008). Time use. In Durlauf, Steven N. and Blume, Lawrence E. (eds). *New Palgrave dictionary of economics* (2nd edition). Palgrave Macmillan, 6654–6657.

Levinson, D., Gillen, D., et al. (2016). *Transportation economics*. en.wikibooks.org July 9, 2016. Print (pdf) version.

Margócsy, D., & Brazelton, M. A. (2023). Techniques of repair, the circulation of knowledge, and environmental transformation: Towards a new history of transportation. *History of Science*, 61(1), 3–18.

Merriman, P. (2009). Mobility. In Kitchin, Rob and Thrift, Nigel (eds). *International encyclopedia of human geography*. Elsevier, 134–143.

Miller, H. J. (2017). Time geography and space-time prism. In *International encyclopedia of geography: People, the earth, environment and technology*. American Association of Geographers/Wiley.

Mollenkopf, H. (2007). Mobility and flexibility. In Birren, James E. (ed). *Encyclopedia of gerontology* (2nd edition). Elsevier, 196–204.

Pronello, C., & Camusso, C. (2011). Travellers' profile definition using statistical multivariate analysis of attitudinal variables. *Journal of Transport Geography* 19(2011), 1294–1308.

Sheller, M. (2004). Automotive emotions: Feeling the car. *Theory, Culture & Society*, 21(4–5), 221–242.

Sheller, M., & Urry, J. (2000). The city and the car. *International Journal of Urban and Regional Research*, 24(4), 737–757.

Smart, M. J., & Klein, N. J. (2018). Remembrance of cars and buses past: How prior life experiences influence travel. *Journal of Planning Education and Research*, 38(2), 139–151.

Van Acker, V., van Wee, B. & Witlox, F. (2010). When transport geography meets social psychology: Toward a conceptual model of travel behaviour. *Transport Reviews*, 30(2), 219–240.

CHAPTER 6

Modes and mode choice

6.1 INTRODUCTION: TRANSPORT MEANS AND ENDS: MODES

Modes are typically defined broadly according to the medium through which they travel: air, surface, and water. They are then broken down further into specific vehicles used, which can include the human body alone, namely walking. Over time, technical, social, and economic change has expanded this list. Air, for example, was not a viable mode of human movement until balloon travel was perfected (the first public exhibition of a balloon flight said to be in France in 1783, though more private efforts preceded it (Fortier 2004)), significantly expanded later with the invention of aircraft. Surface transport has always been with us but has been radically transformed successively by steam power, the railway and the automobile. An entirely new medium was born with pipelines, which are placed underground and underwater and used to transport liquids and gases. Telecommunications is a hybrid mode that moves information rather than people or goods, but often with similar end results economically. It is not considered as a transport mode *per se* but has significant impacts on modes and mode choice, as discussed in sections below. Modes can further be broken down according to types of vehicles used and infrastructure, noting the specific carrying capacity of both (Rodrigue 2020, Section 5.1). (Vehicles and infrastructure are considered in more detail in Chapter 8.) Mode choice can thus be seen as a complex trade-off between time, distance, spatial range, capacity, and reliability/safety (see Box 6.1).

DOI: 10.4324/9781003350866-8

BOX 6.1 INTRODUCTORY CASE: THE RISE OF THE CAR IN AMERICA

While America did not invent the car, that mode certainly dominated transport there. Between 1907 and 1910, passenger car registrations in the US more than tripled from 140,000 to 458,000, rising to nearly 1.2 million passenger vehicles by 1913. By 1916 that figure itself had almost trebled to 3.4 million (McCarthy 2001, 61).

The economic reasons for this early adoption are manifold. In part there was a very large potential domestic market in a large spread out country with even many cities taking up a large spatial footprint in comparison to the denser and more compact countries and cities of Europe. The car met individual transport needs more closely than those of Europeans which, additionally, had economically matured earlier than the US and thus had developed more extensive and intensive urban and regional rail and transit networks.

This demand helped the American car industry reach and reap economies of scale (EOS) more quickly as well. By 1910 American manufacturers were making 1.6 million cars a year, with Henry Ford's assembly line production of the Model T leading the way, helping that firm became a dominant player and creating a genuine nexus between mass production and mass consumption. Vehicle prices fell and the car became a feature of every middle-class household, many of which were locating in urban suburbs (McCarthy 2001, 61). America's rapid economic growth further fuelled a growing market for cars and other consumer durables.

Government policies also played a critical role in enhancing the uptake of the car, especially its petrol and diesel-powered versions. America's entry into World War I created a major government market for diesel and petrol engine trucks and other military vehicles, and a concern with national security spurred the first major American central government investment in improved domestic roads (Sovacool 2009).

After a downturn in domestic car production and consumption caused first by the Great Depression and then World War II, a true automobile "golden age" unfolded in the post-war period. A major economic driver was the demobilisation of millions of US servicemen, re-entering the economy and establishing millions of new households in the process. The Servicemen's Readjustment Act of 1944 provided low-interest, zero-down payment home loans for servicemen returning from the war, while the Housing Act of 1949 allocated $13.5 billion for urban redevelopment and urban slum clearance. These policies, along with the 1956 Federal Highways Act that launched the construction of a national Interstate Highway System (comprising 47,182 mi of roadways as of 2010) privileged car-based suburban development at the cost of inner-city transit-based living (Garceau et al. 2013, 44). An explosion in car buying, manufacturing, and travel ensued. These built upon interwar trends and policies at the local level which had also favoured the car and relative sprawl over the older compact densities.

The uptake of the automobile in America is thus a multifaceted and multi-causal story with a lot of what economic historians refer to as "path dependency", i.e. small incremental changes often having long-term shaping momentum. There is also a strong guiding government hand in various car-friendly policies, both direct and indirect. The dominance of the car cannot thus be boiled to a simple individual rational maximisation process. From the perspective of an individual trip at a given location and point of time, it may look like this. But the choices themselves have been constrained by many external social and institutional factors (Sheller & Urry 2000, 738).

Particular modes can carry passengers, freight, or both, depending on their technology and context. The pipeline medium is for freight only (though somewhat analogous and earlier pneumatic modes of transit existed which did not catch on); and some vehicles are freight only, such as the container ship (although occasionally small numbers of passengers are carried as a sideline). A basic breakdown of mediums and corresponding modes is provided in Table 6.1.

TABLE 6.1

Travel media and modes

		Surface			
Medium →	Air	Road	Rail	Water	Pipeline
Modes → (Selected – Passenger exclusively or used for either freight or passenger)	Plane	Car Taxi Van/ coach (bus) Motorcycle Scooter Bicycle Walking	Passenger train	Ferry Cruise ship	N/A
Modes → (Selected – primarily or exclusively freight)	Cargo plane	Lorry (truck)	Freight train	Cargo ship Tanker "Ro-ro" ferry	Oil and gas pipelines

Source: Adapted from Rodrigue (2020, Section 5.1).

TABLE 6.2

Modes arranged by power source/medium and major trip purpose, with examples of each. See text for further explanation

Modal power source/medium →	Human power/surface ("active")	Mechanised surface – road	Mechanised surface – rail	Mechanised – water	Mechanised – air
Major trip purpose ↓					
Passenger carriage (examples)	Walking, cycling	Car, local urban, intercity coaches (buses), etc.	Streetcar, subway, regional, commuter rail, etc.	Motorboat	Plane
Human services (examples)	Doctor or nurse doing rounds	Fire, ambulance, construction, etc.	Hospital train during wartime	Ferry, water taxi, etc.	Helicopter
Cargo carriage (examples)	Delivery person on foot	Lorries (trucks) etc.	Freight train etc.	Container ship etc.	Plane

Table augmented by helpful suggestions by Glen Weisbrod. Some "minor" modes, such as sailing boats, are excluded from the table.

Modes can also be arranged according to their major (generic) trip purpose and their motive power source and primary medium. Table 6.2 provides a basic initial arrangement along these lines.

Some modes dominate for some purposes, notably road modes in the human services category, mainly because they offer the optimal trade-offs in accomplishing their aim given current infrastructure and technology arrangements. Other spaces have more available choice sets. The core model suggests that this is mainly due to optimising economic forces. But many institutional rigidities and human quirks affect these trade-offs as well.

6.2 MODE CHOICE

In transport analysis, the travel choice is simplified and broken down into two major components. The first is whether to travel or not, as considered in Chapter 5. The second is mode choice (also called modal choice) which, given an affirmative decision to travel, refers to the traveller's calculations of how to get to where they are going (freight movements have their own complexities considered in Chapter 16). The two choices are interrelated and the presence or lack of suitable or efficient modes can be a key factor in deciding to make a trip or not. If no transit or car is available for a 200 km trip then that trip is very unlikely to be taken at all, even if the activity being travelled to is highly desired. (Travel for its own sake is obviously another matter.) However, unless otherwise stated, theoretical framing of mode choice implicitly assumes a suitable choice of available modes.

Modes can be substitutes or complements to one another (see Chapter 3). This relationship depends on many contextual factors, including traveller characteristics and objectives, available infrastructure and service, and relative mode speed, technology, and operations. Transit might be a substitute for car travel in dense urban areas during business hours, when road congestion and high parking costs make the latter too expensive, or it may be a complement in outlying suburban areas where people drive to park-and-ride facilities to switch to take the train to their employment. And when transit service shuts down overnight (as it does in most cities, except a very few, like New York), the car may be the only alternative for long distances. These relationships will vary by user, with rich travellers, for example, having more feasible options than poor ones. Communication technology can serve as a substitute for actual travel, with a Zoom meeting replacing a face-to-face meeting, for example. But it can also be a complement, enabling communication before, during, and after a trip, increasing the productivity of travel and perhaps encouraging more of it (Anas 2008).

6.3 TRIP HIERARCHIES

Demand for travel by consumers is generally posited as being a hierarchy of linked choices. At the top of the hierarchy are decisions about where to work and where to reside. These necessarily come first and change slowly. Travel choices then flow from these anchors to generate a set of origin-destination pairs, which may link to one another through a series of linked trips, sometimes referred to as a trip chain (Anas 2008). Thus once an agent has chosen a place to live and gotten employment, one major origin-destination pair has been established, i.e. the Journey to Work (JTW). Subsidiary trips can then flow-on from this primary one in order of priority and necessity. If an agent has school-age children, getting them to and from school may be a major subsidiary trip to the JTW. A parent may drop a child off to school and then go to work, constituting one overall major origin-destination pair – home to work – with inserted links in between – home to school and then school to work. There are also trips lower on the hierarchy, such as discretionary travel, e.g. a trip to a park, whose frequency can be modulated, down to zero if needed (that is no trip being taken). Factors that enter into this hierarchy include the time of day during which a trip is made and the combination of sequential links chosen, the overall arc being referred to as a tour. (Trips not linked sequentially by the user are treated as separate journeys) (Anas 2008).

6.4 MODE CHOICE AND TRAVEL TIME

Travel time is a critical part of generalised cost and hence mode choice. As mentioned in Chapter 5, agents are assumed to have relatively fixed travel time budgets which they "spend" on travel, with mode selection flowing from their optimal allocation of time (and money). But some argue that the travel budget should be divided into that portion supporting essential activities (fixed) versus "free" activities (flexible), with each portion likely to vary for each individual over a day, a week, and a lifetime. If this is so, mode choice, and travel choice more generally, may well be much more dynamic than it is generally assumed to be because of the close and variable relationship between mode, trip choice, and personal preference for activities (Banister 2011, 955–956).

Indeed, actual mode choice in the field seems to be more nuanced that the generalised cost-minimisation exercise suggested by theory. As mentioned in Chapter 5, past travel choice and travel habit are fairly strong predictors of current mode choice for many users. Subjective perception of modes is also very important, coaches (buses), for example, often being perceived as inferior to trains, even in cases where the travel time, fare, and amenity may be comparable. Indeed, perception is often stronger than reality, especially with social status and expectation thrown in. Young adults often see car travel as a mark of adulthood, and may dispense with transit, even if more convenient, as a way of signalling and practising their independence and avoiding the disrespect of their peers. Perceptions of personal safety are also very important, with negative perceptions often discouraging transit use, especially by certain groups, such as women (Pronello & Camusso 2011, 1295–1296).

Agents may not always be rational about mode choice in other ways. Escape theory has been posited as motivating some leisure travel, with travel opportunities sought out to evade everyday environments and pursue novelty. In some cases the mode is part of this, with long hikes, cycle rides, or car trips being a major component of the adventure (Banister 2008, 74). Car manufacturers especially have long played on this aspect to market their wares. Early on in the history of the automobile, Henry Ford undertook a series of highly promoted nature outings with the inventor-entrepreneurs Thomas Edison and Harvey Firestone to show how cars could be used to get back out into nature in ways that trains, with their fixed railways and schedules, never could. Early advertising promoted car trips as a cheap, safe, and amicable family affair as opposed to trains. Other marketing campaigns focused on specific needs of specific groups, in each case emphasising the supposedly "universal service" cars allowed, ignoring the relatively limited and poor state of roads at the time (Sovacool 2009, 422).

Having said all this, mode choice is still generally treated primarily as emerging from a hierarchical set of calculations that boil down to maximising utility with a minimised generalised travel cost, of which time is a major component. This may suffice if the majority of travel being assessed is utilitarian in the way the core model frames it. But reality does not always fit easily into purely economic constructs.

6.5 THE FOUR-STEP MODEL

Most travel demand modellers operationalise mode choice using a simplified template called the four-step model. A given travel activity zone (TAZ) is defined, which sets out a particular spatial area containing travellers (e.g. households) who make trips, along with locations (e.g. employment centres) that generate trips to be made by travellers. Across a given set of TAZs, total travel demand is typically calculated using these four steps:

1. Trip generation (each TAZ generates a set of trips by purpose across all travellers)
2. Trip distribution (a potential flow of trips across a transport network is estimated given the relative "attractiveness" of each zone based on purely physical characteristics such as shortest distance)
3. Mode choice (travellers choose their desired travel mode to minimise their generalised cost across their trip distributions)
4. Trip assignment (actual paths taken across the network are generated given estimated traveller preferences and economic constraints) (McNally 2007; NCHRP 1998).

There is much variation in how this model is actually applied, but the template of a four-step process is widely employed for mode choice analysis. The generalised cost model underlying this analysis (introduced in Chapter 5) assumes that lowest generalised cost modes are better than higher-cost ones for making trips. Thus less time-consuming modes, like automobiles, are generally preferred to more time-consuming ones, like walking and cycling (Button 2010).

How often this logic holds is subject to debate. The optimal form of travel mode is not always reducible to travel time saved alone nor is the decision to travel itself as mechanically simple as the generation and distribution steps above suggest. Some of these issues have already been touched on in earlier chapters. The mode decision itself can be bound up with non-economic factors. Litman (2004), for example, poses the provocative question of what people would say when offered the choice of losing their ability to walk or losing their ability to drive. Walking in particular is somehow fundamental to being a human being and not completely reducible to choice of the speediest and lowest-cost mode. These issues will be considered in a bit more detail in the section of active travel later on and periodically throughout the book.

6.6 SURFACE MODES: ROAD

A common underlying requirement for the modern transport system, and thus for mode choice, is infrastructure. Human travel on earth surfaces is ancient, but road travel is comparatively modern. It is true that paved roads appear as early 3,000 BCE in Mesopotamia, and that the Persian Empire had built a functional road system of 2,300 km in the 5th century BCE. Meanwhile the first known use of pavement asphalt is in Babylon around 625 BCE (Rodrigue 2020, Section 5.2). As noted in Chapter 4, surface caravan routes were key parts of intermodal trade links. And, of course, there were the famous Roman roads of the Roman Empire of the 1st through 3rd centuries of the Common Era (see Figure 6.1).

It wasn't until the 18th century, however, that improved roads and road systems, capable of carrying regular and heavy surface travel, became a normal feature of many national and regional economies. The French and British had respectively built stagecoach routes of 24,000 km and 32,000 km by the late 18th century, and both countries, amongst other European nations, had established regular mail services, a major impetus to building such networks. Technical improvements, beginning with John Loudon McAdam's innovative ways of laying, compacting, and binding crushed stone to make durably smooth road surfaces, known collectively as macadam, made roads cheaper to build and maintain and able to carry larger volumes of traffic. Road innovations continued to come with road design adapted to carry the new invention of the automobile at notionally ever faster throughput speeds. Germany's autobahn system, begun in the 1930s, was a notable example here,

FIGURE 6.1
Roman bridge in Alcantara, Spain, built circa 98 CE.

Source: Image from Watson (1927, Plate 27, 47). Book and image are in the public domain.

considered as the first to systematically use specifications such as restricted access, overpasses, and road separation (Rodrigue 2020, Section 5.2).

On the modal technology side, the major advance has been, of course, the car and its extensions such as lorries and coaches (trucks and buses in American parlance). The penetration of the car in modern modal usage has been phenomenal. The US can rightly be seen as the pioneer of automobile usage and there, between 1945 and 2009, the vehicle ownership rate rose from 222 per 1,000 people to 828 per 1,000 people, with a total of approximately 240 million vehicles (in 2010) covering close to 3 trillion mi a year. Vehicle miles travelled (VMT) per capita more than quadrupled during that time, from 1,650 to just under 10,000 in 2010, showing that travel growth grew well beyond vehicle ownership rates (Garceau et al. 2013, 44). Adoption of the automobile was prodigious, if not quite as strong, in developed countries other than America. In the UK, for example, 70% of the population held driving licences with nearly 23 million licenced cars in 1999 (Dant 2004, 68).

Car production has increased to meet (and stimulate) growing demand. Annual global car production expanded from around 34 million to 40 million vehicles in the 1990s to surpass 60 million in the 2010s, though with ups and downs along the way. In 2017, the number of registered automobiles worldwide was more than 1 billion, a first, double that of 2000 and quadruple that of 1990. There are now estimated to be eight people for every car in circulation and motorised surface transport has taken a firm hold in the developing as well as the developed world. More than 2 million cars were sold in China in 2003, growing to more than 9 million in 2008, 22 million in 2013, and an estimated 26 million in 2021. The US is no longer the largest or fastest growing market, stabilising at a sales rate of around 15 million per year (Rodrigue 2020, Section 5.2).

Cars are thus the mode of choice for most individual point-to-point trips. In the 28 countries of the European Union (EU-28) in 2016, there was an estimated 6.8 trillion passenger kilometres (PKM) travelled across all motorised vehicles, with 71% of this on cars. At the same time 3.7 trillion tonne kilometres (TKM) of freight were moved, with 49% by the road and 32% by inland waterways (Noussan et al. 2020, 20).

However, as with all modes, cars dominate only over certain distance ranges. US data indicate that approximately 80% of all car trips take place for distances of less than 20 km, with close to 96% taken at 100 km or less (Rodrigue 2020, Section 5.2). A total of 20 km is the length of the typical JTW, while 100 km is a more typical leisure trip or perhaps a series of chained trips (trips from an origin to multiple destinations before returning) in particularly spread out areas. The US data are indicative of wealthy country patterns overall.

This dominance is not solely due to the rational maximisation dynamics of neoclassical economic theory. There is a significant "lock-in" effect once infrastructure networks and mode technology uptake reaches a certain critical mass, further buttressed by work and residential development patterns. Institutions and planning policies also play an important role, as Box 6.1 at the opening indicates. Box 6.2 discusses the role that broader social dimensions can play as well.

A mention must be made of another major motorised passenger mode, namely the motorbike and its variants. The car came early enough in the developed world that its major competitor in the beginning was the bicycle, motorbikes coming in tandem with, rather than prior to, the car. Motorbike usage did rise with car usage, but was generally more confined to niches and its relative usage rate declined dramatically from the 1960s. The car was the big winner almost everywhere with, for example, the private car accounting for 77% of all passenger miles travelled in the UK in 1970 (Gunn 2018, 11–12).

BOX 6.2 CAR CULTURES

Car usage is definitely part of a large complex including not just the vehicle and its driver, but the petrol company, road operator, and a whole other host of institutions. It is from this complex that "automobility" arises, which consists not just of technology but a whole series of meanings and social markers that, as some social theorists have argued, have made the car a social need, whatever else its transport role may be (Dant 2004, 68). From this social complex arises the "car culture". There is no single definition of the term but it broadly refers to the shared beliefs, values, meanings, and language of a set of car users, large or small. These are most pronounced and defined amongst specialist groups such as self-identified car enthusiasts. But there are also general car cultures, varying by country, that define both "in" and "out" groups, especially those with and without access to a vehicle.

In France, for example, there were 2.7 million cars in France in 1954, but roughly 27 million ten years later. The ubiquity of the car led to a corresponding ubiquity in auto-focused social discourse, from adult conversations through to daily newspaper reporting. France's biggest popular weekly *Paris-Match* (which sold 1.8 million copies a week in 1958) would devote several pages each issue to the new models to be presented at the *Salon de l'Auto* (that is the car show, which were often visited by entire families), the annual race at Le Mans, new motorway construction, the opening of new assembly lines, the latest technical innovations, and the luxury cars of celebrities. This was also part of the content of the weekly cinema "newsreels", where racing cars in particular were presented as exhibiting new performance enhancers that would supposedly be coming soon to the ordinary motorist (Lemonnier 2013, 744).

Indeed, the social meaning of the car was a prominent feature of its introduction and adoption early on. The 20th century was seen as an era of ever-expanding technical progress that would bring social and political progress as well, and the car's novelty and rapid and on-going improvements was seen by both elites and the person-in-the-street, as a way of participating personally in an exciting phase of "progressive" human history (Sachs 1983, 357). The car was also identified with freedom from the snares of outmoded social tradition, aided by the fact that the car did actually provide personalised mobility to increasing numbers of people, especially in isolated areas, and appeared to provide much more flexibility and accessibility to the urban masses who were dependent on urban transit "traction trusts" and railway monopolies.

Even as some of the car's less attractive externalities, such as air pollution, became increasingly clear early on, the technology's promise inspired various claims that these were not problems at all but new benefits.

New York City health commissioner Royal S. Copeland, who later became a US Senator, claimed in 1922 that the car would improve physical health rather then hurt it because flabbiness set in from the waist upwards and the steering wheel of a car would fight such flabbiness better than walking because walking focused on the legs. Unsupported claims such as these were widespread amongst doctors and other health professionals, some of them secretly in the direct pay of the car industry, mainly because the car was seen as an inevitable force for progress, as was technology in general (Ladd 2008, 20–24).

There was resistance to the car, just as there was resistance earlier to factories and mechanisation during the early days of the Industrial Revolution. Stone throwing was recorded in Germany, Switzerland, and the Netherlands, amongst other places. Farmers would often throw dung at urban roadsters passing through their farms and disturbing livestock, and they sometimes ploughed roads to block cars (as happened in a widespread way around Rochester, Minnesota between 1904 and 1906), or digging ditches across roads: in Sacramento in 1909 13 cars fell into them. Sometimes ropes and wires were tied between trees, and in one terrible incident outside Berlin in 1913, a couple was beheaded during a Sunday drive when they unwittingly drove through a strung wire (Ladd 2008, 14–28).

Still, the car, like the factory in earlier industrialisation, prevailed. As usual, economic functionality played a big role – the car did improve on speed, access, and mobility of earlier modes. But the car was part of a general reshaping of culture which also has helped entrench the car further, supported by changes in social and economic institutions, and influencing them in their turn.

In the Global South, things have been somewhat different. There cars tended to become dominant after motorbikes, moto-rickshaws, and the like had taken hold. This latter class of vehicle was obviously much cheaper to own and operate than a car, which was generally inaccessible to most of the population in most developing countries. Additionally, the poor state of both rural and urban roads tended to favour more nimble vehicles, especially in highly congested streets in densely populated cities. Bicycles also were a very popular mode (discussed more under the section on active transport). In the poorer two-thirds of the world, car dominance came later and pushed out motorbikes in many places. But it did come, claiming more and more of both the road and overall traffic (Gordon 2012).

6.7 SURFACE MODES: ACTIVE TRAVEL

Active transport refer to any means of transport that does not require an energy source external to human power, basically walking and cycling. It may seem surprising given that it is a fundamental element of human physiology, but walking as a transport mode has actually been falling somewhat precipitously over the last few decades. Between 1995/97 and 2012, British survey data suggest that walking fell from 27% to 22% of all trips in that country with walking seen as less safe and "normal" than it was in the past. Walking is often just an adjunct to longer trips by transit or by car, unavoidable but not preferred in and of itself (Gunn 2018, 3). The longer-term picture is even more stark, with personal travel on foot falling in Britain from 34.8% of all trips in 1975/76 to 23.5% in 2005, and walking to school by children aged 5–10 falling from 73.5% to 49% (Pooley 2009, 146). Data gathered in 2008 show that walking accounted for only 11% of journeys in the US, lower than the average 20% in Europe, though there is considerable variability across countries (Noussan et al. 2020, 15).

Large dense cities in England have resisted this trend somewhat, with 2015 data suggesting that the number of "walking all the way" trips rose by 9.3% between 2008 and 2014. However, population grew at the same rate over this period, so per capita walking rates were stagnant (Gunn 2018, 3). Still, for very short trips walking dominates, with 70% of all journeys of less than 1 mi being on foot. But even for short trips, walking is not always the default option, especially in high auto-traffic environments (Pooley 2009, 146). However, data on walking is often based on surveys, and these tend to under-report walking done as part of multimodal trips. A study of Mexico City, Bogota, Santiago de Chile, Sao Paulo, and Buenos Aires found that walking-only trips accounted for approximately 30% trips in the analysed cities – a fairly high rate globally; but when adjusting to measure walking time across all trips, an increase of between 73% and 217% in daily walking time was estimated (Delclòs-Alió et al. 2022).

As an aside, one-third of all children's trips were on foot in Britain in 2005, though these trips were generally relatively short. Indeed, one of the most important trips for children is going to school. These were once walking trips as a matter of course when families lived and worked near school and when pedestrian landscapes were viewed as relatively safe by parents. But this has changed in more recent times. Illustrative is a Manchester (England) survey that found 50% of travel to school by children aged 10/11 was on foot in 2002/3 as compared to 76% in the 1940s (Pooley 2009, 146).

Cycling is the other major active mode. Some countries like the Netherlands, Denmark, and Germany have very high cycling rates (25%, 18%, and 10%, respectively, in 2008). France, the UK, and the US had 3%, 2%, and 1%, respectively, in that same year (Noussan et al. 2020, 15). Overall cycling in the rich countries accounts for a minority of trips taken and is generally considerably less than walking in most places. This is in stark contrast to the situation during the first half of the 20th century. In Germany the bicycle accounted for 15%–40% of the modal split in most German cities in the 1930s and was 60% in Berlin. In 1930s and 1940s Britain, 20% of journeys to work were undertaken by bicycle. This usage rate fell dramatically after the end of World War II, though. Cycles accounted for only 5% of German travel in the late 1960s, and only 1.3% in 2005 Britain. When adjusted for distance travelled, these figures tend to look even worse: cycling accounted for only 0.6% of total traveller kilometres in 2005 in the UK. And while the Netherlands cycling mode share was 25% in 2008, cycling still only accounted for 6.6% of traveller kilometres (in 2005) (Pooley 2009, 147–148).

The developing world is currently more in the position of developed countries before and just after World War II, with higher cycling and walking shares, but with the car penetrating quickly. Shanghai has become a major global cycling headquarters hub, supported by manufacturing facilities in many other parts of China. China produced close to 40% of all bicycles internationally in the early 1990s, rising to 60% by 2000. But while Chinese cities were once iconic for their throngs of bicycles, between 1990 and 2002, Shanghai's cycling share of all trips fell from 70% to 17% and in 2003 the municipal government banned bicycles from some major commercial streets, to clear space for cars and coaches (Rodrigue 2020, Section 5.2). Indian cities are not quite as far along in this downward trend, with 1999 data in Delhi indicating cycling accounting for over 38% of trips (Pooley 2009, 148). But here too the automobile, in addition to the motorbike – and, to a lesser degree transit – is becoming the preferred mode as income and economic development rises.

Although both walking and cycling are considered active modes, the two are quite different, since the latter requires mastery and use of a relatively sophisticated mechanical apparatus that has the potential for more serious accidents. Interestingly, on average, around 100 million bicycles are produced each year, versus 70 million cars. This discrepancy is largely due to the relative inexpensiveness of cycle purchase and storage as compared to cars. Many cycles are bought, and many of them sit idle.

6.8 SURFACE MODES: RAIL

The railway is the iconic industrial transport innovation of the 19th century, effecting dramatic effects on the economy and the society of that time. A major impact was on travel speed, the railway providing average speeds of over 40 kph as compared to 5 kph (walk) and 10 kph (horse). Over particular stretches trains could travel much faster than this and also carry much greater volumes (Banister 2011, 951).

Rail technology is relatively simple in concept, consisting of a vehicle moving on wheels along parallel tracks. A big advance was the development of the steam engine which allowed for fast and efficient carriage of large volumes over large distances at relatively low cost. Until the advent of the car, rails dominated medium and long-haul travel markets, and many shorter ones as well, for both freight and passenger movements. Rail is still quite important in freight movement (see Chapter 16) and rail technology is a major component in much urban transit (see section below). When considered for intercity and regional movements rail carried 8% of passenger transport in 2016, with the highest shares in India (39% of total passenger travel), China (with 27%), and Japan (11%) (Noussan et al. 2020, 10).

High Speed Rail (HSR) has been the major growth component of global passenger travel by rail. HSR refers to a maximum travel speed rather than a specific technology and is not strictly defined. A system is typically considered to be HSR if it can travel at speeds of at least 250 kph, though the average speed over a route will usually be lower than this depending on stops, traffic, and topography. This speed is gained through carriage and engine design and by laying very straight tracks, segregated from other railways, on long flat runs. The most basic and most common technology is an extension of the traditional rail mode of "steel on steel", with steel wheels on steel rails and electricity as a power source. Magnetic levitation ("Maglev") is a more sophisticated approach, pioneered in Japan, in which magnets using reverse polarity literally lift and carry the train above the tracks with minimal friction. While Japan once had the most extensive HSR network, China has long since overtaken it, primarily using steel-on-steel, with the longest network in the world and continuing to grow. In 2016 China accounted for about two-thirds of global HSR activity, with Japan at 17% and the European Union at 12% at that time (Noussan et al. 2020, 10).

Economically rail is much more efficient than road transport on the basis of capacity and footprint. A single rail line, as compared to a standard four-lane highway, occupies less than half the space and has more than double the capacity (and for typical specifications could carry a notional 335,000 TKM per day versus 150,000 TKM for a road). Both are capital-intensive modes requiring an expensive infrastructure and substantial on-going maintenance and operating costs. But road transportation is much more flexible in terms of its spatial reach, with roads relatively easy to build at various scales penetrating as deeply as needed, and cars can be driven when and where as desired by the operator, and hence very economical for point-to-point travel. This is why railway passenger travel in advanced economies has declined significantly since the end of World War II (Rodrigue 2020, Section 5.3.1). Road transport has also made significant inroads into short-haul freight movement and even long-hauls, considered more in Chapter 16.

6.9 MARITIME (WATER) MODES

Movements across oceans, rivers, and lakes are almost as ancient as walking. Maritime movements remain extremely important for global and some regional freight. But until the 20th century, ship movements were equally important for passengers, especially those moving internationally. For much of history these were exciting and dangerous times for the sea traveller (and often the river traveller too, though these are somewhat less chronicled, with notable literary exceptions such as Joseph Conrad's *Heart of darkness*). Early maritime travellers often had to rely on multiple vessels as the one they started on might break apart in a storm, run aground, or otherwise fail in some way, with repairs far from home often impractical. As noted earlier, around 15% of early modern travellers from Europe to the East Indies never made it to their destination, dying either of disease on board or in shipwrecks (Margócsy & Brazelton 2023, 5).

These problems were largely overcome by the end of the 19th century. The steamship *Great Western* is considered to be one of the first ocean liners in 1838, completing a passage across the Atlantic in just over 15 days. The main advantage of steamships was reliability, since, unlike sailing ships, they need not be delayed by dead winds or diverted by unfavourable ones – though storms were still a problem and refuelling stops were needed. The earliest steam liners used paddle wheels for propulsion and typically had to have sails for supplementary power since early engines and designs were so fuel-inefficient. Passenger capacity was usually 200 passengers or less and thus while steam gained niches in particular markets, sails still dominated through the middle of the 19th century, especially since technical advances in sailing ships markedly improved their speed (Rodrigue 2020, Section 5.4).

However, the introduction of iron hulls, compound steam engines, and screw propulsion in the 1860s reduced crossing times to around eight to nine days and allowed for a vast increase in capacity up to 2,000 passengers. The early 20th century was a golden age of the liner dominating long-distance passenger movements as speeds increased and ticket prices fell sufficiently to cater to most socioeconomic classes (though with obviously quite different levels of service). The liner industry settled into using ships carrying 1,500–2,000 passengers across the Atlantic in five days, carrying many immigrants from Europe to America in the process, as well as increasing numbers of leisure travellers. The ocean liner quickly declined in the face of advances in commercial aviation. By the late 1960s the regularly scheduled passenger liner had fallen into obsolescence with only cruise shipping remaining as the main maritime passenger mode (Rodrigue 2020, Section 5.4).

The maritime mode of ferries, however, are still important, especially where there are many small islands to go between locally and regionally (e.g. Indonesia and the Philippines); complex urban harbour topography with limited or inefficient land access (e.g. Sydney and, to a lesser degree, New York City); or major urban and regional river systems (e.g. Bangkok). Their importance has declined though from earlier times when roads were poor quality and road transport was slow (Tanko & Burke 2017).

6.10 AVIATION

A mere 11 years separated the most successful prototype flight in 1903, by the Wright brothers of North Carolina in the US, to the first scheduled flight with a paying passenger (from Tampa to St. Petersburg across the bay in Florida) in 1914. Though the most chronicled, there are earlier claimants to the "first flight" outside the US. Be that as it may, only 22 years later, in 1936, the American-built Douglas DC-3 made its maiden voyage between New York and Chicago. This plane could carry 28 passengers, attain a top speed of 310 kph, and fly 2,400 km without refuelling. With three-stops, the plane could fly America coast-to-coast (Rodrigue 2020, Section 5.5).

Growth in US air passengers quintupled from 462,000 to 1,900,000 between 1934 and 1939. But airfares were still too expensive for the average traveller, with a 1936 Pan American World Airways return flight between San Francisco costing $US 1,438 (about $US 31,522 in 2023 dollars). After World War II, commercial air travel exploded. By 1956, operating efficiency had increased and fares had fallen sufficiently so that more people in the US travelled between cities by air than by all classes of train. In 1958, airlines surpassed ocean liners in the number of people they carried across the Atlantic (Rodrigue 2020, Section 5.5).

In the UK the number of air passengers increased from just around 1 million to 6 million between 1950 and 1960. Heathrow airport was opened in 1946, and Gatwick in 1958, setting the stage for another 30 years of prodigious aviation growth, the volume of international passengers travelling from UK airports increasing from 5 million in 1970 to 14 million in 2000, with passenger miles rising by a factor of 7 (Gunn 2018, 14, 20).

A big reason for this expansion was the increase in speed that the jet engine brought, as well as a sizeable boost in passenger capacity of the planes themselves. The Boeing 707, the Douglas DC-8, and other jets of the late 1950s doubled the speed of air travel, increased flying range, lowered unit operating costs, and, most importantly from an economic point of view, lowered fares. By the middle of the 1960s, direct flights covered a global network of major cities, and the refuelling stops used for long-haul flights in the 1950s, such as Gander, Canada, and Recife, Brazil, dropped from itineraries, similar to how earlier passenger steam liner efficiencies allowed for dropping stops at coaling stations (Rodrigue 2020, Section 5.5).

Interestingly, other than the brief niche reign of the supersonic Concorde between 1976 and 2003, the fastest regularly scheduled airliners have cruising speeds similar to the B707s of the early 1960s. What has changed is that planes are much larger, lighter on a passenger-kilometre basis, and more fuel-efficient, allowing for more international non-stops at a lower cost. A total of 20 US cities in 2018 had such services to one or more destinations in Asia, as compared to 13 in 1998. In shorter-haul markets, the number of unique city pairs with commercial air service doubled between 1999 and 2019, numbering around 22,000 in the latter year (though often requiring transfers) (Rodrigue 2020, Section 5.5).

Particularly outstanding has been the increase in safety. There were nine fatal civil aviation accidents across the world in 2018. If early 1960s per-million departures accident rates had prevailed, there would have been three per day (Rodrigue 2020, Section 5.5). This is not to say that safety can be taken for granted. Increasing congestion in the air and on the ground increases the risks of collisions between aircraft, and there have been concerns expressed at various times about economising on maintenance and defects in manufacturing leading to deterioration in safety over the longer run. These developments have not yet become systemic, but that doesn't mean that vigilance and continued effort are no longer required.

Economically, aviation dominates certain ranges and trip purposes, both for passenger and freight. Airlines, as already noted, have taken over most international travel and much domestic medium- and long-haul travel. For very short trips, such as within metropolitan areas, obviously aviation is irrelevant, except perhaps for very rich travellers with private jets or helicopters. For medium-range trips, say between 100 km and 800 km, the choice to take a plane depends on a number of factors. Where there is good, fast rail service, such as with HSR systems, rail often is preferred to air, particularly when downtown-to-downtown origins and destinations are involved, since transfers to and from airports often add considerable time and inconvenience. However, where these alternatives are absent, air travel tends to be preferred, especially for business travel.

6.11 MIXED MODES: TRANSIT

Normally a discussion of urban transit would be placed under a consideration of surface modes as indeed most travel in this mode is on the surface. However transit is actually a medley of multiple modes that travel on various media (though almost not at all by air) and cutting across a number of technologies including rail, road, and ferry, but with a shared purpose of providing relatively low-cost, short-haul common carriage of passengers mostly in urban areas: hence the term of art, urban public transit (UPT).

The earliest form of UPT was the horse-drawn omnibus – from which the modern term "bus" is obviously derived – which was essentially a carriage capable of carrying a relatively large number of passengers, for a fixed fare on a fixed schedule. The main market for the omnibus was the growing urban middle classes going to and from burgeoning "office" work and fares were set with this market in mind. The omnibus established a transit "habit" that was built upon in later decades (Young 2015).

Mass growth in transit came with mechanisation, first with the use of rails, and then, in the late 19th century, with electrification. Innovations in carriage design led to the creation of much higher capacity vehicles that came to resemble the streetcar (or tram, to use a synonymous term). Putting this vehicle on rails, at first still using horses, provided for smoother, faster, and more efficient transport of passengers within cities. But electricity allowed for true mass urban networks. Prior to this limited use of the stream engine was attempted but was too dirty and unreliable for urban transit although steam power did work when powering underground cables to pull cable cars. Electricity ushered in the golden age of the urban streetcar in Europe and America between 1890 and 1915. In the US in 1890, 2 billion annual streetcar trips were made; in 1905 the number was 5 billion. Technical innovation continued throughout this period, with the building of underground subways (generally referred to as metro systems in Europe) (Young 2015).

UPT however peaked by the second decade of the 1900s. Only 1 billion annual trips were added in the US between 1917 and 1923. Transit ridership across all modes peaked in 1926 (outside of an anomalous spike driven by World War II and its immediate aftermath during in the 1940s and early 1950s with petrol and other rationing) at more than 17 billion passenger trips, a number never attained again. Declines in American transit growth took place in the context of a huge uptake of automobile ownership, with the petrol engine penetrating transit as well: bus companies arose in the 1910s and took hold in the 1920s when they first established service to new outlying suburbs beyond the reach of streetcar networks. In 1924 one survey counted around 1,000 buses on American streets, and more than 20,000 in 1932. Streetcars declined as a result, with 70,000 operating in 370 cities in 1912, but only 1,200 in 7 cities in 1962 (Young 2015).

In this way the petrol engine has often been antithetical to transit adoption, especially in the US. The car was much more efficient for point-to-point trips and the need for such trips expanded as car-based employment and residential development grew, creating more and more origins and destinations outside of fixed rail networks with lower densities less and less economical for transit companies to service. But the coach, which was lower-cost to operate, proved to be an unpopular alternative with riders. As it became a replacement for streetcar lines – which were rapidly torn up and decommissioned across the US and, to a lesser degree in Europe – transit ridership fell along with transit company operation revenues, resulting in service cuts and further reduced transit usage in a vicious circle. In the US absolute numbers of annual passenger transit trips bottomed out in 1973 but per capita rides continued to fall (Young 2015). In Britain between 1966 and 2005, 40.3% the percentage of all journeys that were undertaken by bus or train fell from 40.3% to 8.2% (Pooley 2009, 148).

Granted, the US (and to a lesser degree the "Anglosphere" of Britain, Canada, Australia, and New Zealand) is something of an outlier. In 2005, 38.8% of work trips were on UPT in Europe, compared to only 9% in the US. Motorised private transport accounted for 88.5% of all American trips and 79.1% of Australian and New Zealander journeys. But the figures in the rest of the world that year were not quite so dire, with respectable shares in the Middle East (55.9%); Western Europe (49.7%); High Income Asia (41.6%); Low Income Asia (35%) (and similar for Latin America); Africa 32.3%; and Eastern Europe 26.8% (Pooley 2009, 148).

In the developed world, transit, especially rail-based Metro commuter rail systems, is still very important in big cities, even within the US. For example, European metro systems across 46 cities carried 10.8 billion passengers in

BOX 6.3 COVID-19 AND TRANSIT USAGE

The Covid-19 pandemic hit urban public transport hard. Bus systems in Europe and the US had average ridership declines of between 40% and 80% during the first year of the pandemic. New York's subway and commuter rail ridership was down 80% and bus ridership was down 50% in the first week of July 2020, coming off a peak subway ridership decline of 94% in late March.

While ridership has since risen substantially, in many places transit usage has not yet recovered to its pre-pandemic levels. Is this a permanent change? Or will transit ultimately make a full comeback? While it is too early to make definitive predictions, initial indications are that even in some high-transit ridership cities some subtle shifts that have taken place. Bikesharing in New York City, for example, has rebounded more strongly than subway usage, partly as it is seen to be less prone to exposing the rider to disease, and perhaps also because some who began using shared bikes during the pandemic have become habituated to continued utilisation. From a longer-term perspective, the pandemic has clearly cemented a shift towards working from home. This obviously affects ridership across all modes. But the closure of many downtown offices has hit transit harder in many cities because rail systems in particular are still oriented towards commuting to central business districts (CBDs), while cars are not so locked-in. Quite a few people have also moved out of cities entirely, either to suburbs or more remote communities, sometimes relying on telecommuting exclusively.

It must be noted that much research has been concentrated on the rich countries of the Global North. For the poorer countries in the South, the picture is more complex. These countries still generally have lower car and higher transit penetration and some of them, especially in Africa, were affected quite differently by Covid-19 than elsewhere. There were disruptions but they varied quite widely and don't seem as persistent.

Transit is very unlikely to require an epitaph, given its necessity in dense urban areas especially. But the trajectory it was on before 2020 has been deeply altered in ways that remain to be seen. When and whether it will come back to its pre-pandemic growth trajectory is still unclear. (Some of the larger issues arising from Covid-19 and communicable disease more generally are considered in Chapter 16.)

(Discussion above is based on Karner et al. 2023; and Wilbur et al. 2023)

2017 (Noussan et al. 2020, 20). And buses carry additional passengers to places that rail does not serve. The Covid-19 pandemic did, however, cause a major rupture in this and the sector has not yet recovered to pre-pandemic levels (see Box 6.3).

In the developing world, transit remains more utilised. By the end of the 2000s, Mumbai motorised public transport modes accounted for 40.9% of all travel (versus 9.3% by motorised private travel) and in Chennai (Tamil Nadu) 44.5% (versus 8.8%) (Pooley 2009, 148). Some of the biggest new transit starts are in countries outside the Global North. In South and Central America bus rapid transit (BRT) was present in 55 cities, carrying more than 20.5 million passengers per day, a 60% share of global travel by that mode. One of the longest fully automated rail transit systems opened in Dubai in 2009, while a huge new and technologically advanced subway is being built in Riyadh, Saudi Arabia, exploiting advanced technology to face the harsh weather conditions in the region, which includes intrusion of sand in the vehicles and extreme temperatures requiring robust cooling systems. There are also a number of rail and BRT systems that have been opened in Africa (Noussan et al. 2020, 24). However "informal" transit systems, unregulated and operated by independent entrepreneurs, still dominate in many countries.

These facts indicate that technological innovation is as present in transit as it is in other transport modes, though not always "high tech". BRT uses buses, a technology over a century old, but delivering speed and capacity equal to, and yet more cheaply than, most light rail transit (LRT) by using dedicated infrastructure, advanced signalling and ticketing, and automated operations wherever possible. Indeed, LRT itself could be said to be a relatively simple, though streamlined, update of the streetcar.

REFERENCES

Anas, A. (2008). Urban transportation economics. In Durlauf Steven N. and Blume Lawrence E. (eds). New *Palgrave dictionary of economics* (2nd edition). Palgrave Macmillan, 6139–6197.

Banister, D. (2008). The sustainable mobility paradigm. *Transport Policy*, 15(2), 73–80.

Banister, D. (2011). The trilogy of distance, speed and time. *Journal of Transport Geography*, 19(4), 950–959.

Button, K. (2010). *Transport economics* (3rd edition). Edward Elgar.

Dant, T. (2004). The Driver-car. *Theory, Culture & Society*, 21(4–5), 61–79.

Delclòs-Alió, X., Rodríguez, D. A., Medina, C., Miranda, J. J., Avila-Palencia, I., Targa, F., Moran, M. R., Sarmiento, O. L., & Quistberg, D. A. (2022). Walking for transportation in large Latin American cities: Walking-only trips and total walking events and their sociodemographic correlates. *Transport Reviews*, 42(3), 296–317.

Fortier, R. (2004). *The balloon era*. Canada Aviation Museum.

Garceau, T., Atkinson-Palombo, C., Garrick, N., Outlaw, J., McCahill, C., & Ahangari, H. (2013). Evaluating selected costs of automobile-oriented transportation systems from a sustainability perspective. *Research in Transportation Business & Management*, 7, 43–53.

Gordon, C. (2012). The challenges of transport PPP's in low-income developing countries: A case study of Bangladesh. *Transport Policy*, 24, 296–301.

Gunn, S. (2018).The history of transport systems in the UK. In *Future of mobility: Evidence review foresight*. Government Office for Science, Centre for Urban History, University of Leicester.

Karner, A., LaRue, S., Klumpenhouwer, W., & Rowangould, D. (2023). Evaluating public transit agency responses to the Covid-19 pandemic in seven US regions. *Case Studies on Transport Policy*, 12, 100989.

Ladd, B. (2008). *Autophobia: Love and hate in the automotive age*. University of Chicago Press.

Lemonnier, P. (2013). Auto-anthropology, modernity and automobiles. In Graves-Brown, Paul, Harrison, R., and Piccini, A. (eds). *Oxford handbook of the archaeology of the contemporary world*. Oxford University Press, 741–755.

Litman, T. (2004). Economic value of walkability. *World Transport Policy & Practice*, 10(1), 5–14.

Margócsy, D., & Brazelton, M. A. (2023). Techniques of repair, the circulation of knowledge, and environmental transformation: Towards a new history of transportation. *History of Science*, 61(1), 3–18.

McCarthy, T. (2001). The coming wonder?: Foresight and early concerns about the automobile. *Environmental History*, 6(1), 46–74.

McNally, M. G. (2007). The four-step model. In *Handbook of transport modelling* (vol. 1). Emerald Group Publishing Limited, 35–53.

NCHRP (1998). *Travel estimation techniques for urban planning*. National Cooperative Highway Research Program Report 365. Washington, DC: Transportation Research Board.

Noussan, M., Hafner, M., & Tagliapietra, S. (2020). The evolution of transport across world regions. In *The future of transport between digitalization and decarbonization*. Springer Briefs in Energy. Springer.

Pooley, C. G. (2009). Mobility, history of everyday. In Kitchin Rob and Thrift Nigel (eds). *International encyclopedia of human geography*. Elsevier, 144–149.

Pronello, C., & Camusso, C. (2011). Travellers' profile definition using statistical multivariate analysis of attitudinal variables. *Journal of Transport Geography* 19 (2011) 1294–1308.

Rodrigue, J.-P. (2020). *The geography of transport systems* (6th edition). Routledge.

Sachs, W. (1983). Are energy-intensive life-images fading? The cultural meaning of the automobile in transition. *Journal of Economic Psychology*, 3(3–4), 347–365.

Sheller, M., & Urry, J. (2000). The city and the car. *International Journal of Urban and Regional Research*, 24(4), 737–757.

Sovacool, B. K. (2009). Early modes of transport in the United States: Lessons for modern energy policymakers. *Policy and Society*, 27(4), 411–427.

Tanko, M., & Burke, M. I. (2017). Transport innovations and their effect on cities: The emergence of urban linear ferries worldwide. *Transportation Research Procedia*, 25, 3957–3970.

Watson, W. J. (1927). *Bridge architecture: Containing two-hundred illustrations of the notable bridges of the world, ancient and modern*. W. Helburn.

Wilbur, M., Ayman, A., Sivagnanam, A., Ouyang, A., Poon, V., Kabir, R., & Dubey, A. (2023). Impact of COVID-19 on public transit accessibility and ridership. *Transportation Research Record*, 2677(4), 531–546.

Young, J. (2015). Infrastructure: Mass transit in 19th-and 20th-century urban America. In *Oxford research encyclopedia of American history*. Oxford University Press.

CHAPTER 7

Cost

7.1 INTRODUCTION: THE MEANING OF COST

Cost in a generic sense refers to a sacrifice made to obtain a goal, or a sacrifice imposed by circumstances, or both. In economics, the term cost also refers to this sacrifice but is more specific in referring to real resources actually used and, in the consumer case, the loss of satisfaction (disutility) that such sacrifice entails. Since the core theory posits that agents are always maximising and thus always weighing potential alternatives, a concept of opportunity cost arises, which refers to the value of the "next best" alternative given up to pursue the option actually chosen. Transport cost, however, requires much more elaboration, given its importance to travel behaviour. While the theory speaks of agents generically, even in theory these agents can be in very different positions, and the way in which they incur and bear costs can be very different as well (Box 7.1).

The core model itself distinguishes between transport suppliers and transport demanders. Assuming these are completely separate activities by different sets of agents, it is already clear that the supply side will have a very different relationship to cost than the demand side. The discussion thus far has been framed explicitly in terms of derived demand. But suppliers of transport do not face the cost of travel but the costs of supplying it, a basic cost of doing business. These costs obviously need to be minimised, but that minimisation is tied up with production technology (such as whether there are increasing returns to scale (IRS) or not) and market environment (such as the level of competition), not based on a supplier's own preferences and any associated disutility. Also, unlike the demand side, higher levels of travel are

DOI: 10.4324/9781003350866-9

BOX 7.1 INTRODUCTORY CASE: THE COST OF HORSES

During the early period of industrialisation, the horse was a primary mode for many journeys. In 1815, Sweden had a horse ownership rate of around 1 per 6 people, Great Britain had around 1 per 10, and Belgium about 1 per 16. As late as 1900, US per capita horse ownership peaked at 1 per 4 people (Marchetti & Ausubel2001, 23). Granted, the horse was used mostly in rural areas and on farms. But it increasingly made its way into the growing cities of the 19th century for urban passenger and freight carriage. The horse was the motive force of early mass transit in the form of the omnibus, a large horse-drawn wheeled carriage similar to a stagecoach, serving the general public at a fixed fare. Omnibus service originated in Nantes, France, in 1826, spread to Paris in 1828, and then to other French cities and London by 1832. A similar service began in New York in 1828 and was present in Boston, Philadelphia, Baltimore, and other American cities by the 1840s (Young 2015).

The omnibus ran on streets. Its successor, horse streetcars (colloquially known as horsecars), ran on rails, allowing for larger cars carrying three times as many passengers as the omnibus and providing a faster, quieter, more comfortable ride. The horsecar also had a lower operating cost per passenger mile, allowing for cheaper fares, around 5 cents per ride in the US as compared to 12 cents for an omnibus. Horsecar service penetrated most major and many secondary cities in the US by the 1860s, and by the 1880s, almost 20,000 horsecars rode on over 30,000 street railways across the country, although European uptake was somewhat lower (Young 2015).

Horse-powered urban transport, however, began to decline by the end of the 1800s. Electric streetcars had almost totally replaced horsecars in the US by 1917. And the automobile was rapidly replacing the horse for personal use and urban deliveries by then as well. This development arose largely because of the greater efficiency, speed, reliability, and capacity of the new modes. Motorised lorries could haul four times as much produce as horse-drawn vehicles per square foot of street space and hence could be accommodated by existing streets much more easily than horse carriages (Foster 1979, 368, 372). A horse team might cover 18–20 mi over the course of a day but at an average speed of between 3 and 5 mph, requiring frequent stops for water and rest (Sovacool 2009, 413). Motorised and electrified transport could do much better than this.

But the shift away from horses also occurred because of the shift in cost structures that using horses for transport on a large scale brought. Once horses were pressed into carrying people and goods in growing dense cities, their normal operating features began to cause significant problems. Manure and stable flies were one thing on farms or in small towns. In quantity on city streets, masses of manure caused stench, hazards to walking, and increased street maintenance costs due to manure removal (Foster 1979, 368). Additionally, horses died at especially high rates in difficult urban conditions where they were usually driven too hard. Carcasses were usually simply left to rot on the street, with very negative amenity and health consequences. New York City disposed of an average of 15,000 horse carcasses every year, a costly exercise in and of itself, made even worse by disease outbreaks. The worst episode in North America was the 1872 equine influenza epidemic, known as the "Great Epizootic", concentrated on the eastern seaboard and killing many thousands of horses, creating a crisis for the horsecar industry, which saw much of its fleet wiped out (Young 2015).

Horses themselves were also very expensive to buy and even more expensive to maintain. They required regular attention and care, and a whole host of skilled tradesmen were needed to keep them fit for transport duty, such as stable hands, blacksmiths and veterinarians. They typically ate their value in feed each year and, even if well cared for, would have a work life of only around five years. If treated poorly, as many were, they expired considerably sooner. Substantial infrastructure in the form of stables and yards was needed, taking up scarce urban land that could otherwise be used for more valuable pursuits and requiring substantial direct expenditures for operations and upkeep. These facilities also were unsanitary and had to be sited well away from residences and businesses (Young 2015).

In short, horse travel on a mass scale incurred increasing operating, maintenance and capital costs which newer modes addressed more efficiently. Even the bicycle seemed preferable on these terms when it became widely used by the 1880s, requiring less maintenance, limited space for parking and storage, and much less cost to buy and run (Sovacool 2009, 414). Once streetcars and then cars came into being, the contest with horses was finished, at least for urban transport. The use of horses continued on in rural areas and for niche use in cities, but as a mass mode, its time was over.

good for suppliers since this boosts sales and revenues and hence potential profitability.

The core model treats transport demand and supply as independently formed from one another, but in fact, their interaction is constant and dynamic. For example, transport demanders often provide at least some of their own supply of transport. At one extreme, walkers use their own bodies to power and move themselves around. But even with motorised transport, travellers make substantial investments in supply, such as maintaining their private car (with carsharing and other collective modes adding another wrinkle to the picture). Freight and cargo supply and demand and the markets they operate in are quite different from passenger markets, as is the nature of costs.

Even when supply and demand are independent, what does it mean to supply transport? Does this consist merely of providing vehicles? This is so for some individual transport companies, but obviously not from a system perspective since infrastructure, such as roads, is needed, and these are often provided by varied parties with varied cost structures. Sometimes these parties are governmental or public–private, with very different ownership structures and incentives and cost relationships from purely private commercial enterprises.

The initial default in this chapter, following the core model, will be to assume independence of supply and demand. "Cost" will be defined as referring to any changes in actual resource positions and, where relevant, changes in utility that these underlying alterations lead to. Accounting changes (referring to alterations in accounting statements such as a balance sheet) or financial changes (referring to changes in monetary positions) are not the focus and are discussed in Chapter 10, unless otherwise noted. (It is true that financial and accounting changes are generally based on economic changes. But their function is to point to resource positions, and they are not the changes themselves, which is what economists are focused on.)

Economists make a distinction between "direct" or "internal" costs that are captured in market transactions and taken into proper account by relevant decision-makers and "external" or "indirect" (or "social") costs that are not fully internalised by markets and market actors and thus not fully reflected in market prices and decisions. This chapter focuses on direct internal costs, with external indirect costs considered in more detail in Chapter 13. The discussion below begins with supply and then moves on to demand.

7.2 TRANSPORT SUPPLY COST: SPECIFIC, JOINT AND COMMON COSTS

A distinction can be made between specific, joint and common costs of production. Specific costs are those that are fully identifiable and attributable to a specific input and activity in production. In a transport setting, the wages paid to stevedores unloading a ship are an example of a specific cost, completely identifiable as an input expense separate from any other expenses. Joint costs are those in which the production of one output necessarily results in the production of another output, and thus the cost incurred in producing the first output necessarily leads to the costs incurred in the second. A classic transport example is a cargo ship that carries goods to a port and then must eventually return home. The return trip out is an inevitable outcome of the outbound trip. The only way to escape a joint cost such as this is to avoid production entirely (Button 2010, 133). In this example, the joint cost would be avoided only by the cargo ship foregoing the entire journey. The cost of the first trip is thus not just the sacrifice made for that trip but the costs of the return trip itself, and it is that return trip that might make all the difference between profit and loss. A "dead run" return where nothing is carried back to the starting point for further trips can be especially costly. But these costs may be defrayed by using that return trip for some useful end, such as carrying personnel back to a rail terminal after they have been gathered together from other lines (Levinson et al. 2016, 146).

A common cost refers to two different outputs jointly produced from a single activity which are not fully separable from that activity. A classic example of a common cost is a plane that provides both cargo and passenger service on each round trip. The round trip cost of these two services is joint, but there is some ability to adjust the cargo and passenger trip costs since the number of passengers and cargo carried can be varied by the operator to some degree, though constrained by market conditions such as demand. Facilities that are often used to produce more than one transport service simultaneously are another example, as when a terminal services both freight and passenger journeys and/or multiple modes. Common costs sit between specific and joint costs in terms of their separability (Levinson et al. 2016, 146–147).

Transport services more generally are sometimes jointly produced to some degree by both consumer and producer. One could say that in these cases there might be common and joint costs shared across producers and consumers. This presents some interesting conceptual issues, to be touched on in the sections dealing with user costs.

7.3 TRANSPORT SUPPLY COST: TIME-FRAMES

The dynamics of the passage of time are not explicitly modelled in the augmented core model which, by default, has no time. Instead, economic theory defines time implicitly with respect to production costs by referring to a "long run" in which all factors related to production can be adjusted and a "short run" in which only some factors related to production can be. In general, the shorter the time-frame, the less the possible adjustment. There is not a specific length of calendar time associated with short or long (or intermediate) runs since they are defined according to relative ability by a producer to adjust factors and thus adjust costs, and this will be highly contextual. At the extreme short-run of an hour, very little can be adjusted. Even cancelling worker shifts would be unlikely to be feasible in such a time-frame. On the other extreme of, say, a century, almost everything, including fundamental production technology, can conceivably be altered.

Economists thus use the terms fixed (FC) and variable cost (VC) to refer to a cost that has to be taken as given – fixed – within a given time-frame versus those that can be varied – variable – within that time. FCs do not vary with the level of activity (put another way, such costs are constant for every level of activity). FCs are also sometimes referred to as sunk costs because, it is argued, from a decision-making point of view, they are "sunk" into the background, i.e. irretrievable and not adjustable. The initial cost of building a railway track, once it is built, cannot be varied any more, however much or little that track is used (Button 2010, 118–119). In practice, however, FCs are not necessarily sunk costs if the facilities built can be used for other activities. A rail terminal building might be redeveloped into a tourist destination, for example, and its initial costs thus "recovered" in a sense. Thought of this way, sunk costs can be said to be FCs that also cannot be used for any other activity. In general, FCs have a very clear meaning, while sunk costs can be said to have more nuance. (Thanks to José Manuel Vassallo for this insight.)

Contrasted with this is VC, which does vary with the level of activity. Operating costs associated with running the trains in the example above vary with the level of service provided and can be adjusted accordingly, at least within the constraints of the market and the resources of the operator. Only VCs are a true decision variable at any given point in time. This would include repurposing of assets that were built with past expenditures, with repurposing costs being variable. However, the presence of a useful asset within a current portfolio nonetheless can shape the decisions of agents, even if its purposes and costs are totally fixed. For example, if one already owns a car, one may use it rather than alternatives, even if those alternatives might be cheaper, simply because one already has the car. This would be considered flawed rationality in the core theory, but the case is obviously arguable.

Transport producers often face a problem of unit cost-minimisation across multiple time-frames at once. Consider, for example, a railway company which owns both its rails and its wagons and engines. Such a company is typically operating with a high proportion of FCs in the form of the rails themselves, which may have useful lives measured by 50 years, wagons that may last for 10–20 years, signals and other technology that may need to be updated every 5–10 years, and significant labour requirements that can be adjusted within 1–3 years depending upon contract requirements and labour availability. By comparison, a trucking company may have little long-term FC, using public roads, with the trucks themselves an FC but only for a few

BOX 7.2 THE RELATIONSHIP BETWEEN SHORT- AND LONG-RUN COSTS

Economists provide a template for analysing costs that arises directly out of the economic theory of production. A cost function is a microeconomics concept used to analyse the relationship between the production of goods and services and the cost incurred by their production. Just as producers aim to maximise the profit obtained from selling goods and services into a market given their production function, they simultaneously aim to minimise their overall costs given that same production function. Formally speaking, the latter problem is the observed side of the former, with the production function generating a corresponding cost function.

A generic cost function might look like this:

$$C = f(Q, T, P_f, F)$$

where
Q = quantity produced
T = production technology used by the producer
P_f = factor (input) prices (e.g. for labour) (these being the source of much VC)
F = fixed factors – factors of production that cannot be changed in the production period, e.g. plant and equipment (the source of much FC).

A very simple (linear) example of such a function is of a bicycle manufacturer that pays $6,000 in rent and an average of $8,000 for labour and other costs each month to produce each bicycle. The cost function for one month of production is C(Q) = 6000 + 8000Q. Technology is implicit as a given and embedded in these figures. If this company produces 10 bicycles, its total cost (TC) for the month will be 6000 + 8000(10) = $86000.

Cost functions such as these can be graphed to yield corresponding cost curves. Figure 7.1 shows such a graph to illustrate the relationship between cost time-frames, in this instance using a typical depiction of nonlinear cost functions. In the short-run, there are TCs yielding short-run average cost (SRAC) and long-run average cost (LRAC) relationships. (There are also short- and long-run counterparts of marginal costs not depicted here.) What a graph like this purports to show is how SRAC changes over time, tracing out an "envelope" of LRAC curves. This particular graph shows an archetypal U-shaped pattern in which average costs first fall, then flatten and then rise over the long-run, indicating changing EOS and other business patterns. This diagram is illustrative, not prescriptive, as many different patterns are possible (Harrison & Snavely 1961, 109–112).

How these curves actually morph into one another over time is implicit. The relationship between short-run costs and how these accumulate into long-run ones may appear to be a simple exercise of adding up the former into the latter, as the graph suggests. But as time-frame changes,

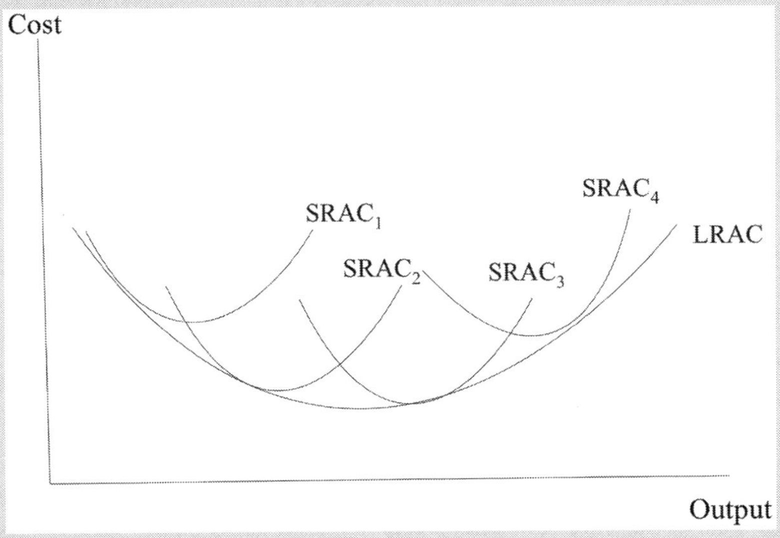

FIGURE 7.1
The "envelope" of short-run and long-run cost curves.

more costs become variable, and their behaviour changes as a result. A standard assumption behind a graph like this is that a variable factor of production (such as labour) is continuously available over time and that there are perfectly competitive markets in both input and output markets. These conditions often do not hold in reality, and they are particularly dynamic over time. Actual relationships between short- and long-run costs thus usually need to be treated heuristically and empirically. Button (2010) captures this idea in his phrase of "temporal divisibilities" with respect to fixed and variable costs, an interesting phrase though not in general usage (118).

years or so, and labour perhaps being adjustable over months if freelance workers are used. These are indicative, not actual, figures. The point is that the proportion of FCs and VCs will range widely depending upon context and change over time.

This dynamic can be encapsulated by the term life-cycle costs. This can be one reason that operators sometimes (in some instances mandated by regulators) only operate one aspect of a business. For example, in Europe and some other countries, the standard is to have rail networks owned and operated by one company and rail services delivered by another company. This simplifies the optimisation problem by narrowing the time-horizon that separate managers need to focus on (Mizutani & Uranishi 2013).

The relationship between short- and long-run costs can theoretically appear fairly clear-cut, but not always so easy to work out in practice. Box 7.2 provides a basic exposition of the standard economic theory on how short-run costs add up to long run ones.

7.4 TRANSPORT SUPPLY COST: ACTIVITY LEVELS AND SCALE

Costs may vary continuously or discretely with different levels of output or expenditures. That is, a particular production cost may change in a continuous manner along with an input. For example, total fuel costs can rise continuously with kilometres travelled by a truck (given a set speed of travel), so if a litre of diesel costs $1 and a truck can go 10 km per litre, then costs will rise across every minute fraction between $0 and $1 and every fraction above that, no matter how small, between 0 km and 10 km and beyond (*ceteris paribus*, of course).

However, many costs do not change continuously with activity but change in chunks from one amount and then up (or down) to another. A simple example of this would be a driver hired by the hour for a fixed wage rate of $30 per hour, paid regardless of how much work is actually done during that hour. Costs here would rise by $30 for each hour of contracted driving, and costs would rise by steps of $30, $60, $90, etc. This sort of change pattern of discrete "lumps" is hence referred to as "lumpy" (a phrase also used in a different context in Chapter 4, but in both cases referring to some degree of intrinsic indivisibility). Lumpy costs (and returns for that matter) are quite typical in many transport operations, especially over the longer-run when infrastructure costs are included (Levinson et al. 2016, 148, 155).

Total production costs over any given period of time are defined as follows:

Total cost (TC) = TVC (total variable cost) + TFC (total fixed cost).

Total cost (TC) and its components can also be expressed as averages. If Q refers to some quantity of output or activity, then average cost (AC) can be expressed as follows:

$$AC = TC/Q$$

which is referred to as unit cost. AC can be broken as follows:

AC = AVC (average VC) + AFC (average FC)

which can be further broken down as follows:

$$AC = TVC/Q + TFC/Q.$$

Note that as the level of Q rises, AFC falls (arithmetically because TFC remains constant in the numerator, while Q increases in the denominator). Changes in TVC/Q cannot be predicted without contextual information.

Finally, there is marginal cost (MC), which refers to the change in TC for a given change in Q. This is how much additional (i.e. incremental or marginal) cost is entailed by producing one more "unit" of output. MC = MVC (marginal VC). Note that there is no marginal FC since FCs are completely unrelated to the level of activity.

As far as transport production goes, many factors affect the variation of costs across activity levels, including capacity utilisation, returns to scale (RTS), economies of scale (EOS), and technical change. EOS is especially important in any transport production that involves the construction and maintenance of large infrastructure facilities and networks and/or utilises large, expensive and sophisticated vessels and supporting technology. For example, maritime shipping generally has increasing EOS because of RTS in its technology, as ever-larger ships can carry more cargo for decreasing costs per unit and the ability of large firms to obtain and maintain market dominance. International maritime shipping is thus dominated by an oligopoly of large global firms, with some variety of small firms in local markets (see Chapter 16 for more discussion of this sector).

The interaction between RTS, EOS and cost can be seen by looking at the simple example of the economics of the shipping container. Figure 7.2 compares two notional containers, one with a volume of $20m^3$ and another with a volume of $160m^3$. The larger "box" has eight times the capacity arising out of a mere doubling of linear dimensions, a very simple example of an increasing RTS due purely to the simple arithmetic of volumes. However, the EOS is determined not just by this technical reality but also by the economy of buying and selling services in the marketplace. If one assumes that the TC for loading, shipping and unloading the smaller container is, say, \$600 per trip, and for the larger one \$1800, then increasing EOS is present since the smaller container has an AC of \$30 per square metre versus \$11.30 for the larger one. As one can see, if these costs change, an increasing RTS may not necessarily translate into an increasing EOS.

This discussion highlights that, in general, transport operators will have ranges of activity over which RTS, EOS and costs will change. Formally, in the case of constant EOS, MC(Q) = AC(Q). That is, for any output/activity level, MCs will equal unit costs and be constant, however much (or little) activity

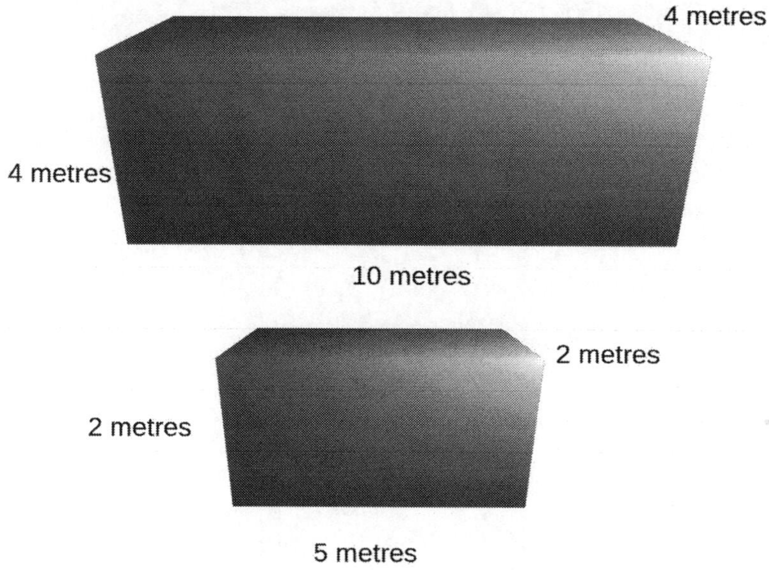

FIGURE 7.2
An example of the RTS, EOS, and costs of shipping containers (see text).

there is. For positive EOS, the pattern will be one of MC(Q) < AC(Q), i.e. MCs fall as Q increases. For negative EOS, MC(Q) > AC(Q). CRS – constant returns to scale – is the default assumption about RTS in the core theory. In the perfectly competitive model, RTS collapses to constant EOS since all producers ultimately are driven down to identical prices for both output and input.

In the real world, in most sectors, and especially transport, RTS and EOS are not typically equal, and increasing or decreasing EOS are common over various ranges of production scale. In actual practice, just as there are multiple time-frames involved in transport production cost, there are typically multiple EOS and RTS dimensions to manage as well, as Box 7.3 illustrates.

7.5 TRANSPORT COST ALLOCATION AND COST ESTIMATION

The ability to accurately trace specific costs to specific activities and actions is actually extraordinarily complex. The formal term for making these determinations is known as cost allocation and refers to the traceability of final costs to their initial drivers (Button 2010, 133). As mentioned in Section 7.2, transport operations are prone to many common and joint costs. As these can be hard to disentangle conceptually, they can be equally hard to trace

BOX 7.3 AIRLINE HUB-AND-SPOKE NETWORKS

After the deregulation of American and then European commercial passenger aviation between the 1970s and 1990s, airlines implemented an extensive "hub-and-spoke" network in which flights from larger destinations were fed into other intermediate destinations before heading on to a final destination. Direct point-to-point service still remained but tended to be confined to very large market pairs, such as New York and Los Angeles, or Rome and London.

There are many reasons for this development, but economically it could be said to have arisen out of a balancing of various RTS and EOS across different aspects of flight production and distribution. On the face of it, hub-and-spoke flying increases some marginal costs (MCs), e.g. overall mileage flown between chosen origins and final destinations, additional take-offs and landings and the terminal and other costs these engender, and the increased possibility and costs of delays along the way. These additional costs were avoided on direct routes (Kockelman et al. 2013, 1.9–1.10).

On the other hand, the hub-and-spoke system ended up serving the airlines well in a number of ways. There were some positive EOS garnered through fleet management and consolidation of demand by gathering it up and distributing it across multiple points on one plane rather than having to individually service smaller markets with single flights (Kockelman et al. 2013, 1.9–1.10).

In some cases, certain airlines also gained oligopoly or monopoly advantages within their respective hubs, such as United Airlines out of Chicago O'Hare and American Airlines out of Dallas/Fort Worth. Smaller regional and budget carriers, meanwhile, took advantage of lower operating costs at smaller and more distant airports to establish their own hubs at these airports and fly to other secondary airports near primary ones. For example, the US carrier Jet Blue established its core hub at Salt Lake City and flew into secondary urban airports around larger cities where possible. Southwest Airlines perfected this strategy, often flying exclusively in and out of such airports. Hub-and-spoke networking thus shows how managing, exploiting and optimising EOS and the associated cost advantages that can result is a multidimensional and dynamic exercise.

and hence allocate. However, cost allocation is a key aspect of trying to plan for cost control in future scheduling of services or setting prices.

There are various methods used to estimate and allocate costs, including econometric estimation of large data sets to establish cost parameters and cost equations in predictive functional forms and data envelopment analysis (DEA), which takes operations data from various internal and external

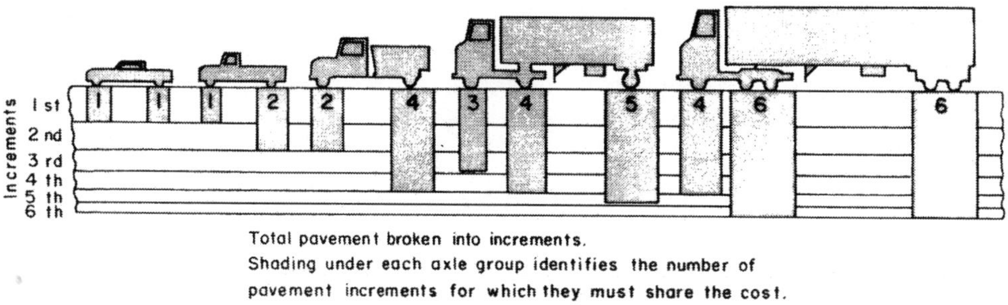

FIGURE 7.3
A conceptual example of highway cost allocation for axle weight.

Source: Image from Wong and Markow (1984, Figure 3, 14). Book and image are in the public domain.

operators to establish efficiency benchmarks against which different cost estimations and allocations can be made and assessed (Button 2010, 153–154; 157–160).

But even sophisticated entities sometimes need to use informed guesses about percentages to make allocations across different cost drivers. This shows that even if full aggregate information is available, its analysis is not always straightforward. One example of this is the determination of the burden that transport users place on infrastructure. Clearly a truck wears out a road more than a car. But by how much? Tracing costs to each category is not easy, requiring a lot of evidence-gathering, analysis and modelling.

As an example, Small, Winston and Evans (1989) estimated the durability of US highways with respect to their ability to bear axle loads from various vehicles and used these estimates to argue for pricing to internalise such costs with the vehicle operator. The simple conclusion was that heavier vehicles should pay more for using the roads than lighter ones. Policymakers in general agree with this premise, and this is why there is a substantial amount of effort devoted to highway cost allocation. The methods for doing this are varied and can be complex, but the conceptual exercise is fairly simple, as shown in Figure 7.3. Engineers look across the various vehicles that use a given roadway and segment them according to axle and weight. Data are collected on the differentials between them in terms of the damage they cause to the road surface and road bed over time. Axle weight is a primary factor here, and, as the figure shows, wear is allocated to vehicles on that basis. However, this wear is also a function of traffic conditions, such as congestion and local climate, and these factors must be accounted for in determining a final maintenance expenditure allocation and setting a level of price for each vehicle (Wong & Markow 1984). In actual practice, road toll settings still often employ the blunt image of axle-pricing on the basis of the number of axles a vehicle has, simply because a full allocation is difficult to estimate and to capture in a price.

7.6 COST AND "EFFICIENT" TRANSPORT SUPPLY PRICING

Obviously cost is critical to the price-setting for transport services. The core model demonstrates (given all its assumptions) that in a perfectly competitive market, the price (P) of any good will ultimately be equalised to the MC of producing it. This formula (P = MC) denotes the "efficient" price because the competitive pressures of the marketplace will keep producers efficient and close to consumer preferences, with an optimum achieved for both sellers and demanders, given existing resource constraints and overall distribution of resources. P = MC is thus the formula often used for establishing the most efficient price to set in lieu of the market price if transport is being delivered in an imperfectly competitive or other flawed market. This is known as MC pricing (see Box 7.4).

Given the difficulties of cost estimation and cost allocation in transport markets, however, it is often very difficult to truly know what the efficient market price would be if the market is not competitive or not fully functioning. A practice that arose under transport and other pricing regulation was the reasonable rate of return rule, in which regulators estimated how much a monopoly service provider should be expected to reasonably earn on its assets if markets were competitive and then worked out what price would provide that return, adjusting it at regular intervals based on changing market conditions over time. A variant on this idea is cost-plus pricing, which has a similar thrust but in which a supposedly reasonable revenue margin is added on to known production costs (Button 2010, 134). This latter formula is still used in some public–private contracts in which the government contracts out services to a private provider (see Chapter 10).

A big issue in all these approaches is the availability of accurate information. Truly competitive markets in the core model sense generate full price information and hence, implicitly, cost and return information as well. But these types of markets exist primarily in textbooks. In general, transport supply markets are not all that competitive, especially because of the wide range of EOS and RTS that predominate. And even a regulated company has many ways of concealing true cost and profit data from regulators. Direct government provision of a service gets around this particular problem but raises others, including the greater potential for the intrusion of politics into operations.

BOX 7.4 THE THEORETICAL BASIS OF MARGINAL COST PRICING

Is what is profitable for a transport supplier necessarily efficient in the economic sense of maximum unit output for minimum unit input and maximised total consumer utility ("welfare") overall? The core theory says "yes", assuming that there are perfectly competitive markets, and given all the other assumptions of the core model outlined in Chapter 2.

Total profit (TP) = total revenue (TR) – total cost (TC). Arithmetically one can show that TP is maximised for a producer where marginal cost = marginal revenue (i.e. MC = MR). The intuition behind this is if MC < MR, the firm is clearing more revenue on each unit than it costs to make it. Therefore, the firm can make more profit by producing more units. If MC > MR, the firm is losing money on each unit and should cut back production.

Since the profit maximisation condition for all private profit-maximising producers is MR = MC, this means that the perfectly competitive market will set a price delivering a productively efficient outcome in equilibrium. Demand (D) is satisfied at this price. Thus, the condition D = MR = MC = P holds, and one can analytically show (proof not shown here) that since D is the sum of all consumer preferences at the margin and consumers are always maximising their utility given their constraints and since producers are all maximising profit and efficiency at MR = MC (given the competitive pressures they face) and since P equalises all these, maximum output for minimum output is being supplied through the market and in the form of just the array of goods and services that maximise consumer welfare. This result is known as the fundamental theorem of welfare economics.

Even if good information is available, MC pricing in transport is actually not quite this simple because all transport links occupy a unique space and, by virtue of that spatiality, attain some measure of monopoly power, even if there is an otherwise perfectly competitive market in place. This may not always be of much practical significance, where there are alternative links, routes, and carriers. But it can be an issue in critical instances, making the setting of a single "ideal" price problematic, perhaps necessitating an array of prices instead (Levinson et al. 2016, 107). In practice, there is no preconceived one-size-fits-all answer that will answer any and all conundrums, although the MC pricing at least provides a benchmark to work with.

7.7 TRANSPORT DEMAND: THE "COST OF TIME" FOR TRAVELLERS

Switching from the supply side to the demand side, core theory posits a traveller whose demand for travel is derived and whose aim is thus to minimise travel cost. As already noted in Chapter 6, the most unique aspect of transport cost is on the agent utility side, rather than from production. Each user has a generalised cost of travel which can be conceptualised as follows:

$$G = g(c_1, c_2 \ldots c_n)$$

in which G refers to generalised cost and c refers to various types of costs incurred (indicated by the numbered subscripts 1 through n).

This can be operationalised with the following equation:

$$G = \Sigma(i)M(i) + \Sigma(j)T(j)$$

This simply says that generalised travel costs equal the sum of the monetary (M) and the non-monetary (T) costs of travel, which here refers to time spent travelling. (The bracketed "i" and "j" terms simply refer to the cost items indexed for each individual expense.)

The transport demand function can be expressed as follows:

$$Q_d = f(G)$$

which says that the demand (d) for a quantity (Q) of travel is a function of G (Button 2010, 143–144, Equations 5.4 and 5.5).

Money costs for motorists include annual registration, fuel, parking, tolls, fines, insurance costs, and other taxes associated with vehicle purchase and ownership. Non-monetary costs involve the time spent taking a journey and the value of that time for each agent. These costs are especially affected not just by time spent but by the experience of the journey itself, such as reliability, comfort (what economists refer to as "amenity", as discussed in Chapter 15), and the loss of the possibility of doing other activities during the trip (i.e. opportunity cost). A trip by HSR may offer much more value to travellers than a trip by a local bus, for example, and in this way be less "costly" from a generalised cost perspective.

The version of generalised cost presented in Chapter 6 – $G = p + u(w)$ – is another way of stating these relationships functionally but here explicitly adding the variable of network service levels as a factor in determining indirect cost. Direct cost (p) is objective and can be objectively measured, although data may be limited. A standard estimate for car ownership is that, accounting

BOX 7.5 INCORPORATING ROAD TOLLS INTO CONSUMER PRICES

User fees and tolls have been an increasing feature for roads and other facilities as a way of pricing efficiently and for operators to cover their costs. Official government measurements of inflation are meant to capture the impact of this pricing on consumers. Transport pricing certainly does increase measured inflation, captured through price change indices, the consumer price index (CPI) being of most importance to assessing the "pocketbook" impact of overall price changes on the person-on-the-street.

Yet, interestingly, the impact of tolls on overall inflation may not always be fully captured in CPI. There are a variety of reasons for this, but an important one is the salience of tolls to those who pay them, i.e. how much a particular item stays in one's consciousness. The rise of electronic tolling has caused the salience of toll payments to fall in drivers' minds, mainly because their collection is so automatic. This can have an effect on CPI measurement, which tends to rely heavily on consumer surveys in which people are asked to keep diaries of their spending, a method that may well underestimate tolls because of their relatively low salience.

Indeed, a study of the US CPI compared actual toll collection data with the toll payment information garnered through the Consumer Expenditure Survey (CES) undertaken by the US Bureau of Labor Statistics (BLS). This study found that tolls were under-reported by around 50%. This obviously does not translate into a proportionate understatement for the overall CPI since that covers many more goods and services than tolls. But it does imply that, in the US at least, the CPI is lower than it would be if tolls were properly accounted for.

This problem is not as bad for non-consumer price indices such as the producer price index (PPI), which does not draw from CES data and which, measuring producer costs, generally is more representative of actuality since businesses generally are much more aware and accurate in their collection of data about their expenses (discussion based on Peters et al. 2015).

for all of the owning and operating, cleaning and maintenance costs, a car owner on average spends 1600 hours a year supporting their vehicle (Sovacool 2009, 411).

However, even here it is not always clear that transport users always correctly perceive their direct costs. Because much travel is habitual, people often become hazy even about actual monetary costs they are bearing. Insurance, tolls and other transport fees are often billed automatically and pulled directly from bank accounts and not very front-of-mind for payers.

Behavioural economists refer to the concept of salience to indicate how notable a particular bit of information is to cognitive and perceptual processes. Many transport costs are not very salient because of their automaticity, even though the actual information is available to the party incurring the costs. Even government statistical agencies may not always be properly recording such costs as a result (see Box 7.5).

7.8 TRAVEL DEMAND: TRAVEL TIME VALUATION ISSUES

While direct costs are observable, at least potentially, indirect disutility cost "u(w)" (as per the generalised cost equation in Chapter 6) is obviously not and must be estimated in some way. One standard metric used by transport economists is the concept of value of travel time (VOTT). VOTT is affected by a number of things, such as travel mode, trip time of day, trip purpose (e.g. business or leisure), trip quality, and characteristics of the traveller, such as their income. This value can also be affected by the variability of travel time, with unexpected time losses potentially creating more disutility than expected ones, since the latter is built into decision-making, while the former is not. Time in motion also likely has a different value than time spent waiting. There are a wide range of VOTT estimates, one average estimate for the US being $US50 per hour by air and $US30 per hour by car, with business trips more valuable than personal ones (Levinson et al. 2016, 198–199).

This utility variability makes estimating VOTT difficult because time valuation cannot just use observable market prices to measure the opportunity cost of travel. Values of time can vary greatly among consumers due to both wage rate and opportunity cost differentials, implying that consumers who undertake similar trips frequently incur vastly different opportunity costs. Averages of values for different broad classes of users are often used (e.g. business versus leisure travellers), but much can be lost in this averaging process. Even average valuations are far from straightforward and often the subject of debate. And there are issues in aggregating individual preferences as well (Anas 2008).

The "w" term in the "u" function also complicates matters further. Congested time increases with traffic flow on a network (whether that is a road or a railway track or some other facility), and this varies by time-of-day, state of the network, and many other factors. Even if preferences and utility are known, overall estimation of "u" is difficult because it varies with "w", and w may not always be observable or clearly measured (Levinson et al. 2016, 190).

BOX 7.6 "EFFECTIVE" SPEED

Estimation of VOTT requires an estimate of "TT" first, i.e. the travel time itself. Traditional VOTT looks solely at costs incurred from the duration of a point-to-point journey alone; the time spent earning the money needed to buy and service the vehicle used to attain this journey is generally ignored. One study took the average wage rate in the US, calculated how many hours of work would be required to cover vehicle operating costs for the typical car whether it travelled or not, and then added these hours into car travel journey time to get an adjusted average travel speed that accounted for these "overhead" expenses. This adjustment suggested that for US motorists, the average car trip had a "net effective speed" of 9.7 mph as opposed to an existing estimate of 25 mph as the probable US average for cars.

This method of calculating the amount of time that must be spent earning money to buy and service a vehicle itself and then adding it to actual journey time is referred to as "social speed" or, more widely, "effective speed". This metric can be applied to any mode, of course. But the effective speed of the vehicles most expensive to buy and maintain will obviously be more impacted than less expensive ones. The standard formula of speed equalling distance divided by time is still used. But travel time measurement is expanded to consider time costs of acquiring and maintaining the mode of transport in addition to time spent moving.

There are various estimates. One, again for America, is that 1,600 hours of earnings time are necessary to get a total of 7,500 mi driven, yielding an average car speed of less than 5 mi per hour for the period studied. By these measures, the "effective speed" of a bicycle could be faster than a car. Under this rubric, there will also be multiple travel times across different vehicles, in different countries, by different socioeconomic groups, at different times. But in principle this is no different from standard travel time estimates, which are also affected by variables such as traffic congestion and socio-demographic differences in mode choice and availability.

There are obviously objections to be made to effective speed. One can accept the argument that information about earnings and time required to obtain a means of transport is relevant and should be collected and reported. But it is also fair to claim that, even so, the mode acquisition and trip/mode choice decisions are separate and should be treated separately. And injecting earnings time into travel time may be combining apples with oranges. For particular trips clock time, such as a 300 km journey that needs to be completed today, may be the critical objective in many cases, even when effective speed might suggest that a bicycle is "faster" than a car.

This is not to dismiss effective speed or other variants of it, for there is nothing sacrosanct about standard speed and cost measures, and every measure has its strengths and weaknesses. Transport does have a wider social and institutional context, and the multiplicity of metrics that attempt to capture this is a good thing. (The discussion above (except for the critique) is drawn from Tranter and Tolley (2020).)

And market prices themselves may be distorted when markets are imperfect in some way. For example, the core theory assumes that since workers agree to work for a contracted pay rate, this is the value they themselves place on time spent working under that contract. But that result assumes perfectly competitive labour markets in which people are paid for the true marginal product of their work effort (see Chapter 12). Yet labour markets are often not perfectly competitive, and wages paid may thus not capture true opportunity cost value. Households also assign a value to home time generally different from work time, with value variations within each category (such as time eating versus listening to music) jointly determining the optimal combination of activities an agent chooses to participate in. In other words, value and activity choice can be seen being set simultaneously, quite different from the sequential VOTT-setting assumed theoretically (Gronau 2008). This is why averages and other heuristics are often used. These may be good enough in practice but are also open to challenge in many instances.

Some critiques of VOTT are more fundamental than this. Already mentioned is the underlying assumption that travel is a "necessary evil" that creates disutility for consumers. If this is the case, minimising travel time is obviously desirable; if not, then things are not so straightforward. Where travel has a positive utility, the VOTT measure obviously gives a distorted picture of the true benefit of a given transport improvement or of travel time more generally.

Banister (2011) makes a more fundamental point about travel time in the context of sustainability. He argues that a single-minded focus on a limited clock-time metric ignores key societal and personal dimensions and, in so doing, biases analysis and decision-making towards certain mechanised modes which excel on this reckoning but which might have other costs and distortions that should be taken into account: "The central concept in all transport analysis has been desire to 'save travel time'. Transport appraisal is almost totally (80%) dependent on the user benefits resulting from travel time savings ... hence the overwhelming desire to speed up traffic" (955).

Banister further notes that time is "embodied and relational" in the sense that people experience it not just in isolation but in relation to themselves as beings with bodies interacting with other beings with bodies. Time is also "culturally constructed" through meanings and values formed in the larger society in which agents sit. This leads not just to individual differences in the experience of time but also social differences within and between groups.

> "This overriding concern with time savings needs to be balanced with a richer interpretation of the many different constructs of time that might begin to increase our understanding of travel decisions, the quality of time and the benefits of slower not faster movement.
>
> (957)

Box 7.6 discusses some of these "social" aspects of travel time. (Chapter 15 discusses the many issues that arise from time valuation in the evaluation of transport programs.)

7.9 TRANSPORT DEMAND: COST AND MODE CHOICE

Standard theory suggests that mode choice, once the choice to travel has been made, is based on the mode that has the lowest cost. The overall choice set can theoretically be described using a low-cost envelope which captures mode-trip bundles that have the lowest generalised cost (G). Thus, travellers with a high value of time will choose faster transport modes with higher direct costs to slower ones with lower direct costs, involving implicit and explicit trade-offs between the value of time and money across different modes. Various studies have come up with a variety of estimates for these trade-offs. One finding that seems relatively robust is that commuters value their travel time at around 1/5–1/2 of their average wage rate, while the value of walking and waiting time is around 2.5–3.0 times greater than in-vehicle time. On average, travellers will prefer to be moving in a faster rather than a slower mode of transport, or waiting on either one, *ceteris paribus*. Travellers also prefer what are perceived to be more comfortable modes (e.g. a train) than less comfortable ones (e.g. a coach), with the disutility cost of time increasing along with the length of the trip (Gronau 2008).

As already indicated, a major share of travel continues to be by car (though varying widely by region), somewhat invariant with respect to operating costs. To use economic parlance, the demand for driving seems to be fairly inelastic (see Chapter 2). There are many reasons for this, including a lack of viable modal alternatives in some places and user treatment of the car as an investment that must be used rather than a service to be employed on a per-trip basis – whatever the logic of "sunk cost" might suggest. Dynamic simulation models also suggest that travellers choose departure–arrival times simultaneously, making time valuation and mode choice much more dynamic than portrayed by static theory (Anas 2008). While mode choice and cost trade-offs can be captured within the core model, in reality mode choice (and travel choice more generally) cannot be completely boiled down to rational cost-minimisation within an optimal equilibrium of a rationally maximising system. Direct costs should be the most amenable to rational choice, but there are limits to this at the level of ability of agents to fully assess their situation in real time. Beyond this, mode choice and cost are often heavily constrained by contextual and environmental factors such as existing infrastructure. Many of these issues are discussed in Chapter 9.

REFERENCES

Anas, A. (2008). Urban transportation economics. In Durlauf, Steven N. and Blume, Lawrence E. (eds). *New Palgrave dictionary of economics* (2nd edition). Palgrave Macmillan, 6913–6917.

Banister, D. (2011). The trilogy of distance, speed and time. *Journal of Transport Geography*, 19(4), 950–959.

Button, K. (2010). *Transport economics* (3rd edition). Edward Elgar.

Foster, M. (1979). City planners and urban transportation: The American response, 1900–1940. *Journal of Urban History*, 5(3), 365–396.

Gronau, R. (2008). *Value of time: From new Palgrave dictionary of economics* (2nd edition), edited by Steven N. Durlauf & Lawrence E. Blume.

Harrison, W. C., & Snavely, W. P. (1961). *Intermediate economic analysis*. McGraw-Hill Book Company, Ltd.

Kockelman, K., Chen, T. D., Larsen, K., & Nichols, B. (2013). The economics of transportation systems: A reference for practitioners. University of Austin, TX, *Texas Department of Transportation*, Project 0-6628.

Levinson, D., Gillen, D., et al. (2016). *Transportation economics*. en.wikibooks.org July 9, 2016. Print (pdf) version.

Marchetti, C., & Ausubel, J. (2001). The evolution of transport. *The Industrial Physicist*, 7(2), 20–24.

Mizutani, F., & Uranishi, S. (2013). Does vertical separation reduce cost? An empirical analysis of the rail industry in European and East Asian OECD Countries. *Journal of Regulatory Economics*, 43, 31–59.

Peters, J., King, D. A., Gordon, C., & Santiago, N. T. (2015). For whom the consumer price index tolls: Reporting of road pricing in the consumer expenditure survey. *Transportation Research Record*, 2530(1), 55–64. https://doi.org/10.3141/2530-07

Small, K. A., Winston, C., & Evans, C. A. (1989). *Road work: A new highway pricing and investment policy*. Brookings Institution Press.

Sovacool, B. K. (2009). Early modes of transport in the United States: Lessons for modern energy policymakers. *Policy and Society*, 27 (4), 411–427.

Tranter, P., & Tolley, R. (2020). *Slow cities: conquering our speed addiction for health and sustainability*. Elsevier.

Wong, T. K. F., & Markow, M. J. (1984). *Allocation of life-cycle highway pavement costs*. Final report. US Department of Transportation, Federal Highway Administration, Report FHWA/RD-83/030.

Young, J. (2015). Infrastructure: Mass transit in 19th-and 20th-century urban America. In *Oxford research encyclopedia of American history*. Oxford University Press.

CHAPTER 8

Transport and the human body

8.1 INTRODUCTION: THE HUMAN BODY AND TRANSPORT

The core model assumes disembodiment by default. Transport economics relaxes this assumption, but only at a very basic level of indivisibilities and a footprint in time and space. Human mental and physical particularities are not explored beyond the very simplistic assumptions made about economic agents such as rationality etc. Even when human embodiment of some sort is posited, it is fairly minimal, usually focusing on mental and cognitive features, such as the anomalies of behavioural economics (BE), rather than corporeal ones such as body memory or motility (Gordon 2015). The far more nuanced realities of human embodiment are largely ignored (except in specialised areas like active travel and public health, considered later) (Box 8.1).

There are a number of dimensions to transport and the human form. First, there is the purely physiological aspect, the fact that bodies are born, grow, age, get sick, recover, get sick again, and ultimately die. To put it technically, human morbidity – incidence of illness – and mortality – incidence of death – are affected by changes to the transport system and by advances in transport technology. To summarise, transport affects human health.

Second, the physical embodiment of the body overall must be accounted for and designed around. Many of these issues are considered at length in Chapter 19 on human factors, but an introductory discussion of this is provided here.

DOI: 10.4324/9781003350866-10

BOX 8.1 INTRODUCTORY CASE: THE HUMAN BODY IN SCIENCE FICTION

Many interesting issues of the future have been wrestled with in the science fiction of the past. One interesting dimension that the genre has engaged in is that of the human form. For example, episodes of the popular television series *Star Trek* depicted periodic encounters with beings of pure energy and intelligence, sometimes benign, sometimes not, that would have to take on some embodied means of communicating and interacting with humans. These episodes sometimes illustrated the superiority of non-embodiment, such as an ability to move across physical space and even whole dimensions in an instant; other times the advantages of the human form were emphasised instead, with pure energy beings pining for the physical and emotional pleasures such as hedonism, love, and connection that their human counterparts had in abundance.

In some scenarios, these disembodied forces would seek to take over human forms for their own, sometimes nefariously. A particularly ominous vision was presented in the film, *Invasion of the Body Snatchers* (originally made in 1956 and remade in 1978), in which an alien presence took over individual human beings once they fell asleep nearby one of the pods containing this presence that had come down from outer space. In this case the advantages of the human body, such as communication, mobility, and ability of physical action, were co-opted in the service of a relentless weed-like colonisation by a monolithic consciousness, with other human aspects, especially emotionality and physical attachment, discarded as inhibitions to the alien purpose.

Much science fiction involves space travel, which takes the human being completely out of its earthly environment. A lot of detail is provided about how space vessels are adapted to the human body and vice-versa. This generally involves a complete recreation of earth system essentials such as gravity (for resting environments), nutrition, respiration, physical exercise, and mental engagement, along with complex computer systems to maintain total control over all aspects of a journey, sometimes with human input, often without. Stanley Kubrick's 1968 film, *2001: A Space Odyssey*, about an ill-fated space mission to Jupiter, graphically depicts astronauts as tiny specks overwhelmed by a technical apparatus that ultimately attempts to destroy them and almost succeeds bar for one soul who manages to overcome the machinations of the hyper-intelligent computer *HAL*. Andrei Tarkovsky's 1972 film, *Solaris*, has a somewhat similar outlook except here humans have lost their emotional and psychological bearings within a system that appears to have a benign intelligence that attempts to recreate the desires of the travellers on the ship. The aforementioned *Star Trek* series by contrast shows human beings more firmly in control of the vessels they inhabit, except when things go wrong, which they often do.

These tales illustrate that the human form has manifold and subtle particularities. Transport activity requires the cooperation and participation of the human being, in its bodily form, with requirements to be designed around, and catering to, it. The physical body is of paramount importance in transport, and human mental and physical health and well-being should be at the forefront. This is not always the case, however, with significant consequences for individuals and society at large.

Third, there is the mind-body complex. The core model and much transport analysis typically treat processes in the brain as the main motor of relevant transport perception, cognition, and decision, implicitly separating these out from the rest of the body, and treating the body as a sort of container for the brain. However, "mind" is not necessarily reducible to the brain (though behaviourists and modern neuroscience effectively does just this), with the brain and body intimately connected.

Fourth, and related to the third point, the fact of the human body has implications at the collective as well as the individual level. The core model posits rational and atomistic agents, with no embodiment, while that model modified for transport has very lightly embodied agents. But agents with human bodies are automatically related to other human beings in a basic corporeal sense and these bodies have many unconscious, subconscious, visceral, and non-rational faculties that shape relations with other human beings and affect cognitive and other mind processes as well.

Fifth, and finally, there is the subjective experience of the body. How important is this dimension to both the personal experience of transport and the decisions that transport users, and perhaps transport suppliers make?

8.2 EMBODIMENT AND THE PHILOSOPHY OF DECISION-MAKING THEORY

Philosophically, embodiment is defined as "the identification of an abstract idea with a physical entity". A more specific form of embodiment is incarnation: "When such ideas are identified in the flesh, we say they are incarnate"(MacLachlan 2004, 2). The actual existence of human form is unchallengeable (except for certain metaphysical traditions that hold that physical existence is merely an illusion, as in Hinduism, which are obviously well outside the scope of this book). But its importance to understanding the workings of the world have been quite contested in Western philosophy in particular. Going back to the ancient Greeks, Plato posited that the physical world we sense consists only of pale earthly reflections of true ideals (Plato called them "forms") existing in a sort of pure thought world. In this construct, incarnation and embodiment were seen as inferior copies of a pure disembodied and essential reality. Platonic thought served as a foundation for what developed into a mind-body split (discussed below), systematised by the French rationalist Rene Descartes, whose famous Latin syllogism "*Cogito ergo sum*" ("I think therefore I am") put mental activity, separated from any corporeal form, at the centre of existence. These traditions have largely triumphed in Western scientific method and analysis and the analytical paradigms about human behaviour and society that have side-lined the human body itself, making it either irrelevant or an obstacle or a bit of both (Thomas 2014).

The core economics theory provides a framework of utility maximisation in which agent decisions are driven by acquisition of inputs that will lead to maximum output of satisfaction (utility) given resource constraints. (Producers have their own equivalent to this which is analytically similar but does not involve utility since objective quantities, namely profit, are the maximisation objective.)

The formal problem for a single agent (a) looks something like this:

$$\text{Max } U_A = \max U(x_1, x_2 \ldots x_n), \text{ s.t. } I = p_1x_1 + p_2x_2 \ldots + p_nX_n$$

In other words, agent "A" chooses quantities of input ("x") subject to (s.t.) a budget constraint ("I" = price times quantity bundles of all desired inputs) that maximise utility ("U_A") given A's individual preferences. With multiple agents competing against one another, the formal problem gets more complex. But the basic aim always is the maximisation of satisfaction across an entire society, which is equivalent to the sum of all individual utilities reached by individual maximisation processes. This aggregation may be complex but it is still just an additive process. In this construct the posited agents, however they process information, deal with constraints and come to make choices, are all disembodied. In other words, the one thing that is common across all human beings – the human body – is mostly absent from the theory.

Does this matter? Economists would generally argue that it does not, so long as the theory generates predictions that match reality with the explanatory theory being as simple as possible. This latter criterion is often referred to as Occam's razor after the medieval philosopher of the same name who is credited with first formulating it. The basic argument is that if realistic assumptions about human embodiment can be discarded without sacrificing accuracy in theoretical predictions, then the simpler theory should prevail.

Bringing this back to transport economics, there are two distinct questions to consider,

1. What consequence does physical existence (embodiment) have for human transport?
2. What consequences does human embodiment have for human transport?

The implications of the first question have already been touched on, namely that physicality leads to space and time, travel, and location. If agents and transactions consisted of pure "energy", so to speak, they would not need to be located anywhere, go anywhere, move any place – in fact "place" and "time" would be irrelevant concepts. This is the situation in some of the science fiction described in the opening case.

Once some sort of physical embodiment is introduced, time and space become more substantive realities to grapple with. Physical entities need to locate somewhere and their basic characteristics, such as the indivisibilities previously mentioned, will make some locations economically and practically preferable to others. Gravity models (Chapter 5), in which goods and people flow along lines of least physical resistance (i.e. lowest cost), directly spring out of physical embodiment and that area and weight and spatial friction that travel across distance entails. Things like agglomeration economies arise because embodied agents involved in similar activities, when located close to one another, produce spatial economic synergies.

Physicality automatically introduces some kind of temporal process. Chapter 4 discussed the fact that structures, such as infrastructure and housing, require fixed costs to create and, once built, are subject to processes of change and deterioration over time that have economic consequences. Structures are "lumpy", i.e. are added to and subtracted from in discrete increments, and they cannot be immediately dismantled or moved without physical effort and duration. They have definite useful lives and because of the costs of creating and destroying them, they often sit in place, providing services, but becoming obsolescent in quality and location over time, requiring agents to optimise around them and limiting and directing spatial and investment choices. The presence of structures, facilities, and activities at definite physical locations in space creates the panoply of transport requirements grappled with in economic geography, spatial economics, transport economics, and urban economics.

Thus it can be said that the relatively lightly considered question in economics is not so much (1) but (2). Economists have obviously had to recognise the physical dimension of human beings in some contexts. But they still have mostly not gone that extra mile in incorporating the specific differences between human physicality and pure object physicality. Human beings are not just objects of weight and volume that are costly to move but are in very special forms deserving very specific attention.

If physical form is fleshed out as human (pun intended) then a whole raft of unique issues arise. Travel itself is a distinctly human activity, not just utilitarian in a disembodied utility maximisation sense but involving choice of means and ends that is partly driven by a human bodily need for stimulation and discovery and exploration. Limitations in accessibility and mobility thus have not just economic and physical dimensions but embodied social ones as well. This is the essence of social inclusion and exclusion (Chapter 14) which refers to damage done to human beings when they cannot get to activities and social connections easily or sufficiently. During the Covid-19 pandemic, this issue was brought to the fore when people were physically locked down, most interactions were online, and face-to-face contact (the phrase itself is significant) was largely prohibited. Even though required, the disruption and disconnection lock-downs created would not have been as great or as intense if we were also not inhabiting human bodies, with all the strengths and limitations these entail.

The study of social forces is an additional example of the subtle role that human embodiment plays in transport behaviour. The modern paradigm is to use maximal engineering design of transport systems to optimise traffic safety and efficiency. This assumes that technological and mechanistic guidance and control is superior to human intuition, gut-feel, judgement, and perception. But there is some evidence that engineering controls can lead to an automaticity in human decision-making that is actually sometimes more flawed than more informal forms of navigation and coordination on streets and roads. This is particularly the case in environments where traffic consists of mixed pedestrian and motorised modes that are moving at relatively slow speeds. In some cases flow and safety have been improved by removing traffic signals and road lines, leaving people to sort things out with one another with greater attention and consideration. This suggests that the human body has a wisdom that goes beyond mere cognition and mental reasoning (Wang et al. 2022, Sections 1.2–1.3).

The focus in this chapter is therefore on several key ways that transport enquiry is changed when including a consideration of how human form affects transport decisions and activity. One is to take a more "minimalist" route and assume, as in classical decision theory, that human decision-making, about transport and other areas, is primarily cognitive in nature, and then see how aspects of the human body might affect the way in which humans go about carrying out their cognitively based decisions. Another approach is to see how the human body *in toto* is involved in decision-making, cognitively, and otherwise. Finally, and not mutually exclusive to either approach, is the consideration of the implications of human body particularities in specific body-related arenas such as health and safety.

8.3 THE BRAIN AS A HUMAN COMPUTER: BOUNDED RATIONALITY

The modern history of computer science contains many attempts to study human decision-making and behaviour to apply to computer programming design, and vice-versa. A seminal effort in this regard was the work of Allen Newell and Herbert Simon. They studied how students actually went about solving maths problems and observed that these students approached matters by taking "short-cuts", i.e. trial and error methods which focused on "promising" areas of attack which were followed up on and expanded if they worked, discarded if they didn't, and modified as problem-solving proceeded. This approach Simon and Newell referred to as "heuristics" (rules-of-thumb), from which they inferred that analysis and problem-solving required time and processing effort, and that this was in limited supply, which was why short-cuts were employed to solve a problem in the first place. Such strategies were not optimising in the sense of the core model but instead traded off optimality of method again human rational processing constraints, termed as "bounded rationality" (Hjeij & Vilks 2023).

Information gathering and processing consume time and energy, things which embodied entities do not have in unlimited quantities and which must be conserved. The physiology of the human body imposes a limited overall energy budget, thus providing the brain with a limited portion for cognition, calculation, and decision-making. Heuristics indicate distinctly human ways of shaping logic and rational thought to these constraints. Rationality is still assumed to be the general default but now recognised as having "bounds". (They also contain heavy doses of uniquely human "gut feel" and intuition, aspects that Newell and Simon did not dwell on, of which more below.)

8.4 BOUNDED RATIONALITY AND "BEHAVIOURAL TRANSPORT"

Bounded rationality and heuristics are the impetus of the field now known as BE, which retains the standard neoclassical dictum of rational maximising agents but allows for human physical limitations in decision-making. The brain's particularities, derived from many generations of evolution, are seen as giving rise to cognitive "biases" that often lead to less than rational and less-than-optimal choices by agents. The use of Newell–Simon type heuristics applied to practical choices as a result of rational processing bounds are part of this but so too are cognitive distortions "hard-wired" into the human brain.

Transport economics still generally defaults to the core model's assumptions of a rational actor without processing or other cognitive limits. Marginal cost pricing (Chapter 7) of transport services and facilities is a classic example of a recommendation based on the assumption that once the price signal is set, agents will automatically calibrate their actions to help attain a simultaneous personal and collective optimum. Even where reality deviates from the assumed conditions (such as imperfect competition), it is still held that agents would optimise perfectly if circumstances allowed them to do so.

The decisions of transport agents in practice, however, do not always conform to this pattern even when the conditions they operate in are favourable. This has led to the rise of the field of behavioural transport (BT) which applies the findings of BE, and of cognitive psychology more generally, to understanding transport choices in the field. Some of this has already been alluded to in earlier chapters without using an explicitly behavioural rubric. Habit, for example, has been long recognised as being a significant part of travel choice, both in terms of trips and modes. In many settings, such as parking, travellers can be seen as "satisficing", a term which means that one is making a "good enough" choice rather than the "best" one simply to save time and effort. This "predictably irrational" behaviour (perhaps one should also say "predictably non-maximising") has been recognised by transport analysts as being fairly widespread (Riggs 2022, 90).

The rise of "Big Data" and smartphone apps has been used by researchers to find out what systematic biases and heuristics exist and design "nudges" to guide people towards more "efficient" outcomes. The term "nudge" refers to the idea that agents need a little help to reach the optimal rational choices that they are essentially aiming for but fall short of due to limits of the human brain (FHWA 2015). But nudging can also be about enabling people to make more sophisticated and up-to-date optimisation decisions using real-time information processed and delivered to the traveller in a useful and useable form when they need it. In this sense modern technology can, in theory at least, partly compensate for innate limits in human information processing.

There are many examples here, but a few involving shifting mode choice towards more active and "sustainable" options are illustrative. Officials in

Durham, North Carolina in the US gave people an active travel app that provided them with personalised maps of walking and cycling alternatives to their single-occupancy vehicle defaults, along with information about much weight they could lose and how much health benefit they could gain by travelling via an active mode. This is an example of providing and processing relevant information to aid people in making decisions based on more data and knowledge than they would otherwise have. Other cities in the US, and internationally, have used similar approaches augmented by financial incentives to increase the nudge. Other strategies use implicit or explicit peer-group norming to influence behaviour (e.g. providing data to a target group showing the active travel habits of people with similar socio-economic and demographic characteristics to the group). Since people often alter their actions to conform to those whom they consider their fellows, either competitively or cooperatively, these social signalling schemes can be quite motivating (Riggs 2022, 92–100). Well-known cognitive biases towards social comparison are thus used to shape decisions towards more beneficial ends.

BT and BE are not without criticism. For one thing, the long list of heuristics and biases that have been compiled is interesting, but it is not always clear how important these really are in given situations, or how consistent they necessarily are across different groups and circumstances. Context may matter much more than the theory implies. Policies designed on the basis of BT/BE therefore may not always be as effective as intended and may even have unintended consequences at times.

Questions have also been raised about whether nudges and other decision-shaping instruments are always benign, even if intended to be. A parallel can be drawn to tech platforms, like Google and Facebook, that use algorithms to direct groups to certain information and not to others. These policies have not been without controversy and the same is arguably applicable to BT. In other words, there is an inherently political element to BT that is not always admitted or recognised, and which should be more explicitly admitted, analysed, and discussed. Privacy in the use of large data sets is an additional concern.

Nonetheless BT does have utility within proper limits. The recognition that human beings do make mistakes and have human limits inherent in their choice making is an advance over more simplistic and mechanistic notions about purely rational actors making optimal choices in a "neutral" environment. The realities of at least some aspects of the human brain in transport behaviour have been acknowledged and incorporated into theory and practice, however, imperfectly.

8.5 BRAIN WITHOUT BODY

While the cognitive/behavioural approach adds some real-world subtlety to models of transport decision-making, it still is primarily brain-based, with relatively little recognition of the workings of the rest of the body except as a mechanism for obtaining and digesting information from the outside world, bringing it back to the neural networks of the brain, which then decides on actions that all this processing suggests. A standard textbook treatment of cognition and perception posits that there are stimuli in the external environment within which an agent operates and which are sensed by the agent through various bodily faculties. These are converted into electrical impulses or signals to receptors within the brain which are, in turn, structured into mental perception, cognition, and experience of that outside world. All this is then processed by the brain to lead to decisions about action. Once these decisions are made, the brain directs the body to carry out the actions with the bodily instrumentalities (such as feet and hands) available. Over time, experience accumulates into knowledge about the world and this knowledge interacts with the other processes to shape cognition, perception, and action (Goldstein 2010, 5–13).

The body obviously plays an important role in all this and shapes the abilities of the brain to detect, respond, and interpret experience. The eyes, ears, olfactory organs, and cutaneous systems, using their uniquely formed facilities, are constantly taking stimuli from the world around them, with the brain making sense of it in the ways described above (Goldstein 2010, Chapters 4, 11, 14, 15). But bounded rationality and heuristics, useful as they are, persist in seeing human beings as brains with quirks, with the body as mostly an accessory to mental processes. A fuller understanding of the brain's functioning would incorporate the quirks of the other faculties as well; for example cognition is dependent upon attention and attention is affected heavily by what the human eye is able, or not able, to see, beyond what happens cerebrally. This is indeed much of what human factors in transport deals with, though often in very narrow functional terms (see Chapter 19).

This particular model, which is simplistically but provocatively referred to here as essentially a "brain without body" template, does have its merits. The brain clearly is extremely important to human choices and actions. Cognition, perception, and experience are very much structured by the human mind and increasing knowledge about the human brain and its neural workings has been very useful in the design of transport systems and associated innovations.

However, there are limitations to this approach even if its basic premises are accepted. Perception and cognition are defined as conscious processes (Goldstein 2010, 17–18). But even Newell and Simon implicitly recognised that the heuristics they observed often appeared to be "unconscious", and Arthur (1994) notes that many mundane actions and decisions (he specifically mentions walking or driving) are subconsciously directed and argues that these realms are best represented by subconscious "pattern cognition maps" that are directly played out into physical actions, arguably as much through other parts of the body as much as in the brain. Arthur's reference to driving is especially pertinent here since much travel behaviour relies on machines whose safe operations actually require a suppression of some parts of conscious processing, with a heightened emphasis on others, all taking place with a lot of background unconscious and subconscious processing. His reference to "maps" also recalls the notion that travellers have "mental maps" of the spaces they navigate that are critical to much travel behaviour, sometimes even overriding "objective" maps (see Chapter 5).

Nonetheless, Newell and Simon and Arthur (and many others) still see the "unconscious" and "subconscious" as extensions of, and adjuncts to, conscious mental processes, fitting very much into the stimuli-decision-action model laid out at the opening of this section. Thus there is a tendency to dismiss visceral "fight-flight-or-freeze" instinctual responses as necessarily inferior to front-of-mind cognitive ones. The typical discourse of BT and BE is that the modern world's configuration has meant that more "primitive" adaptive responses that once served well "in the wild" are now maladaptive and inefficient and misleading and thus need to be overridden somehow, either mechanically or by devices such as behavioural "nudges" and fuller information sets delivered through smartphones. This is no doubt sometimes true, but not always, for body sensing and instinct draws on non-mental responses that can be more immediate and sometimes more accurate than conceptual mind processes are, even those that are unconscious.

8.6 BODY AND MIND

Indeed, one may ask, could it be that parts of the body other than the brain are critical in directing cognition, beyond just being important input–output devices? Newell and Simon and other computer scientists writing in the 1950s and 1960s believed that they were on the threshold of a brave new world in which computers could do anything humans could do and more. They were active pioneers of "Artificial Intelligence" (AI) which revolves around the idea that intelligence resides in the brain, and that the brain behaves like a computer.

But despite all the on-going hype, the AI agenda has run into persistent problems for decades now. Computer problem-solving ability continues to advance significantly, especially with problems that are well-suited to modelling and solution by algorithm. But with respect to seemingly ordinary tasks, such as walking (one of Arthur's "pattern cognition maps in action"), and even basic cognitive tasks, such as natural language creation and chess play, computer science has reached significant limitations. Granted, algorithmic sophistication and massive expansions in processing power and data storage have led to good simulations of many of these processes, producing apparent outcomes that *seem* highly intelligent, language translation and game-play being good examples. But human beings are not disembodied processors external to their world but are in fact human embodied forms deeply intertwined with it, with human intelligence being much broader than its "artificial" counterpart (Dreyfus 1992, 38–40). In the transport realm, this seems to be indicated by that fact that progress in areas like self-driving cars, which require bodily as well as conceptual intelligence, has been more challenging than expected (see Chapter 19).

A broader question is, how do we "know" things? Textbook cognitive models hold that knowledge is the result of the brain's structuring of experience and remembering of this structuring over time. This may be so in a sense. But while we can have "knowledge" without a body, only with the body do we have "know-how". "Know-how" often involves a significant amount of "muscle memory", as any car driver or bicycle rider can attest. This is also quite true of many navigational functions which are at least as much physically based as mentally. Especially after a route has been traversed numerous times, the traveller often uses embodied "feel" to get from one point to another or to deal with unplanned diversions and interruptions. This becomes quite clear to anyone who has given verbal directions to someone else only to recall omitted twists, turns, and landmarks once they follow the route themselves (and wish, with regret, that they could go back and tell their questioner of the correct itinerary) (Dreyfus 1992, 40–45).

AI also depends almost totally on programming. But computer coding and human language are very different affairs. For example, even congenitally blind people use gestures when they speak. Language is thus not just a conceptual affair but a physical one, with physical nuances being critical, including elements such as voice tone, pitch, inflection, and speed (MacLachlan 2004). Neural networks in the brain are very critical to all this, of course. They are also highly "plastic" and are constantly evolving in response to changes in the body and in the environment with multifaceted causality. This indicates that the brain is not just disembodied "mind" but intimately tied up with the human body. Indeed, computer programming techniques that utilise "neural networks" and other "connectionist" protocols have had greater success in problem-solving than heuristic and other disembodied formalisms. Thus the boundaries between brain, mind, and body are variable and subtle (Drefyus 1992, n15–20) (see Box 8.2).

8.7 WALKING – THE ORIGINAL GRAVITY MODEL

In the very beginning, there was only walking – the human body unencumbered or augmented by any technical apparatus, save things like bags to carry or animals to ride on. Before the invention of the wheel, there weren't even carts to pull along. This was, to be sure, a very limited world as far as transport goes. The ambit of walking is at the most perhaps 30 km per day, if one is able-bodied, has a good walking track and level topography, and is carrying a light load. For these reasons nomadic societies in particular travelled light while more settled ones limited regular travel to the ambit of what most individuals considered to be absolutely necessary.

To put this another way, pre-industrial transport was heavily limited and affected by the forces of gravity, with human beings, being embodied physically, obviously quite affected by this basic law. Maupin (1993), the inventor of the bodywork method of "Rolfing", which involves deep tissue massages and manipulations of the human form to improve mobility and function, posits gravity as "the most basic fact...pressing us against the earth" (8). The basic elements of the truly remarkable human skeleton and the nature of three-dimensional space interact together to determine each individual's orientation to gravity as the body moves in and adapts the space it inhabits.

Maupin sums things up thusly:

> "Every physical creature is subject to the effects of gravity throughout life. It is the one unrelenting stimulus to which we must relate. The skeleton has evolved primarily in response to the various demands placed upon it by different systems of dealing with gravity (that is, a quadrupedal skeleton differs from a biped's in ways which are predictable on the basis of their different relations to the ground). Gravity determines what is physically efficient or inefficient. When the human body is inefficiently organized, effort is required to resist the effects of gravity. Eventually gravity wins, and the tragically bent bodies of some elderly people are the results. When the structure is efficiently organized, the flow of gravity can be a source of energy.
>
> (8)

BOX 8.2 VARIOUS BODY-MIND UNITIES

"Cartesian dualism", so prevalent in Western philosophy and named after the French rationalist René Descartes of the 18th century, posits an insuperable split between mind and body, with the former dominant over the latter. This has been referred to as the "ghost in the machine" in which the activity of the mind supposedly animates and drives the various mechanisms of bodily form.

There are various conundrums this model raises. Causality is one of them. Does the mind command the body or is it the other way around? Freud said that "the ego is first and foremost a body-ego", indicating his view that physical embodiment was much more dominant than is often supposed. Thus many mental conflicts were experienced as expressed as physical ones, such as "conversion" hysteria in which psychological issues are expressed in the form of bodily ailments and complexes. Indeed, the very word "psychosomatic" suggests a close link between the human psyche and the somatic system. Modern research shows that the relationship is complex, with many psychological conditions triggered by physical cues and changes, such as relapse into addiction when a clean and sober addict finds themselves in physical environments closely associated with old acting out behaviour. This can be a place where the desired substance is readily available, such as a pub, where a slip is more understandable. But it also can be triggered by exposure to smells or sounds or other seemingly unrelated stimuli that are not directly related to substance use and abuse, but which embody some aspect of past "acting out" behaviour for individuals through the environments that they once inhabited as active addicts.

Indeed, the whole phenomenon of "trigger points" is rife with the complexity of the mind-body connection. This is not just confined to addition but includes a whole range of immunological disorders in which non-biological aetiology (such as stress, personality type, and cultural factors) play clear, if not entirely transparent, roles. "Phantom limbs", in which amputees feel pain and other sensations in limbs long since lost, exemplify this complexity further. And in a transport setting, the issue of "simulator sickness" is well-known. Here there is a mismatch in some individuals between what their mind and body are experiencing, resulting in an imbalance expressed in physical terms.

In the current age, the default explanation for many of these "oddities" is neurological, namely that changes within the chemistry and/or architecture of the brain cause the physical manifestations. But this is just an update of the Cartesian dualism. The issues are not settled just because changes in the brain can be observed (and the brain is far from being definitively mapped or understood in any case, so many neurological hypotheses are just that, not firm truths). In fact, the lines drawn between body and mind are not as clearly drawn as philosophers and scientists often make them out to be.

(The discussion above is drawn from MacLachlan 2004)

In other words, gravity affects every earthly object. But human bodies are affected and adapted to this force in very particular ways (see Figure 8.1).

Engagement with the gravity-bounded body was obviously quite universal in early human history. The well-known human health benefits from energy expenditure were realised from moving around without having to think about it. But with modernity things are not so simple or automatic.

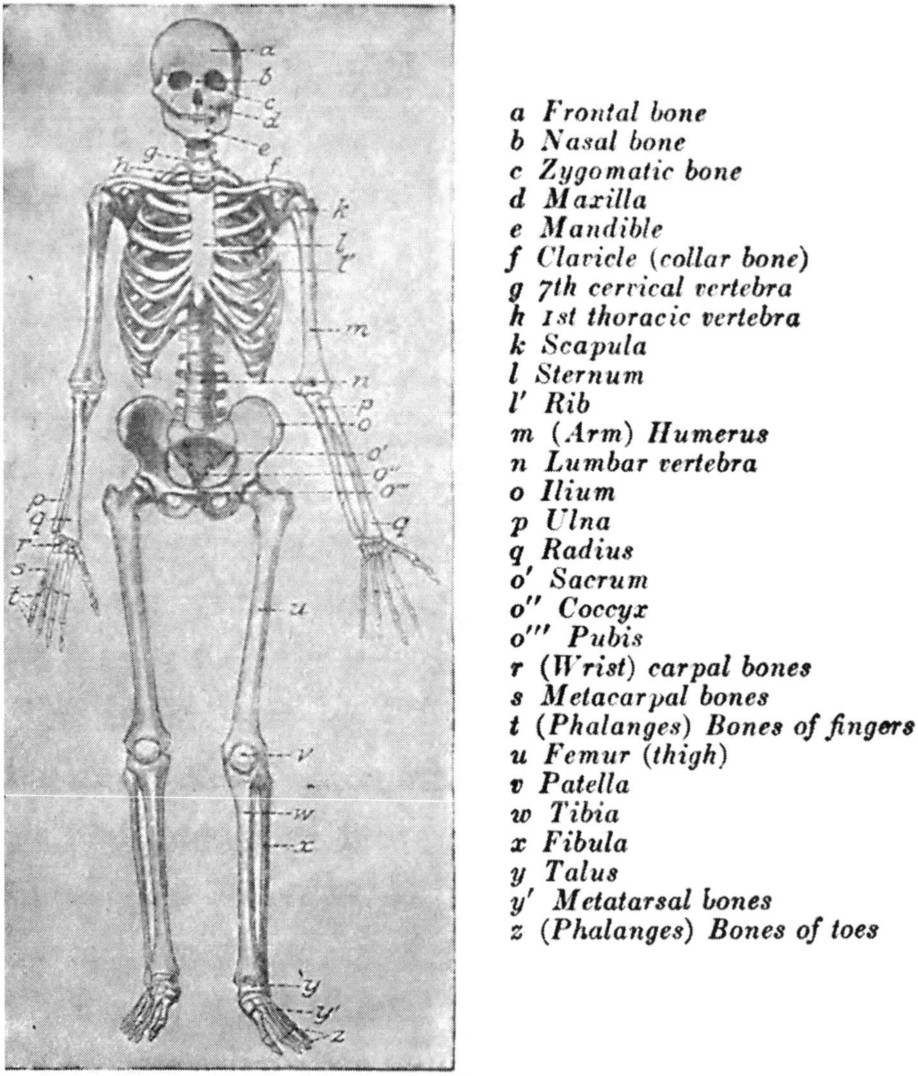

FIGURE 8.1

The bones of the skeleton, held in their natural position.

Source: Image from Stopes (1926, Figure 3, 18). Book and image are in the public domain.

Sallis et al. (2004) define "physical activity" as "any form of muscular movement that produces energy expenditure" (252). It is now well-known that this energy expenditure, up to a point, decreases human morbidity and mortality. This reality is in obvious contrast to the standard assumptions about transport as purely a derived demand which implicitly considers expenditure of energy by individuals to be part of a "disutility," or cost. When utility is derived solely from consumption, any human "work" or "effort" which is needed to attain this consumption, including transport, is a sacrifice, not a pleasure. And since travellers are implicitly disembodied in the core model, and only lightly embodied in its basic extension into transport economics, the basic energy expenditure-health relationship is not present at all.

However, active travel in the form of walking and cycling has definite and positive impacts on human health. The optimal form of travel mode is thus not reducible to travel time saved alone but must account for the contours of human physiology. The non-human powered modes of modernity have sped up and made transport more efficient and expanded the available trade-offs between speed, range, and capacity, as discussed in Chapter 6. But they have done so in a way that has de-privileged human physiology. More efficient transport increases access to many more activities and encourages more motion, *ceteris paribus*. But that motion does not generally employ the human body very much, a gain in core model "efficiency" terms, but a loss physiologically.

Younger et al. (2008) thus argue that there is a predominant focus on technology improvements in transport, such as increased fuel efficiency, rather than system design that expands the choice to more easily include, or even encourage, active travel. Sallis et al. (2004) have made similar points, noting clear evidence that neighbourhood design attributes and transport options are associated with physical activity levels, higher or lower, which is, in turn, associated with morbidity and mortality outcomes, better or worse. Interestingly, high levels of motorised traffic alone, apart from broader travel environment, can create "barrier costs" that prevent or discourage a baseline volume of walking and cycling in urban areas, defined as "the volume of walking and cycling that would take place if people were able to choose their mode of transport according to their preferences in a situation where motorised traffic did not cause insecurity and other inconveniences" (Sælensminde 2004, 603).

8.8 TRANSPORT SYSTEMS IN OPPOSITION TO THE HUMAN BODY

What this discussion points to is that advances in mechanised transport have not been neutral in its relationship to the human body that employs energy expenditure by the human form, in a sense side-lining that form entirely, with some deleterious physiological effects. We are however human beings with human bodies. How to bring make the transport system more benignly aligned with that body is something worth considering more.

It is true that transport improvements are not all negative for human health, with access to medical care, medicines, healthy food and beneficial exercise programmes, and facilities made much easier and much less costly for many in the population. But beyond the discouragement of active travel already discussed, the modern transport system has sometimes been dangerous for the human body. The World Health Organisation (WHO) reported in 2023 that almost 1.2 million people died on the world's roads, the ninth leading cause of death globally and the leading killer of young people aged 15–29 years. Annually, road crashes also cause between 20 million and 50 million non-fatal injuries. Trends have been downward, fortunately. But this toll is still the rough equivalent of French battle deaths during the entire World War I being lost every year and equals all battle injuries during that war (World Health Organisation (WHO) 2023).

Pollution and other transport system externalities (see Chapter 13) also have numerous deleterious human impacts. Automobiles emit numerous chemicals, including carbon monoxide, benzene, formaldehyde, and tiny suspended particles known as particulate matter. There is surprisingly little broad research on this topic, but studies of people living close to highways show health effects of such emissions ranging from lung disease, cancer, and respiratory diseases such as asthma, with children and the elderly particularly hard hit (Zhang & Batterman 2013).

Transport modes have more subtle effects on the human body as well. Prolonged exposure to transport noise, whether from traffic, airports, or other modes such as trains, has been shown to affect cardiovascular health and sleep and to reduce performance in concentration and analytical skills, especially in children. Additionally, vehicle vibrations have real, if diffuse and complex, effects on human beings, including potential for long-term muscle damage and psychological and cognitive impairment. Some impacts are especially hard on operators of particular types of vehicles, especially motorcycle, coach, and truck drivers, where there is often sustained long-term exposure to vehicle vibrations (NIOSH 2006).

Transport professionals are by no means unaware of these physical effects and have studied them and have tried to address them in various ways. There are benefits as well as costs to all technical advances and a purely negative focus on the latter can come close to a modern form of Luddism. Nonetheless, it is well to ask whether current and projected transport technologies, policies, and investments might have gotten ahead of the strengths, limitations, and needs of the unique physical form of human beings and whether we might not want to go back to this source, understand more about its subtleties, and adjust and redesign our transport accordingly. Chapter 19 delves into some these issues more deeply.

REFERENCES

Arthur, W. B. (1994). Inductive reasoning and bounded rationality. *The American economic review*, 84(2), 406–411.

Dreyfus, H. L. (1992). *What computers still can't do: A critique of artificial reason.* MIT Press.

FHWA (2015). Behavioral economics and transportation. US Federal Highway Administration Publication No. FHWA-HRT-15-035, April 2015. www.fhwa.dot.gov/advancedresearch/

Goldstein, E. B. (2010). *Sensation and perception* (8th edition). Wadsworth/Cengage.

Gordon, C. E. (2015). *Behavioural approaches to corporate governance.* Routledge.

Hjeij, M., & Vilks, A. (2023). A brief history of heuristics: how did research on heuristics evolve? *Humanities and Social Sciences Communication*, 10(64). https://doi.org/10.1057/s41599-023-01542-z

MacLachlan, M. (2004). *Embodiment: Clinical, critical and cultural perspectives on health and illness.* Open University Press.

Maupin, E. W. (1993). *The structural metaphor: An introduction to structural integration.* International Professional School of Bodywork.

NIOSH (2006). *Proceedings of the first American conference on human vibration (June 5–7, 2006).* US Department of Health and Human Services, Centers for Disease Control and Prevention, National Institute for Occupational Safety and Health.

Riggs, W. (2022). Chapter 5: Behavioral economics and social nudges in sustainable travel. In *Innovations in transport.* Edward Elgar Publishing.

Sælensminde, K. (2004). Cost–benefit analyses of walking and cycling track networks taking into account insecurity, health effects and external costs of motorized traffic. *Transportation Research Part A: Policy and Practice*, 38(8), 593–606.

Sallis, J. F., Frank, L. D., Saelens, B. E., & Kraft, M. K. (2004). Active transportation and physical activity: Opportunities for collaboration on transportation and public health research. *Transportation Research Part A: Policy and Practice*, 38(4), 249–268.

Stopes, M. C. (1926). *The human body.* Blue Ribbon Books.

Thomas, J. (2014). *The minds of the moderns: Rationalism, empiricism and philosophy of mind.* Routledge.

Wang, W., Wang, L., Zhang, C., Liu, C., & Sun, L. (2022). Social interactions for autonomous driving: A review and perspectives. *Foundations and Trends® in Robotics*, 10(3–4), 198–376.

World Health Organisation (WHO) (2023). *Global status report on road safety 2023*. World Health Organisation.

Younger, M., Morrow-Almeida, H. R., Vindigni, S. M., & Dannenberg, A. L. (2008). The built environment, climate change, and health: opportunities for co-benefits. *American Journal of Preventive Medicine*, 35(5), 517–526.

Zhang, K., & Batterman, S. (2013). Air pollution and health risks due to vehicle traffic. *Science of the Total Environment*, 450–451, 307–316.

SECTION 3

Transport supply

CHAPTER 9

Infrastructure and vehicles

9.1 INTRODUCTION: THE INFRASTRUCTURE–VEHICLE NEXUS

History demonstrates that the demand for transport modes and their technical variants is not a simple matter of a disconnected demand "out there" being met by a passive supply response. Technical factors are important: petrol cars, for example, could traverse the large physical extent of America and the need to cover long distances across rural areas, which early EVs could not handle (Box 9.1).

But there is also a close connection between infrastructure and vehicle development early, petrol-powered cars having an insurmountable advantage due to the US road building and design choices that gave preference to petrol rather than electric charging stations. The choice to build petrol trucks for the war effort during World War I further created a large new pool of additional petrol vehicles which was added to the growing private output of petrol vehicles more generally, further tipping the balance away from electric power transport.

9.2 TRANSPORT AND LATENT DEMAND SATISFACTION

In the core model, demand for transport and supply of transport interact with each other via a market to set an optimal price that delivers an

DOI: 10.4324/9781003350866-12

BOX 9.1 INTRODUCTORY CASE: THE FIRST FALSE START OF ELECTRIC VEHICLES (EVS)

Little remembered today is the fact that electric vehicles (EVs) initially held the advantage over petrol-fuelled alternatives during the first decade of 1900s. Electricity was already powering streetcars, electric motors were well established, and battery technology had made significant strides, making for viable electric cars. The Electric Carriage and Wagon Company, set up in 1896, operated electric taxis in New York City in 1897, while the Pope Manufacturing Company was in the market that same year offering the first EV for sale. EVs produced neither steam nor soot like its petrol (and, for a little while, steam) competitors and were considerably quieter as well. This made them especially attractive for use in dense urban residential neighbourhoods, including noise-restricted affluent ones. They were popular with women who favoured its push-button start and easy gear changing. And they also appealed to commercial operators, with many suppliers of commodities, like ice and coal, already using them for consumer distribution. At this time, the electric truck's operating range was also greater than its petrol-powered alternative (see Figure 9.1). Meanwhile the electrical grid was expanding and improving rapidly (416). (The discussion in this section draws on Sovacool 2009 and the page references which follow in this section are to this article).

EV usage peaked in the US in 1901 and 1902, however, at a 62% share of all motorised vehicles, then began a slow but steady decline to mere 2% market share in 1920. EVs constituted 10% all commercial vehicles in America in 1913, going down to 3% in 1925 (416).

The rapid rise and fall of EVs in the US derived from multiple factors. While electric powered cars had some technical advantages over petrol-powered ones, they had some disadvantages as well. Batteries were improving, but their charge held for only limited ranges and the predictions of a "miracle battery" never eventuated. EVs could at most travel only around 25 mi between charges; recharging was time-consuming, and speeds topped out at less than 15 mph. They also performed poorly on hills, mountains and rough roads, or carrying heavy freight. Gasoline vehicles had a 70-mi range and top speeds of 40 mph as early as 1905 (416–417). The potential market for electric cars was thus more limited than petrol ones. Both were well suited for short trips in cities with extensive charging networks. But petrol engines were additionally suitable for rural and non-urban use, for longer trips, and for heavy item carriage.

Price was a further factor since early gasoline automobiles cost $1,000–$2,000 as compared to $1,250–$3,500 for electrics. This caused EV manufacturers to focus on luxury markets, leaving downscale markets to petrol vehicles. The latter would prove to be the larger market, helped along by major oil discoveries in the US in 1901

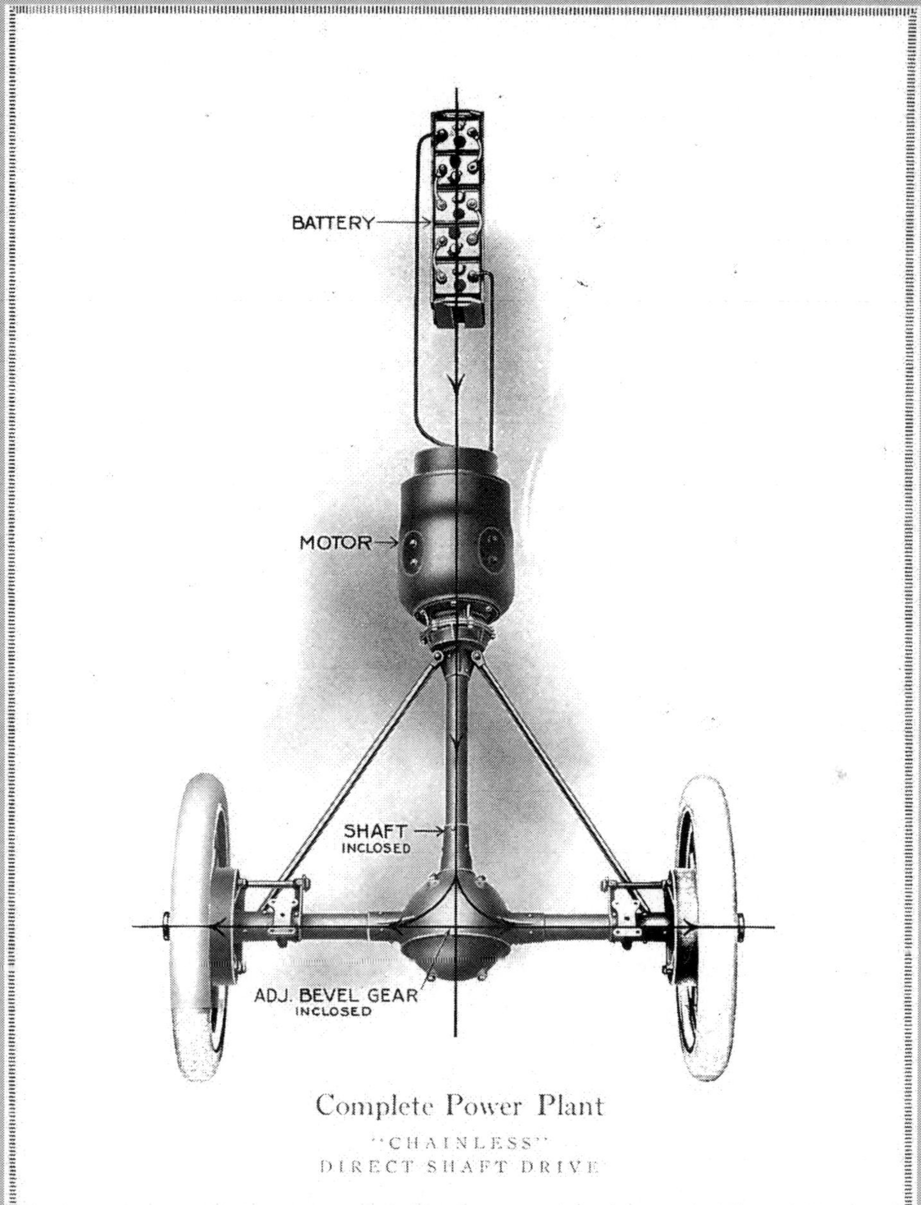

FIGURE 9.1
A 1911 electric car power plant.

Source: Image from Anderson Electric Car Company (1911, 35). Book and image are in the public domain.

that dropped crude oil prices below 5 cents per barrel, lowering the relative operating costs of petrol cars (418).

These initial incremental differences began to accumulate, especially once mass production took hold in car manufacturing. The petrol engine car now became a mass-produced item, and the huge Economies of scale (EOS) achieved in its production led to sharply falling sticker prices that ultimately outcompeted the EV across all categories of consumer. Interestingly, Henry Ford had worked for Thomas Edison and knew a great deal about the electric engine and could have easily focused on producing those in great quantities. But apparently he found the internal combustion engine a much more edifying challenge, perhaps because he didn't know them as well, and from there the die was cast (418).

Once Ford managed to churn out low priced petrol vehicles in great numbers, the contest between electricity and gasoline was largely over. After a certain point, the momentum became self-propelling: the more petrol vehicles there were, the more the roads were filled with them, the more petrol stations built for them, and the more people wanted to obtain them. By 1912, American roads carried 30,000 EVs as compared with more than 900,000 internal combustion vehicles (417).

Other factors were at play too. The outbreak of World War I, and America's entry into it, was a major "exogenous" event (to use the economics term) in this period and had it not occurred America might have emerged with a "dual" market in which electric cars dominated within cities and petrol cars dominated outside them. After all, there were existent charging and petrol networks already established side-by-side, and substantial fleets of, and established user bases for, both vehicle types. World War I however created a huge new government demand for gasoline-powered trucks that flooded American markets when they were demobilised after the end of the war, this alone dramatically lowering petrol car prices overall (417). The US federal government had judged EVs, particularly trucks, as ill-suited for military applications, and during the War, public subsidies were aimed at making gasoline trucks the *de facto* default for the military. Technical differences were key here, since military standards for speed and range were much greater than what EVs could deliver. Before America's entry into the War, the European Allied powers turned to the American truck industry for imports, providing a major prod to increased production of gasoline-engine trucks and realisation of EOS. Sharp shortages of coal in the cold winter of 1918 highlighted a need for freight modes to supplement rail and only petrol-powered vehicles could meet these long-haul and heavy weight trip requirements. Indeed, it was partly this experience which caused the government to build an improved and expanded road network, built with petrol-powered trucks, not EVs, in mind. Once the War ended, America found itself with a factory base standardised for petrol vehicles and masses of demobilised army personnel trained to drive them. All these policies greatly aided the internal combustion engine at the expense of its electric alternative, with the Great Depression finally bankrupting the remaining manufacturers of commercial EVs (420–421).

Meanwhile oil and petroleum companies ran aggressive campaigns for the establishment of gasoline filling stations. The 1916 passage of the Federal Aid to Roads Act provided matching funding from the Federal government to State road building efforts. A total of 700,000 mi of highways were constructed by 1930, encouraging the building of service stations and motels all along them (421). If this legislation had come a decade earlier, many or all of these stations might have had electric charging capabilities. But by this time, the trends were clear and EVs found themselves locked out of the road-based refuelling network and headed towards ultimate extinction.

efficient amount of transport service supply to meet a corresponding transport demand. This happens simultaneously and immediately in the supply–demand framework. The relevant concept here is latent demand, which refers to a Willingness-to-pay (WTP) for a good or service that remains unrealised because supply is not being offered in the market. For example, some neighbourhood residents would buy cappuccino in an upscale cafe but do not do so because such a cafe does not exist. Once the cafe opens, this latent demand can be met and realised. The analogy in transport is a set of travellers who would travel if the means for travel were available. If there is no change in transport infrastructure and/or service, this demand remains latent, i.e. existent but unmet. But if a facility is opened, or adds capacity, new travel may occur over and above what existed before because this latent demand can now be realised; or, to use the more technical parlance, induced. In this case, one could thus loosely speak of the increment in travel as representing the latent demand for travel that the new facility capacity releases (Fulton et al. 2000).

Figure 9.2 diagrams the basic economics of such a situation. There is supply and demand for travel in some market. Assuming a perfectly competitive market with proper pricing (i.e. the marginal cost of travel is fully captured by prices, including appropriate tolls), there will be an equilibrium quantity of travel at an equilibrium unit price where the supply of transport equals demand. There is, however, demand for transport that exists but which remains unrealised (latent) because of supply constraints. If the supply of transport were greater, this demand would then become induced demand, i.e. realised demand that is generated (that is, induced, or "drawn out"), in this case because of transport system improvements. Until that supply is added, such demand will remain unrealised.

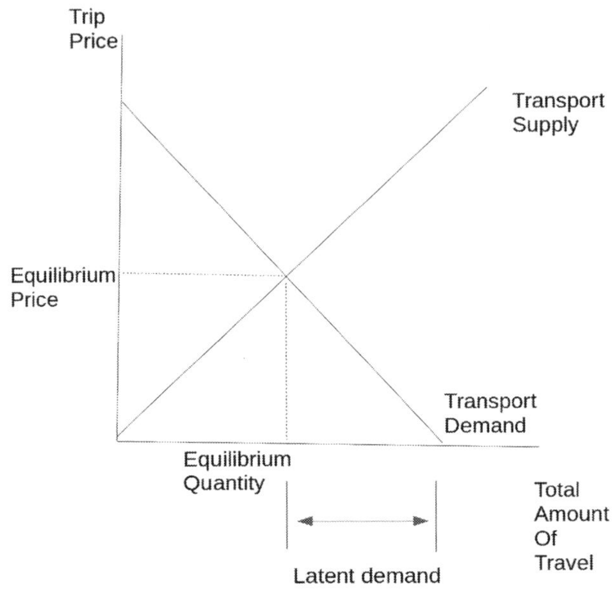

FIGURE 9.2
A diagram of latent demand for transport (by author).

This textbook model can be operationalised to allow planners to forecast latent demand with more specificity. Here is a simple example. Imagine that the demand for transit is captured by the function V = 2500–350t, where V indicates transit demand and t indicates travel time. If current average travel time given the existing transit system is 5 minutes, then current transit demand (V) is 750 daily trips. The theoretical maximum number of trips that could be taken with shorter transit times is 2500 (if t = 0). The maximum latent demand would be the difference between this maximum demand and the current demand or 2500–750 = 1750 (Kumares & Labi 2007, 56–57).

9.3 TRANSPORT DEMAND SATISFACTION COMPLEXITIES

This does not mean that all latent demand should be met by a supply response. According to the core model, a market equilibrium is by definition economically efficient and it would be therefore inefficient to meet remaining unmet demand if the market is behaving as it should.

But real-world transport markets rarely conform to the assumptions of the core model. Transport service generally requires both extensive infrastructure and mass production and distribution of vehicles, with all the facilities needed to support them (e.g. fuel stations for the relevant energy source). As

Chapter 4 noted, infrastructure has indivisibilities across time and space (i.e. it cannot be divided into continuous quantities) and this makes it a "lumpy" asset which can only be altered by increments, often with significant lags. At a particular point in time, therefore, even a market that meets all the other requirements of the core model (such as perfect competition, constant returns to scale (CRS) and so forth) may nonetheless provide an inefficient supply of infrastructure for a significant period. There could either be undersupply (in which case there is latent demand) or oversupply (in which case demand is insufficient). Passenger vehicle supply production and distribution has its own supply lags and lumpiness, as the EV example shows. In theory, these rigidities will be corrected by the market, but this could still entail a very long transition interval. Potentially the lags might never all be perfectly ironed out at all, especially in an environment of regular technological and economic change.

The "P" (price) and "Q" (quantity) of the standard supply and demand template is also not fully applicable to actual transport markets in a number of ways. Production of transport, "Q", consists of multidimensional and heterogeneous outputs, both in terms of quality and quantity, with a spatial component always present. The typical measures of such outputs illustrate this (e.g. tonne-kilometres, passenger-kilometres, and so forth). Quality is typically variable in a dynamic sense, with travel times, for example, being typified by peaking, seasonality, and reliability (Levinson et al. 2016, 126). On the demand side, consumers do not just demand a "trip" but also a route, a mode, and a time of day when they "consume" a particular transport "Q". Thus "P" cannot be simply reduced to a transit fare or vehicle opportunity cost because the generalised cost of travel includes consumer disutility (as covered in Chapter 7) meaning that consumer WTP is variable according to trip purpose, time-of-day, etc. (Button 2010, 78–81; 85–86). A market in equilibrium under these conditions, even when functioning "perfectly", may not easily reach a fully settled optimum.

The fact that transport demand is derived from innate demands for other goods, services, and activities is part of the problem here. Key features such as price elasticity are altered not just by the usual "background" characteristics of user income and cost, but by a sometimes dynamically shifting bundle of desires for other goods and services, the desirability of which can be affected by the relative availability and cost of transport at a particular time. For example, one may very much want to go to a film, but not if it is too hard to get to. Thus some other things that are easy to get to at that certain moment may become more valued as a result. All of this can change as travel conditions alter (e.g. whether it is raining out or not) and as supply availability adjusts (e.g. before or after a subway shuts down for the night).

Even assuming relatively fixed preferences on the part of consumers, transport P and Q demanded comes out of a calculation of multiple optimisations across directly demanded goods and indirectly demanded transport which is a product of that direct demand and which affects and is affected by it.

Already noted is the fact that transport itself is often effectively co-produced between demanders and suppliers. If travellers own their own vehicle, like a cycle or a car, then they are providing some of their own inputs into the production process, without which the trip doesn't happen (Button 2010, 82–84). By the same token, infrastructure is needed for most modern trips and in a sense suppliers can be said to co-creating demand for their services. The EV case shows this rather strikingly.

All of which means that the standard supply–demand "cross" is by itself not especially applicable to a full understanding of many transport markets, except perhaps as an initial starting point or frame. At a minimum the economics of supply of infrastructure and vehicles must be fleshed out more, to which the discussion now turns.

9.4 INFRASTRUCTURE ECONOMICS

Transport in most cases requires a network in order to be consumed or produced at all. This is why transport is often referred to as a network good. Networks require a lot of infrastructure building, maintenance, and development. But with transport infrastructure, there is a chicken-and-egg situation. A new transport technology, like the automobile, requires infrastructure to move on to make its use viable. But which comes first? Historically this is a back-and-forth dynamic with expansion tending to see-saw with major facility growth driving more vehicle sales which in turn leads to more facility provision. The EV history presented at the start of this chapter is a good illustration of this.

In the core model, the market coordinates a series of decisions by agents to build up a network in a decentralised fashion while ultimately providing a network that optimally allocates resources in an efficient manner. Historically, however, network building has often initially been carried out or significantly assisted by government. The reason for this is that while there may be sufficient collective benefit to infrastructure provision in many instances, there is generally not sufficient profit to be made in privately providing it until a network exists and getting one up to critical mass where the market can then sustain itself requires nonmarket intervention.

Transport networks are also inherently spatial. Thus in addition to the positive Economies of scale (EOS) often found in transport markets, there also can be density economies which refer to declining costs when output increases but the network extent (e.g. total number of kilometres) is held constant. The dynamic here is that with networks that are already in place, the more users there are, the cheaper it is to service each one. Thus economies-of-density refer to declining average network costs per user as opposed to the declining average costs coming through increased production levels that typify EOS. There is obviously a great deal of interaction between economies of density, EOS, and capacity utilisation (i.e. how much of a network's total capacity is used, 100% being the maximum). Density can affect capacity utilisation and some links in a network may be congested, while others may be underutilised (e.g. an urban road versus a rural road in a national highway system). Of course there are capacity limits to any existing network at a point in time. When this limit is neared, average costs will rise due to congestion. This tipping point will vary by network and user (Levinson et al. 2016, 152–154).

Network designers face various questions at initial design and build stages. For example, scale economies will suggest that it will be cheaper to provide more capacity rather than less at the outset (e.g. three runways versus two) even though this may mean that excess capacity may need to be maintained at great expense for a long period of time. How much that latter expense will amount to depends on future trends in network demand, something very hard to predict. The initial capacity decision will also affect the potential utilisation economies discussed above (Levinson et al. 2016, 169–170).

Efficiency, however, is not always the only relevant consideration in infrastructure investment. The EU, for example, has programmes to fund facility building aiming to balance development across the bloc, knitting economically peripheral regions more closely to developed core areas (EC 2024). This is more about regional equity than efficiency (see Chapter 14). But it does have efficiency implications since more balanced activity across a region can potentially also reduce capacity overload, bottlenecks, and other network strains.

9.5 VEHICLE PRODUCTION

Vehicle supply is a separate but related issue. In pre-industrial times, much less travel was needed because activities often remained confined to very small areas, like a household, farm, or village, and there was less activity to choose from. Much transport was self-provided or done on a small scale. Animal-drawn carriages and human-borne bundles carried by walking individuals were the main surface mode. Even local water carriage was often done on small vessels operated by individual operators (Casson 1994).

This is not to say that there was an insubstantial amount of organisation involved in these "primitive" times. Especially for long-distance trade routes and major undertakings such as trade fairs, human beings proved themselves to be especially resourceful. The basic capacity and speed of walking, on a well-maintained level path and carrying 18 kilos, yielded a 30 km coverage over a period of about 8 hours. Using beasts of burden, and carrying 125 kilos, including the rider, by horse and, again under ideal conditions, was twice as fast or more as walking. These basic modes could be considerably leveraged to higher levels of cargo carriage, though not much increase in speed (Rodrigue 2020, Section 1.3).

With the emergence of mechanisation and industrialisation, all this changed substantially for all modes of travel. Vehicles became larger, more complex, and powerful and produced and distributed by specialist manufacturers. These coalesced into complete industries with their own complex microeconomic and macroeconomic dynamics (see Boxes 9.2 and 9.3).

BOX 9.2 THE RISE OF THE BRITISH CAR INDUSTRY

Cars were manufactured in the UK as early as 1896, with Austin, Rover, and Sunbeam all launched before World War I. Large motoring organisations like the Royal Automobile Club were already in existence by 1905 exemplifying an established motoring culture (Gunn 2018, 11–12).

The British car industry's origins differed from its American and French counterparts (the other major producers of the era) because of its roots in the bicycle industry (see Chapter 19). But its overall arc is indicative. Coventry became Britain's car manufacturing capital, analogous to the dominance of Detroit in the US and Paris in France. Overall, 89% of new car firms located in the Coventry/Birmingham area between 1895 and 1900 had prior experience in cycle production and related businesses. Coventry had become the centre of the UK's bicycling industry in the late 19th century and bikes had been made there since 1868 (Boschma & Wenting 2007, 222–223).

The British industry continued to grow and it consolidated relatively quickly. The number of carmakers was very high until after the early 1920s, although new entrants began to tail off around 1913. Between 1922 and 1932, the number of automobile manufacturers in Britain dropped from 147 to 40 and ultimately three firms dominated: Morris, Austin, and Singer, accounting for 75% of car production by the late 1920s (Boschma & Wenting 2007, 219–221).

However, even with the Great Depression, which was not as severe in England as elsewhere, the country having already gone through a sustained economic slump in the 1920s, there was nonetheless enough growth and competition that the country ended up with the "Big Six" of Morris, Austin, Ford, Vauxhall, Rootes, and Standard. These companies realised large EOS, and by the end of the 1930s, Britain was behind only America in auto production and exports. This market configuration was relatively stable until 1968. Still, the total number of British car manufacturers remained high compared to France, Germany, and the US, mainly because of a number of small surviving niche luxury producers, a pattern that was reflected in some other British industries, perhaps because of a persistent class system and high relative income and wealth inequality segmented the market more than other places. But like car industries elsewhere, a few leading companies produced most of the cars, although geographically the industry was more spatially dispersed with Coventry/Birmingham not dominating quite like Detroit in the US (Boschma & Wenting 2007, 222–223).

Domestically the car industry reached a peak in 1958, producing over a million cars, and employing over 500,000 workers by 1965. Motorcycle production also blossomed, peaking in the early 1960s. Between 1955 and 1971 around 1 million workers were employed in motorised vehicle manufacture overall, this falling over the 1970s to three-quarters of a million. The numbers of lorries doubled in the 1950s and 1960s, and car ownership grew by a factor of 5 between 1950 and 1970 (Gunn 2018, 11–12, 20).

However, vehicles required roads to ride on and here Britain was a laggard. Partly because it had adopted rail so early and had such an extensive network, intercity road building had not been an immediate priority (Hugill 2009, 431). There was a national road system with service classifications in place by 1922 and a Road Fund established in 1920 using automobile excise duties and licence sales revenues for road improvements. But the first true extended motorway, the M1, only opened in late 1958 and 1,000 mi of motorway were completed only by 1972 (Gunn 2018, 11–12). Britain had lagged behind its developed country competitors considerably, even Germany, which itself had been a laggard until the 1930s, when it began to catch up, though under very different institutional arrangements (see Box 9.3). The close link between industrialisation and vehicle development is clear in both cases.

Contrary to the independence of supply from demand suggested by the core model, mass car production everywhere arose from varied mechanisms for stimulating mass demand. For example, American automobile manufacturers cut deals with banks and finance companies to develop and sell their new product: automobile insurance against theft, fire, vandalism, and accident liability, through manufacturer dealers. Auto shows became

BOX 9.3 THE LATE MOTORISATION OF GERMANY

Although highly industrialised, Germany in the first part of the 20th century had a population slow to warm to cars. In 1935, only 1.6% of the populace in Germany owned motor vehicles, while 4.9% owned them in France, 4.5% in Britain, 4.2% in Denmark, and 1.8% in Ireland. To be sure, Europe as a whole was way behind America and its 20.5% ownership rate. But Germany was close to the bottom within rich Western Europe (Evans 2005, 325).

The Germans did try to close the gap, doubling car production between 1932 and 1933 and again by 1935. More than 250,000 cars were produced annually in that year, with falling prices and rising numbers of cars on the roads, going from 500,000-plus in 1932 to just below 1 million in 1936. By 1938 Germany car output was the fastest growing in Europe. But even then there was only one motor vehicle per 44 inhabitants, versus 1 per 19 in Britain and France. Like Britain, most freight and passengers relied on the country's excellent rail network, but with a still far greater dominance than in England (Evans 2005, 326).

Hitler found this situation unacceptable once he came to power in 1933 and he attempted to kick auto production into high gear under government direction. On the one hand, the State undertook construction of a massive programme of high-speed intercity national road construction in the form of the vaunted *autobahns*. On the other hand, a new "People's Car", the Volkswagen, was established, in collaboration with the industrialist Ferdinand Porsche, offering a supposedly low-cost, efficient, and widely distributed car for the masses. This effort was launched with a huge advertising campaign encouraging workers to put a portion of their wages aside each week as down payments to help fund mass production of this new mass vehicle. More than 340,000 people invested in this scheme, contributing millions of Deutschmarks (Evans 2005, 338).

However, not one of the people got a Volkswagen in the end. The money was diverted to rearmament, and the plant dedicated to Volkswagen production was converted to war production at the beginning of World War II. Many of the high-quality autobahns were built, as these had immediate military purposes as well as civilian ones. But Hitler's economic regime was always single-mindedly focused on war-making and passenger cars did not fit this priority. Germany's auto catch-up would come in the post-war period, along with most other countries, when a booming economy and an explosion in car production, including of the Volkswagen, motorised the entire developed world.

a regular marketing event by the 1920s, widely publicised, the largest of which exhibited 500 vehicles while attracting 40,000 attendees. Company dealerships were designed to be luxurious modern buildings encased in glass, offering test drives – a novelty – along with service plans and occasional gifts to walk-in customers, such as flowers. Dealer finance became a regular feature of car sales, and General Motors established its own finance arm, the famous General Motors Acceptance Corporation (GMAC) in 1919, offering one of the first consumer instalment plans in which customers could take the vehicle away but pay for it in monthly instalments over an extended period (Sovacool 2009, 419–420).

9.6 FLEET MANAGEMENT

An additional wrinkle is whether vehicles are managed as individual units or as purposeful collectives. Implicitly, economic theory defaults to individual agents making individual trips using individual vehicles (or no vehicle at all in the case of walking). However, vehicles are often managed as fleets and operated as such (though with individual operators running particular vehicles). These range from delivery trucks run by freight companies, to taxis operated by taxi firms, to the coaches and trains of public transit. Individual cars become part of fleets when managed by distribution networks such as Uber or Deliveroo, to name a couple of the major players as of this writing.

Fleets thus have their own economic dynamics, related to, but separate from, those present in infrastructure and vehicle production. These include economies of vehicle size, of distance travelled, of energy consumption, and of speed, in addition to the economies already discussed. These all add up to economies of fleet size, which vary widely according to context. With fleets, economies-of-density across the fleet are especially important. For road transport, vehicle size economies tend to increase up to a certain optimal point, while the speed, distance, and energy economies tend to be diminishing and then negative at fairly low ranges. This is largely because of the rising average costs in fuel and operations that come with increased speed and distance, at least given current technologies. These can sometimes be made up for with reaping of positive economies in other domains such as fleet size (Levinson et al. 2016, 155).

Economies-of-density (and of scale) obviously vary according to fleet size, size of network, mode, and utilisation of existing capacity. Available research suggests that bigger is not always better, at least for coach operations. With intercity coaches, for example, there seems to be a limit to efficient scale (when there is some degree of competition, that is) with small- or medium-sized firms exhibiting CRS. The length of routes run by larger operators may account for this in part since there is low ridership on some connecting segments within the network as opposed to heavier utilisation of more compact networks of smaller operators. There may also be diseconomies in managing sprawling fleets as well as limits on reaping density economies in both profitable dense markets within a network (e.g. congestion in large cities countervailing returns garnered from a big customer base) and sparsely used rural routes (which have less congestion but fewer customers over longer distances). After deregulation of intercity bus firms in the US and the UK, the number of operators dropped sharply, and the very few large firms that remained moved to a sort of hub-and-spoke network, analogous to the airlines, to improve density economies. These statements are, however, qualified, because available studies overall suffer from various methodological limitations (Levinson et al. 2016, 160).

Different modes have quite different operating economies. For passenger fleets (freight is covered in Chapter 16), rail-based transit generally has greater returns to density than road modes. While rail systems have higher fixed costs, their variable costs can be reduced by, for example, reducing headways between successive trains, something less possible with roads where there are safety and congestion limits to headway reductions (though conceivably "smart" highways may change this – see Chapter 19) (Anas 2008).

Overall, railways seem to reach CRS at around 500 mi or so, at least using US data. But there is the potential for substantial economies of density in large networks through more intensive utilisation of capacity, assuming, of course, there is sufficient demand. These particular data apply to freight operations, though there is some general applicability to passenger operations as well. The problem with passenger travel, however, is that demand at profitable fare levels is not always feasible given the available modal alternatives (Levinson et al. 2016, 162).

9.7 THE INFRASTRUCTURE–VEHICLE URBAN DEVELOPMENT NEXUS

Different vehicles require different kinds of infrastructure which, in turn, have differing impacts on land and spatial development from both an input and an output perspective. The quantity of streets, highways, and public transit and rail rights-of-way all use land that is taken out of usage for other purposes such as housing and production. *Ceteris paribus* this raises land prices and shifts the incentives shaping economic geography. In very rural areas, this shift is generally of little consequence. But in dense cities with very limited land supply, transport infrastructure expansion and modification is constrained and often quite expensive. Many times capital is effectively substituted for land by the use of tunnelling under, or raised roadways over, existing routes (Anas 2008).

This trade-off appeared quite early in the early history of transit. Even in the US, where cities developed later than in Europe, rapid population and density growth caused the earliest commuter railways during the 19th century's second half to seek alternatives to running on existing surfaces. Transit companies in the New York and Chicago areas built elevated railroads using steam power above large urban streets, totally separate from the mixed traffic below. The New York Elevated Railroad Company carried 500,000 daily passengers between lower Manhattan and the Bronx in 1893. Chicago's elevated line opened in 1892. Electrification widened the possibilities to running transit trains in tunnels because electric motors did not generate the noise, smoke, and boiler explosion risks of steam. Boston began to build the first underground subway in America in 1894. Urban train transit ended up consisting of a combination of on-street, elevated, and underground tracks, typically with differing vehicles operated by differing companies (Young 2015).

The London Underground was the pioneer here, opening in 1863. Gas-lit carriages made of wood were pulled by steam engines, and opening day patronage was 38,000. The system expanded prodigiously from there. Heat and pollution from the engines was a long-standing complaint of passengers, although operations were generally safe and passenger growth strong. Electrification came in the early 20th century (Day & Reed 2005 [1963]).

On the output side, different vehicle infrastructure combinations had long-lived impacts on urban economic structure, shape, and form. Transport network and operator characteristics radically transformed transport operations, broadening economic options. The capital intensity and the locational monopoly advantages of streetcars quickly led to consolidations across a very few operators in most major urban markets, with monopoly service delivery in particular areas, and the rise of corporate forms that were especially well suited for raising large amounts of capital. There were also substantial cross-linkages between transport and non-transport industries, with electrical utility companies in some instances also being transit providers, while some transit companies had substantial electricity investments (Young 2015).

There are many examples of infrastructure-vehicle investments shaping economic geography more immediately. During the 1960s in the UK, a major confluence between the M4 motorway running east-west and the M5 running north-south was constructed around 10 mi north and west of the centre of Bristol. In 1972, British Rail opened the Bristol Parkway station well outside the Bristol central business district (CBD) but less than a mile from the M4 corridor in a bid to service the city's growing northern suburban fringe. As a result of this location choice, development in the centre of Bristol ceased for several decades. Similarly, in the 19th century, the Bridgewater canal, which halved the cost of coal in Manchester, turned the network of canals in Birmingham into a motive force for its economic growth (Lowson 1998, 14–15). Indeed, industrialisation has been accompanied by a series of "transport revolutions" with each successive modal innovation giving birth to new infrastructure, new finance models, new corporate forms, and new alterations in the shape of economic space. Thus canals and canal boats gave rise to a canal building boom in waterway rich countries like the US and the UK. This was followed by many railway booms across the planet, with similar infrastructure and vehicle upsurges, and then came the automobile which is still altering the economic landscape now over a century on.

The flow-on effects of roads and cars on economic structure and geography have been particularly profound. Retailers of all sorts adapted to mass car ownership and highway building by developing fewer and larger outlets close to road exits, in the process closing many of their smaller inner city locations (though some of these remained open because of the higher margins available in very dense areas). The iconic shopping "mall" is a direct creature of the car in which multiple retailers found a way of combining "big box" scale economies with an attempt to replicate the diversity of consumer offerings that cities offered (Knowles 2006, 407–408).

This potted history illustrates the importance of "path-dependence" in transport infrastructure and vehicle change, whereby small initial changes can accumulate into large shifts that can be "locked in" since long-lived infrastructure investments and vehicle adoption are difficult to dislodge unless a major "exogenous" effect, like a new technology, major provider failure, or geopolitical event occurs. However, conditions can shift even in the absence of such events. Indeed, shopping malls have more recently closed in their thousands and many "big box" retailers have failed, even as the private automobile has retained its dominance. Changes in lifestyle and work–life balance are among the many drivers here, showing that economic change is a multi-causal affair that is not entirely transparent.

Whether all this ultimately leads to some sort of "steady-state" long-run spatial equilibrium is not clear. Bruegmann (2008) argues that the fast-growing, low-density regions of the American West are increasing in density, while the higher-density older urban areas in the American East, and Europe too, are declining in density. These now appear to be converging to

5,000–15,000 person per square mile range that might be a new urban norm. The reason claimed for this is that these are densities high enough to support traditional urban amenity while allowing for continued widespread use of automobiles. But if true, this is a developed world pattern, still emerging, with future trends being speculative.

9.8 THE MAINTENANCE DIMENSION

Modern transport infrastructure-vehicle complexes offer many benefits but come with large direct costs in the form of massive on-going maintenance expenditures. Systematic estimates of this burden are not available but certainly they could easily run into the trillions of dollars given the huge capital stock and operating loads that transport systems carry. Maintenance has become industrialised and centralised, just like everything else. Entire large-scale mode-specific industries have arisen, as with the automobile and flight sectors that are built on anticipations of regular and constant repairs and part replacement. Aircraft maintenance and repair spending is now comparable to airplane production itself (Margócsy & Brazelton 2023, 2).

This rise in maintenance scale and scope has arisen because transport has become much more complex, extensive, and intensive. But it has also come about because safety in passenger carriage and reliability in freight carriage has become paramount. To maintain the chance of airplane or railway crashes at their current levels of around 1 in 10 million, vehicles and networks must be extraordinarily well-maintained and this entails a great deal of money spent keeping everything in a high state of repair (Margócsy & Brazelton 2023, 5–6).

The long distance ocean travel of the past also had high repair and maintenance burdens. But the options were more limited, and the tolerances for failures considerably higher. Multiple ships could be sent out in the hope that at least one of them would get through with little incident. But this was quite costly and most sailing ships simply carried with them extra materials and tradesmen to fix broken masts and sew up torn rigging. This still was very expensive, as the books of the well-provisioned English Royal Navy attest. But this was still generally the lowest cost strategy, and a version of it carried over to the early age of car travel when there were few mechanics outside major population areas and drivers carried their own tools and repair materials (Margócsy & Brazelton 2023, 5–6).

Sailing spanned the globe and maintenance and repair did as well. Stocks of materials were often stored at various points along a passage so that following ships could avail themselves of them to fix the many problems that could and did arise on most voyages. A whole network of repair stations with local expertise emerged, along with spatial concentrations of experts for particularly complex repairs and modifications. Bombay (now Mumbai) became a global centre of ship repair and alteration in the early 17th century, with Parsi shipwrights especially skilled at their craft, applying their knowledge towards repairing and rebuilding English ships, effectively making them into new composite vessels in the process. Even back then there were vigorous debates about this early offshoring and outsourcing of maintenance, with English lawmakers sometimes claiming that Indian wood and talent was not as trustworthy as what domestic sources could provide. Nonetheless, spatially distributed repairs were necessitated by the nature of sailing and the state of current technology (Margócsy & Brazelton 2023, 7).

Indeed, for those who think in terms of historical progression being from simpler to more sophisticated, from primitive to advanced, the global ship industry should give them pause. Shipbuilding and ship repair were large-scale industries involving high skill levels and coordination across a worldwide network at a time when communication was considerably slower. Additionally, available materials were much more prone to wearing down, and with hazards that are irrelevant today, such as the shipworm *teredo navalis* that bored into the hulls of ships making them leak and sink. This problem was addressed in various ways, such as using timbers that were less susceptible, and coating hulls with protective paint or lead or copper sheathing. None of these strategies were wholly successful and all entailed enormous additional costs. The early railways had comparable problems in India and much of South and Southeast Asia where white ants and other parasites bored into wooden sleepers and structures (Margócsy & Brazelton 2023, 11–13).

In many ways the modern maintenance complex is grappling with similar problems in different guises. What has changed considerably is standardisation and centralisation such as the use of computer diagnostics and standardised, computerised modules and components made in large-scale production facilities which are then provided to local repair centres that often are essentially swapping out old sub-assemblies for new ones. This trend has become prevalent across the transport sector, from bicycles to cars. Indeed, DIY repairs are rapidly becoming a thing of the past. This is not without controversy, since poorer socioeconomic groups and those in poorer countries can be heavily burdened by the need to buy expensive components from suppliers with oligopoly or monopoly power, rather than tinker on their own with salvaged spare parts. This can be problematic even for the relatively well-off, though perhaps not as burdensome in a relative sense (Margócsy & Brazelton 2023, 8). There is also the question of how sustainable the centralised approach is, with is bias against reuse and repair and towards discard and replace. Issues of sustainability are addressed in Chapter 17.

9.9 PARKING

A discussion of vehicles and infrastructure is not complete without a discussion of parking, i.e. space and place to store idle vehicles. One of the seminal works on this topic is Shoup (2005), who noted that, as of that book's writing, 6.1 billion people owned 735 million vehicles across the world. Storing all these vehicles as they made their daily rounds would be space-consuming enough. But Shoup noted that parking, especially in the US, is highly subsidised via government planning policy requiring provision of on-street and off-street parking spaces, often for free, and that if US policies applied across the globe, space to park 4.7 billion vehicles would be required, roughly equivalent to the size of the country of France. Not all countries subsidise parking as much as America, but most provide some sort of inducements, with the net result being that much valuable land is devoted to the relatively unproductive, if necessary, use of parking cars.

Shoup's overall solution to this problem can be boiled down into two words: market pricing. That involves things like removing urban planning requirements for providing parking as part of real estate development, and fully pricing the spaces that are available at their marginal cost. Shoup estimated that the total subsidy for off-street parking in the US 2002 was at least $127 billion, and perhaps as much as $374 billion, the larger number accounting for 3.6% of GDP. At the time 99% of parking in America was free, heavily paid for by non-drivers whose tax revenues and opportunity cost made it possible. This lowered the cost of driving and therefore increased overall driving to inefficient levels.

Shoup's analysis has been highly influential and has led to some change in both planning laws and, even more, pricing of parking, with both governments and private entities (like universities) charging for parking as a matter of course. However, as with road pricing, the existence of a price does not necessarily mean that it is set at an efficient level or that prices are charged at the right physical spaces. On the one hand, some planners now limit the amount of parking provided with each new development, supposedly to encourage less driving. But this only is effective if reasonable transit or active modes are available to get people to where they want to go. If not, illegal parking and suboptimal mode choice will result.

And the placement and price of parking spots should ideally optimise traffic flow and set price according to the WTP of those using it. For example, delivery vehicles often waste a lot of time looking for parking spaces as they do their runs, adding to traffic congestion and emissions, while often incurring infringement fees for parking or idling illegally. Meanwhile, many spots they could be using are filled by residential vehicles parked for the day or even longer. A more systematic planning approach would reallocate property rights to on-street parking and reset pricing for those spots, perhaps giving priority to business operators during some hours (Rooney 2020).

The need for parking is one example of how modern transport systems and facilities actually require a lot of physical space, much of it in the form of idle capacity much of the time. One cannot have car transport without parking space and garages, or trains and trams without terminals and rail yards, etc. But, as with all other transport elements, these too need to be factored into system design and priced accordingly.

REFERENCES

Anas, A. (2008). Urban transportation economics. In Durlauf, Steven N. and Blume, Lawrence E. (eds). *New Palgrave dictionary of economics* (2nd edition). Palgrave Macmillan, 6913–6917.

Anderson Electric Car Company. (1911). *The Detroit Electric*. Anderson Electric Car Company.

Boschma, R. A., & Wenting, R. (2007).The spatial evolution of the British automobile industry: Does location matter? *Industrial and Corporate Change*, 16(2), 213–238.

Bruegmann, R. (2008). Point: Sprawl and accessibility. *Journal of Transport and Land Use*, *1*(1), 5–11.

Button, K. (2010). *Transport economics*. Edward Elgar Publishing.

Casson, L. (1994). *Travel in the ancient world*. Johns Hopkins University Press.

Day, J. R. & Reed, J. (2005 [1963]). *The story of London's underground* (new edition). Capital Transport Publishing.

Evans, R. J. (2005). *The Third Reich in power*. Penguin.

EC (2024). EU regional and urban development: Territorial cohesion. European Commission. https://ec.europa.eu/regional_policy/policy/what/territorial-cohesion_en

Fulton, L. M., Noland, R. B., Meszler, D. J., & Thomas, J. V. (2000). A statistical analysis of induced travel effects in the U.S. Mid-Atlantic region. *Journal of Transportation and Statistics*, 3(1), 1–14.

Gunn, S. (2018). *The history of transport systems in the UK. Future of Mobility: Evidence Review Foresight*, Government Office for Science, Centre for Urban History, University of Leicester.

Hugill, P. J. (2009). Trade, transport and communications, historical geographies of. In *International Encyclopedia of human geography*. Elsevier, 338–344.

Knowles, R. D. (2006). Transport shaping space: Differential collapse in time–space. *Journal of Transport Geography*, 14, 407–425.

Kumares, C. S., & Labi, S. (2007). *Transportation decision making*. Wiley.

Levinson, D., Gillen, D., et al. (2016). *Transportation economics*. en.wikibooks.org July 9, 2016. Print (pdf) version.

Lowson, M. V. (1998). Surface transport history in the UK: Analysis and projections. In *Proceedings of the Institution of Civil Engineers-Transport*. (Vol. 129, No. 1, pp. 14–19). Thomas Telford.

Margócsy, D., & Brazelton, M. A. (2023). Techniques of repair, the circulation of knowledge, and environmental transformation: Towards a new history of transportation. *History of Science*, 61(1), 3–18.

Rodrigue, J. P. (2020). *The geography of transport systems*. Routledge.

Rooney, R. (2020). Trouble with the kerb. *Smart Parking*. www.smartparking.com/uk/latest/2020/november/trouble-with-the-kerb. Accessed 12 December 2024.

Shoup, D. (2005). *High cost of free parking*. Routledge.

Sovacool, B. K. (2009). Early modes of transport in the United States: Lessons for modern energy policymakers. *Policy and Society*, 27(4), 411–427.

Young, J. (2015).Infrastructure: Mass transit in 19th-and 20th-century urban America. In *Oxford research Encyclopedia of American history*. Oxford University Press.

CHAPTER 10

Finance and funding

10.1 INTRODUCTION: REAL VERSUS MONETARY VARIABLES

The opening historical example (Box 10.1) is illustrative of the fact that institutional arrangements are central to transport finance, changing over time along with the underlying society and economy. These organisational subtleties are not captured in the core model. But that model does set out a useful framing of the function of finance in an economy.

The core model is explicitly about the "real" economy. "Real" in this context refers to actual resources of some sort or another (what accountants often refer to as "tangible"). The real economy is where physical goods and services are produced and consumed and is obviously fundamental. But a monetary (or financial) economy exists as well and sits on top of the real economy. This refers to the flow of money in the economy as opposed to the resources that underlie them. Indeed, the opening example depicts a shift from an economy based heavily on real resource flows, such as labour levies by feudal landlords on their tenants, to one where money, first through charitable donations and then through taxation and private investment, became increasingly central to transport system finance.

Chapter 2 provided a template for depicting the real economy, namely the circular flow concept.

Figure 10.2 shows the circular flow diagram presented in Chapter 1 but with financial markets in place and with money intermediating between real economy resource movements.

DOI: 10.4324/9781003350866-13

BOX 10.1 INTRODUCTORY CASE: HOW LONDON BRIDGE (AND OTHER BRIDGES) WERE KEPT FROM FALLING DOWN

In a riverine territory like the British Isles, water crossings are particularly important. In fact, many transport historians argue that bridges actually contributed the most to efficient movements of goods and people there, especially in the mediaeval period (221). (The discussion in this section and page references all refer to Harrison (2004).) During the Middle Ages, travel on English roads was slow and often impassable without bridges to ford the frequently encountered watercourses.

However, bridges were expensive. They required mobilisation of large amounts of capital to build, with further periodic infusions required for upkeep and upgrade. Some bridge building was undertaken for strategic and economic reasons, led and funded by the Saxon kings. (The Romans had similarly earlier built a quite good English road and bridge network, but this network had long since fallen into disrepair.) Major bridges were initially closely related to fortifications, often co-located and deeply integrated with each other. Fortifications relied on the ability of the Anglo-Saxon states to compel landholders to provide a labour force to build and maintain them. These wartime levies expired after the Norman conquest, but many of these work liabilities remained tacitly, in other guises, for the maintenance, improvement, or replacement of existing bridges at existing sites (185–189).

However, labour levies more and more became *de facto* money levies as local landowners increasingly hired paid craftsmen rather than extracted work from the local peasantry. Charitable donations soon became especially important, with gifts of money for bridge building and maintenance becoming a major source of funding by the early 13th century. Charitable giving was typically from landed, wealthy parties who had excess funds and particular needs, such as a merchant without heirs leaving a large bequest to build a bridge in his local area or a lord bridging a stream to benefit his own estate but with benefits to the surrounding community as well. As English per capita incomes grew during and after the Middle Ages, such surplus income became more widely available, leading to more road and bridge building and more charitable giving to support it. These investments, although self-serving for particular individuals or estates, generally turned out to be shrewd from a wider economic point of view. Substantial bridges were mostly built not in idiosyncratic, out-of-the-way places but at critical points in the economic geography of the era. Most bridges remained well maintained, a further indication of their economic and not just charitable utility (224–225).

Churches were also very important in the upkeep of mediaeval bridges, either because of charitable missions, obligations attached to monastic lands, or because church-related artifices, such as chapels, were attached to bridges. Hospitals,

FIGURE 10.1
The old London Bridge, circa 1209.

Source: Image from Watson (1927, plate 26, 62). Book and image are in the public domain.

typically religious institutions in these days, were also usually charged with care of the nearby bridges. By the 14th century, however, the London Bridge, Harnham Bridge, Salisbury, and Trent Bridges were no longer maintained by the wardens of nearby hospitals. The English Reformation, of course, killed ecclesiastical bridge oversight completely with the government takeover of the Catholic Church in England and the appropriation of most Church assets (204–205).

During the Reformation period, the Estate Trust arose as a financial mechanism for bridge fundraising and operations. Charitable bequests by individuals were increasingly put into these mechanisms to better manage risks and rewards collectively and in accord with increasing government regulations (205–206). Bridge trusts and estates became the norm, beginning in the 12th century onwards, especially for big and important bridge projects. These were akin to limited liability corporations, pooling funds under formalised administration to oversee spending and operations (184–186). Many of these bridge estates became quite wealthy. The London Bridge estate had the largest income: 796 pounds in 1537 (roughly 550,000 pounds in 2024 terms). Rochester Bridge was also quite well off. Many bridges did not have formal estates or trusts, but many still had property which generated income that benefitted from bridge investments and helped pay for their maintenance (206). Substantial bridges, such as the London Bridge, also often sited buildings and enterprises along their span, spinning further income for operations (see Figure 10.1).

The period between 1530 and 1760 marks a new phase in the English bridge finance system. The 1530 Statute of Bridges reinforced the principle of placing burdens of repair on local property owners. But it also added a county rate to finance maintenance of new bridges, effectively establishing a property tax. The Chantries Act of 1547 suppressed the religious guilds, and along with the dissolution of the monastic estates, this brought an end to church finance (213–214). By the time of the Industrial Revolution, bridge (and other infrastructure finance) in England looked more like its modern version, with a mix of public charters and incentives mixed with private shareholder corporation investment. This trend can be traced back to the *Magna Carta*, which undermined the English government's ability to impose new obligations based on feudal traditions, slowly shifting to the use of money rather than labour levies. Modern transport finance had thus already arrived by the onset of the Industrial Revolution in England. The voluntary charitable donations and trusts that had once filled funding gaps were replaced by government tax finance and what are now referred to as public–private partnerships (PPPs).

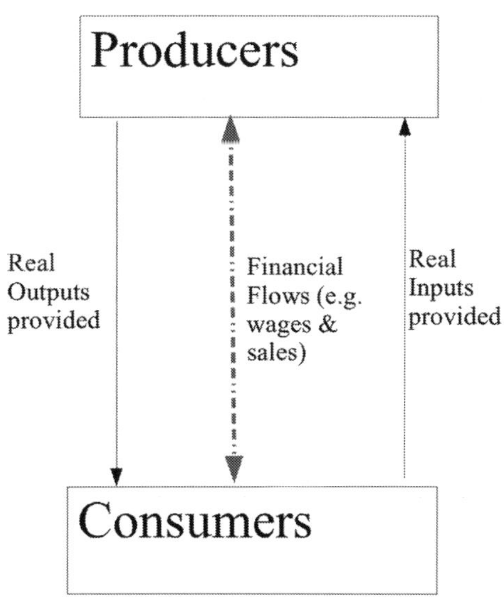

FIGURE 10.2
Circular flow with financial markets.

Economic theory suggests that a real economy with money is a lot bigger and more efficient than one without. The standard claim is that money was invented because it is useful for expanding the reach of the marketplace and all the benefits that result from such a marketplace. If there were no money, the story goes, there would only be real exchange or barter (of which the labour levies above were a forced version). The number of market transactions under such a system would be limited to those where one party could offer exactly what another wants. So a musician who wants a haircut would have to find a barber who wants to hear a song, a process formally known as finding a "coincidence of wants". With money, this one-to-one correspondence is no longer needed, and there can be many more mutually beneficial transactions possible, with a corresponding increase in overall consumption and production. The historical evidence for this particular story is actually rather contested. But there is little doubt that money does make day-to-day transactions more efficient.

10.2 FINANCIAL INTERMEDIATION

There is something else that money makes more efficient, and that is trade-offs between consumption and production across time. Rather than having an economy consisting primarily of production, consumption, and trade in the present, money allows the possibility of trading consumption and production between now and later. Functionally, a money economy greatly expands savings and investment. Both consumers and producers can choose to defer consumption or production now and get more of both later. Alternatively, both can borrow from future consumption and/or production to have more of both in the present. This function is aided by the use of money and leveraged by "financial intermediaries", such as banks, that provide for "financial intermediation" between real and financial sectors to increase the potential (and often the actual) productive capacity of the economy by facilitating present–future resources trades via the medium of money and markets for money known as financial markets.

The early 20th-century economist, Irving Fisher, the father of the field of modern financial economics, developed a model of how these financial processes expand the real economy. Referred to as the Fisher separation theorem, a simplified graph is presented in Figure 10.3.

The diagram is interpreted as follows. Three trade-offs are depicted between future and present consumption (in this case using simple linear forms, though multiple forms are possible). Without money, in a pure barter

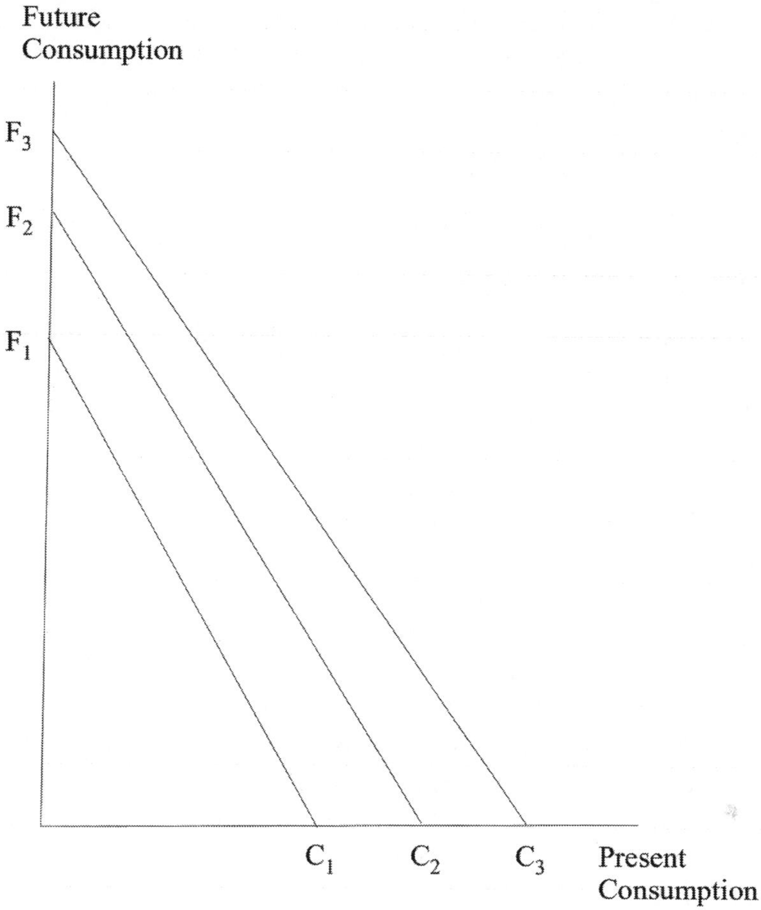

FIGURE 10.3
A Fisher separation theorem diagram (image by author).

real economy, the trade-offs between present and future consumption are limited to the line F_1C_1. In other words, it is feasible to save resources today in order to obtain more tomorrow (or, conversely, spend resources today by committing oneself to sacrifice more resources for the privilege in the future). But, according to the theory, finding the necessary coincidence of wants to barter between agents, along with the fact that some commodities (such as food) can only be stored so long, limits the future–present trade-offs to a maximum possible boundary between F_1 and C_1.

With money introduced, transactions in the real economy become more efficient, and the trade-offs possible are now expanded to the line F_2C_2. Money gets around the physical limits of barter. The ability to save and consume across time periods increases as a result to a maximum boundary of F_2 and C_2. With financial intermediation, money is leveraged further by specialised financial institutions to create an even more expanded trade-off line F_3C_3 and a maximum boundary of F_3 and C_3.

10.3 THE CONTINUUM OF TRANSPORT FUNDING AND FINANCE MECHANISMS

Financial institutions, money, and money markets play an important role in enabling the expanded trade-off sets suggested by the Fisher separation theorem and the building and maintenance of transport infrastructure, which, by definition, is a very long-run undertaking. The English bridges example shows that this is far from new. Although the context has changed radically, the task is still the same, namely to shift resources across time periods to fund desired transport goals.

Certainly the resource need is great at present. \$2.5 trillion was estimated to have been spent globally on economic infrastructure, of which transport is a major part. An annual average of \$3.7 trillion between 2017 and 2035, \$70 trillion over the period or 4.1% of world gross domestic product (GDP), is one analyst's assessment of the amount needed to sustain current economic growth rates (Gupta et al. 2022). Not all of this money is for transport, and actual needs may actually be lower (or higher). But either way, a lot of transport investment is required for the modern economy.

A distinction must be made between funding (obtaining and committing scarce resources to a particular purpose) and financing (the form in which funding is delivered, e.g. debt versus paying out of current income). In an economic sense, funding refers to the transfer of real resources between present and future. Financing is simply the choice of monetary means to deliver that end. The two terms are used interchangeably in practice and can have the same meaning depending upon context. But their economic meaning is quite different, and financiers and politicians often confuse matters, sometimes intentionally, by referring to financing mechanisms as somehow being "new money", which they are most definitely not.

The institutional methods for finance and funding of transport can be depicted as being along a continuum (Figure 10.4). At one end is direct government provision of transport infrastructure and services using traditional public debt and taxation methods. On the other end is purely private provision, using private debt and expenditure. In between are a whole range of public–private or "mixed" finance and provision mechanisms.

FIGURE 10.4
The public–private finance continuum.

10.4 ECONOMIC PRINCIPLES OF TRANSPORT FUNDING AND FINANCE

Funding and finance choices are driven by many factors. The core theory suggests that any funding choice and related financing scheme should be economically efficient, expanding the resource base of present and future economic activity as much as possible in a way that is least distortionary. Because of the strong simplifying assumptions and structure of the core model, purely privately provided transport is considered the most efficient since it arises entirely out of market competitive supply and demand processes.

Reality is rarely this simple, and even in pure private provision, some intervention outside the marketplace must be utilised, and so more explicit operational principles are required. Forkenbrock (2008) argues that efficient transport finance and charging

> is capable of ensuring a stable stream of revenue to provide adequate funding for the...system...[having] a low evasion rate, efficiency in relation to the cost of collection for the agency and the user, convenience and ease of use, and, above all assurance that the privacy of ... users will be protected.

Transport financing mechanisms, like anything else, should be designed to garner the required revenue (no more and no less) and do so in a least-cost manner. But from a public policy perspective, any mechanism that is developed must also be equitable and fair, outcomes that markets will not attain, except by accident. (Equity and justice are discussed in Chapter 14.)

Revenue raising is only part of the transport funding process. Equally important is how revenues are spent. Little is gained for the transport system if, say, road charge receipts are diverted from their intended purpose of operating and maintaining the road. For this reason, it is generally seen as desirable to have a revenue source that matches closely with intended expenditures. For example, road tolls depend upon the level of usage of the road being tolled. There is thus a clear justification for ploughing these revenues back into the road and hence a clear matching of revenues and expenditures. This is referred to generically as the "user-pay principle": that those benefiting from an investment are the ones paying for it. This method also is least distortionary if the price is set equal to marginal cost.

This may not always be possible, however. Some necessary and economically efficient facilities and services may nonetheless yield insufficient revenues to cover their costs and may require subsidy from elsewhere. Or fairness and equity concerns may dictate subsidies for certain users or for the provision of a service below its marginal cost. While the principles outlined may need to be deviated from, the economic efficiency implications of doing so should always be kept in mind.

The administrative issues that arise with actual transport facility provision are neglected in the core model since market exchange transactions between atomistic agents are deemed to yield optimal results all by themselves. In the real world, administration of some sort is required, and evasion and errors are bound to happen under any financing scheme, public or private. Entities charged with managing revenue processes have to minimise leakage from the system to collect the intended revenue. But this requires investment of resources into enforcement and collection systems. Enforcement, while necessary in terms of improving collections or reducing violations, is generally an expensive affair. Some expense can be recouped through penalty payments imposed on user infractions. But usually not entirely.

There is thus a trade-off between collection rates and enforcement and monitoring costs. In some cases, it may make sense to allow a certain amount of violations to occur in the system as long as the cost of collection for violations outweighs the revenue generated in the collection process. An important caveat to this argument is that if it becomes known that violations are tolerated and not pursued aggressively, then the rate of violation may increase because there is an incentive for users to infringe. Therefore, the ultimate balance is to establish an acceptable rate of slippage as measured against enforcement costs. One does not want to spend more on violations collection than the yield in revenue from such collection (Peters et al. 2003).

10.5 GOVERNMENT PROVISION AND PUBLIC TAXATION

The discussion thus far has focused on collecting revenues for on-going facility operations and maintenance. But how is financial capital accumulated to build the facility in the first place? In the rarefied world of the core model, economic agents will be able to accumulate such capital in advance based on the future expected returns of a particular project. How this actually happens is not detailed explicitly.

In actual fact, much advanced facility finance has to be arranged at least partly outside market dynamics. One means of transport service and facility provision is direct government delivery using taxation. Taxation refers to the power of the state to compel private individuals and entities to surrender a portion of their resources to the public treasury. As the introductory case study shows, government taxation and provision are actually much more modern and commonplace than they were in much of the pre-industrial past, where states were often weak or fragmentary in comparison to non-state entities (though much of the ancient world's large-scale building was conducted by large empire states, often using slave or other forced labour).

Public taxation diverts resources from production and consumption in the real economy to other purposes. Since economic theory holds that private sector activity is productive and efficient by definition, this diversion is deemed inefficient in the first instance. This is not necessarily bad as long as those productive resources are put into activities which are at least as productive or, perhaps, less productive but with socially beneficial activities that the private sector finds uneconomical to undertake.

But even if revenues are efficiently invested, taxes themselves introduce distortions into the market. Without taxes, a producer sells a good to a consumer at the market price, and both pay (or receive) the same price. In the core theory, the market price is also the optimal efficient price for both sides of the transaction. With taxes, however, this direct correspondence no longer holds. Now there is a pre-tax price and an after-tax price, the former being the market price and the latter being that price plus the tax payment to the government, the latter not being a direct participant in either transaction but intervening in it through its taxation authority. This difference between prices is called a tax wedge. Without taxes, buyers and sellers make a deal, and, in a market operating under all the standard assumptions, the price and quantity they agree to will match the true costs of production and true value assigned to that production by the consumer. With a tax imposed, this equilibrium no longer holds. Respective buyer and seller prices are no longer identical, as in the tax-free market, but different, the difference between the two being determining the amount of the tax wedge (see Figure 10.5).

The figure shows the tax wedge that occurs if a tax is imposed on the buyer of a commodity. This is often the case with transport excise taxes, such as a petrol tax. This is a tax on demand. (Some of the labelling of the figure would be different if this were a tax on supply, but the underlying economics would be the same.) Without a tax, the competitive market yields an equilibrium price and quantity of P_E and Q_E. With the tax imposed, there are now two prices – an after-tax and a pre-tax price. The buyer pays a price of P_{E+t}, which is the equilibrium price plus the amount of the tax. The seller

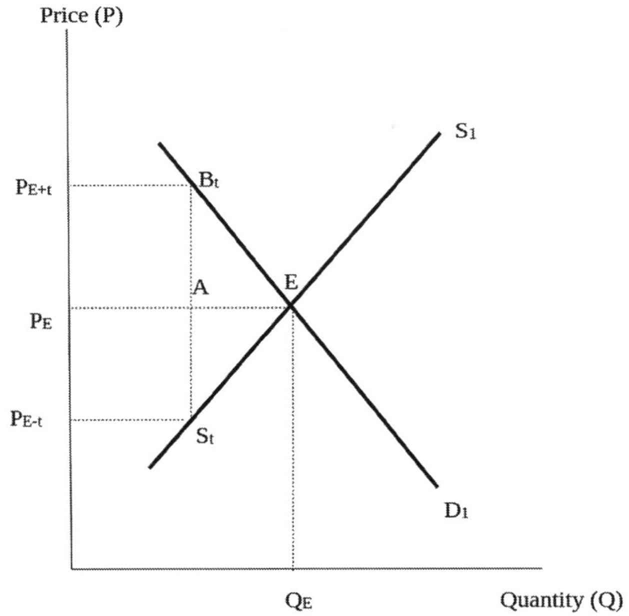

FIGURE 10.5
A tax wedge.

receives a price of P_{E-t}, which is the equilibrium price minus the amount of the tax. The government takes the revenue from the tax, which is equal to the rectangle $P_{E+t}B_tS_tP_{E-t}$. The diagram suggests that roughly half of this amount is paid by the buyer and half by the seller, represented by the squares of $P_{E+t}B_tAP_E$ and $P_EAS_tP_{E-t}$, respectively. The proportionate amounts will change depending upon the elasticities of supply and demand. In technical terms, the burden of these payments is referred to as the incidence of the tax.

A tax wedge is considered by economists to be distortionary because the prices paid by the buyer and seller are now different, and their respective calculations of gains to exchange are no longer in sync. This causes a new equilibrium between supply and demand that is not the market equilibrium, and by the lights of the core model, inherently inefficient. This is due to the fact that a third party, namely the government, is now part of the transaction but outside the market exchange and market price-setting processes. The government does collect the tax revenue and hopefully provides needed and valuable services with it. But there is an economic efficiency cost, and this is shown by the triangle B_tES (often referred to as a welfare triangle). This consists of producer and consumer surplus (inframarginal revenue and inframarginal utility to each, respectively) that would have been garnered at the pre-tax equilibrium but which are now lost entirely, what economists refer to as a deadweight loss.

This is not to say that taxes should not be imposed at all, since many government services are essential, with tax revenues used for what are hopefully beneficial activities that have greater value than the deadweight losses and/or meet desired social objectives. But those services are not directly provided through, nor directly priced by, the market. Taxes by definition impose a burden on those who bear them. Part of this burden is intentional, as a way of funding government activities paid through the imposition of a tax. But the tax wedge imposes an additional, unintended "excess burden" because it causes a shift in equilibrium supply and demand. This excess burden is equal to the distortionary effects of the tax. Thus, total tax burden can be broken into intended burden and excess burden.

Economic theory suggests that taxes should be designed to minimise the deleterious effects on economic efficiency of excess burden represented by the tax wedge. Some basic economic and financial principles for optimal tax design follow from this:

Economic efficiency: Taxes should be designed so that their excess burden, with its inevitable distortionary impact of a tax on private economic activity, is minimised.

Neutrality: Relative after-tax incentives to different types of consumption and production should be as similar to pre-tax incentives as much as possible (i.e. taxes should change relative prices as little as possible).

Simplicity: Taxes should be simple to understand and simple to pay; this ensures that taxpayers spend a minimum amount of time dealing with the administrative burden of taxes, that mistakes in filing are few, and that there is little ambiguity about who should file and when. This minimises the transaction costs entailed by taxation.

Administrative efficiency: Taxes should be easy and cheap to collect and enforce by the collecting authority. This minimises administrative costs of taxation.

Equity: Those whom society feels should have a greater burden should be taxed relatively more than those whom society feels should not be (this is called vertical equity). Also, taxpayers in similar situations to one another should be taxed similarly (this is called horizontal equity).

A critical issue in tax efficiency is the tax base, which refers to the body of individuals subject to a tax directly and/or indirectly. For example, almost all national governments and many subnational ones impose taxes on personal and corporate income. These are considered to be broad-based taxes because a high proportion of the tax base is subject to them. Other taxes have more narrow bases. Excise taxes are an example particularly applicable to transport, such as petrol or diesel taxes. Only drivers are subject to this tax, rather than all income-earners, and so its base is more narrow; though given that there are many drivers, it is still a relatively broad-based tax.

There is not a straightforward relationship between the tax base and the outlined optimal taxation guidelines. Broad-based taxes in general tend to be less distortionary than narrow-based ones (*ceteris parabus*) because their impacts are spread so widely and thus more likely to maintain neutrality. A broad base typically also allows for low unit tax rates, thus minimising the tax wedge (i.e. the difference between pre-tax and after-tax prices). Narrowly based taxes fall on smaller sub-groups and thus change incentives faced by these groups relative to the untaxed population and may require higher unit rates to raise a given amount of revenue. But, on the other hand, narrow-based taxes can often more closely tie revenues to beneficiaries. And badly designed broadly based taxes will affect many more taxpayers and markets than badly designed narrowly based ones, resulting in potentially greater efficiency losses. Context matters a great deal here.

Sometimes taxes are designated according to the public budgetary categories from which they are drawn. "General fund" taxes typically refer to public expenditures drawn from broad-based taxes, like a personal income levy that is designed to fund "general purpose" spending. "Special fund" taxes typically refer to those narrowly raised from more limited bases with revenues dedicated to "special purpose" spending. Many transport expenditures are funded by special fund taxes, like excise taxes on petrol that are devoted to the maintenance and expansion of road systems. This terminology is not economic but derived from public budgets which have their own specialised and varying vocabulary. Much policy discussion does refer to terms like this as a proxy for tax economics principles, however.

Actual assessment and collection of taxes occur at what are known as collection points. The government often picks collection points where revenue collection is least costly and enforcement potential is greatest. This is why excise taxes are so popular, especially in the transport arena. A diesel or petrol tax collected at the pump is administratively efficient, with economies of scale (EOS) in assessment and collection and relatively minimal evasion by taxpayers. This does not mean that such taxes are always the most economically efficient, as this depends upon multiple factors. But at least it makes the tax collection job easier and cheaper.

Transport finance analysts have come up with a wide range of possible tax schemes to raise needed system revenue in an efficient, sustainable and relatively low-distortion way. Sometimes multiple purposes are aimed for, such as raising transport revenues while lowering emissions at the same time. Box 10.2 provides some examples of such multipurpose transport taxes.

BOX 10.2 SELECTED MULTIPURPOSE TRANSPORT TAX TYPES

There are a wide variety of transport taxes meant to accomplish a variety of policy ends while simultaneously raising revenue for transport tasks. A few of the more widely used and discussed ones are:

Sales taxes: A sales tax is a levy on sales of a specified set of goods and services. A general sales tax (GST) has a very broad base, often with exemptions for certain goods based on policy aims (e.g. exempting food to lower the burden on low-income consumers). Sales taxes are levied on final sale transactions. Many governments impose a value-added tax (VAT) levied on transactions made at different stages of production instead. A single-item or narrow-category sales tax is referred to as an excise tax. Some governments dedicate a portion of their sales taxes to transport. A variant some US states and localities have employed is called a local-option sales tax. This allows for local jurisdictions to add a supplemental tax on top of the regular sales tax and dedicate the revenues to specific local transport needs. For example, if a state sales tax is 6%, a local option programme might allow qualifying local governments to add an additional 1% to the sales tax on each transaction and claim the supplemental revenues as their own for the purposes they desire, such as upgrading cycle lanes.

Freight weight taxes: A freight weight tax refers to a tax or charge that increases as gross vehicle weight (GVW) increases. New York State in the US, for example, has a ton-mile tax (TMT) calculated by measuring the weight of each truck for each trip, arriving at a gross weight which is then assigned a tax rate which is multiplied by the miles of travel. The levy is applied to vehicles with maximum gross weights of at least 18,000 pounds. Taxes like these are meant to indirectly recompense governments for the extra wear-and-tear that heavy vehicles impose on roads and other infrastructure (see Chapter 7).

Dedicated taxes: A dedicated tax is not so much a special levy but a budgetary device whereby revenues collected from a given source are directed to a particular purpose or entity. One example, again from New York State, is a 2009 dedicated payroll tax in which a small percentage levy was imposed on the total wage bill of employers in the 12 counties served by the Metropolitan Transportation Agency (MTA) in order to cover budget shortfalls that the agency was experiencing. While it was referred to as a regional "mobility" tax and was purportedly meant to spread the burden of MTA operations to those benefiting from its services but not necessarily paying for them, it obviously is a very indirect tax and potentially incentivises employers to reduce their payrolls. An alternative idea is to dedicate portions of transfer taxes (a tax on any gain made from a sale of an asset, financial or real) to pay for transport projects and operations. A broader based transactions tax such as this is likely to be less distortionary (Gordon & Peters 2013).

10.6 PUBLIC DEBT FINANCE

Tax finance is sometimes referred to as pay-as-you-go finance because it takes money from current period income and devotes it to current period spending. However, government, like any other entity, has the option to draw on future income for present spending. The primary way to do this is through the issuance of debt, the usual instrument being a bond. Bonds are sold to raise a certain amount of principal, which is then repaid over time with a series of interest payments ending with the repayment of the principal to the bondholders. Bond financing is often necessary for the very large amounts required for large infrastructure projects.

Analogous to taxes, bonds can have narrow or broad revenue bases. Some bonds are referred to as "general obligation" (GO) bonds, which are paid out of general revenues, i.e. all taxes and other revenues collected by the government, whatever the source, during a given period. Others are "revenue" bonds paid out of the cash flows generated by the project itself. Thus, a public toll road financed with revenue bonds would pay back the bondholders through the toll revenues generated by the road once it is up and running.

GO bonds have the advantage, from the bondholder's point of view, of being backed by the "full faith and credit" of the issuing entity because, in effect, all government revenues from whatever source are notionally held as repayment collateral. But revenue bonds can sometimes be deemed as more secure since they contractually obligate project financers to devote a portion of project revenues to bondholders, and these are quite traceable and potentially more recoverable in a court of law. GO bonds lack this specificity, and when a government finds itself unable to repay its obligations because of insufficient tax collections, it may choose to default on specific bonds, and the bondholders have little specific to chase after for recovery except the government itself. Legally this is not typically a very promising recourse. Revenue bonds are thus more limited in what bondholders may claim in the event of default. But they can also be more enforceable in the event of default. The desirability of one over the other, for both issuer and bondholder, depends on circumstances.

According to the core theory, debt is not as potentially distortionary as taxation is. The reason is that debt is issued through financial markets and financial intermediaries which supposedly operate according to the same competitive market dynamics as real product markets and thus are more likely to deliver optimal results. Also, buyers of bonds or issuers of loans are not, in theory, compelled to offer their surplus capital and can negotiate terms with the debtor. In practice, financial markets can fail, and there are various asymmetries in available information that can make such markets inefficient. But these issues are not considered here.

10.7 PRIVATE INVESTMENT AND PRIVATISATION

On the other end of the spectrum of financing and transport provision is private investment. A great deal of transport is actually provided by and for private actors. This is especially true in the freight sector, as covered in Chapter 16.

However, much passenger transport is still under the purview of public authority, and government is often involved in various aspects of much transport service, even freight in some cases. But public provision does not always mean direct provision or funding by government. A transfer of management, ownership, and/or control of any aspect of an enterprise from the public (governmental) sector to the private (nongovernmental) sector is referred to as privatisation.

Privatisation runs a gamut from large-scale to small-scale and from full public transfer to the private sector to more limited partial transfer. The purest example of privatisation is the outright sale of a governmental asset or operation to a private corporate entity. Infrastructure assets such as roads and airports are often in this category, having in many cases been built, owned, and operated by the government, which then decides, perhaps many years later, to sell the asset to a private operator. The asset may be directly sold, in which case the method of transfer is referred to as an asset sale; alternatively, the shares of an incorporated entity that holds the asset for the government may be floated on public share markets, or those shares may be sold to selected private entities, in which case the method of transfer is referred to as a trade sale.

An alternative method of public-to-private transfer is a concession or lease arrangement. For example, suppose a government decides to transfer a public commuter rail to a private entity. As noted above, the government could sell the rail line directly (an asset sale) or sell the shares of a governmental corporate entity that owns the rail line (a trade sale). But a third alternative is for the government to retain ownership of the rail line but lease the line to a private entity for some period of time, after which the line reverts back to public ownership (referred to as a lease-back arrangement). If the lease term is long enough (20 years or more, with 75- or 99-year leases quite common in the infrastructure field), the government has *de facto* (i.e. in fact), though not *de jure* (i.e. by law), transferred ownership because the long-term lease effectively gives control over the asset to the private entity even though the government nominally owns it. Leases and concession agreements can have many different legal provisions through which the degree of privatisation can be modulated. For example, shorter or more limited lease terms can allow the governmental owner to retain more management control over the privately managed asset.

Leasing is an example of a widely used method of privatisation known as contracting out. In this case, a service or activity (as opposed to an asset) is paid for by the government but is provided, by means of a service agreement, through a private entity. Almost any conceivable example of public service can be provided in this way, though some, such as transit and information technology services, are more widely contracted out by governments than others, such as police protection. Outsourcing is another label often used to designate contracting out, though the former term is broader in that it is used for both public-to-private and private-to-private transfers of responsibility. If the service is outsourced to a provider in another country, then it is sometimes referred to as offshoring.

This continuum of privatisation has led to the development of the PPP mentioned earlier. A broad definition of the term refers to working arrangements based on a mutual commitment between a public sector organisation and any organisation outside of the public sector. The common theme of privatisation and a PPP is some sort of blending of private and public institutions and missions. However, privatisation refers to some definite transfer of activity or authority from the public to the private sector, whereas a PPP can also include joint public–private efforts that are more blended.

Privatisation can be completed in one step or through a series of intermediate steps. Corporatisation, in which a public operation is first transferred to a new corporate entity that is governmental but is typically run outside of governmental budget and policy frameworks, is often a step on the road to complete privatisation. For example, when the Australian central government decided to privatise a number of airports that it owned and operated, it first transferred ownership of, and responsibility for, those airports to a purpose-built entity called the Federal Airports Corporation (FAC). The FAC operated these airports for a few years before putting them up for sale, mostly utilising trade sales (Gordon et al. 2009). Even if corporatisation is a final outcome, the final effect may be much the same as privatisation if that corporation operates much like a private company even though technically a governmental entity retains ownership and control.

Governments choose to privatise for numerous reasons, the major stated rationales being that the private sector operates more efficiently and cost-effectively than the public sector in many instances; that government can achieve better overall outcomes by focusing on its core missions and core competencies while giving peripheral activities and programmes outside its skill set to capable private operators; that privatisation allows access to private capital which would otherwise be unavailable; that the method shifts risk to market-based entities better able to handle them; and that greater flexibility in operations is achieved (Gordon et al. 2013).

Maintenance of the public interest is a prime concern with any privatisation, and a potential lack thereof thus constitutes one of the main counterarguments against its use. It is not a given that the public interest will be maintained when private parties with perhaps countervailing interests take over. A related issue is that of fairness: private operators are generally return-driven and inclined to charge market rates and/or cut costs to maximise returns. This may be inequitable if service cuts or charges fall upon groups deemed to be disadvantaged. In general, economists note that there is a difference between an actual gain in resources and a mere transfer of resources from one party to another. Government budgets may see a gain from privatisation, but other parties, such as workers or consumers, might see a loss, with no real net efficiency gain realised. This is especially a problem where a natural or other monopoly exists and in which price and quality are not subject to much competition, often the case with large transport facilities. Privatisation can be said to enhance efficiency only if the gains are above and beyond any shifts of resources across different groups (Weisbrod & Gordon 2008).

There is no *a priori* case for or against privatisation, so the matter rests on evidence, and this is mixed. There are examples of very successful privatisations that have delivered superior outcomes for both public and private sectors (e.g. Japan Rail, mostly completed by the 1960s); those that did poorly on both counts (e.g. the initial privatisation of British Rail); and many much more ambiguous cases. Probably the most overall successful set of privatisations has been the transfer of state-owned enterprises (SOEs) to private enterprises in some developing countries. When SOEs run large losses, being corporate in form, there seems to be little economic reason to keep them in public hands. Even here, however, there have been failures and transfers back to the public sector in a few cases. In general, it is clear that privatisations, being negotiated arrangements between governmental and nongovernmental entities, will be successful only if the agreements are sound and well implemented and, in some cases, regulated afterwards. Some transfers, such as of an SOE, will be relatively straightforward to sell to the private sector, while others, such as complex public services spread across multiple entities, will be more difficult. Privatisations certainly have wide applicability and do offer one of many alternatives for governments to use in providing services, but to work, they need to be designed properly and may not always be the best available method of reform (Rindyawati & Gordon 2010).

10.8 DISTANCE-BASED AND OTHER "GREEN" FINANCING MECHANISMS

Financing methods that both raise revenue and address environmental problems have become more widespread in recent years, especially with the rise of new information technologies that were not available in earlier periods. One example is the vehicle miles travelled (VMT) (or, in metric units, vehicle kilometres travelled (VKT)) charge in which all miles (or kilometres) travelled in a vehicle are tracked and taxed. The Oregon Department of Transportation (ODOT) in the US conducted a field experiment of the charge, utilising an on-board vehicle GPS system to track mileage and usage patterns of individual drivers. The data collected was retrieved from the on-board units at technology-equipped gas stations. The test was conducted in spring 2006 and involved 260 vehicles equipped with mileage recorders and 2 service stations equipped with readers. If the fuel pump detected that a road price on-board mileage recorder was present, the pump then deducted the existing state fuel tax from the bill to the consumer and then added the cost of the road mileage charge. This swapping was done because the idea of the trial was to test using a VMT tax instead of the existing and obviously much less targeted petrol tax (Gordon & Peters 2013; Oregon DOT 2007).

The Oregon project had a number of limitations with regard to its immediate applicability to transport finance. Firstly, the project assumed that the tracking technology on board the vehicle would be supplied by the auto manufacturers at no cost to the state. Secondly, the test used volunteers that were willing participants in the project, and no significant measures were used to prevent tampering or fraud in the system. Finally, the test utilised only two petrol stations, and even then, there were a number of operational problems that occurred during the test. Still, the test represented a good attempt to model the operational issues of distance charging as well as providing a baseline estimate of costs to deploy this kind of system (Oregon DOT 2007).

Distance charges have very high potential system start-up costs. The large number of users to be monitored, as well as the large number of payment sites and the cost of tracking technology installation, generally entail high fixed costs. There are also significant privacy issues since, by definition, distance charging relies on monitoring trips. It is possible to anonymise this data to an extent, but this is not necessarily sufficient to protect user confidentiality.

On the other hand, distance charges do have large revenue potential and, unlike fuel taxes and tolls, directly capture all the relevant travel activity, i.e. actual distance travelled. Such schemes could incentivise people to make economically efficient levels of trips and potentially make them move out of environmentally more costly modes (like automobiles) to less costly ones, like transit, while generating significant revenue for investments in these more ecologically friendly alternatives (Gordon & Peters 2013). As of this writing, however, distance charging schemes are still mostly conceptual or in the trial phase, mainly because of their cost and current technological limits.

"Green" charges are another category of financing mechanism which aims to capture the environmental cost of transport usage and put it back on the user. Distance charging can be put under this rubric, though its intent is to capture direct costs, such as wear-and-tear, as well as "external" costs. A carbon emissions tax is a more direct example of a "green" charge. Taxes like these can create problems if not uniformly applied, however. If a tax is applied in one market and not in others closely situated, then there will be an incentive to create a black market in the taxed product and smuggling of the good from the low-tax market into the high-tax market. This is commonly observed in products such as cigarettes and in alcoholic beverages subject to tax in one jurisdiction but not in another one nearby. Black markets are generally not too problematic given the nature of transport services, but there have been examples of informal cabs and transit vehicles that have evaded government price and operations regulation and, in some areas, black markets for petrol.

10.9 ECONOMIC DEVELOPMENT, VALUE CAPTURE, AND VALUE UPLIFT

One aspect of financing and pricing that has particular importance is their effects on economic development. Transport infrastructure affects accessibility and mobility, which in turn changes the spatial layout of economically desirable locations for work and home. Vadali (2008), for example, studies the effect of new toll roads on property values around Dallas, Texas, finding that these created some significant accessibility premia for prices of properties located near the road. Boarnet and Chalermpong (2001) found similar effects for toll roads in Orange County, California. There is a huge literature on the effects of public transit infrastructure investment on property values and development, especially around train stations and rail transit stops, with a growing literature on buses, especially bus rapid transit (BRT), as well. This literature finds property value changes to be positive overall but ranging from falls of 18% to increases of 120%, affected by a variety of factors including quality and frequency of service, mode, broader economic geography, and measurement methods used by particular studies (Saxe & Miller 2016).

These economic development impacts have importance in their own right. But from a financing point of view, when transport system investment raises land values – referred to as value uplift – this provides a basis for leveraging some of that future increase towards funding facility building in the present – referred to as value capture. This is an example of the Fisher separation theorem (Figure 10.3) in action, i.e. trading future asset value rises for present investment today via monetary channels.

Value uplift works on the principles of spatial economics outlined in Chapter 4. Travel time savings delivered by transport infrastructure improvements reshape economic geography, making some locations closer to stations more accessible and hence more valuable. These effects are capitalised into the future land prices of these locations, which will be higher with the project than without it. These accessibility-driven increases in value can be further augmented by knock-on effects such as a concentration of businesses around a rail station, and these can be encouraged by policies that redesign transit nodes to encourage and shape concentrations in ways desirable to consumers, producers, and residents. When this is done around transit stations or corridors by policy design, it is referred to as transit-oriented development (TOD). Value capture involves structuring financing around the expected value uplift that a new (or expanded) facility will bring. The basic concept is to use taxation incentives and/or PPPs built around the uplift that is directly associated with the new facility to help pay for that facility (Gupta et al. 2022; Saxe & Miller 2016).

Value capture is not a cure-all for transport system funding needs. For one thing, it mostly applies to major new investments or major expansions. Maintenance, normal upgrades, and on-going operations are not amenable to the method. Additionally, not all projects will have sufficient amounts of, or sufficient certainty around, value capture to attract private finance. And there will be, of course, cases where the value uplift might be negative, i.e. the facility, may cause value in some locations to fall rather than rise. This can happen for various reasons, such as operations creating their own disamenities, such as vehicle noise or emissions, or a new station having purely transport utility rather than development potential, such as a transfer station built in an otherwise isolated area. There are also limits to value capture since density has costs (e.g. crowding) as well as returns. Finally, value capture arrangements can be complex, and a badly executed or designed deal can allow the private participants to capture more of the value than their investments are entitled to. This is true of PPPs more generally, where, as the old saying goes, "the devil is in the details". Having said all this, value capture is a significant recent transport financing tool.

REFERENCES

Boarnet, M. G., & Chalermpong, S. (2001). New highways, house prices, and urban development: A case study of toll roads in Orange County, CA. *Housing Policy Debate*, 12(3), 575–605.

Forkenbrock, D. (2008). Policy options for varying mileage-based road user charges. *Transportation Research Record*, 2079, 29–36.

Gordon, C., Hughes, M., & Read, A (2009). *Australian Airport Privatisation: Impacts on Operations and Customers*. Unpublished working paper.

Gordon, C., Mulley, C., Stevens, N., & Daniels, R. (2013). How optimal was the Sydney Metro contract?: Comparison with international best practice. *Research in Transportation Economics*, 39(1), 239–246.

Gordon, C., & Peters, J. R. (2013). Funding urban transport in New York: Revenue potential of VMT and carbon taxes in New York State. In *Transport Research Board, 92nd Annual Meeting Proceedings*, Washington DC, Paper No. 13-0443.

Gupta, A., Van Nieuwerburgh, S., & Kontokosta, C. (2022). Take the Q train: Value capture of public infrastructure projects. *Journal of Urban Economics*, 129, 103422.

Harrison, D. (2004). *The bridges of medieval England: Transport and society 400-1800*. Oxford University Press.

Oregon Department of Transport (2007). Road User Fee Task Force Final Report. www.oregon.gov/ODOT/Programs/Pages/Road-User-Fee-Task-Force.aspx

Peters, J. R., & Kramer, J. K. (2003). The inefficiency of toll collection as a means of taxation: Evidence from the Garden State Parkway. *Transportation Quarterly*, 57(3), 17–31.

Rindyawati, Y., & Gordon, C. (2010). Partial Privatisation in Banking: The Indonesian Experience. In *Proceedings of the 23rd Australasian Finance and Banking Conference* (Sydney, Australia).

Saxe, S., & Miller, E. J. (2016). *Transit and land value uplift: An introduction*. Urban Informatics for Sustainable Metropolitan Growth.

Vadali, S. (2008). Toll roads and economic development: Exploring effects on property values. *The Annals of Regional Science*, 42(3), 591–620.

Watson, W. J. (1927). *Bridge architecture: Containing two-hundred illustrations of the notable bridges of the world, ancient and modern*. W. Helburn.

Weisbrod, G., & Gordon, C. (2008). The challenge for public-private financing of transport: Aligning benefits, costs and sustainability. In *Proceedings of the12th International Congress on Transport in the Developing World*, Hanoi, Vietnam (November 12–14, 2008).

CHAPTER 11

Planning, management, and governance

11.1 INTRODUCTION: TRANSPORT PLANNING VERSUS MANAGEMENT VERSUS GOVERNANCE

The opening case (Box 11.1) graphically illustrates *in extremis* the many perverse incentives and unintended consequences that arise from the poor design of institutions and organisations. These are suffused throughout modern economies and their transport systems, and their planning, management, and governance are their lynch-pin activities, needed to keep them running and, hopefully, carrying out their intended missions.

Planning generically refers to deciding on a goal and laying out a set of actions to attain those goals, sometimes supplemented with a set of predictions of future events and circumstances. Management generically refers to the act of controlling and organising activities. Governance broadly refers to the procedures, processes, and institutional structures that assist with carrying out the acts of management. These concepts/actions are obviously all quite interrelated.

Strategic planning entails the setting of high-level goals and a programme of suggested actions to attain them. The term's broadest sense, derived from military theory, refers to the design and execution of a master plan. Below this is tactical planning, in which different means towards desired ends are evaluated for their relative efficacy with respect to achieving the master plan. Operational planning takes tactics and strategy as given but sets out and

DOI: 10.4324/9781003350866-14

BOX 11.1 INTRODUCTORY CASE: SOVIET PLANNING, CARS, ROADS, AND THE ONE-TONNE NAIL

Before it collapsed in 1991, the Soviet Union had organised its economy around central planning by the State. Most production and distribution decisions and resource allocations were made according to a central plan designed by an agency colloquially known as "Gosplan" and carried out and executed by various state instrumentalities giving direction to state-run factories and manufacturers (see Figure 11.1).

Soviet car production was a product of this system, with the state largely monopolising production of motor vehicles using, as was the case for most production: very large-scale factories with cradle-to-grave services provided to employees who often lived in purpose-built

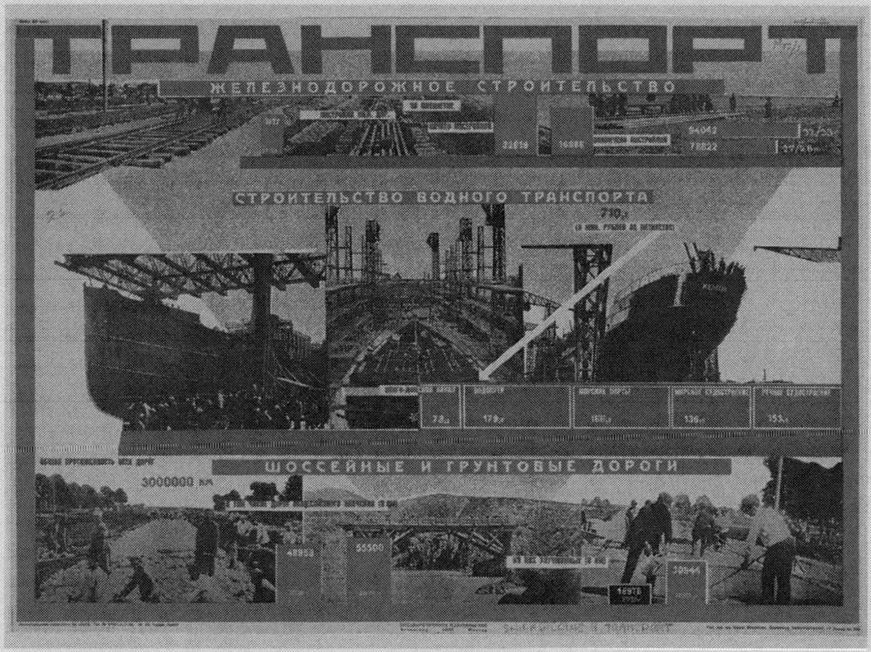

FIGURE 11.1
A Soviet poster on outcomes of one of the Five Year Plans in the transport sector (ca. 1930).

Source: Image from National Library of Scotland. https://digital.nls.uk/74506120 Item description: "Coloured photomontage poster showing projected increases in construction in the various sectors of the transport industry during the Five Year Plan". The physical item used to create this digital version is out of copyright. Image is used under a Creative Commons Attribution 4.0 International Licence.

neighbourhoods (and sometimes entire cities); the government allocation, rather than sale, of cars to citizens; and government planning imperatives in production, dictating a preponderance of trucks versus passenger cars in the total motor vehicle fleet, reflecting a general bias against consumer goods that remained until the 1960s. The Soviet Union also had a very underdeveloped road network poorly suited to motorised travel until well after the end of World War II. For decades large sections of the country effectively had no roads, especially in the wet seasons of spring and autumn, when mud made what tracks there were impassable. Central planning did close these gaps, tripling paved road mileage over the course of 12 years during Stalin's reign, and producing considerable amounts of passenger cars so that by the 1980s these were no longer scarce items of privilege, although they were nowhere near as ubiquitous or of a quality as found in the West (Siegelbaum 2008). This was part of larger and very rapid, if sometimes brutal, industrialisation of what was still a largely backward country at the time of the 1917 Bolshevik Revolution which, combined with the country's victory in World War II, ended in its attainment of 40 years of global "superpower" status along with the US.

Soviet central planning was not economically efficient, involving a great deal of resource misallocation and waste. Eggertsson (1990) mentions an old Soviet political cartoon showing a factory with a huge one-tonne nail mounted on the wall and a caption under it entitled "This Month's Plan Fulfilled". The joke here is that Soviet state planners would have performance plans for factory managers where output was specified in tonnes. Thus, Soviet steel, glass, paper, cars, and most other things were often heavier than they should have been. The Soviets produced all manner of things but most of these were of relatively poor quality and the predominance of clunky and unwieldy central planning was a prime reason for this. While planning may have helped rapidly industrialise Russia in its early stages, ultimately its inefficiency and inflexibility was a major reason that the entire system collapsed.

Still, maximising of tonnage was arguably better than a target economising on it. Products like paper and steel would have been too thin and hence almost completely valueless under such a maximisation criteria, even though resource use would have been lower. At least thick product can generally be used. In this case it just wasn't very good.

organises actions to ensure smooth execution "on the ground". It is at this lowest level where governance mostly applies, being in the realm of concrete and regularly repeated actions to keep going concerns going. But governance system design definitely also has strategic and tactical dimensions.

Strategic management involves defining "an organization's attempt to set a direction and to implement and evaluate it in light of its external environment and its internal capacity...[in which] managers seek to develop... advantage and create a successful future by managing all the organization's resources" (Roberts & Menker, 2000, 562). Tactical and operational management refer to control and implementation at the lower levels of generality discussed above.

The STO (strategic/tactical/operational) framework, developed by Van de Velde (1997), applies these different elements to the various roles of transport stakeholders, especially operators, and overseers such as regulators. The framework tracks (S) with the setting of overall transport policy, (T) with system planning, and (O) with service delivery. Well-done STO fundamentally aims to align all three dimensions to achieve three "E's" of efficiency, equity, and environmental sustainability combined with the three "A's" of accessibility, affordability, and availability (Hensher & Potter 1998). It is critical to make sure the incentives, authority, and accountability are all at their proper levels. For example, operational goals related to service delivery are generally best handled by transport providers not policy-makers, with the latter focused on strategic, not tactical, goals. Indeed, many problems often are at the tactical level with conflicts between regulator and operator often muddying the waters.

11.2 THE CORE THEORY AND THE AGENCY PROBLEM

Soviet planning had an all-encompassing purview in which strategic, tactical, and operational levels were combined. This offered the purported advantage of completeness but at the cost of rigidity and over-specification, particularly problematic when information was imperfect and predictions about the future turned out to be wrong, both obviously inevitable at one point or another. Although management and governance were nominally separate from planning, the authoritarian nature of Soviet institutions meant that "The Plan" was the tail that often wagged the implementation dog, leading to further inefficiencies and unintended consequences, like the "one tonne nail".

This is obviously an extreme. But so too is the idealised world of the core model, in which the market is the mechanism used by atomistic agents to accomplish all strategic, tactical, and operational planning, management, and operations. The core model, even with modified assumptions to account for the presence of time, space, embodiment, and complications such as imperfect competition, does not explicitly address institutional issues. Even atomistic agents clearly need to work with one another to coordinate, plan, and manage beneficial activities, and to derive gains from trade and production, often over long-time periods. However, with all actors assumed to be individually atomistic, rational, maximising, and selfish, such coordination will be problematic because these characteristics are antithetical to trust. It is true that in the short-run, temporary alliances can arise for specifically arising instances of immediate and clear mutual collective gain and optimisation for participants. But these are not necessarily stable, coming apart as soon as market dynamics and conditions change. If conditions are such that disloyalty and betrayal pay, then agents will be disloyal and betraying, even to a temporary alliance that they themselves helped form.

The core model assumption of completely autonomous and independent agents, acting independently, is unrealistic in many ways. Interdependence refers to the general fact that people need to rely on others with skills and endowments that they do not possess to accomplish almost anything in business and life. This is true even for the otherwise hard-headed selfish rational realists posited by neoclassical economic theory. Thus, there are returns to interdependence, rather than just mutual gains from individual trade (Gordon 2015, Chapter 2).

The economic need for interdependence presents a problem for the core model because trust and reliance of some sort is required which is not automatically captured by market processes. For example, an owner of surplus capital may buy a railway because it has the highest possible rate of return of all investment alternatives. But if this owner has no expertise in running such a railway, recruitment of a manager with the requisite skills will be needed. The owner is referred to as the principal and the manager as the agent. The principal seeks to maximise value (V) received from the agent's services minus the payment (P) made to the agent, i.e. maximise the net value of V – P. The agent wants to deliver as little V as possible given agreed upon P, i.e. minimise V – P. Thus, their value maximisation problems are misaligned. This is referred to as the agency problem (or the principal–agent problem) (Besanko et al. 2013, Chapter 12).

Principals and agents will operationalise their relationship and aim to solve this problem with a management contract. The design of this contract will seek to optimise returns to interdependence and align principal and agent maximisation. The core model assumes that all agents possess identical information and that everything that could be known is known by all market actors, a condition referred to as complete, symmetric, and perfect information. The core model also assumes there are perfect and complete property rights, i.e. inviolate legal ownership and control over owned assets and activities with transferability of that control/ownership seamless from buyer to seller.

In the core model, principal/agent goal misalignment need not be a problem with these two assumptions in place. Both know the other's maximisation equations and have all the information necessary to draw up a binding contract that will be worth it for both of them to maintain, and perfectly enforceable if breached. Such conditions can be approximated in thick, deep, and competitive markets for standardised services. In that case the market mechanism itself generates a dynamic and wide information base on principal and agent performance and incentives, captured in the prevailing "price" for agent services and clear willingness-to-pay (WTP) for agent services by principals. The on-going frequent transactions in such markets can thus generate a set of functional workable contract terms, easily replicated and enforced, supporting well-functioning property rights and generating complete and symmetric information. Such a market would simultaneously inform and constrain principals and agents in their dealings and contractual obligations with each other. With both easily replaceable in the marketplace, there is a clear cost of breaking or gaming contracts as word would spread quickly and the price that unreliable agents could command for their services would fall, while the fee that unreliable principals would have to pay would rise (Gordon 2015, Chapter 2).

However, information and property right imperfections abound in the real world, especially in cases such as non-tradable goods and services that have no market at all, markets that are thin and not very competitive, and markets that can only handle "bundles" of services or goods where inefficiency might arise in contracts for a piece of that bundle. These sorts of conditions hold in many transport markets, especially given that transport is a derived demand and its markets are characterised by imperfect competition and information lacunae.

11.3 ORGANISATIONS AND TRANSACTION COST ECONOMICS (TCE)

The core model also assumes that there are no "transactions costs", i.e. that economic transactions like contracts are costless. Production and consumption of course entail sacrifices of resources, but these are directly linked to productive activities. But the costs of exchange, such as purchases and sales, or the administration of things like execution and monitoring of contracts, only indirectly support efficiency, relating to costs of background enabling transactions which the core model omits by assuming them to be without cost. This is obviously completely unrealistic, and such costs are often considerable.

The field of transaction costs economics (TCE) consists of the core model with the assumption of costless transactions relaxed. Its primary implication is that the presence of transactions costs creates a divide between "external" transactions, conducted by agents in the marketplace, and "internal" ones conducted within organisations. Coase (1937) claims that the existence of positive transaction costs is the very reason that organisations, including private firms, exist, namely as devices to minimise transactions costs.

In the core model, any undertaking involving collective action across agents could potentially be reduced to the necessary pairwise gains from mutual trade, just added up to the whole that makes up the sum of the parts. But if transactions have even small costs, there will be cases where this will not be feasible, though the opportunity for returns to collective action remain. Organisations will thus arise to deliver stable and long-lived arrangements to minimise overall transaction costs if the gain from that minimisation is lower than the returns to be realised. There are other explanations for the existence of the firm in particular. But transaction costs minimisation is the one that the core model offers, a fix that can leave the rest of the economic model untouched (Gordon 2015, Chapter 2).

11.4 FORM, FUNCTION, MANAGEMENT, AND GOVERNANCE

If providers of capital calculate, in the presence of positive transactions costs, that their returns are better if they stand together and pool their resources to create a new entity, what shape does the entity take, and how does it run and what ensures it reaches its desired goals? The core theory covers external interactions between private firms competing against one another subject to the external pressures of the marketplace. But understanding planning, management, and governance of the firm's internal workings requires the development of more theory. These issues are considered under the rubric of firm structure, or form, sometimes referred to as "organisational architecture". As the term implies, conscious and intentional institutional design is required, distinct from the impersonal workings of the market's "invisible hand".

The institutional design problem requires getting right the structure of organisational coordination of internal firm activities, especially the flow of information to ensure formulation and achievement of objectives, and control, which requires setting the location of decision-making and rule-making authority within some sort of hierarchy of authority. Thus are born the basic tasks of planning, management, and governance themselves. Organisation design aspects apply to all levels within the firm: individual, team, and organisational. From the economist's single-minded perspective, all the observed varieties of corporate form arise from the balance between minimisation of transactions costs and the necessary mobilisation of resources to maximise competitive advantage and profitability of the firm in the marketplace. Within the neoclassical framework the criteria for design success is one where structures minimise transactions costs and align principal and agent incentives as effectively as possible. This is particularly important for decisions pertaining to firm integration across its value stream such as vertical/horizontal, upstream/downstream, and make/buy (sourcing) decisions (Williamson 1985).

TCE thus presents a dichotomous marketplace model, between external market behaviour in competition and internal markets of the firm. Agents in both cases remain rational, atomistic, selfish, maximising. So how do they manage to stick together in the internal market? Milgrom and Roberts (1992) coined the term "influence costs" in this context to refer to the cost of management activity devoted to lobbying within organisations about allocation of internal nonmarket resources to various uses. Once principals provide capital to a firm, it becomes "internal capital" and its allocation within the firm has an obviously political flavour, indicating that as far as pure theory is concerned, the firm itself is not a perfect market setting where decisions are driven by "pure" economic forces. But influence costs will be higher for some organisational forms than others and this, balanced against task- and mission-efficient cost and benefit drivers, will result in a choice of organisational form that hopefully maximises net benefit for the firm as an entity, and for its principals (Meyers et al. 1992).

Firm structure and form are not synonymous with governance of that form. One can design a good watertight ship but if the captain sails it into an iceberg all that design is for naught. Still, form does interplay with governance in critical ways. Economists study how form acts as a means of minimising the costs and information management within the organisation and effective means of executing strategy outside of it. The TCE perspective is that to plan, manage, and govern effectively within an institution comes down to two things: choosing the right institutional form and choosing the right decision-making procedures within that institution. "Right" in this case refers to organisational outcomes meeting strategic and programmatic objectives, operating in an efficient manner, and successfully competing in the external marketplace. Whether this actually happens in practice, even for firms in competitive markets, is debated even by some economists (see Box 11.2). But the theory does have a lot of structure and useful predictions to help guide decisions and test against reality.

BOX 11.2 ARE COMPETITIVE FIRMS ALWAYS EFFICIENT?

The classic assumption about firms is that they exist to maximise profits because this will maximise the value of that firm for their owners. Since owners (principals) are rational maximisers, they will choose managers (agents) that will maximise profits. However, this may not always be the case, even within the core model. Firm owners may derive utility from things other than profits. An example of a firm owner's utility function is the following:

U = f(profits, firm size, prestige)

In this case, the firm owner gets utility from three things: profits, the size of the firm, and the prestige of being an owner of a prominent enterprise. Of course the firm has to be a going concern and firms which focus on more than profits may be driven out of business by leaner, meaner competitors. But this may take years or even decades: the core model is agnostic about how long because the passage of time is not explicitly detailed. Further, firms operating in imperfectly competitive markets may not need to maximise profitability to survive, with principals able to trade off some profit for attaining other aims without threatening firm viability. The agency problem further complicates the picture because managers may be able to arrogate some control from the principal to their own behalf, maximising things like the size of their own staff and salaries. Even if this is not viable in the longer run, such a state of affairs can last awhile.

Liebenstein (1966) has found empirical evidence of considerable slack in the way actual firms use available resources, finding cases where dramatic increases in productivity were obtained with no changes in technology or inputs, only to formal management protocols. Liebenstein argues that this could be evidence that firms are often utilising their inputs inefficiently, referring to this under-utilisation as "X-inefficiency". He speculates that this could be because, contrary to theory, inputs and outputs do not always have a determinate relationship but vary widely according to the management and market environment in which they occur, with managers needing to experiment a great deal to find an ever-shifting "sweet spot". They thus need to have some resources in reserve due to some inherent variability in production–cost relationships, in addition to general market uncertainty. X-inefficiency suggests that the core economic theory of production might be missing something, at least in some instances. These are gaps that TCE does provide a partial answer for.

11.5 THE ECONOMICS OF OPTIMAL GOVERNMENT DESIGN

In transport, government is often the provider and/or manager of transport services. Public management and governance is not the same as for its private counterparts, especially given its relative separateness from market processes. There may be "internal" markets for all organisations of any size. But the public sector typically has much less exposure to "external" markets and their "ownership" is quite different as well. In representative democratic systems public authorities are meant to reflect the preferences of the greater populace, a majority at least. Even in authoritarian regimes the state is meant to work on behalf of the "people". The government of the Soviet Union was, for example, at least notionally working towards a greater good, even though deviating far from that in practice.

The core theory abstracts away from governmental realities and political theory to treat public institutions in the same way as private ones. Agents in both realms remain selfish, atomistic, rational, and maximising, including politicians, public servants, and voters, with individual preferences that they seek to have met. The economic theory of public choice thus analyses government form, operations, choice, and "collective action" by applying the standard assumptions about economic agents to everyone in the public sphere. With democratic systems the "marketplace" is the voting arena where politicians craft their policies to appeal to just enough voter preferences to attain a majority. Once in government, decisions are carried out by self-interested bureaucrats, constrained by politicians, but still seeking to maximise their own objectives of accumulating power – the agency problem in the public sphere.

Public choice and its applications are considered more in the discussion of political economy in Chapter 18. Here the focus is on the economics of optimal" design of government institutions, denoting a form and function that accurately encompasses voter preferences and meets those preferences in an economically efficient manner. This is effectively supply and demand analysis transferred to the public sector. In this case the demanders are the voters, while the supplier is the government.

The relevant economics field here is fiscal federalism. Federalism refers to any system of government in which a larger political jurisdiction, usually a nation, shares political sovereignty with two or more subsidiary levels of government. For political theorists, sovereignty refers to the ultimate source of legitimate authority and power of action given to the State. Some countries, like the UK, have unitary government in which sovereignty rests with the central government. There is some devolution of authority to local governments, but these entities and their powers are purely creations of the central government. Thus, London currently has a powerful local directorate with a strong mayor. But this was only formally created by an Act of Parliament in 1999 (taking effect in 2000) after a roughly fifteen year period in which London was managed by separate local councils (Blunkett et al. 2016, 556–557).

Other governments have explicitly federal structures in which sovereignty is constitutionally shared between the central and "lower" levels of government and which cannot be altered without fundamental change to the constitution. Germany, the US, Canada, and Australia are major examples of federal systems. Transport delivery has both strategic and operational aspects and even unitary governments usually devolve operational authority to localities while making strategic decisions nationally (Box 11.3 compares three different federalist models of transport policy across the world).

In fiscal federalism the word "fiscal" refers to a study of resource flows across systems of shared political sovereignty, while "federalism" in this context "lays out a general normative framework for the assignment of functions to different levels of government and the appropriate fiscal instruments for carrying out these functions" (Oates 1999, 1121). Normative is a term that refers to policy prescriptions implied by the theory that are purportedly drawn from more "positive" (i.e. "objective") findings about government operations drawn from theory and evidence. The main principle to come out of this literature is that levels of government, and the jurisdictions they serve, should be designed to ensure that the beneficiary of local services should as much as possible bear the cost of these services and that jurisdictions should have boundaries and functions that accomplish this purpose (Musgrave 1969).

A primary question considered in this literature is optimal jurisdiction size. When economists speak of optimal, they mean the lowest-cost way of meeting actual citizen preferences, in which citizens are thought of mainly as consumers of public goods and services. All the usual core transport economics assumptions apply, with an additional explicit premise of perfect mobility of individuals (voters) across space and between political jurisdictions. The basic idea is that households sort themselves according to their preferences about housing and government services into communities of voters with largely homogeneous shared preferences. This is economically efficient since each household moves to the jurisdiction that maximises its own utility by providing the most preferred bundle of public goods and services relative to the taxes they pay, with policy choices guided through the electoral process. The fact that agents can "vote with their feet" ensures that government, through the pressure of constituent mobility, will give their residents what they want at a minimum unit (average) cost (AC). For each political jurisdiction there

BOX 11.3 TRANSPORT FEDERALISM IN AUSTRALIA, THE US, AND THE EUROPEAN UNION

A textbook definition of federalism is "a system of government in which powers are shared between a central (national) government and regional (state) governments". This same book defines a federal system as "a means of dividing the power and functions of government between a central government and a specified number of geographically defined regional jurisdictions". This is to be distinguished from a confederation ("a league of sovereign states in which a limited central government exercises few independent powers"), and a unitary system ("one in which all authority is derived from a central authority") (Bowman & Kearney, 1999, 5, 24).

The distinctions between confederation and federalism system are particularly relevant for a case comparison of transport policy-making across three different federal systems: Australia, the US, and the EU. The first two are the most similar in their governmental design. The US was created by agreement between 13 independently sovereign breakaway English colonies, with details hammered out in a written constitution that created a new central government. The US Constitution explicitly spells out, in broad strokes, powers reserved for the federal government and those reserved for the American States (which is what the colonies became in the new union). Very broadly speaking, the federal government was meant to focus on affairs that were purely national, namely those cutting across State boundaries. The States retained traditional sovereignty over their own internal affairs.

The delimitations between the two were not entirely clear and were clarified only with a major Civil War between 1861 and 1865 simultaneously abolishing slavery across the country and affirming that States did not have a right to secede from the Union. Much evolution took place after that. As far as transport is concerned, the current American central government sets policy objectives and division of responsibilities through laws passed by the US Congress and regulations and programmes directed by federal agencies designated to carry out those laws. The 50 States are largely responsible for making the actual transportation investments, operating transport facilities, maintaining infrastructure within their individual boundaries, and managing operations for their residents (such as licencing of cars). Much of this shared policy-making and implementation is done through federal grants with conditions set by the federal government and through an array of national agencies like the US Department of Transportation (Gordon 2005, 295–296).

Australia has a similar history, with six independent colonial governments uniting in 1901 under a formal written constitution (now encompassing six Australian States and two Territories). As in the US, these are the two sovereign levels of government.

Local governments in both places are the construct of the States, with their authority devolved from above. Australia actually based its constitution on the US model, while also drawing on elements of the British parliamentary system from which it was then operating under a template sometimes called the "Washminster" model, combining the words "Washington" and "Westminster". Because the Australian union came much later in history than in the US, the Australian constitution is much more specific about delegations with respect to transport policy. Sections 90, 92, and 117 establish a common market, removing barriers of movements of goods and people across State boundaries. Sections 106, 107, and 108 protect the integrity and independence of the States. Section 51 defines the powers of the Australian Government and leaves the residual powers (those not assumed by the Australian Government) to the States. Section 109 provides that where there is a conflict, central Australian Government law prevails. As in the US there is considerable variety of transport policies across States but privatisation plays a bigger role in practice in Australian infrastructure building than in the US, which is a reason that States actually often exercise considerable independence in the building of major urban infrastructure facilities there. As in the US, Australian states do most of the transport spending. But, also like the US, the Australian Government uses many financial and regulatory levers, as well as planning mechanisms, to try to ensure that the national network and corresponding areas of national need are properly served, with grant funding often serving that role (Gordon 2012, 223–236).

The EU appears similar at first glance to both the American and Australian unions. But on closer inspection it is a quite different animal. The EU emerged out of treaty agreements between already sovereign nations, and formally it remains more of a confederation of equals rather than a federal system with different levels of government with differing degrees of inherent authority. In the EU there is not a central government *per se* but a European Commission and Council of Ministers that sets very detailed transnational plans and an elected European transnational Parliament that is meant to reflect public opinion across the bloc. But these do not have the same powers or sovereignty that the public executive and legislature have in the US and Australia. In transport policy, however, there are similarities, with the EU "centre" formulating policies and plans across countries and coordinating and implementing these through grants, policy directives, and various specialised transnational technical bodies. Thus, for example, the European Commission launched the Trans-European Transport Network (TEN-T) project to connect and interoperate national infrastructure networks, focusing on key transnational corridors. Much of this effort has been technical, with some EU financial incentives and funding. But implementation and much of the financing is left to the individual countries involved (Gordon 2005, 298–303). Still, underlying these arrangements is a fundamental EU allowance of the free movement of goods, capital, people, and services within the European single market, without discrimination. This principle, buttressed further in EU countries that have adopted the single currency of the Euro, makes the EU something of a hybrid between confederation and union (Barslund & Busse 2014).

In all three cases, the common aim is to dynamically balance central and local authority in transport policy-making and execution, delegating strategic planning to "higher" levels of government, and implementation to "lower" levels that are nominally closer to the citizenry. How well this actually goes is a matter of on-going debate and practice.

will thus be an "optimal" population size (n*) for that community, within a region of various communities and jurisdictions, each one with populations consuming a preferred government-provided goods bundle at minimum average cost (AC*). Figure 11.2 shows this optimum condition, which can be applied both as a metric for individual communities and across the set of communities as a whole (Tiebout 1956).

This conclusion is dependent upon many additional simplifications to those of the core model, such as exclusion of "politics" (outside of rational preference maximisation), an absence of any local differentials that might affect either choice of community (such as existing job base or natural amenities) or differences in the production technology of government goods and services (such as a nearby cheap natural energy source that might lower government costs). And there is no particular empirical consensus on optimal jurisdiction size except that housing costs, land availability, land price, transport costs, and tax policies, amongst other things, change the optimal size and mix of communities and division of function across levels of government (Gordon 2013).

Since these grand issues are so difficult to settle, much of the fiscal federalism literature focuses on the more narrow question of how to efficiently achieve policy ends within a federal system. One recommendation is the provision of national grants to lower levels of government to achieve larger strategic goals that are not in the purview or interest of local governments. These can be in pursuit of both efficiency goals, e.g. grants that align spatial areas containing constituents who receive the benefits of local public goods with actual jurisdiction boundaries; and equity goals, e.g. grants that redistribute resources from communities with more ability to pay, to those in communities less well-off. Cost-sharing between levels of government is generally recommended to incentivise private choices in lieu of direct government action. One historical example is the US Federal Highway Act of

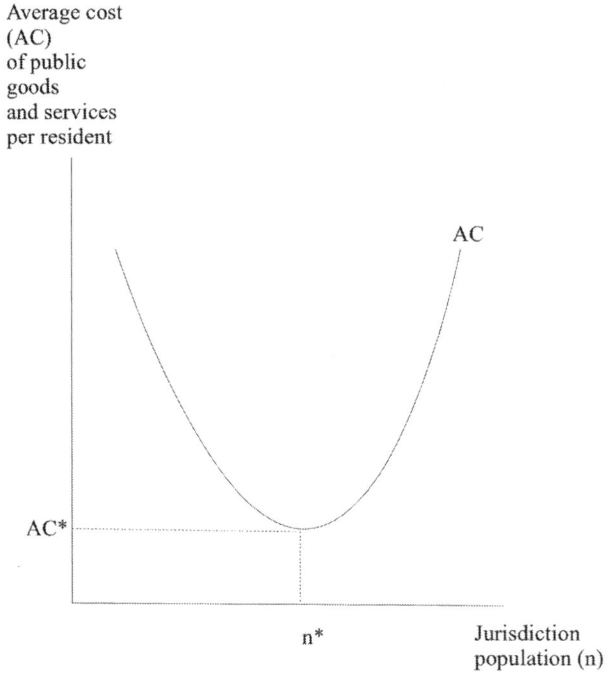

FIGURE 11.2
"Optimal" jurisdiction size according to fiscal federalism.

1921, in which the national government appropriated $75 million per year to build roads but did so requiring that US States provide a dollar match for every federal dollar. Partly this was because of constitutional issues about powers delegated between the national and State governments. But it was also designed to provide incentives that made the governments partners in road building rather than setting up a scheme that could be easily "gamed" by States. This "federal aid highway system" set the pattern for national road funding models for the rest of the 20th century (Dilger 2015, 6–7).

11.6 TRANSPORT GOVERNANCE AND DESIGN GUIDELINES

From the core model perspective, there are three primary criteria for institutional design and governance: (a) technical efficiency, defined as maximum output yielded from minimum inputs (the focus being solely on the technical and material transformation of raw inputs into final products and services for sale, anywhere along the production chain); (b) economic efficiency, defined as the maximum welfare benefit yielded from minimum resource cost (incorporating not just technical efficiency but maximum desired outcomes); and (c) agency efficiency, which refers to the minimising of transaction, coordination, and agency costs arising from internal markets. This last item is the critical governance aspect. Oliver Williamson (1985) calls the balancing of these three efficiency levels across a vertically integrated firm "economising". This process consists of deciding on the optimal mix of transactions undertaken through the market and internal transactions negotiated and conducted within the entity. Key tasks for any organisation are to (a) pick the right level of integration across activities, essentially an organisational architecture design choice, and then (b) provide efficient governance across that level of integration, which basically amounts to implicit and explicit contract (read: incentive) design.

Government is more complex than this for reasons already mentioned, and transport has its own particular nuances, especially with infrastructure. Table 11.1 provides a template for sorting out some of the economic design issues of transport organisational management and governance.

The template can be used to guide and assess both new and existing programme design and delivery. As an example, suppose a local government is planning to expand its existing bus service by integrating and merging it with a neighbouring jurisdiction's operations. This proposed move could be analysed by using the rows and columns of Table 11.1. In this example, on the rows, services provided could be "local buses", the service area consisting of a newly expanded region across two local jurisdictions, the physical assets referring to the bus fleets, depots, etc. of the merged operating entity, management design referring to form, structure, and function of the combined entity, and fiscal capacity noting the local financial resources available to it. As for columns, the first would spell out the overall objectives that the merger

TABLE 11.1

Transport programme management and governance considerations

Provision dimension	Strategic objectives	Scale	Scope	Structure
Services provided				
Service area (geographic, etc.)				
Jurisdictions involved				
Physical assets				
Management design				
Fiscal capacity				

Source: Adapted from Gordon (2002).

is supposed to achieve arrayed across the dimensions spelled out in the rows, i.e. how they tie into scale (of provision etc.), programme scope, and the relevant administrative structuring issues. This is an indicative example. The various categories can be adjusted as desired, but some core aspects of institutional design in transport are highlighted. More detailed data or analyses could be linked to in the background as desired.

11.7 THE RISE OF PROFESSIONAL TRANSPORT PLANNING

Planning in a formal and administrative sense has an ancient pedigree, arising, it seems, with the appearance of empire-states. The need for explicit plans and officials to carry them out probably emerged with the rise of concentrated cities within extensive political jurisdictions. Rome in particular built and administered an extensive surface transport network across the Empire for military and political subjugation and control, an apparatus that required extensive planning and management. Other early empires such as China, Egypt, and Mesopotamia were all very concerned with generating and distributing agricultural surplus inside and outside their empires and building and operating integrated transport systems for doing so. The Roman Empire's planning administration made the Mediterranean a true economic region, a path-breaker in that regard. The planning foundation it built, however, largely fell away in Europe after the Empire's end, not to be picked up again for many centuries (Hugill 2009, 339).

Planning as a specialist expertise specifically tied into attaining economic growth and development is of more recent vintage, being roughly 300–400 years old; planning of urban road and other transport systems in the technical sense we have of it today really dates from the middle of the 19th century. European governments launched public works projects on an unprecedented scale in the middle of that century onwards, driven by the desire to incentivise the domestic and international capital investment so critical to the modern industrial system of economic growth. A whole series of new ministries of public works to supervise and strategically plan spending programmes were launched, in Portugal, Spain, and, most notably, the Second Empire in France, the archetypal "developmental regime". There was also a big increase in the establishment of state statistical offices focused on measuring the "national economy". Formal planning like this required data, leading to the formulation of data categories and collection, carried out by new bureaucracies, dramatically redefining most problems as technical ones with technical solutions (Clark 2012, 177–185).

11.8 AUTOMOBILES AND HIGHWAY PLANNING

The invention of the automobile added a new problem to contend with for both urban and transport planning, the two fields increasingly fusing together. Indeed, automobiles threw into question the very necessity of cities since, unlike even urban mass transit, there now seemed to be economically viable alternatives to the concentration of population, trade, and industry in a single very dense place. Planners began questioning how compact cities should be. This question was bound up with assessments of which modes to privilege for urban carriage. Underneath both was the question of costs, both of potential solutions and current and projected problems.

These conflicts were most prominent in the US, the vanguard of automobile adoption. Even before the car, American cities in particular generally had little in the way of modern right-of-way rules, even for horses, so when cross-traffic met through-traffic, the result could be a mess, with considerable danger for pedestrians who crossed streets at any point they chose. Streetcars further complicated this situation, but at least these were on fixed trajectories and, in some cases, running above or below the street. But cars made things truly chaotic. Cars could be parked anywhere there was space, including footpaths (sidewalks in American parlance) and traffic lanes. And there were few limits on their speed of travel and no rules-of-the-road (Brown 2006, 14).

This was bad enough for the ordinary citizen but devilish for business interests and city political leaders seeking economic development. As car uptake increased, congested streets became gridlocked, and motorists were often unable to park and shop. Land developers in particular began to split into camps, between those already with a great deal of inner city assets, and those without. The planning profession split as well. The urban planning profession was initially dominated by "City Beautiful" and "Garden City" strains that were based on predominantly pedestrian and transit-based cities. The former emphasised urban core plans with broad thoroughfares, lots of inner city parks, and generous spaces for walking and mingling. The latter had a vision of satellite cities, much smaller than main ones, but with similar amenities, located along intercity train lines, but nestled within the still relatively untouched green land outside conurbations. Both visions recognised the challenges of urban congestion and density and sought solutions for them. But one axis of the urban transport-development debate asked whether urban growth should continue to be centralised and pedestrian-focused, while the other asked whether it should become more decentralised and car-focused (Fishman 1998).

By the 1920s it was clear that the car was the wave of the future, destined to ultimately replace even the relatively new technology of streetcars, and requiring much more of scarce available urban space to operate, for both roads and parking. Soon a "City Practical" (also known as "City Functional") school of urban design arose, seeking economical and functional solutions to urban congestion, conceding city space to autos rather than emphasising costly aesthetics (Brown 2006, 6). A debate then ensued amongst planners about whether cars or transit were the solution or the problem when it came to solving congestion. In the end the sheer number of cars on city streets caused a planning focus on autos as both (Foster 1979, 369–370). That ended up in the rise of the professional transport planner (and its adjunct, the highway engineer) and the dominance of that profession in the urban planning space, a trend that lasted for decades.

Emphasis shifted towards urban decentralisation over centralisation, and a car-, not a streetcar-based version. Soon grade-separated classes of roadways were designed and built in metropolitan areas throughout the US, allowing for segregated high throughput roads with limited access to surrounding feeder and circulator streets. Thus was born the "freeway" which eliminated the "frictions of movement" within cities, reducing congestion, increasing travel time, and reducing accidents at crossing points, previously the most dangerous point in urban circulation. Aesthetics and social concerns were not entirely absent from this shift in focus. Freeways developed for suburban pleasure drives by urban travellers, called "parkways", were often beautifully landscaped. But the primary aim remained the speedy, low-cost, and safe throughput of motor vehicles through and around urban cores. Transport planners and engineers focused mostly on this particular problem, while urban planners were more concerned with the effects that these corridors had on shaping the future development of the city, while trying to integrate them with local streets and businesses. Either way the car and the road were the common focus of achieving a goal of "efficient" motion (Brown 2005, 4, 7–8).

The obvious policy and planning imperative in a framework such as this was to improve roads and their management, rather than shifting mode choice, travel behaviour or land use patterns. This was what the freeway was about and what various 20th century inner city road schemes were about also, with double-decked street systems, like Chicago's Wacker Drive, and, much later, interstate highway bypasses and throughways going straight across urban neighbourhoods aiming to deliver maximum throughput of auto traffic (Foster 1979, 379).

With the end of World War II, the American transport planning became dominated by the traffic-service vision of engineers, soon becoming widespread across Europe and the developed world, though with lags and adaptations for older cities and development patterns (Brown 2005, 8). The now familiar level of service (LOS) measures to evaluate traffic conditions arose out of this, still with us today, in which a letter grade designation is assigned to road performance, ranging from LOS A (no congestion or free flow) to F (maximum congestion). Roadway segments and intersections receive specific LOS grades based on a calculated ratio of traffic volume on the facility divided by its capacity, i.e. a volume to capacity (V/C) ratio, with a V/C ratio of 0.9 or higher indicating heavy congestion and a grade of LOS E (Zhang 2010, 149).

These concepts are meant for arterial and other high-volume roads. Local streets are another matter, given that they are meant to circulate people over very small neighbourhood areas. There has been a recognition in urban and transport planning that pedestrians must be given greater consideration. Box 11.4 provides an example of how US localities deal with planning for local streets, an example that also illustrates some of the issues discussed earlier about fiscal federalism and institutional design.

11.9 PLANNING FOR PEDESTRIANS

The early auto-focus of planning has reversed considerably over the past five decades or so. Partly this has been driven by a major backlash against "urban renewal" coming from relatively well-off urban neighbourhoods whose communities were better able to fight highways being run through their streets and homes than the poorer and less politically connected places that had been decimated by the first waves of urban highway building. Jane Jacobs became a *cause celebre* in the US and an influential theorist of an urban planning model that evoked the earlier "City Beautiful" movement with its emphasis on liveable and walkable communities encouraging tight social bonds, a theme that has been picked up more recently by the "New Urbanists". However, these ideas have been criticised as containing an idealised image of the past that applies only in a relatively few, mostly older cities and in mostly affluent locales (Fishman 1998).

There have also been many moves to bring pedestrians back into city centres. This was the first line of government policy response to the backlash against urban arterials as a solution to all urban transport problems. In the UK, for example, many city centres were pedestrianised after 1970 with Reading and Leeds being early excluders of cars from their central zones (Gunn 2018, 4). There are many other examples in many other places. These initial moves were not particularly successful, especially when downtown decline and continued suburbanisation were at their heights, which was the case when most of these measures were implemented. Instead of revitalising

BOX 11.4 A (VERY) BRIEF HISTORY OF THE PLANNING AND POLICY CONTEXT FOR LOCAL STREETS IN AMERICA

An influential 1911 US book, *The Width and Arrangement of Streets*, argued for a local street classification and standardisation scheme that later would evolve into a complex hierarchy of roads and service level classifications. A follow-up 1916 text, *City planning*, called for the classification of streets as either main thoroughfares or minor streets. In both cases, the aim was primarily about the diversion of danger and nuisance from vehicle through-traffic off of local roads and on to larger arterials (Brown 2006, 6). In a real sense local streets were seen as afterthoughts left to the local city engineer and the local politicians to sort out.

This has remained the pattern in federalist America. There are many programmes, policies, and funding mechanisms for national, state, and county roads in the US. But when it comes to local streets, sidewalks, and curbs, these have mostly been the responsibility of localities. National and State planning programmes for local streets in the US remain highly fragmented and focused on very particular needs such as safe routes to school, cycle-ways, and pedestrian facilities specifically augmenting transit (Gordon 2018). For example, the US State of Maryland listed eight separate grant programmes in 2014 with very narrow and specific foci such as access to heritage and federal lands, paths in community parks and bicycle lane retrofits. Of course it does make sense that local streets would and should be primarily a local affair (Peters et al. 2017).

But planners have increasingly recognised that the condition of local streets affect both urban form and the performance of the larger transportation network. Because many trips begin and end on local streets, and because those same streets can have a significant effect on land development and mode choice (e.g. a lack of footpaths will generally discourage active travel modes and favour automobile travel), there is an argument for a broader funding and policy framework at higher levels of government. The "Complete Streets" framework in the US recognises these linkages, defining such streets as those designed to meet the needs of the broadest possible range of users, across all manner of modes and trip purposes. However, perhaps because of this very local focus in the framework, there is as of yet no specific federal funding in America to support Complete Streets (outside over very narrow single purpose money) and states are not much interested either. Local streets in the US at least remain locally designed and provided, not necessarily a bad thing, but perhaps leaving some broader synergies unrealised at times (Peters et al. 2017).

urban cores or encouraging walking, many pedestrian zones saw upticks in crime and squatting, and some later reopened to cars. However, as cities overall saw a return of significant economic activity to their centres (somewhat, but not entirely, reversed by Covid-19), and as pedestrianisation took more integrated forms, including using traffic calming and better design and integration between footpaths and roads, the positive economic and environmental effects have been much more pronounced (Brownrigg et al. 2023).

There has also been a renewed focus on making transit a greater part of overall pedestrian mobility. Walking distance guidelines for transit have been adopted in many places to ensure that service is at least notionally easily accessible to those within its service area. American LRT systems have guidelines ranging between 400 m (0.25 mi) and 800 m (0.5 mi), with an average walking distance to suburban stations of 649 m (0.4 mi) and central business district (CBD) stations of 326 m (0.2 mi) (Kim et al. 2007, 513). However, many urban places still have no reliable or regular service, and walkability criteria do not do much in such cases. Moreover, the overall urban environment is very important for transit usage. A station may be "walkable" but still inaccessible if, for example, getting to it requires crossing a busy highway or other impediment.

The building of Park and Ride (P&R) facilities is another attempt to increase transit use and walking to encourage transit use. P&R facilities have grown significantly in many countries, the Netherlands being a leader. The first official P&R opened in 1979 in Schagen, north of Amsterdam and ten years later more than 50 official P&R facilities were in use, with 386 by 2003. However, even in the cycle- and walking-friendly Netherlands, the impact of these facilities is ambiguous. Dutch and broader European evidence suggests that the main effects of P&Rs might be spatial traffic redistribution rather than reduction in car travel. This is not necessarily bad, especially if it relieves road and other congestion at choke points. But it does not appear to be an effective strategy for major mode shift (Mingardo 2013, 7–8).

However, the developing world is in a much different situation compared to its richer counterparts. For one thing, in many cities walking is still a very important means of travel, with cities such as Dar es Salaam and Nairobi having around a 46% share of all trips, and greater in rural areas, even for long journeys. And the institutional arrangements are generally quite different as well. Nonetheless transport planning in these places tends to mirror those of the Western world, often shaped by requirements and advice of international aid and lending institutions such as the World Bank (Pooley 2009, 146). Urban environments are often quite chaotic in terms of mixed traffic, with people walking in spite of, rather than because of, the environment, mostly out of economic necessity. Even though walking may still predominate in many cities in lower income countries, this does not mean that the policies enabling such walking cannot be improved to make that activity safer and more attractive, and more desirable than driving where that is a socially and economically desirable goal.

11.10 TRANSPORT PLANNING, MANAGEMENT, AND GOVERNANCE IN THE MODERN WORLD

One thing that has shifted considerably over the 20th century and into the 21st is the complexity of planning. This chapter has focused mainly on surface transport along roads, especially cars and pedestrians, mainly because this affects vast numbers of travellers. But there are entire fields devoted to aviation planning, both for air movements and on the ground (especially airports), and for maritime transport, trains, and urban public transit (UPT), amongst others. Some of the issues pertinent to these fields are covered in other chapters. Full discussions of them as planning modes in their own right are omitted here simply because of space constraints.

At the same time the objectives of transport planning are much broader than was the case earlier. Environmental impact, equity, liveability, amenity, and finance, amongst other things, are now judged as important, and sometimes more so, than the single objective of efficiency in movements. Planning now thus often requires multi-objective strategy formulation and execution. Intermodalism is also recognised as the new norm, for both passenger and freight transport, with planning taking this a starting point in the form of mobility delivery paradigms such as Mobility as a Service (MaaS) (see Chapters 16 and 20). Additionally, the links between urban and transport activity are more recognised than ever, with planning practice evolving accordingly.

Institutions have grown more complex too, with public–private partnerships (PPPs) and blended finance/delivery models complicating transport governance, management, and delivery considerably (see Chapter 10). Much efficiency can be gained by these organisational innovations. But new management challenges are presented as well, especially in balancing responsibility and accountability across numerous entities for ultimate results. The management of mega-projects, like entire new rail lines, can be particularly difficult to conduct when there are multiple public and private entities involved in construction, maintenance, and operations over long periods of time. Corruption – roughly defined as the abuse of institutional power for private benefit – and maladministration – a term difficult to pin down but encompassing a whole set of often unintentional administrative failures and malfunctions – are long-time potential scourges that have grown more subtle and complicated in a complexifying environment (Gordon 2006).

From an economic theory perspective, the goal of getting maximal outcomes from the minimum possible resources remains a primary aim of transport planning, management, and governance. Achieving this on practical level has always been hard, and is now more nuanced, but is as important as ever.

REFERENCES

Barslund, M., & Busse, M. (2014). *Making the most of EU labour mobility*. CEPS Task Force Reports.

Besanko, D., Dranove, D., Shanley, M., & Schaefer, S. (2013). *Economics of strategy* (6th edition). John Wiley & Sons.

Blunkett, D., Flinders, M., & Prosser, B. (2016). Devolution, evolution, revolution … democracy? What's really happening to English local governance?. *The Political Quarterly*, 87(4), 553–564.

Bowman, A. O., & Kearney, R. C. (1999). *State and local government* (4th edition). Houghton-Mifflin.

Brown, J. (2005). A tale of two visions: Harland Bartholomew, Robert Moses, and the development of the American freeway. *Journal of Planning History*, 4(1), 3–32.

Brown, J. (2006). From traffic regulation to limited ways: The effort to build a science of transportation planning. *Journal of Planning History*, 5(1), 3–34.

Brownrigg-Gleeson, M. L., Monzon, A., & Cortez, A. (2023). Reasons to pedestrianise urban centres: impact analysis on mobility habits, liveability and economic activities. *Sustainability*, 15(23), 16472.

Clark, C. (2012). After 1848: The European revolution in government. *Transactions of the Royal Historical Society*, 22, 171–197.

Coase, R. H. (1937). The nature of the firm. *Economica*, 4, 386–405.

Dilger, R. J. (2015). Federalism issues in surface transportation policy: A historical perspective (Report # 40431). US Congressional Research Service.

Eggertsson, T. (1990). *Economic behavior and institutions*. Cambridge University Press.

Fishman, R. (1998). Beyond utopia: Urbanism after the end of cities. *Urbanitats* 7.

Foster, M. (1979). City planners and urban transportation: The American response, 1900–1940. *Journal of Urban History*, 5(3), 365–396.

Gordon, C. (2002). S...S...S...S Marks the "Spot": Who should do what, when and why in the provision of regional infrastructure. In *Proceedings of the conference, "Maintaining and Financing Public Infrastructure in Tough Budgetary Times,"* jointly sponsored by the Federal Reserve Bank of Chicago and the National Association of State Budget Officers, Chicago, IL, September 25, 2002.

Gordon, C. (2005). Transportation policy in the European and American Unions compared: Lessons in transportation federalism. *Public Works Management and Policy*, 9(2), 292–304.

Gordon, C. (2006). Costing and curing corruption in public transit agencies: A preliminary assessment of New York and Los Angeles. *Journal of Financial Crime*, 13(4), 442–455.

Gordon, C. (2012). Urban transport management and financing elements. In Wellman, Kath and Spiller. Marcus (eds). *Financing and managing Australian urban systems*. Wiley-Blackwell, 235–255.

Gordon, C. (2013). An economic theory perspective on optimal design of government of regional infrastructure in Australia: The case of national transport.

In *Proceedings of the 42nd Australian Conference of Economists*. Economic Society of Australia.

Gordon, C. (2015). *Behavioural approaches to corporate governance*. Routledge.

Gordon, C. (2018). Economic benefits of active transportation. In Larouche, Richard (ed). *Children's active transportation*. Elsevier, 41–48.

Gunn, S. (2018). The history of transport systems in the UK. In *Future of mobility: Evidence review foresight*. Government Office for Science, Centre for Urban History, University of Leicester.

Hensher, D. A., & Potter, S. (1998). Competition, ownership and wider transport policy issues: Workshop 5. In competition and ownership in land passenger transport: The fifth international conference. *Transport Reviews*, 18(4), 342–347.

Hugill, P. J. (2009). Trade, transport and communications, historical geographies of. In *International encyclopedia of human geography*. Elsevier, 338–344.

Kim, S., Ulfarsson, G. F., & Hennessy, J. T. (2007). Analysis of light rail rider travel behavior: Impacts of individual, built environment, and crime characteristics on transit access. *Transportation Research Part A: Policy and Practice*, 41(6), 511–522.

Meyer, M., Milgrom, P., & Roberts, J. (1992). Organizational prospects, influence costs, and ownership changes. *Journal of Economics & Management Strategy*, 1(1), 9–35.

Mingardo, G. (2013). Transport and environmental effects of rail-based Park and Ride: Evidence from the Netherlands. *Journal of Transport Geography*, 30, 7–16.

Musgrave, R. A. (1969). Provision for social goods. *Public Economics*, 124–144.

Oates, W. E. (1999). An essay on fiscal federalism. *Journal of Economic Literature*, 37 (September), 1120–1149.

Peters, C. E., Peters, J. R., & Gordon, C. (2017). Who should pay for local streets? Who does?: Survey of New Jersey municipalities. *Transportation Research Record*, 2670(1), 24–32.

Pooley, C. G. (2009). Mobility, history of everyday. In Kitchin, Rob and Thrift Nigel (eds). *International encyclopedia of human geography*. Elsevier, 144–149.

Roberts, N. C., & Menker, J. (2000). Strategic management in the federal government. In Rabin, Jack, and Miller, Gerald J. (eds). *Handbook of strategic management* (2nd edition). Marcel Dekker, 561–593.

Siegelbaum, L. H. (2008). *Cars for comrades: The Life of the Soviet automobile*. Cornell University Press.

Tiebout, C. (1956). A pure theory of local expenditures. *Journal of Political Economy* 64(October), 416–424.

Van de Velde, D. (1997). Entrepreneurship and tendering in local public transport services. Paper presented at the 5th International Conference on Competition and Ownership in Land Passenger Transport (Thredbo 5), Leeds, United Kingdom.

Williamson, O. (1985). *The economic institutions of capitalism*. Free Press.

Zhang, M. (2010). Can transit-oriented development reduce peak-hour congestion? *Transportation Research Record*, 2174, 148–155.

CHAPTER 12

Operational issues

12.1 INTRODUCTION: OPERATIONS IN THE FIELD

Economic theory tends to take a high-level and abstract view of matters. This is a necessary simplification designed to give a clearer view of essential elements. But transport in actual environments consists of many mundane actions taken in often volatile and messy circumstances. Theory can provide a broad guide for transport operations, but success or failure is determined in the field (Box 12.1).

The issues discussed in this chapter focus on nitty-gritty things such as staffing, training of personnel, compliance with policies and regulations, receiving public input, suicide prevention, crime, and the handling of large and/or special events, expected and otherwise. This is not a comprehensive list, but many of the major issues are included. This chapter also focuses on the passenger transport sector. Freight sector issues are considered in Chapter 16. Broader issues that impact on operations but are not operational issues *per se*, such as pollution, are touched on at other points in the book. Two major operational categories are covered:

1. Passenger operations
    a. public involvement
    b. staffing for service delivery
    c. large events (planned)
    d. weather management

DOI: 10.4324/9781003350866-15

BOX 12.1 INTRODUCTORY CASE: THE EVOLUTION OF HIJACKING

The invention of the airplane and subsequent rise of the aviation industry was obviously a watershed moment in transport technology development. But, as with any new transport mode, creating and then operating an aviation system was a learn-as-you-go effort. This was true of all aspects of the business. But the most unanticipated was the possibility of hijacking of a plane.

Hijacking is a term that appears to be American in origin, first used to indicate an act of theft against someone travelling on a public road, traditionally termed as highway robbery, later updated to refer to stealing goods from a lorry in transit, and then extended to the seizure of ships for the purposes of theft or extortion. The term was applied to the taking of planes after the first recorded hijacking of an aircraft in Arequipa, Peru in 1931.

This incident, and later ones, mostly bombings of aircraft for damages which were recouped through insurance fraud, made airline operators aware that the security of their craft was an area that needed to be managed. But relatively little was done, even with a raft of worldwide hijackings between 1947 and 1953, mostly by Europeans escaping from Communist countries and seeking political asylum in the West. Airline interest in the issue grew however as hijacking activity increased. Between 1960 and 1974, there were 240 hijacking attempts, successful and otherwise, involving Cuba alone, at first mainly by Cubans escaping Fidel Castro's new regime but soon with fugitives seeking asylum in Cuba. The US Department of Transportation recorded 364 total hijackings globally between 1968 and 1973, occurring at a rate of one every two weeks during its most intense period.

This marked the beginning of an evolution of aviation security operations that would become increasingly stringent. Passenger screening by metal detector was mandated by the US in 1973, and in 1974 the US passed the Anti-Hijacking Act, one element of which was to create a Sky Marshal programme, placing armed guards on routes deemed to most high-risk, to combat what was now known as air piracy or skyjacking. Additional inspections and electronic passenger screening procedures were implemented at selected large US airports and overseas stations, and tougher penalties were imposed on hijackers themselves. Of course individual airlines could impose their own additional measures. These efforts were spotty and none matched the extremely tight procedures imposed by the national carrier of Israel, *El Al*, after a 1968 hijacking of a flight en route between Rome and Tel Aviv.

Security managers soon found that hijackers evolved along with security measures. The Air Marshal programme was largely wound back after a flight carrying both Marshals and FBI agents was hijacked, showing that prevention of boarding of flights by hijackers was much more effective than thwarting attempts in the air. A series of parachute hijackings in the early 1970s, in which people would ransom the flight and then jump out after they obtained what they wanted, led to engineering measures to stop the rear air stairs from being lowered in flight. Catering and other ground crew were soon required to pass through metal detectors after hijackers used them to infiltrate guns and explosives on to the plane. Bombing attacks on various facilities (most of them non-aviation) in the US and abroad led to the 1995 imposition of a 300-ft zone at US airports around airport terminals and air traffic buildings where vehicles were not allowed to be parked or unattended. The 9/11 attacks created a whole new flurry of intensified security measures, both in America and around the world (and which will be discussed later in this chapter).

The evolution of aviation measures to combat hijacking shows that operations in any transport arena is a dynamic affair. Many problems cannot be anticipated until they are well upon an enterprise and the effectiveness of solutions are often known only after considerable retrospection. Even successful measures are often only temporary, with changing conditions requiring constant revisions. There are also economic trade-offs to consider, with some solutions at times costing more than they deliver in benefits. Yet operations is the stuff of transport services, which have to be delivered one way or another, even in a dynamic environment with many uncertainties.

(The discussion in this box is drawn from Klenka 2019)

2. Passenger safety
    a. crime
    b. suicide prevention
    c. system security

12.2 CONTRACTING THEORY

Still, one might ask what the economic theory context is. In one sense, there is relatively little. The core theory as applied to transport deals only with lightly embodied economic activity where the notion of "operations" is highly abstract. But the economics of strategy has more relevance here. It is not so much a separate theoretical strain but a collation economic concepts and models (such as transaction costs and market structure) applied to the workings of firms and other entities (Besanko et al. 2013). This template has already been applied at various points throughout this volume. But as the name suggests, this analysis is done at a strategic and sometimes tactical level, not generally at the minutiae of operations.

One potentially useful core model framework is contracting theory. As Chapter 11 presents, imperfect information and costly transactions lead to a separation between principals, i.e. economic agents with specific objectives and their own resources committed to achieving these objectives; and agents who are hired by principals to help them with various functions that the principals are unable to do directly. The need for negotiated agreement, implicit and explicit, between actors is clear. Contracts in a legal sense are binding agreements between parties towards achieving specific agreed-upon ends using agreed-upon means (the latter being spelled out with varying degrees of specificity). More generally a contract is any agreement between parties that is potentially enforceable, by law or other means, of delivering rewards and punishment for degrees of compliance and non-compliance with its terms. Contracting theory examines the economic nature of all such agreements. The theory holds that the contract, often tacit, is the basic structure governing agreements in the "internal markets" of organisations, whether they are public or private, scaling down to as minute a level as required, including operations.

Although this frame is typically applied to higher-level phenomena, it is possible to examine operational issues with it. In these terms all aspects of governance and implementation, public or private, including low-level actions, can be reduced to a constrained optimisation problem in which scarce resources are allocated to achieve an efficient outcome that cannot be improved upon materially at any given point in time (Shleifer & Vishny 1997). Contracts, formal or otherwise, provide the incentive structures to align principals and agents and ensure optimal outcomes within the internal markets of organisations mirroring those that the market supposedly achieves on its own outside them. They must be designed properly and then enforced and monitored efficiently. Operational failures under this construct could be said to result from a design or implementation failure in the contract covering the specific area in question.

While this is a plausible construct, and applicable in a general way, its explanatory power is often too limited to use for issues that result from the messiness and randomness of human life and work. Thus contracting theory is noted here but for information rather than applied to operations. It will enter into the picture again in Chapter 18 on political economy.

12.3 PASSENGER OPERATIONS – PUBLIC INVOLVEMENT

In the core model, determination of transport user preferences, and meeting them effectively and efficiently, is taken care of by market processes. That is, the market will deliver outcomes generating optimal well-being, measured by utility, to market participants. However, markets are not always able to meet transport needs, with government meeting them instead. In this case determination and fulfilment of the will of the majority of citizens, with protection and due consideration of minority views, is a fundamental tenet of democracy. Involvement of the public in the planning and implementation of direct and indirect government provision of transport is essential. The "public", i.e. the larger base of actual and potential users for a particular service, cannot be taken for granted (Grossardt et al. 2003).

Indeed, modern transport development has been punctuated with many protest movements against particular projects and policies. Some of these have been successful in their aims, as with the campaign against the Westway (A40) in London and the ensuing cancellation of a proposed Motorway Box around central London in 1973 (Gunn 2018, 11–12). The occurrence of mass protest can be taken as a sign that public preferences were not adequately taken into account for initial policy, programme, and project formulation. "Public involvement" (or, synonymously, "public participation") broadly refers to any method of bringing relevant groups of users in to help formulate, design, and evaluate service delivery and objectives and other related aims. This is distinct from "public information", which is simply delivering messages and content to users for a larger aim such as safety (and which is discussed further in the context of transport suicides below). Information delivery is part of public involvement, but as the basis of a dialogue between providers and "customers". The intent is to have users collaborate in the production of transport services, to better meet genuine public preferences. The methods for doing this vary widely, including taking regular user surveys, holding periodic focus groups on specific issues, convening user discussion forums, and establishing permanent user advisory committees. These can applied to oversight of regular operations, proposed changes to policies or service levels, or major new projects (Maier 2001).

Commitment to public involvement is one thing. Drawing the public in, getting the word out, and making policy and plans truly informed by that public is quite another matter. Analysts have long recognised that there are differing degrees of public involvement and that it can be difficult to get an effective level of engagement. Participatory processes can be expensive, unwieldy and, if designed poorly, may yield little useful output or, worse, exacerbate existing divisions. Therefore, it is important to deliver a process suited to the problem at hand (Arnstein 1969; Maier, 2001).

Moreover, the "public" is multifaceted and often split, with some segments more powerful or more vocal than others. Capturing a true picture of public desire under such circumstances is difficult enough with coherent, strong, and unified government. But if government is divided or, worse, dysfunctional, then public involvement becomes problematic. There are times when the public is clearer about what it wants than transport authorities are willing or able to accommodate (Westin 2022).

There is also the issue of perception. Users may not always clearly perceive transport outcomes, sometimes underestimating or overestimating quality and quantity. Public coverage of transport outcomes in the media also affects user knowledge and perceptions of service delivery (Daniels et al. 2012). But this limitation applies to operators as well. Operators do collect a wide variety of metrics on their service delivery, and often think this is sufficient. For example, an improving "on-time" arrival and departure metric may be seen as a job well-done. But users may instead experience deficiencies in the way the metric is defined (e.g. the train may leave its initial origin and arrive at is final destination on time but may be regularly off-schedule at intermediate points) and point out problems that the metrics don't easily capture (e.g. a lack of cleanliness or security). Ideally operators and users should work on measuring and delivering outcomes together (TRB 2010).

An implicit premise of much of the public involvement literature is that various public media, ranging from print to internet, are interactive conduits between government, interest groups, and the people at large, not interested and involved parties themselves. In this schema, the media are mostly "facilitators" of information flow rather than "producers" of it (Wolman & Page 2002). There is now much debate about how neutral media organisations are, with public trust in them at historic lows. The fields of media studies and media culture focus on media as an entity unto itself and as a powerful institution with interests of its own. Interestingly, the public choice approach of economics would rather similarly model these institutions as self-interested rational maximisers. The role and motivation of media institutions is a very important consideration, but out of scope of the present discussion.

The common thread here is performance in delivering services. This is something that all providers, public, private, and hybrid, have to focus on. But the picture is complicated by multiple objectives, not all of which are consistent with efficient operations. Accessibility for groups with particular needs and requirements to have equal access for all are standard legislative requirements across the world. Public involvement is about meeting operational requirements on the ground, while ensuring other public objectives are met, as well as regularly reviewing and renewing the objectives themselves (see Figure 12.1).

FIGURE 12.1
A humorous take on public involvement in transport.

Source: Image from FHWA (2001, 29th page). Book and image are in the public domain.

12.4 PASSENGER OPERATIONS – STAFFING AND SKILLS MANAGEMENT

Transport operations generally require large labour forces. An estimated average of 298 million people worked in the transport and tourism industry annually worldwide between 2019 and 2022, a figure estimated to rise to 449 million by 2034 (Statista 2024). These numbers measure direct employment. In one sense it is an overestimate since tourism encompasses many non-transport activities such as accommodation and customer service. On the other hand, there are many other workers performing transport functions outside the transport and tourism sector, such as in-house employee shuttle services for non-transport enterprises, that would not be counted in these figures. Either way, how are all these people identified, recruited, put in the best job for their skills and inclinations, retained, and properly remunerated? How do the organisations hiring them get the best possible "rate of return" on their "human capital" investment?

The core theory does have a framework for explaining all this, which is the competitive market for labour, in which supply and demand determine

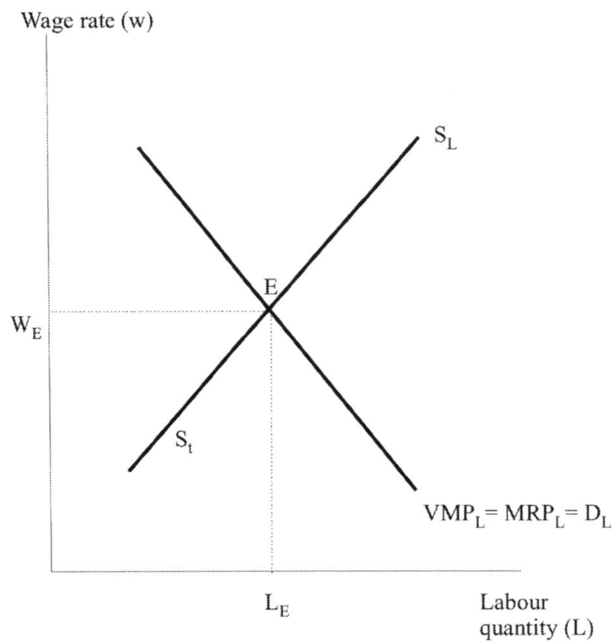

FIGURE 12.2
The market for labour and the setting of wages.

equilibrium employment levels, and wage rates that are optimally productive. This is depicted in Figure 12.2.

This theory says that labour is a commodity like any other and thus traded as such. Producers are the demanders for labour, and their collective demand is represented by a downward-sloping curve. That curve is labelled $VMP_L=MRP_L=D_L$ to indicate that employers base their hiring decisions on the value of marginal product (VMP) that each "unit" of labour produces which translates directly into the producer's marginal revenue product (MRP) that it receives from the use of labour in the production process. By assumption there are diminishing returns to VMP and MRP, i.e. the first unit of labour is more productive than successive units. Meanwhile, workers provide their units of work individually, and the sum of these units collectively constitutes the upward supply curve of labour. That curve is upward sloping because, by assumption, workers have increasing disutility as they work more and thus require an increasing wage for each successive unit of labour they provide. In equilibrium a wage rate of W_0 and an employment level of L_0 is set and this is optimal from a welfare point of view (Liebhafsky 1963, 335–338).

How accurate this model actually is remains a topic of debate. Labour is arguably not just like any other commodity such as soap or sugar, and treating it as such, especially on the demand side, can be problematic. Also, the core model has no institutions and all employment decisions, both supply and demand, are treated as if they come out of a never-ending succession of separate pairwise transactions between suppliers of labour and demanders. As Chapter 11 has shown, much economic activity takes place within the "internal markets" of organisations, in which information asymmetries and principal–agent problems abound. Additionally much transport employment, especially passenger service, sits directly or indirectly within governments. Therefore, one needs to go beyond the core model to consider institutional realities.

Recruitment, retention, and performance is one place where contracting theory has something to offer. In the rarefied and highly formalised realm of Arrow and Debreu (1954), literally every possible aspect of reality across all time periods can be measured and evaluated and put into contract terms. These are referred to as "complete" contracts and they contain terms covering all the appropriate incentives for all relevant agents and principals providing exactly the right rewards and punishments to induce economically efficient performance on all sides.

It should be obvious that this can be a tall order in all but an ideal world. In practice, incomplete contracts are the norm, when they are feasible at all. Just as individual contracts will be incomplete, background contract law itself will be too. This is due to a number of factors. Information is typically lacking in some way, both in the present (e.g. with information asymmetries between parties), and in the future (with inevitable uncertainties about what might transpire sooner or later). Information may be private or propriety and thus unavailable to all parties even if it exists somewhere in the system. Contract law itself is dynamic and will evolve in ways that cannot always be foreseen. Natural language itself, the stuff of contracts and law, has ambiguity, an important limit to exact performance specifications. Finally, the physical embodiment of things and agents, with all the variety and specificity that entails, limits contract completeness since physical things have a related but separate reality from the symbols of words and numbers used in formal documents and even informal agreements.

Still, performance contracts, metrics, and incentives are very much recommended by contracting theory as aids to efficiency. Performance contracts and recruiting based on them have the advantage of making things explicit and tying performance to explicit incentives. They are also, however, very hard to get right and often lead to unintended consequences, such as managers aiming to maximise their metrics even at the cost of good delivery on the ground (Poister et al. 2013; TRB 2010).

In passenger transport, especially urban public transit (UPT) and local and regional roads that are publicly provided and/or regulated or managed, historical factors play a big role in labour practices. Much human resources (HR) policy in these domains still remains engineering-focused, which is obviously essential but which doesn't always include the "soft" aspects of service delivery such as communications skills. Additionally, in government following of process is sometimes as important as results. Partly this is because of the nature of government itself, which is bound by many procedures to ensure goals other than efficiency in performance, such as equity and public integrity. These organisations can also be buffeted by sometimes fractious politics (see Chapter 18).

Transport HR is thus highly contextual. A major US study of transport sector "Systems Operation and Management" (SOM) reviewed the nature of job levels, titles, and skills for high-level functions and found a number of broad-level core functions and related competencies used within American organisations. These included policy and strategic considerations, programme planning, systems development, and project management, with required competencies such as business process management, contract oversight, procurement, and risk assessment (NCHRP 2012, 19–20). There is some variation in this across public authorities in different countries, especially those with more centralised governmental authority than what holds in the relatively decentralised and federalised US (Kepaptsoglou et al. 2012). But public transport agencies tend to be organised in a manner that is less "strategic" and more "task"-oriented than the mostly private logistics and supply chain sector, which is focused on profitability.

Thus HR managers in private operators in freight are highly influenced by a template known as the Business Logistics Management (BLM) framework (Poist 1984). This widely used template aims to measure the desired knowledge, attributes, and skills that a senior-level logistician should possess. It consists of three sub-inventories:

- Business knowledge and skills, consisting of direct business skills (e.g. marketing, accounting) and indirect business skills (psychology, public relations)
- Logistics knowledge and skills, consisting of "traditional" freight skills (e.g. transport, warehousing, forecasting) and "non-traditional" ones (customer service, parts support)
- Management knowledge and skills, which consist of traditional skills (e.g. planning, organising, supervision, and motivation); non-traditional skills (e.g. ability to adapt to change and time management); and personal characteristics (e.g. assertiveness) (adapted from Razzaque & Sirat 2001, 377).

This personnel management framework is obviously much less process-oriented than that identified for public transport authorities. The presence of market-related functions as encompassed in the business knowledge and skills category is notable. But people remain people wherever they are, and training, recruiting, retaining, and compensating them, while accounting for their differing skills, psychologies, and proclivities, is a core focus in both settings. Moreover, the management of the "internal" markets of organisations is similarly critical, whatever the core mission is.

12.5 PASSENGER OPERATIONS – LARGE EVENT PLANNING

Planning for large (expected) events can be a difficult undertaking. (For unplanned events, such as those associated with climate change, it is even harder. These issues are deferred until Chapter 17.) An NCHRP (2003) survey of transport planning for such events defined them as occurrences that "abnormally increases traffic demand", focusing on road demand and management for relatively frequent happenings for sport games, musical concerts, national conventions, and so on. These events ranged in size from 1,000 to 1.7 million patrons, and in duration from a few hours to several months. The report identified that transport planning in these instances, especially for very large and/or long events, could involve law enforcement and emergency response agencies, transport authorities, media, the military, politicians, civic groups, and event organisers, amongst others.

This particular study emphasised the need for: detailed advance planning and the use of traffic management tools such as motorist information (e.g. media partnerships, pre-event informational campaigns, and highway advisory radio); active traffic management before, during, and after the event (including temporary lane closures, traffic management teams, reversible lanes, moveable barriers, temporary contraflow, and ramp metering); travel demand management (including park-and-ride lots, and preferential incentives for public transportation and ridesharing); and infrastructure and service investments such as major transit or road improvements (NCHRP 2003, Chapter 4).

This last category is obviously unlikely to be undertaken except for all but the largest events, such as the Olympic Games, which typically result in long-lived investments after the games are closed. These are not always especially useful to the hosting locales after the games are over, however. The monorail in Sydney, built for the 2000 Olympic Games, was torn down in 2013 because it contributed little to urban mobility other than as an on-going tourist experience. Sydney's transport performance during the Games actually relied much more on non-structural enhancements, such as increased bus and ferry service, which overall met increased demand, though not always seamlessly (Hensher & Brewster 2002). The experience of other Olympics in large cities is somewhat similar. Infrastructure expansion can often be justified for areas with dense population and overburdened transport networks. But designing them on the basis of one-off major occurrences generally does not leave a good strategic or operational legacy.

One very interesting recurring event is the Hajj/Umrah Pilgrimage in Makkah, Saudi Arabia. The Pilgrimage has been held every year for centuries and has grown to 6 million visitors each year and more, with 3 million during the week of the Hajj itself and 1 million during Ramadan. Every practising Muslim is required at some point in their life to go on this journey at least once. In this it even surpasses the Olympics in frequency, the latter being held over two weeks in major host cities every four years. Roughly 2 million pilgrims a year come to the Hajj, less than the up to 8 million ticketed spectators moving during an Olympics, not including movements of officials and athletes. But it is still a sizeable event. Currie and Shalaby (2012) note some important transport management differences between Hajj and the Olympics events. Hajj venues remain fixed, which allows for more ability to plan for the future and learn from the past and to make both incremental and substantial improvements in infrastructure and procedures. However, because the Hajj has fewer sites visited by many more people, not only congestion but dangerous overcrowding is possible, and occasional tragedies have resulted. Education and training programmes for participants and spectators for Olympics events are more developed and more formal than for the Hajj, where groups of around 250 pilgrims are led by volunteers. Training and procedures have been improved over time, along with the use of many of the usual traffic demand and supply measures noted above. (Box 12.2 presents a case of a proposed regular major urban event that did not come to pass mainly because of the inability of planners to surmount substantial logistical issues.)

12.6 PASSENGER OPERATIONS – WEATHER MANAGEMENT

Weather, as everyone knows, is highly changeable, with a continuum ranging from very mild and stable to extreme and volatile. Transport system managers must be ready to deal with the gamut of weather effects on operations. (Preparation for, and dealing with, extremely severe weather is

BOX 12.2 PROFESSIONAL CAR RACING COMES TO NEW YORK CITY?

NASCAR (National Association for Stock Car Auto Racing) is an American company that runs the most extensive stock-car racing business in the world. Tens of millions of tickets across over 2,000 races are sold throughout the year. It's audience and image have historically been one of an American southern and rural fan-base, even though the firm has race tracks in Chicago and Los Angeles and has many urban followers (Amato et al. 2005).

NASCAR made a major move to break this rural image by trying to establish a track in New York City beginning in 2005. New York is very dense, with little land available for something as large as a race track. But Staten Island, one of the City's five boroughs, the most iconic being Manhattan, has the smallest population, estimated at around 450,000 in 2005, living on the largest borough in terms of physical area, with quite a few sparsely populated and developable areas. So the company bought a 230-acre plot in Bloomfield, in a relatively unpopulated portion of the Island's north-east corner, for the modest price of $US 10 million (Annese 2006).

Initial public and political response was enthusiastic. The proposed 80,000-seat stadium and associated retail business would bring jobs and economic development to a somewhat depressed part of the Island. And Staten Islanders, considering themselves to be the neglected stepchild of New York City government, relished the prospect of being the site of a national major sporting event. Local politicians endorsed the company's efforts and offered support in securing the necessary and legal approvals (Annese 2006).

However, a major hurdle soon arose: the difficulty of transporting 80,000 race fans to and from the site during each event. It was true that these events would be periodic, only several a year. And the company did offer initial plans for moving people into and out of the site. But while Staten Island may be lightly populated relative to the rest of New York City, its transport capacity across all modes is highly constrained and already overburdened. Transit in the area of the track was largely non-existent and the major roads into New Jersey and Brooklyn (there is no direct road into Manhattan) were already overcapacity at almost all times of day and night. Public and political sentiment quickly began to sour as it became unclear how these episodic but major traffic surges would be handled. Local fans owning cars would have enough trouble. Out-of-towners staying in Manhattan, Brooklyn, or New Jersey hotels and taking transit could well be stranded. And this was under normal circumstances. Sudden and heavy rain storms are relatively frequent in New York's harbour, creating acute traffic snarls. The company had offered to build a ferry terminal near the site to run up to eight to ten ferries across to New Jersey. But these could handle only a fraction of projected demand (Annese 2006).

In the end, the transport issue sunk the raceway. NASCAR could not give convincing answers about how the movement of fans to and from races could be handled, and New York's Byzantine and fractious political style didn't help matters. After it was all over, it seemed to many as if the company had left out an obvious factor in its advance planning and had paid for it as a result (Annese 2006).

The NASCAR case study indicates that even sophisticated private operators can get things wrong in their transport operations planning, and, indeed, the "devil" really is often in the "details". Not that such mistakes should always be judged harshly. Transport operations in urban areas especially are subject to many unknowns and "exogenous" events, immune to even the best advance strategies at times.

generally handled under separate disaster management protocols, considered in Chapter 17.)

Weather impacts transport in a variety of ways. Infrastructure is affected differently by the overall climate (i.e. the longer-term general patterns of weather in a particular area) in which it is placed. Thus areas with high seasonal climatic variations across the year (such as north Asia, northern Europe, and northern parts of North America) have freeze-thaw cycles that stress roads, bridges, and structures in particular ways due to the expansion and contraction of materials caused by moving from cold to hot and back again and the cracking and other strains this results in. This does not occur in consistently hot and wet climates in countries around the equator, or in dry desert areas elsewhere. But facilities in these areas have their own climate-related maintenance and management challenges. Because climate patterns are long-term, these effects can be anticipated and planned for by system managers (e.g. by having large stocks of snow-melting ice and a fleet of snow removal vehicles in cold climes). However, climate change is upending most long-standing weather cycles around the world, presenting a whole new challenge (see Chapter 17).

On a day-to-day basis, weather "events" such as storms can be predicted only over the very short-term and even then quite imperfectly. Such events affect operations in various ways, the most significant one from a user point-of-view being traffic impacts. The three main variables here are as follows: (a) travel demand; (b) traffic safety; and (c) traffic flow. Weather changes travel demand by reducing it (when people cancel trips because of dangerous conditions such as heavy fog) or diverting it to other times of day, to other routes, and/or to other modes. Diversion of some sort is the most common behavioural adjustment and has further flow-on effects depending upon which mode is being shifted to (e.g. from car to transit or from cycling to car), how re-routing rolls out across the network, and how travel across the day is changed. From an operations management perspective, weather events increase uncertainty in system performance, effectively, if temporarily, reducing available network capacity. Estimates of such reduction in the case of heavy rain range between 10% and 20% (Cools et al. 2010).

Obviously, managers make contingencies for such events in the form of built-in redundancy of infrastructure and vehicles and diversion of resources from one area of operations to another. But there are limits to effective response, both because of the inherent uncertainty in weather and because some strategies, such as keeping extra train cars in reserve or using back-up lines, are either too costly or otherwise infeasible. As in other areas of living, weather is a fact of life in transport operations that has to be accepted and adapted as best as one can, while doing so as cost-effectively as possible.

12.7 PASSENGER SAFETY: CRIME ON TRANSIT

The management and prevention of crime presents a great operational challenge on UPT. There are crimes committed on intercity surface modes such as rail and road, but these tend to be confined to property crimes and are less numerous both relatively and absolutely, mainly because public transit usage is overall much greater and more frequent. (Safety of vehicle operations and networks is a different issue, considered in Chapter 19.)

Crime has both subjective and objective dimensions. Even when transit is actually quite safe, if users feel uncomfortable while waiting for service and/or while being on vehicles, then they may avoid using it. On average, women in particular tend to feel less secure on transit than men, older people often feel less secure than younger ones, and these patterns can sometimes be found in other particular socioeconomic and demographic groups. Crime itself can occur at various points along a journey: when a user is walking to and from a bus stop, on a platform or station while waiting for a service to arrive, or during the journey (Ceccato et al. 2022).

Both perception and incidence of crime vary according to many situational and environmental factors that are more or less "criminogenic" to use the technical term. Different sections of stations and platforms can appear to be, and at times might actually be, more or less dangerous, depending on how visible they are to others, including law enforcement personnel, and how well-lit and appealing they are. Transit stops in high-crime neighbourhoods can be perceived as unsafe and sometimes do have more incidences of crime. Similarly, the behaviour of fellow travellers is important, even when not actually criminal. Loud or rowdy behaviour may be intimidating to others, even with no malicious intent, and can sometimes lead to actual infractions (Ceccato et al. 2022).

Transit crime includes offences that may be directed against other users, against transit personnel, and against property. Indeed this last category is often the most frequent, especially vandalism and fare evasion. Some have argued that this sort of activity can lead to a perception of lawlessness inhibiting transit use sometimes leading to a permissiveness for other crimes to be committed. However, there is a great deal of debate about what affects both perception of crime and the commitment of crime itself. Many theories are advocated but relatively little consensus exists (Ceccato et al. 2022).

Detecting crime and punishing violations is an obviously large element of transit operations. More cost-effective and preferable is, of course, deterrence and prevention. Solutions here can be broken into infrastructural and non-structural categories. Examples of the former include transit gates that cannot be easily jumped over or otherwise evaded, platform and vehicle help points, better lighting, and more open and visible waiting spaces. Examples of the latter include greater police presence, including plain clothes officers, higher levels of ticketing and arrests, and public information campaigns. *A priori* justifications can be made for all of these strategies. Their actual effectiveness is not entirely clear, especially since transit crime tends to move in waves that can have more "macro" causes, such as deteriorations or improvements in broader social and economic conditions. Most of these methods are used in suicide prevention, discussed next.

12.8 PASSENGER SAFETY: RAILWAY SUICIDE PREVENTION

Suicide prevention has been a major concern for railway operators internationally since the first reported incident in England in 1852 (Clarke 1994). Selective statistics illustrate the scope of the problem: between 1994–95 and 1998–99 there were 819 cases of over-ground railway suicides and "suspected suicides" in England and Wales; in Sweden between 2000 and 2002, there were 145 railway suicides; in Turkey, there were 326 railway suicides reported from 1997 to 2003 (UQAM 2012). Gough (2012) claims that between 150 and 200 people die each year by intentional self-harm in and around train stations in Australia. In the Sydney metropolitan area, this equates to more than a death a week on the Sydney Trains network (Routley et al. 2004). Ratnayake et al. (2007) note that of the approximately 135 subway systems in metropolitan areas worldwide, suicide fatality rates are lethal approximately 60% of the time.

These are only direct impacts of suicide attempts and deaths. There are additional flow-on effects, such as vicarious trauma to railway operators, other staff, and the general public. While the absolute numbers are still very small by comparison to other forms of suicide such as hanging and poisonings, the violent and public nature of railway suicide can have more far-reaching impact, inflicting detrimental consequences on the psychological well-being of hundreds of people (Krysinska & De Leo 2008). Railway suicide also has significant financial and organisational costs stemming from service delays and railway staff absenteeism (Ladwig & Baumert 2004).

A review of the literature indicates two broad streams of research on the topic of suicide causes and prevention. The first line of enquiry is concerned with the epidemiology of railway suicide, i.e. its incidences, causes, and distribution in a population. These studies provide clues to the different types of behaviour to expect of those planning, or at risk of, suicide. Solutions consist of different types of interventions that can be employed to reduce railway suicide attempts by at-risk individuals (Krysinska & De Leo 2008).

The second line of enquiry abstracts away from individuals and focuses on the operating environment in which suicides occur. Solutions here are varied. Organisational interventions include training of operations staff to identify at-risk persons and intervene to prevent an incident, or giving customer-facing staff a repertoire of mental health "first aid" to enable them to better identify suicide warning signs (Debbaut et al. 2014). Servicescape interventions involve changes to the physical service environment so as to inhibit or prevent suicidal actions, e.g. the use of platform barriers or enhancements in platform lighting (Havârneanu et al. 2015). Communication interventions in this arena focus on messaging the passenger through the use of public address announcements, advertising campaigns, and other means (Salm & Hommers 2013). All these interventions are aimed at trying to modify an underlying health issue, as in the epidemiological approach, but using changes to operational responses and environment conditions to reduce suicide attempts. Table 12.1 provides a summary of examples of the different approaches.

The complex and unpredictable nature of railway suicide requires a flexible and adaptive organisational response employing a variety of strategies varying by context. Organisational, servicescape, and communications interventions are all important individually. A constant across all of them is the balancing of costs and benefits, as unpleasant as this idea may sound in a tragedy like suicide. For example, installation of physical deterrents such as platform barriers can run into the millions of dollars per station but have relatively low impact as compared to alternative policies, since the optimal

TABLE 12.1

Summary of suicide prevention literature

Selected suicide intervention strategies

Organisational	Servicescape	Communication
Help points Education programs for staff Increased staff/police presence Quick response emergency services	Fences and barriers Reduce station blind spots Limit/prevent access Surveillance devices Modification to trains	Signage Social media Advertising Public announcements

Source: Adapted from Keating and Gordon (2018).

aim is to keep those contemplating suicide from even getting to a platform in the first place. Money should be appropriately directed in addressing the problem, and one should have an idea of which strategies are more or less effective (Keating & Gordon 2018).

12.9 PASSENGER SAFETY – SYSTEM SECURITY

Security broadly refers to freedom from danger of threat. That is a negative statement of its meaning. Safety is the more positive statement of the same idea referring to actually being protected from harm. Just as health is not merely the absence of disease, transport security is tantamount to a set of actions to minimise the risk of bad things occurring to users, property, and innocent bystanders.

Transport security is often broken down into three dimensions: physical, cyber, and a recent category of epidemiological (Rodrigue 2020, Section 9.3.1). Physical security can be threatened by deliberate action done for its own sake, such as terrorism, which uses violence to disrupt a political system the perpetrator opposes, or at a much lower level, vandalism which is often a demonstration for demonstration's sake; deliberate action as a means of achieving a discrete ulterior motive, such as theft and other illicit activity such as the running of drugs, immigrants, weapons, or pirated items; or accidents, such as collisions of vehicles on freight platforms or runways. Cybersecurity refers to the management of similar threats of deliberate and accidental disruption of communications technology and networks. Epidemiological security, the newest category, arising out of the Covid-19 pandemic (though the concern is much older than that) refers to management of disease transmission within and by transport modes.

Functionally, operational roles in these areas may be spread across different parts of an organisation and under different names. For example, employee safety is usually managed separately from the security apparatus of an institution, although there may be close cross-coordination. Similarly, cybersecurity is generally mostly separate from physical security functions given the very different technical orientations between the two. Security is thus a cross-cutting feature of many different areas, although each of these areas are generally not reducible to security alone. Transport safety in general is a complex field (covered more in Chapter 19) having a security element but encompassing much more besides.

The job of the security manager in any of these areas is to identify potential threats and system weaknesses and vulnerabilities to those threats; to devise effective means of limiting exposure to risks; and minimising the consequences if security breaches occur. A major focus of much physical security is on terminals, both freight and passenger, because these are heavily used, with passenger terminals generally located in densely populated areas, and channelling movements into narrow areas and choke points such as corridors, platforms, waiting rooms, and gates. These are the most vulnerable to security weaknesses, whether through a terrorist attack, an accident, or crime, and will likely exhibit the greatest impacts if a security event happens (Rodrigue 2020, Section 9.3.1).

But one should not fall into the trap of ignoring vulnerabilities elsewhere which often can rise to a similar level of seriousness. Railway tracks, for example, can be subject to sabotage or serve as points of illicit or other harmful activity (suicides have already been discussed earlier) that may result in serious disruptions or harm. Therefore rail operators do regular track inspection across their lines, often at great expense (Kaewunruen et al. 2019). Other network operators do the same.

Security has many dimensions, including of politics, since it is bound up with the natural human propensity to preserve and protect human life and health. Economic theory and the facts of resource scarcity suggest that there is a trade-off between measures to enhance security and the reductions in harm they bring against the costs that such measures entail. This is very clear for airline travellers and airlines which are the groups most frequently subject to the various security policies and practices that have been brought into effect after the 9/11 attacks in the US and the global Covid-19 pandemic. Security changes here include hiring and training expanded security workforces, development, and purchase of sophisticated screening machines, dedication of more space within terminals to handle security procedures (such as inspection areas and waiting lines), and the introduction of reinforced cabin doors on aircraft. These measures have lowered passenger throughput by an estimated 5% and clearing security is now the largest source of delay in the passenger boarding process. The International Air Transport Association (IATA) estimated that these measures directly cost more than $7.4 billion to airlines in 2018, and there are additional indirect (and disutility) costs to travellers and businesses. To the extent that these costs sometimes divert passengers to less safe modes such as cars, especially on trips over distances of 500 km or less, there is arguably and ironically an offsetting increase in fatalities due to increased exposure to the risk of road accidents (Rodrigue 2020, Section 9.3.2).

Airlines and airports have sought to both reduce and recover these costs (as have other modes and other transport providers). On the operations side, airports have resorted to multiple security lanes, high throughput scanning, and "pre-checked" passenger programmes (usually at an extra charge to enrollees) to speed up security processes and lower at least somewhat their direct and indirect unit costs. Meanwhile, airport security fees have become a standard part of ticketed airfares. These help operators recoup their own expenses but do have economic flow-on effects. One estimate is that an increase of 1% in the costs of trading internationally would cause a decrease in trade flows of between 2% and 3%; in which case that 1% security "tax" could be costing the economy proportionately more than 1% when trade effects are included (Rodrigue 2020, Section 9.3.1).

Having said all that this does not mean that security measures are a *de facto* net burden. Obviously they do have benefits in the form of bad consequences averted. There is also a learning curve on designing more effective protocols that run more efficiently over time. And not everything can be reduced to economic terms, safety having inherent value. Still, security can and should be evaluated economically using CBA and other methods (see Chapter 15). There is currently much more scope to do this than is presently being done.

REFERENCES

Amato, C. H., Peters, C. L. O., & Shao, A. T. (2005). An exploratory investigation into NASCAR fan culture. *Sport Marketing Quarterly*, 14(2), 71–83.

Annese, J. (2006). Putting the pedal to the metal on NASCAR plan Developer to release new traffic proposal details in its challenging race to build an 80,000-seat racetrack. *Staten Island Advance*, Sunday, January 8.

Arnstein, S. (1969) The ladder of citizen participation. *Journal of the Institute of American Planners*, 35(4), 216–224.

Arrow, K. J., & Debreu, G. (1954). Existence of an equilibrium for a competitive economy. *Econometrica*, 22, 265–290.

Besanko, D., Dranove, D., Shanley, M., & Schaefer, S. (2013). *Economics of strategy* (6th edition). John Wiley & Sons.

Ceccato, V., Gaudelet, N., & Graf, G. (2022). Crime and safety in transit environments: A systematic review of the English and the French literature, 1970–2020. *Public Transportation*, 14(1), 105–153.

Clarke, M. (1994). Railway suicide in England and Wales, 1850–1949. *Social Science & Medicine*, 38(3), 401–407.

Cools, M., Moons, E., Creemers, L., & Wets, G. (2010). Changes in travel behavior in response to weather conditions do type of weather and trip purpose matter? *Transportation Research Record*, 2157, 22–28.

Currie, G., & Shalaby, A. (2012). Synthesis of transport planning approaches for the world's largest events. *Transport Reviews*, 32(1), 113–136.

Daniels, R., Gordon, C., & Mulley, C. (2012). The role of media in developing public transport policy through public involvement: Case of Sydney Morning Herald, Australia. In *Proceedings of the 91st Transportation Research Board Annual Meeting*, Washington, DC (Paper # 12-1519).

Debbaut, K., Krysinska, K., & Andriessen, K. (2014). Characteristics of suicide hotspots on the Belgian railway network. *International Journal of Injury Control and Safety Promotion*, 21(3), 274–277.

FHWA (2001). *A citizen's guide to transportation decision making*. US Federal Highway Administration.

Gough, D. (2012). Suicide main cause of rail deaths. *The Age Victoria*, accessed on 28 October 2015 from www.theage.com.au/victoria/suicide-main-cause-of-rail-deaths-20121101-28luk.html

Grossardt, T., Bailey, K., & Brumm, J. (2003). Structured public involvement: Problems and prospects for improvement. *Transportation Research Record*, 1858(1), 59–102.

Gunn, S. (2018). The history of transport systems in the UK. In *Future of mobility: Evidence review foresight*. Government Office for Science, Centre for Urban History, University of Leicester.

Havârneanu, G. M., Burkhardt, J. M., & Paran, F. (2015). A systematic review of the literature on safety measures to prevent railway suicides and trespassing accidents. *Accident Analysis & Prevention*, 81, 30–50.

Hensher, D. A., & Brewer, A. M. (2002). Going for gold at the Sydney Olympics: How did transport perform? *Transport Reviews*, 22(4), 381–399.

Kaewunruen, S., Osman, M. H. B., & Rungskunroch, P. (2019). The total track inspection. *Frontiers in Built Environment*, 4, 84.

Keating, B., & Gordon, C. (2018). Preventing railway suicide: An open-systems perspective and application. In *Proceedings of the Annual Meeting the Transportation Research Board (TRB) 97th Annual Meeting*. The Transportation Research Board (TRB).

Klenka, M. (2019). Major incidents that shaped aviation security. *Journal of Transportation Security*, 12, 39–56.

Kepaptsoglou, K., Meerschaert, V., Neergaard, K., Papadimitriou, S., Rye, T., Schremser, R., & Vleugels, I. (2012). Quality management in mobility management: A scheme for supporting sustainable transportation in cities. *International Journal of Sustainable Transportation*, 6(4), 238–256.

Krysinska, K., & De Leo, D. (2008). Suicide on railway networks: epidemiology, risk factors and prevention. *Australian and New Zealand Journal of Psychiatry*, 42(9), 763–771.

Ladwig, K. H., & Baumert, J. J. (2004). Patterns of suicidal behaviour in a metro subway system. *The European Journal of Public Health*, 14(3), 291–295.

Liebhafsky, H. H. (1963). *The nature of price theory*. Dorsey Press.

Maier, K. (2001). Citizen participation in planning: climbing a ladder? *European Planning Studies*, 9(6), 707–719.

Murphy, P. R., & Poist, R. F. (2006). Skill requirements of contemporary senior-and entry-level logistics managers: A comparative analysis. *Transportation Journal*, 45(3), 46–60.

NCHRP (2012). *Attracting, recruiting, and retaining skilled staff for transportation system operations and management*.

National Cooperative Highway Research Program, Report 693.
NCHRP (2003). Transportation planning and management for special events: A synthesis of highway Practice. National Cooperative Highway Research Program, Report 309.
Poist, R. (1984). Managing logistics in an era of change. *Defense Transportation Journal*, 40(5) (September/October), 23–30.
Poister, T. H., Pasha, O. Q., & Edwards, L. H. (2013). Does performance management lead to better outcomes? Evidence from the US public transit industry. *Public Administration Review*, 73(4), 625–636.
Ratnayake, R., Links, P. S., & Eynan, E. (2007). Suicidal behaviour on subway systems: A review of the epidemiology. *Journal of Urban Health*, 84(6), 766–781.
Rodrigue, J.-P. (2020). *The geography of transport systems* (6th edition). Routledge.
Razzaque, M., & Sirat, M. (2001). Skill requirements: Perceptions of the senior Asian logisticians. *International Journal of Physical Distribution & Logistics Management*, 31(5), 374–395.
Routley, V., Staines, C., Haworth, N., Symmons, M., & Ozanne-Smith, J. (2004). *Rail related suicides in Victoria: Analysis of databases and literature review* (report #215). Monash University Accident Research Centre, Melbourne.
Salm, L., & Hommers, C. E. (2013). New concepts in trauma practice. *Scandinavian Journal of Trauma, Resuscitation and Emergency Medicine*, 21(Suppl 1), A9.
Shleifer, A., & Vishny, R. W. (1997). A survey of corporate governance. *The Journal of Finance*, 52(2), 737–783.
Statista (2024). *Number of travel and tourism jobs worldwide from 2019 to 2023, with a forecast for 2024 and 2034 (in millions)*. Statista. www.statista.com/statistics/1268465/number-of-travel-and-tourism-jobs-worldwide/
TRB (2010). *A methodology for performance measurement and peer comparison in the public transportation industry*. Transportation Research Board, Report 141.
UQAM (2012). *Railway fatalities*. Universite du Quebec a Montreal (UQAM). https://railwaysuicideprevention.com/scientific-literature-review/choose/railway-fatalities.html.
Westin, M. (2022). The framing of power in communicative planning theory: Analysing the work of John Forester, Patsy Healey and Judith Innes. *Planning Theory*, 21(2), 132–154.
Wolman, H., & Page, E. (2002). Policy transfer among local governments: An information–theory approach. *Governance*, 15(4), 577–501.

SECTION

4

"System" policy issues

CHAPTER 13

Externalities and other market failures

13.1 INTRODUCTION: PRIVATE, PUBLIC, AND QUASI-PUBLIC GOODS

The core model predicts that there is an economically efficient equilibrium between transport supply and demand at a price that reflects the marginal cost (MC) that it took to produce those goods and services, summarised by the formula P = MC (see Chapter 7). In the core theory, the market should produce this equilibrium all by itself. But, as has been mentioned often, these ideal theoretical conditions rarely hold in practice.

Economists distinguish between four types of goods, one of which can be efficiently allocated through markets, but others which usually cannot be. There are two relevant dimensions here, both expressed in terms of ability to consume the good in question. The first dimension is rivalry, i.e. whether consumption of a unit can be shared with someone else or not. The second dimension is excludability, i.e. how much the consumer of the good can exclude others from consuming it without their consent. The matrix of these four types is provided in Table 13.1.

Pure private goods are "rival in consumption". This means that if one agent consumes a unit of a fixed supply of X and there are two potential consumers, the other consumer will, by definition, not be able to consume that unit. A pure private good will also be "excludable in consumption", which means that the owner of that unit of X can keep anyone else from

DOI: 10.4324/9781003350866-17

TABLE 13.1

A public and private good matrix

Consumption is	Exclusion is: Feasible	Exclusion is: Not feasible
Rival	Pure private good	Club good
Nonrival	Quasi-public good: common pool resource	Quasi-public good: pure public good

BOX 13.1 INTRODUCTORY CASE: LONDON'S CORDON TOLL

At the turn of the current millennium, London was facing a road traffic problem. Greater London encompassed an area of 45 km by 58 km, with 8 million people living in it. But although the city has iconic transit – think double-decker buses and the Underground – in 2000, 41% of trips in London (carpooling not separated out from driving alone) were done by car, just below 45.0% trips by transit. In Central London, relative transit usage was higher, with a 59% share. But even there 21% – one out of five travellers – still drove (TfL 2006, 47).

Clearly fewer cars needed to be on the city's roads but options were limited. There was little space to build new car routes, while transit expansion was expensive and would take years to build. So London's newly elected mayor, Ken Livingstone, decided that perhaps the economist's solution of pricing should be given a try.

There are two major types of road tolls (the typical road price method): (a) a general toll, which is a flat fee charged to use a particular facility; and (b) a cordon toll, which is a flat fee to enter a particular area at any entry point along its boundary. Livingstone went with the second option, a particularly bold choice because it was (and still is) relatively rare across the world and because such a scheme requires cordoning off an entire region and assessing a toll from every vehicle passing in or out, a much more costly and complex job than charging for entry and exit on a single road, bridge, or tunnel. But cordon pricing has the potential to control traffic more effectively because one cannot avoid the toll by diverting to an untolled pathway.

The idea was very unpopular and Livingstone was a new mayor. But he was fully committed to carrying the policy through to completion, seeing congestion as central problem for the city's future. The legal, planning, and political processes took 30 months (1 July 2000 to 17 February 2003), after which London established its first cordon pricing scheme around a central zone with heavy tolls imposed on vehicles passing into and out of the urban core. The cordon price was 5 pounds and applied from 7:00 AM until 6:00 PM on weekdays. Once the charge was paid, drivers could leave and re-enter the zone as many times as they pleased over the next 24 hours. The congestion charge was enforced by photo recognition of licence plates. Residents of the zone were granted a 90% discount on the charge for one vehicle. In addition, vehicles powered by alternative fuels and electric vehicles were exempt from the congestion charge. The charge was increased from 5 pounds to 8 pounds in July 2005. The zone was expanded westward in February 2007 (TfL 2007).

Livingstone didn't just impose a toll but decided to make large additional investments in transit service to allow riders to more easily shift from their automobile to mass transit. Roughly half of the money collected is spent on toll collection and enforcement. But this left a substantial amount left over for other purposes. Transport for London (TfL), a comprehensive transport agency responsible for the Underground, buses, and the surface road system, was created to coordinate policy across all modes to reduce traffic and promote mobility in London (TfL 2006, 22).

FIGURE 13.1
London's congestion zone since 2011.

Source: Taken from Wikimedia, https://commons.wikimedia.org/wiki/File:London_Congestion_Charge_Zone_since_2011.png, commons, created in 2016 by ed g2s using www.openstreetmap.org, under a cc-by-sa-2.0 license.

The early impacts on travel into the congestion zone were initially dramatic. By 2007 TfL reported a 33% reduction in cars entering the zone from 2002 (prior to charge) to 2003 (post charging). The number of cars entering the zone during charging hours dropped from almost 200,000 vehicles in 2002 to about 125,000 in 2003. Overall, the number of vehicles entering the zone had decreased by 16% as compared to the pre-charging period. Total traffic entering the zone dropped from 378,000 in 2002 to 316,000 in 2006. Meanwhile, mass transit ridership jumped from 32% in 2000 to 36% in 2004 and road travel speeds increased in central and inner London after 2003, though with some congestion creeping back in 2006–2007 (TfL 2007).

The zone has since been expanded and charges increased (see Figure 13.1). The congestion reductions have not been as dramatic, particularly as the London economy has grown. But overall congestion (and associated pollution) levels have remained lower than they would have been without the scheme (Herzog 2023). In general, travel growth in most dense cities experiencing economic growth will find increases in congestion inevitable due to constraints on transport supply and physical space. London's experience shows that pricing can be a powerful policy tool to manage traffic through the use of economic incentives.

consuming that same unit without their explicit consent. Private goods can, as has been seen, be easily traded and priced, thus allowing for viable and efficient market transactions. Thus, if one person is driving a car, then by definition no one else can (back seat drivers don't count), exhibiting rivalry in consumption. It is also feasible for the driver to stop anyone else from "consuming" the car (not letting them drive it or be a passenger in it), and to therefore be able to charge others for the privilege of doing, so exhibiting excludability in consumption.

A pure public good is the opposite of a pure private good. It is nonrival in consumption (i.e. if one agent has access to a unit of X, everyone else can consume it simultaneously) and nonexcludable (i.e. it is not feasible for an agent owning the good to keep anyone else from consuming that unit of X). In a transport setting, a classic textbook example of a pure public good is the light of a lighthouse (though the lighthouse itself is a private good). Once the light is turned on, everyone has access to it – it is nonrival in consumption. And if people choose to "consume" the light, there is no feasible way to stop them from doing so – it is nonexcludable.

It should be noted that technology has been evolving to make excludability more feasible. This is clear in the case of electronic tolling which is much more sophisticated in its abilities to track and variably charge individual users than was once the case. In the lighthouse example above, one could envision some sort of digital signalling in lieu of actual light that would provide navigational guidance only to paid subscribers who had the required transponders and digital mapping devices. None of this invalidates the basic analysis, though it does change its application in practice over time.

Roads would appear to be private goods and in a sense they are. But they are not purely private because they can be jointly consumed with other users. A road can be used (consumed) by multiple drivers at the same time and hence consumption is not purely rival. From an economic point of view, a road has a degree of "publicness" to it. The implication of this nonrivalry is that, after a certain point, congestion sets in and everybody's consumption of the road is degraded; they cannot travel as fast nor as reliably as they did when there was no congestion.

Roads are thus an example of something economists call a "quasi-public good". There are two different categories. Roads are considered a club good, i.e. one which is excludable in consumption (people can be kept from getting on the road) but nonrival to some extent (once people are allowed to consume the good, their consumption of it impacts other people's consumption, congestion in the case of a road).

The other type of quasi-public good is a common pool resource. An example would be a fishing area in open waters. The fish are rival in consumption in that if one person catches one, that is one less for somebody else. But the fishing area itself is nonexcludable in that it is difficult to keep others from accessing the resource. Underground aquifers and oil fields provide similar examples. A road is nonrival in consumption because multiple people can use it at the same time. But it is not a common pool resource because users can be easily excluded from consuming it. Thus, it is a club good, and a toll is one method of such exclusion.

13.2 PUBLIC GOODS AND MARKET FAILURES

It might seem that, nonetheless, the supply of roads and the price for road users will still be efficiently set at P = MC, if roads are privately provided. In a market with purely private goods, the price of the good not only equals the MC of producing the good but it also equals the marginal benefit (MB) from consuming the good. With private goods, it is easy to determine supply and demand: simply add up demand for the good of each individual consumer and the price that each would be willing to pay (which equals each consumer's MB derived from their utility derived from consumption of the good). This aggregate demand can then be matched with available supply to find equilibrium price and quantity. The final equilibrium will be an efficient equilibrium of P = MC = MB.

With any degree of publicness in goods, however, this is no longer an automatic result. With pure public goods consumers become what economists call "price-adjusters and quantity-takers". Since there is nonrivalry and nonexcludability with a pure public good, any consumer can "take" any quantity supplied into the marketplace and pay what they wish for it. Because consumers are assumed to be rational self-interested maximisers, they will do this taking and pay nothing. Which means, in the core model, that supply of a pure public good will also be zero, since rational, maximising, self-interested suppliers will not provide a good for free.

The problem is not quite as stark with the quasi-public club good of a road because some excludability is possible. But in a market where all roads are provided privately, there will still be a degree of inefficient provision because of the element of nonrival consumption. Providers will have to set the price first and then exclude users afterwards rather than have the market set both price and quantity on the basis of competitive processes. The social optimum of P = MC = MB will not automatically arise and some nonmarket intervention will be required to set the price efficiently. (There is also imperfect competition in road provision because of its local spatial monopoly aspects, a further market inefficiency.) Publicness of goods therefore creates what economists refer to as a market failure. Bator (1958) defines such a failure as a situation in which an idealised system of price-market institutions cannot sustain economically efficient activities or stop inefficient ones.

The idealised price-market system noted by Bator is that presented by the core model. In this world a private optimum is reached in terms of maximum total utility across the whole of consumers and efficient production across suppliers. The body of economic theory that purportedly proves that this equilibrium also is a social optimum (as narrowly defined by economists) is referred to as welfare economics. But with market failure, neither a private nor a social optimal allocation can be guaranteed; indeed, resources will certainly be misallocated in some way. Here the field of public economics (in older parlance, public finance) comes in, which considers how specific deviations from the ideal conditions of the core model (of which publicness is one) lead to particular market failures, and ways of correcting or compensating such failures. Figure 13.2 maps out these basic conceptual relationships between core theory, welfare economics, and public economics.

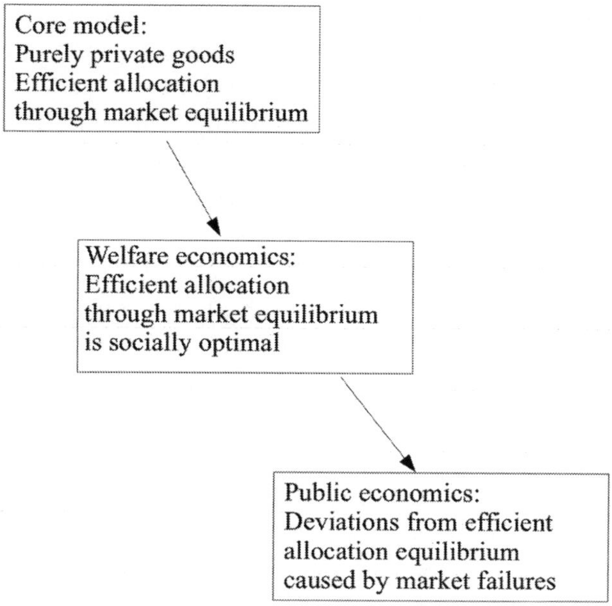

FIGURE 13.2
Relationship between the core theory, welfare economics, and public economics.

13.3 CLUB GOODS, "EFFICIENT" PRICING, AND "FIRST-BEST" AND "SECOND BEST" SOLUTIONS

For club goods like roads, pricing is a solution for correcting market failure. The problem with a purely private market, though, is that the market will not generate, by itself, the correct price. "Congesting" goods like roads (and really any "network" good), being excludable but nonrivalrous, can be managed by externally introducing various degrees of excludability, both by fixing and securing access points, and determining the socially optimal toll (Levinson et al. 2016, 29–30). This is exactly what the London congestion charge aimed to do so by cordoning off an entire area with pricing points and setting a price that was intended to capture, and internalise to the user, the cost that their individual driving generated in terms of congestion (and, first implicitly but later explicitly, the cost of emissions as well).

In intuitive terms, a road can be "consumed" by many people but after a certain point congestion sets in and motorists cannot travel as fast or as reliably. Before that point roads are similar to pure "private" goods in which each individual has full and unfettered access to their portion of the road and the services that the road provides. Once congestion sets in, one driver's use of the road starts interfering with other driver's use of it. Road pricing can fix this problem by establishing a charge that captures the cost that each individual driver imposes on the road, thus causing drivers to change their behaviour to reduce this cost, incentivising them to adjust their use of the road to ensure that overall capacity is smoothly utilised at minimum cost and maximum overall utility (Buchanan 1965).

However, as usual, reality is not this simple. Economists refer to "first-best" and "second-best" solutions. In the core model, the untrammelled operations of the market always yield first-best allocations of resources, i.e. ones that are fully efficient. Even with club goods, there is a "first-best" toll that can be imposed to achieve efficiency, as indicated above. But to get this price one would have to know the distribution of the value of travel time among travellers using the road and then calculate the generalised cost of congestion imposed by each user. As Chapter 7 discusses, neither of these is easy to determine. Additionally, road use, and hence congestion, varies widely and continuously across a day and in theory first-best tolls should dynamically vary with them. But again, in practice, this is not easy to do, even with current advances in information technology. Thus, typically toll road operators use some proxy of average costs to set prices, usually divided into peak and off-peak periods, hopefully a "good enough" approximation of traveller preferences, but certainly not first-best (Anas 2008). The toll set is still going to be too low, or too high, relative to the optimum of P = MC. But the toll will at least yield a second-best outcome moving the equilibrium usage of the road closer to that optimum.

There is an additional issue of administrative costs. These are glossed over in the core model which assumes costless administration. But tolling does have a "deadweight" loss component in the form of collection and other administrative burdens which yield no direct utility to consumers or profit to producers, yet must be paid to have road tolling work at all. Costs of collection and administration for road tolling run in a range of 10%–45% (Peters & Kramer 2003). Pricing on transport facilities is needed to ensure optimal use but the actual act of pricing involves significant and unavoidable pure welfare-reducing dead weight losses.

The "lumpiness" of infrastructure (see Chapter 4) presents another complication. To be efficient, a road must be able to carry the socially optimal amount of traffic. But what if the road's capacity has become inadequate because traffic growth was larger than expected? In this case a socially optimal price is impossible to set in the short-run. Imposition of a higher price at a sufficiently high level to reduce traffic congestion to manageable levels on existing capacity will lessen traffic; but this will not be an optimal outcome because the level of transport service provided is too low. But too low a price allows for continued congestion. This dynamic applies equally for other networks such as train and tram lines. If there is some long-term deficiency in the system that will take significant amounts of time to address, even full-cost pricing will not necessarily yield an efficient transport outcome (Peters & Gordon 2009).

This theoretical discussion is a partial equilibrium analysis. Even if a P = MC condition can be met on an individual road within an individual market, the broader outcome may nonetheless result in a sub-optimum from a general equilibrium point of view. For example, there are subtle and complex issues revolving around changes in economic incentives to business and consumer enterprise that tolls might introduce. High truck tolls on a bridge may be efficient in managing congestion at just that facility in isolation. But that toll might also divert transport to other modes and other routes and also shift the location of warehouses, terminals, and fleet operations, reshaping the economic geography of the region, perhaps in suboptimal ways. All of this means that even efficient partial equilibrium solutions may not yield general equilibrium optimality. In this sense almost all policy inevitably ends up being second-best in reality.

13.4 EXTERNALITY

Externality refers to an interdependence between separate production functions and/or utility functions, a situation representing another violation of the idealised conditions behind the core theory which assumes a complete independence of production and consumptions decisions other than those mediated through market transactions and constraints. This leads to market failure and is typically referred to as a technological externality, to indicate when two or more distinct production or utility "technologies" (or functions) are directly linked through the structure of the function itself or through the direct inputs into those functions. Such an occurrence is a direct violation of the assumption that such technologies are separate from one another and that agents are atomistic. (As an aside, public goods generally lead to externalities, but externalities are not always created by public goods, as discussed more below.)

Interdependencies can be on either the production or consumption sides. Here is an example of a production externality in the following production functions of producers A and B:

$$X_A = f(L_A, K_{A,B})$$
$$X_B = f(L_B, X_B)$$

In this particular case, producer B has a "normal" production technology with B's output of X being solely reliant on the inputs of labour (L) and capital (K) that B obtains. But producer A has a production technology with an externality in the sense that the K that B uses also enters into the output of X by A with B having no direct control over that input. An example might be two shipping firms on a river, one upstream and one downstream. Both firms operate terminals and vessels that pollute the water with slicks and debris. The firm operating upstream is not directly impacted by the other firm; but the downstream firm operates in water polluted by the upstream firm and has its machines damaged by the upstream firm's pollution. Thus, the term $K_{A,B}$ in A's production function indicates the interdependence between A and B's production.

On the consumption side agent utility functions, and hence agent consumption, may also be interdependent. For example, consider consumers A and B and goods X and Y:

$$U_A = f(X_A, Y_A, X_B)$$
$$U_B = f(X_B, Y_B, X_A)$$

In this case, both consumers have technological externalities since the amount of X that B consumes affects A's utility and the amount of X that a consumes affects B's utility. For example, both A and B might have great empathy for one another in that they feel each other's joy and pain, and the more the one has, the better the other feels. By contrast, with envy, a gain by one reduces the utility of the other.

Finally there can be interdependence of production on utility in which one agent's production affects another's consumption utility. Noise from a freight terminal disrupting the peace of households around its perimeter is a classic example of this. (In theory there could also be an interdependency going from utility to production, though it is hard to conceive of a meaningful practical example.)

Externalities can be positive or negative. Negative externalities imply that one party's activities are imposing a cost on other parties; positive externalities imply that one party's activities are providing a benefit to others. Industrial pollution is a classic negative externality: one producer's actions produce negative effects on another's utility and/or production. The spatial externalities mentioned in Chapter 3, such as knowledge spillovers or agglomeration economies, are positive in the sense they generate returns to producers and consumers in their presence, regardless of whether they have contributed directly to them or not. Table 13.2 presents a few examples of negative and positive externalities in transport production and consumption.

TABLE 13.2

Examples of types of externalities in the transport sector

A new training programme by a logistics firm increases the supply of trained labour to the whole industry.	Externality in production – positive through an interdependence in production functions through labour input.
A new shopping mall opens and increases road congestion in the surrounding area.	Externality of production on utility – negative impact on utility of nearby residents due to the impact of activity generated by the shopping mall.
A new freight terminal opens up in a residential neighbourhood increasing local noise and emissions from trucks.	Same as above.
A rail station is refurbished, improving its amenities and user environment but not changing the quality or quantity of transport outputs.	Externality of production on utility – positive on consumers due to an increase in their satisfaction from the improved station amenities.

As with public goods, technological externality can be a problem for one main reason: an agent's production and/or consumption decisions are directly affected by the actions of another agent, without those actions being mediated through the price system. In either case, the market price does not reflect the full benefits and or costs (also known as social benefits or costs) of an activity and yet it this price that parties use to set the level of that activity. This is a market failure.

This can be seen clearly when considering social cost. Social cost and benefit can be formulated as follows:

Social cost = private cost + external cost
Social benefit = private benefit + external benefit

If there is no external cost or benefit, then the equation is reduced into social cost = private cost and social benefit = private benefit, with the problem of maximising net social benefit collapsing to the problem of equilibrium of supply and demand in the private market. Once externality is introduced, however, private net benefit is no longer equal to social net benefit and price no longer reaches a social optimum.

Public goods, by their very nature, lead to some degree of externality. That is because the presence of publicness leads to an interdependence of production (utility) functions for all producers (consumers) using that good. On the other hand, externality does not necessarily imply publicness in the good involved. It can arise, and often does, with purely private goods, like emissions from a factory which involve no public goods at all, on either the consumer or producer side. There are also some externalities that do not present a problem for attaining social optimum in the market. Thus, if envy is an aspect of some agent utility functions there is a utility impact, but it arises solely from the agent's individual psychology. These agents will still find their social welfare maximised through the allocation of resources in market equilibrium, even though the quirks of their preferences might degrade (or augment) the utility they derive from it. That is their individual problem, not a collective issue.

Economists also distinguish between the technological externality of direct interdependence of activities unmediated by the market, and "pecuniary" externality in which the production or consumption activities of one party affecting the production or consumption activities of another, but through the price mechanism. This latter sort of interdependence happens all the time, e.g. a new road raising property values which makes some land owners better off and some land buyers worse off. This is really just a technical statement of the general interdependence of supply and demand working through markets, which is not a failure but exactly how the market is supposed to work.

With technological externality there are changes that are not reflected in price. The example in Table 13.2 of a firm training up people in logistics and improving the quality of labour for the whole sector represents a technological externality rather than a pecuniary one. The firm is making a commercial choice in its own interests but in this case its investment also benefits others in a way that is not fully captured in market prices. In another example from the table, truck traffic creates noise and emissions that disturbs surrounding communities. This is clearly a direct technological externality. But even here, if the new terminal also improves freight movements in the area and lowers operating costs for local firms, these can be seen as mainly pecuniary dynamics, mediated through the market. Here only the non-pecuniary aspects are of potential policy concern (Levinson et al. 2016, 177).

Indeed, pecuniary externalities of transport systems are especially pervasive because the creation of new transport capacity directly affects many things, such as patterns of mobility and accessibility. A transport investment can allow cities to expand to outlying areas that were previously inaccessible and also change the relative accessibility of locations within cities. These changes can be positive (some locations becoming relatively more accessible than before gaining value) or negative (areas made relatively less accessible losing value). But these instances are not considered market failures *per se*, though they do have effects greater than the sum of the parts (Anas 2008).

13.5 COLLECTIVE PROVISION AND THE FREE RIDER PROBLEM

Public goods and externality create what economists refer to as the free rider problem. This is a name for the fact that with public or quasi-public goods, or situations generating externality, there is the possibility of getting consumption or production for less than its true cost. Consumers will want to "free ride" off of others who are paying for the goods from suppliers of that good. Consider an example of a lighthouse funded by a consortium of private shippers to aid navigation for their own ships in a channel used by boats owned by everyone, whether they are members of the consortium or not. These shippers came together to fund the construction of the lighthouse but each could have paid less if the other beneficiaries outside that consortium could have been forced to pay as well for the benefit they receive from the light produced. This was not possible because the light is a pure public good, and once provided everyone can consume it and no one can be excluded. In this example, the lighthouse is built because there is sufficient private interest. But it might not have been built at all if such sufficiency is not present. Or, to continue the example, perhaps the consortium would build the lighthouse but it would be smaller and its light less powerful than the social optimum would require because these free riders cannot be forced to chip in.

The free rider problem is one of the main reasons in the core theory that some nonmarket entity might have to provide public goods and price or regulate externality in some way. This is one reason that the state taps societal resources, usually through taxes, to pay for and provide public goods. This collective provision of a public good is thus one economic justification for the existence of government (though there is the possibility in some cases, like the consortium mentioned above, of nongovernmental collective provision).

Even with the coercive power of the state, providing public goods is not easy. The state has a problem in determining how much of the good to provide, and what price to charge for it because market information is not available. And the more beneficiaries there are, and the more public the good is, the more difficult this information problem becomes, both because of the difficulty of identifying beneficiaries in the first place, and also the difficulty of discovering, without the benefit of marketplace processes, what people are actually willing to pay. One could ask agents, of course, whether they want the good and for how much. But these maximising agents will inevitably provide the lowest estimate of what they think they can get away with, information that a market would otherwise force them to reveal through their

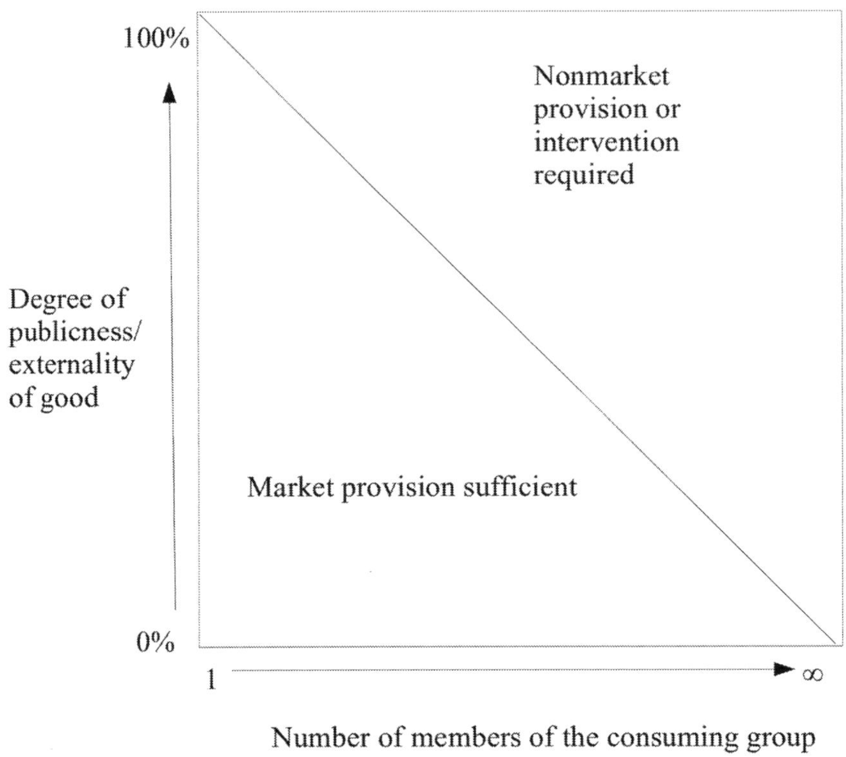

FIGURE 13.3
The free rider problem and collective provision.

transactions. The degree of publicness in the good directly feeds into this as well. At some point an economic boundary is passed where, if it is socially desirable to provide the good at all, it must be provided by government or some other nonmarket institution rather than through the market, or with an external guiding intervention such as a Pigovian tax (see below).

Figure 13.3 presents this trade-off in conceptual terms. The vertical axis indicates the degree of publicness and/or externality of the good, 0% indicating a pure private good and no externality, 100% indicating a pure public good and/or all-encompassing externality. The horizontal axis indicates the number of members in the group consuming the good. If the good is purely private, the market can efficiently provide it to as many members as there might be, even up to infinity. But as the good becomes more public and/or has more externality, then the free rider problem looms larger and larger, with a trade-off between group size and degree of publicness creating a boundary which, once crossed, requires some nonmarket involvement for efficient outcomes. (The line shown here is just for illustration and in reality such a boundary is likely to be complex and highly contextual.) For very small groups of consumers, publicness might still be sorted out through markets since the individual gains from provision are clearer and free riding through concealment of preferences is harder. But with larger numbers and publicness the degree of market failure rises.

Incidentally, there are reasons other than market failure for a nonmarket supplement to, or replacement of, private markets. Even if all private markets are functioning perfectly, and even if all transactions are in pure private goods and services within private markets without externality, the agents in those markets, taken as a collective, form a society and that society does not necessarily simply "add up" to the sum of all individual transactions and preferences. These "system effects" or "synergies" can arise from a variety of sources, such as the social interdependence of agents (which violates the core model assumption of atomism), or, as has already been alluded to above, from general equilibrium effects that make a whole that is greater (or potentially less) than the sum of the parts. To a certain degree agglomeration and other spatial effects fall into this category.

Additionally, society as a whole may have non-economic values which do not correspond to, or may conflict with, the outcomes produced by markets. For example, perfectly functioning markets may nonetheless produce distributions of wealth and income that the social or political order judges to be unacceptable. Related to this, society itself may have values that are not directly "economic", such as an adherence to a particular moral code. Economists refer to these issues under the rubric of "merit wants", as discussed in Chapter 14.

Thus, while in the core theory government primarily exists to step in to correct instances of market failure, in actual fact the state can also ensure that social values and goals are achieved in instances where the market alone is not achieving them; take advantage of systematic "synergies" which private markets might ignore but which are beneficial to society; and deal with non-economic issues which are deemed important to society but which are considered to be adversely affected socially by market impacts (e.g. spatial pockets of unemployment because of distance from work opportunities, that government might address with transport subsidies to qualified recipients).

13.6 NATURAL MONOPOLY

Another cause of market failure emerges from a different quarter. Socially optimal pricing rests upon an assumption of perfect competition in the market. However, roads are clearly not in that category, being single facilities with locational market power. Roads, like many other spatially based quasi-public goods, are therefore prone to some degree of monopoly provision within its local service area. Without some sort of external constraint, such as a regulatory authority or a binding agreement between the government and a private operator, there will almost certainly be pricing above MC that will maximise operator profits but will provide service short of a social optimum. Pricing or tolling regulation is one possible solution, though that involves government intervention introducing some inefficiency of its own.

Imperfect competition in other markets, such as rail, has at times had more vigorous regulation, and sometimes even public takeover, because market power in these instances is judged to be more thorough-going and extensive that the more purely spatially based advantages of local roads. As mentioned in Chapter 3, transport service and infrastructure provision is often subject to increasing returns to scale (RTS) and positive economies of scale (EOS). In the extreme case technically efficient production might be achieved by a single, very large monopoly producer. Such an outcome is referred to as a "natural monopoly".

A monopolist will charge a price for its services well above the socially optimal price, while providing a quantity of service well below the optimum. Thus, economists will often argue that transport enterprises that exhibit tendencies towards natural monopoly be allowed to be operated as such but be regulated by government by setting the prices they charge to ensure that a firm's average costs and a "reasonable" rate of return are covered while keeping the firm from gouging consumers. A related policy is to set transport service prices for users to cover variable operating costs, while subsidising the purchase the fixed inputs, such as right-of-way. These solutions recognise that a monopoly arrangement is efficient but that price and quantity nonetheless needs to be adjusted to get closer to those that a perfectly competitive market would provide. In either case, interestingly, application of MC pricing will actually lead to a below-optimal level of service by leading to provision at an inefficient scale because the fixed costs that yield RTS and EOS will not be covered under such a rule and provision will be inefficient (Anas 2008). Here the second-best is the best that can be achieved.

13.7 "MIMICKING" THE MARKET

Market failure needs to be corrected. While nonmarket institutions may be necessary to solve some of failures, the default argument by economists is that government is the least preferred choice for this. There are various theoretical reasons given for this judgement which are covered in more detail in Chapter 18. Here one can say that in solving market failure, economists tend to favour using the market as much as possible to solve resource allocation problems in society because theory suggests it leads to the greatest possible efficiency. Where it cannot do the job, as with the market failures of technological externality of quasi-public goods, economists prefer techniques which "mimic" the market, using mechanisms that allow as much of the market to remain as possible and applying interventions that themselves operate in ways similar to the market. Tolls and congestion charges are a classic example of this, leaving the market to operate while adjusting the incentives to such operation through a price mechanism.

Another policy that leaves the market relatively untouched while adjusting incentives to correct market failure is the Pigovian tax, named after the economist A.C. Pigou, who came up with it. Suppose car drivers generate emissions that impose an external cost in the form of lowered air quality for everyone around them. This cost will not be internalised by the drivers themselves and they will drive more than they would have if such a cost was recognised by them. In other words, there will be more driving than is socially optimal because drivers are calculating their private optima without taking the external cost into account.

In this case, the socially optimal equilibrium can be restored if an external charge equal to the external cost of the emissions is imposed on drivers, thus internalising the cost to those drivers. Now there is an after-tax price that includes the externality and which the drivers pay. This tax wedge (see Chapter 10) is used for a very definite purpose, namely to shift consumption down enough to maximise net social benefit to reduce the externality. The tax itself still has the efficiency costs that all taxation involves. But hopefully these are outweighed by the efficiency gains of the corrected externality. Such a solution is judged to more efficient than something like a regulation because the efficiencies of market processes are preserved almost intact without introducing the inefficiencies that often come with nonmarket measures.

Meanwhile, the natural monopolies discussed in Section 13.7 have, in the past, often been run by governments, either from the start, or as a result of a public takeover of a private enterprise, to eliminate the inefficiencies – and unfairness – of monopoly power. But economic theory would suggest that more efficient solutions would be to leave a private monopoly in place but regulate or monitor its price and output, preferably as minimally as possible.

These policy prescriptions involve implicit value judgements, however. Box 13.2 discusses how economists consider the treatment of value judgements in their methodology.

BOX 13.2 NORMATIVE VERSUS POSITIVE ECONOMICS

Economists refer to what they typically do as positive economics. This refers to the theory of the way things actually are. Thus, the core model and all its extensions are said to be "positive" in the methodological sense of the word meaning to describe the world as it actually is. The model is greatly simplified, as all models are in some way, and subject to challenge, but nonetheless aims to depict reality.

"Normative" economics represents a different kind of aim to describe a world as it ought to be. The same models may be used and, indeed, usually are. But a positive theory of markets would purport to present a model of actual markets and how and why they function, while a normative theory would define a desirable objective like economic efficiency and describe what the market needs to look like to conform to that desired goal.

Public economics as presented in this chapter is supposedly positive. But the core model has an inherent tendency to privilege efficiency above other values and thus to see the private market as socially privileged as well. This raises the question of where a positive approach ends and a normative one begins. This is distinct from the issue of realism of assumptions and speaks to whether there are underlying biases in the theory itself that are actually more normative than they pretend to be. All theories, being human-made, are subject to this problem and it is basically unavoidable. But it should nonetheless be made as explicit as possible and examined accordingly.

13.8 THE BOUNDARIES OF MARKET FAILURE

Market failure is a very elastic concept in that it essentially encompasses particular phenomena of consumption or production that can be only incompletely captured in market prices and processes. The examples discussed here are not exhaustive. Systemic issues such as climate change are discussed in Chapter 17 under the rubrics of sustainability and resilience because while these can be defined as market failures, arguably they are also much broader than that, requiring a view that goes beyond market efficiency and requiring a longer-term system perspective.

Similarly, transport safety is sometimes considered under the market failure template. It can be considered at least partly as highly related to congestion and general usage level of a network, and thus a symptom of the market failures peculiar to club goods. Accidents also certainly impose costs that markets cannot fully incorporate either in advance or afterwards. This is one reason that there are public insurance liability laws for auto-owners. Insurance of some sort (properly designed – a big caveat) is optimal from a social welfare point of view. But the free rider problem will result in under-insurance and so there is arguably a state role for an insurance mandate or other external intervention into the market. Safety issues are discussed primarily in a human factors context, in Chapter 19. Insurance is discussed in a property rights context in Chapter 17. Thus, market failure is a widely applicable concept but can also be analysed in other broader contexts.

REFERENCES

Anas, A. (2008). Urban transportation economics. In Durlauf Steven N. and Blume Lawrence E. (eds). *New Palgrave Dictionary of Economics* (2nd edition). Palgrave Macmillan, 6913–6917.

Bator, F. M. (1958). The anatomy of market failure. *Quarterly Journal of Economics*, 72(3), 351–379.

Buchanan, J. M. (1965). An economic theory of clubs. *Economica*, New Series, 32, 1–14.

Herzog, I. (2023). The city-wide effects of tolling downtown drivers: Evidence from London's congestion charge. SSRN Working Paper 4404817. https://ssrn.com/abstract=4404817 or http://dx.doi.org/10.2139/ssrn.4404817

Levinson, D., Gillen, D., et al. (2016). *Transportation economics*. en.wikibooks.org July 9, 2016. Print (pdf) version.

Peters, J. R., & Gordon, C. (2009). Results not guaranteed: A tale of road pricing in New York and London. *Journal of Urban Technology*, 16(1), 113–131.

Peters, J. R., & Kramer, J. K. (2003). The inefficiency of toll collection as a means of taxation: Evidence from the Garden State Parkway. *Transportation Quarterly*, 57(3), 17–31.

TfL (2006). *London travel report 2006*. Transport for London.

TfL (2007). *Central London congestion charging impacts monitoring: Fifth annual report*. Transport for London.

Vickrey, W. S. (1963). Pricing in urban and suburban transport. *The American Economic Review*, 53(2), 452–465.

CHAPTER 14

Justice, equity, disadvantage, and social exclusion

14.1 INTRODUCTION: THE FUNDAMENTAL THEOREM OF WELFARE ECONOMICS

South African apartheid and its transport and locational policies are clearly products of a system that everyone sees as morally and ethically wrong. Behind the highly deleterious economic and social effects of the pass laws, Bantustans and other discriminatory actions taken by the Afrikaner government of the time, there is a spine of injustice that is inhumane and reprehensible.

Public policy serves as the instrument for expression of collective values – or in the worst case, placing one group's over another's, as was the case under apartheid. Yet the core model has little to say about values explicitly. Private markets, operating freely, will achieve a social optimum which maximises welfare (utility) across all agents, the core theory predicts. But the paramount social value here is the maximisation of utility across all agents. Government intervention, especially of the heavy-handed nature taken in South Africa, clearly goes against this goal. So, on its own terms, the core model would clearly be against this sort of policy, and any policy at all except those that address a market failure.

But what kind of world does the untrammelled market actually deliver? The market sets a price for all inputs and outputs and the competitive process ensures that this price equalises with the marginal cost of production (P = MC) and also the maximum utility of consumption possible given

DOI: 10.4324/9781003350866-18

BOX 14.1 INTRODUCTORY CASE: SOUTH AFRICAN APARTHEID, THE PASS LAWS, AND BANTUSTANS

South Africa's system of apartheid, which was an official and brutal policy of White racial supremacy and segregation against a Black African majority, had many impacts on those subjected to it. One of the gravest was on transport and location. The Afrikaner apartheid government of the second half of the 20th century, building on laws and institutions used by the British and Dutch colonial rulers of South Africa going back to the 18th century, forcibly relocated Blacks into segregated remote "townships" distant from city centres and employment opportunities that were reserved for the White minority. This extreme form of ghettoisation forced Blacks, who formed the bulk of the unskilled and semi-skilled workforce, to travel long distances to go to and from work, often for hours a day (King & McCusker 2007, 6–7).

The methods of social control needed to maintain this unequal order were considerable, to say the least. The most notorious example was the pass law requiring Blacks in South Africa to carry documents authorising their presence in restricted areas. This too hearkened back to practices of the British Cape Colony whose White government forcibly expelled Blacks to make room for British settlers and then, to alleviate chronic labour shortages, enacted Ordinance 49 in 1828 permitting Black labourers to enter the colony for work only if in possession of official contracts and passes. Other regulations of this sort followed reaching an apotheosis in 1948 with the election of the National Party representing the Afrikaner minority and the promulgation of apartheid as a permanent and institutionalised regime. The Population Registration Act of 1950 classified all South Africans as either Bantu (covering all Black Africans), Coloured (those of mixed race), or White, with a fourth category – Asian (Indian and Pakistani) – added later. This same year, the Group Areas Act formally established officially racially segregated urban residential and business sections from which members of other races were barred from living, owning land, or running a business, with thousands of mainly Black people expelled from Whites-only designated areas as a result. To monitor and control such movements, passes were used, then replaced with "reference books" that were effectively internal passports, including identity information, employment history, employer evaluations, and fingerprints. Black men of at least 16 years of age were required to carry this book at all times, with severe penalties if caught without one, or with a fraudulent document. By the end of the 1970s, the daily average prison population in South Africa was one of the world's highest, with pass offences accounting for the majority of charges. By the time the pass law system was annulled in 1986, shortly before the end of the apartheid regime a few years later, over 17 million arrests had been made under its auspices (Matthias 2024).

Parallel with this, the apartheid government also established "homelands", referred to as "Bantustans", as notionally "separate" political jurisdictions which the various Black tribal groups would be moved into, before the whole system was shut down with the coming of multiracial democracy in 1994. These also could be traced back to colonial-era creations of "reserves" for indigenous populations to be herded into and then drawn upon as a source of cheap, excess labour. Various acts created these separate territories while enabling movements of Blacks into them and enforcing controls on their movements out of them. The Bantu Homelands Citizenship Act of 1970 replaced South African for Blacks with homeland citizenship regardless of whether it was desired or not. Four homelands – Transkei, Bophuthatswana, Venda, and Ciskei – were granted "independence" (though with none receiving international recognition) and six were given "self-governing status". Only around 14% of the country's land area was provided to these new entities, but roughly 3.5 million people were

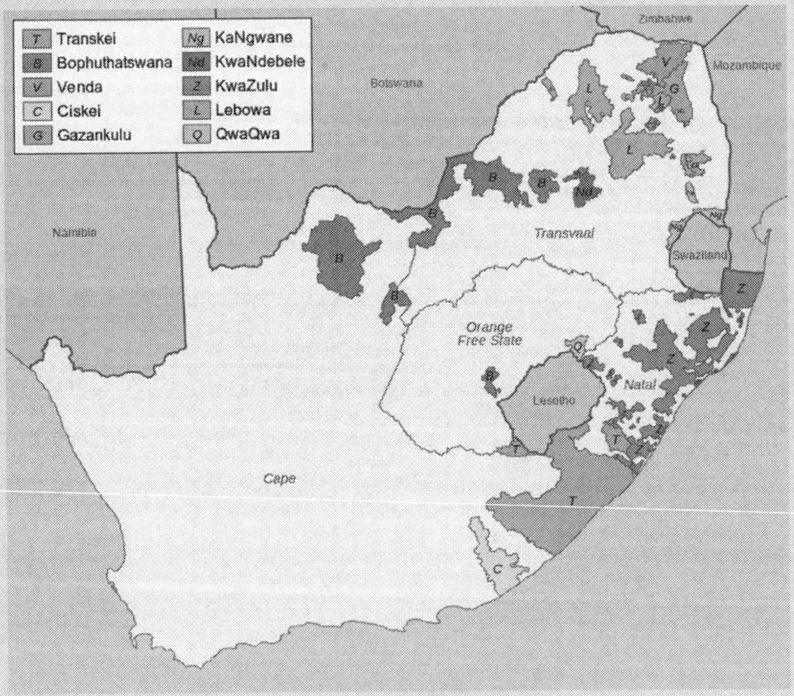

FIGURE 14.1
South Africa's Bantustans.

Source: Image by Htonl, under a CC BY-SA 3.0 license https://creativecommons.org/licenses/by-sa/3.0, via Wikimedia Commons.

relocated, with the proportion of the total Black population living in them rising from 39% to 53%. These were effectively townships writ large, reservoirs of cheap labour, forcing workers to travel large distances under strict controls to get to the work which was so insufficient nearby (King & McCusker 2007, 7–9) (see Figure 14.1).

With these policies in place, the transport system and residential location patterns were thoroughly distorted. A large and shifting sector of informal transit arose to serve both township and Bantustan into and out of "Whites only" city centres and suburbs, and population and employment densities were grossly imbalanced between them. Although apartheid fell by the wayside 30 years ago, its effects are still very much in evidence. Townships such as Soweto, outside Johannesburg, though vibrant, remain overcrowded, distant from much employment and amenities, and reliant on a large and vital but mostly unregulated transit industry. Meanwhile, although the Bantustans no longer formally exist, the spatial economic and population patterns they laid down still persist and some have argued that rightful emphasis on delivering proper services to concentrations of people, such as electrification and housing development, are also unintentionally reinforcing these apartheid geographies (King & McCusker 2007, 10–11). These patterns continue to deeply complicate the efficiency, effectiveness, and equity of South Africa's urban transport system, and much more besides.

available resources, current technology, current preferences, and – most critically for this discussion – existing distribution of resources. In the final equilibrium across all markets, this optimum will ensure that no resources are left idle or wasted, that all inputs are yielding their maximum possible outputs, and that the mix of goods and services being produced are fully satisfying consumer desires within each one's individual constraints, given the initial distribution of income and wealth. This is the essence of what is referred to as the fundamental theorem of welfare economics that equilibrium in a perfectly competitive market (with all simplifying assumptions in place) cannot be improved upon in consumer utility and producer profitability terms. The technical term for this state is a Pareto optimum. Named after the Italian economist Vilfredo Pareto, who wrote during the late 19th and early 20th centuries, this is a state where nobody can be made better off without making anyone worse off in material and utility terms. To use Voltaire's famous phrase, voiced through his eternal optimist character Pangloss, the market yields the best of all possible worlds.

14.2 THE EFFICIENCY–EQUITY "TRADE-OFF"

One can see that a Pareto optimum leaves a lot to the imagination as far as the facts on the ground it actually delivers. In particular, the core model accepts as given the distribution of resources at the beginning and end of the market exchange process. But this distribution will not necessarily be what most individuals would consider fair or equitable. It is possible to have an "efficient" economy where the top 1% of the population consumes 99% of all output, leaving the 1% to feast and the remaining 99% to famine. One could imagine a scenario, for example, where the market-produced material outcomes similar to apartheid South Africa, in which a small minority controlled many more resources than the large majority. Official repression would be absent, but if an apartheid-like economic outcome was product of a competitive economy, the end result would be claimed as Pareto optimal, with redistribution of any sort making somebody worse off and thus welfare-reducing.

A more fundamental question is where did the initial distribution of resources come from? Distributions of resources are at least partly determined, often heavily so, by nonmarket forces and institutions such as social structures, private organisations (like corporations), and government, as well as natural resource endowments of things like water and energy. South Africa is like many post-colonial countries in that it was left with a deeply unequal social and economic order entrenched by centuries of colonial rule and certainly not the product of pure market dynamics. To gloss over the nature of the foundational starting point of resource endowments in a model of resource allocation is analytically questionable and, in many cases, ethically debatable.

The core economic theory deals with ethical content by employing a notional trade-off between "efficiency" and "equity". Equity broadly refers to the distribution of resources across different groups as measured against some socially preferred ideal of fairness. Efficiency, as already mentioned, is the attainment of an allocation of resources that leaves society as materially well-off as possible.

Efficiency is the main focus of economic theory and in the core model the market delivers two primary forms of it: (a) technical efficiency, in which maximum output is obtained from a given set of inputs and technology; and (b) allocative efficiency, which includes this condition as a baseline but also adds that the set of goods and services being produced maximises the "welfare" (satisfaction) of all agents within an economy. Any redistribution to improve equity at this point will necessarily sacrifice some efficiency in the welfare sense of the term. Hence the notion of an efficiency–equity trade-off, which is that equity must necessarily be purchased at the "cost" of efficiency as defined in the core model. And while equity is often the critical element of many debates about how to allocate public resources, economists argue that efficiency should be sought before equity in a first-best world, and often even in a second- or third-best world because attainment of this goal provides the largest possible pool of resources to redistribute afterwards, whatever the desired goals may be.

14.3 SOCIAL WELFARE FUNCTIONS, MERIT WANTS, AND MERIT GOODS

This still leaves the question of what a "fair" redistribution is. Can the theory itself generate an answer to this?

The economist Kenneth Arrow (1950) did try to "solve" this problem analytically, within the sole frame of the core theory, as he did also with other issues such as with agglomerations (see Chapter 3). Notionally a socially ideal redistribution could be determined by weighing up all individual agent preferences and coming up with some "social welfare" function that would distribute resources collectively to those individuals society wants to give more to, and away from those it prefers to have less, analogous to the way in which agents select consumption items in the marketplace to maximise their individual utility. The basic idea is to derive a social welfare function (SWF) that adds up all individual utility functions, weighted according to some "social preference" to determine their relative social importance to yield a "socially optimal" distribution of welfare across agents which would further yield the socially optimal distribution of resources that obtains that welfare.

This function can be expressed as follows:

$$W_s = (U_1{*}W_1 + U_2{*}W_2 \dots + U_n{*}W_n)$$

where W_s refers to the social optimum of welfare, this consisting of all individual utility functions from agent 1 to agent n, socially weighted, with the weights summing to 1 (i.e. 100%).

The logic is clear when looking diagrammatically at the simple case of a two-agent economy of agents A and B, as provided in Figure 14.2.

The "utility frontier" (curve AB) for a two-agent economy (with agents A and B) is a mapping of the array of combinations of potential utility between A and B with a given overall stock of resources available at a given point in time. Point A represents A having maximum utility (taking the most

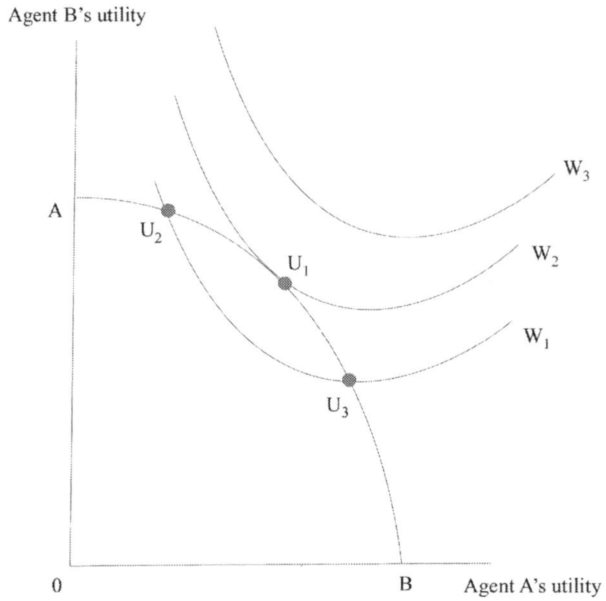

FIGURE 14.2
A social welfare function (for a two-agent economy).

possible) and B minimum utility (in this case zero). Point B represents the opposite case of B getting maximum utility and A getting zero.

What point along the utility frontier is optimal from society's point of view? The market by itself will not generate the answer since selfish, rational, atomistic, maximising agents will aim to get the lion's share for themselves and the core model takes initial resource distributions as given. An "efficient" distribution of utility will result from market processes, but likely not a socially preferred one. If there were some "just" economic planner that could sit above the situation, this planner could theoretically devise appropriate social weights for each agent's utility to capture social preferences about the total utility received by each agent. The SWF explicitly does this, generating various iterations of utility trade-offs that arise from different distributions of resources, as shown by the curves marked "W". Three are shown here as W_1, W_2, and W_3. Of these three, W_3 is infeasible since it can only be obtained with a stock of resources that is beyond what is available. W_1 is feasible and generates two possible resource distributions that achieve points on the trade-off curve, U_2 and U_3. But these are not the ideal preferred utility distributions since they do not yet optimise social preferences. U_1 is the ideal, the point that W_2 touches on the frontier and which cannot be improved upon. This is what economists (ironically?) refer to as the "bliss point".

Putting aside the difficult question of how this redistribution would be carried out, it turns out that a suitable SWF is impossible. Arrow considered various procedures for determining social preferences (such as various types of voting rules) and found that unless completely restrictive, and totally inapplicable assumptions were used, there was no way of determining social preferences coherently enough to derive a SWF at all.

Although theory cannot provide the answers to specific ethical quandaries like the optimal distribution of resources, society still must grapple with these issues. To attempt to bring these ethical issues into neoclassical theory, Musgrave (1969) proposed the concept of "merit wants" to refer to social desires that could be satisfied by goods provided by the government, these being referred to as "merit goods". These goods may not necessarily be public goods in the sense discussed in Chapter 13. They might be excludable and rival in consumption. But nonetheless private markets may still not provide sufficient quantities to satisfy these wants and there may be a justification for government to step in and provide them, or at least subsidise their provision (and/or redistribute resources to allow markets to provide the desired quantities and qualities). Basic access to health care and education are classic examples of merit goods that are provided in many places as part of a basic government "safety net".

This concept is not an economic argument for doing such things, but rather a rationale for why such things might be done. Provision of merit goods will, according to the core theory, almost certainly result in efficiency loss (unless they are provided as a countervailing solution to an inefficient market failure). If the utility reduction caused by diverting resources to merit wants can be more than compensated for by gains in utility from meeting merit wants, there is an economic argument for doing so. The same can be said for pure redistributions of resources from one group to another, such as from the very wealthy to the very poor. But either way, sometimes there may be social values that are compelling even though they sit outside of an efficiency framework.

14.4 MORALITY, ETHICS, SOCIAL VALUES, AND ECONOMICS

Moral standards (which define what a society considers to be "right" or "wrong") and ethics (which refers to the application of moral standards) are drawn from social "values" which refer to a shared background of beliefs and notions about what is important to the way that individuals, groups, and societies act (Jaspers 2016). Where do these standards and values come from?

There are some economists who argue that because the market is theoretically the most efficient mechanism of allocating resources and meeting individual preferences, it is also, therefore, the most equitable (ethical) system as well. SWFs are not only theoretically incoherent by this reckoning; the setting of social weights for individual preference functions is objectionable, as is the intervention into markets to provide merit goods, because private utility maximisation, collectively and individually, is also the social ideal and anything negating, it is thus inherently wrong. This is not to say that "bad" things don't happen in markets, just that market interventions make things worse.

An example of this sort of thinking is provided by economist Gary Becker who analysed racial discrimination and the persistence of a Black–White wage differential in the US by framing it as a matter of supply and demand between economically rational players. In competitive equilibrium Becker claimed that discrimination arose out of individual preferences, which for some people involved racism. But competitive markets also created consequences for both the people being discriminated against and those engaged in it. Discrimination depressed the wages of Black workers relative to Whites, but it also, he claimed, increased the wages that had to be paid to White workers because discriminating employers were hiring from a smaller (White) labour pool. Becker further claimed that Black workers would over time gravitate to employers that did not discriminate, thus slowly reducing the negative impacts that discrimination had against them while providing productivity benefits to those non-discriminating employers who, at least initially, could get Black labour cheaper than equally productive White labour. While racial discrimination is objectionable, Becker admitted, market equilibrium would eventually settle at a place that at least would reduce, though not necessarily eliminate, discriminatory differentials in wages (Becker 1971).

This framing is problematic in a number of ways, especially the unconditional acceptance of a "taste" for racism that many would argue should not be accepted so readily. But this follows naturally from the consumer sovereignty assumption of economics which holds consumer preferences, whatever they are, as sacrosanct. And it endorses, at least implicitly, public policy that leaves the market to "work things out" with the least possible government interference. It also enshrines a sort of majoritarianism in which majority preferences are accepted *in toto* over any minority ones, an implication which follows from the core model and its focus on maximising of the sum of individual preferences, with those with more purchasing power literally "counting" more than those with less.

In fact the core model does have implicit ethics consisting of consequentialism, utilitarianism, and materialism. There is a distinction in philosophical ethics between deontology and consequentialism. In the former, ethical standards are derived from pre-existing absolute principles. This is the position of philosophers such as Plato and, most notably, Immanuel Kant. Consequentialism refers to the idea that no objective standards exist but that actions should nonetheless be judged by their consequences. This latter position was most famously elaborated by the 19th-century political economist Jeremy Bentham, who is the father of the variant known as utilitarianism, adopted by many of the earliest economists and still the implicit ethical standard of much economics today. Bentham posited that people aim to maximise their satisfaction (which he argued could be objectively measured in units that he labelled as "utils") and that ethics amounted to maximising the total amount of utils (utility) across agents in a society; hence the term "utilitarianism" and, in Bentham's famous phrase, a favouring of any policy that provided "the greatest good for the greatest number" (Gordon & Zimmerman 2009). Economists have dropped the notion of being able to count and actually add up "utils", but most still adhere to a utilitarian philosophy.

Classical ethicists also make a distinction between intrinsic value and instrumental value. Something with intrinsic value has value in and of itself. Something with instrumental value is of value only because of the consequences that it leads to (i.e. it is an instrument of such consequences). Deontological approaches focus on intrinsic values, and judge actions according to those values (such as justice). Consequentialist systems like utilitarianism focus only on the instrumental outcomes of actions. Outcomes are considered in both approaches, but with differing emphases. A deontological system would judge a favourable instrumental outcome achieved by means considered intrinsically immoral as ethically unacceptable. For a consequentialist the outcome would ethically unacceptable only if the means cost more instrumentally than the ends. Because consequentialism looks mostly at material outcomes, it is generally considered to be materialist in philosophical terms. Intrinsic ethical systems, because they emphasise ideals, are generally spoken of as being idealist.

The debates about which ethical standard is "better" is an unsettled debate, unlikely to be closed any time soon since it has been going on literally for thousands of years. But it is important to note that the core theory itself does actually embody ethical standards even though this is usually more implicit than explicit. As such these standards can and should be subject to debate, like any other standard.

14.5 DEFINING AND MEASURING EQUITY IN TRANSPORT: LORENZ CURVES AND GINI COEFFICIENTS

There are two standard dimensions of distributional equity: horizontal and vertical. Vertical equity is defined as fairness in the treatment of people in a differing social position (usually different levels of income or consumption). Horizontal equity is defined as fairness in the treatment of people holding roughly the same social position. With either concept, "equitable" is a value-based term which implies some favoured pattern of resource allocation as socially preferred to others. But one can at least measure distributions of resources or burdens and compare them against a benchmark of perfect equality, i.e. every member getting the exact same amount. This does not imply judgement of equality as preferred, but merely a measure of how unequal a given distribution is. There are basic distributional measures that assess how resources are spread across either a given total population (the vertical dimension) or across selected groups of people with similar characteristics (the horizontal dimension) (Di Ciommo & Shiftan 2017, 140–141).

The standard metrics of distributional equity in this sense are the Lorenz curve and the Gini coefficient. The basic idea is to choose proportionality in distribution as a unit of measurement. Proportionate shares are measured in ways invariant to shift in units of measurement and can be applied to various concepts (e.g. income or wealth). A benchmark of exact proportionate cumulative equality across a population is chosen as a reference standard of perfect equality, with every person receiving the same share of the resource being considered (such as income). One then measures actual proportionality of distribution of a resource (typically income) across the reference and compare the divergences between the two to see the extent of inequality. This process is operationalised through the Lorenz curve (Karner et al. 2024) (see Figure 14.3).

A Lorenz curve plots the relationship for a given population of the cumulative distribution of a resource in question (such as income) and compares that to the reference standard of exact proportionality in distribution which will be shown as a straight line. The level of inequality in data will show up as a convex curve, with a more pronounced convexity indicating greater levels of inequity. Gini coefficients express the Lorenz curve relationship as a metric of distortion, with a Gini coefficient of 0 indicating no inequality (all members have the same share of income) and a Gini coefficient of 1 indicating complete inequity (one member has all income). In this figure the Gini coefficient = (Area A)/(Areas A+B).

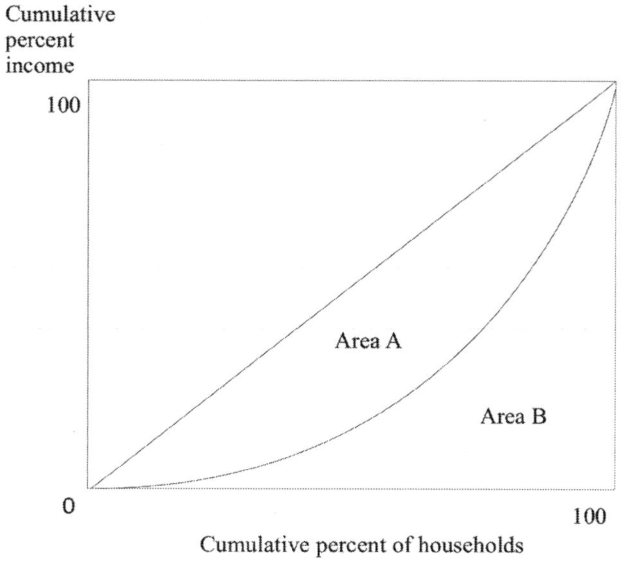

FIGURE 14.3
A Lorenz curve.

Lorenz curves and Gini coefficients are not the be-all and end-all. In particular, comparing different unequal distributions with each other (as opposed to the equality benchmark) is metrically and conceptually fraught (Atkinson 1971). In addition, the causal factors behind unequal distributions, and judgements about the fairness of measured inequalities, cannot be settled by plotting of a Lorenz curve alone (Bronfenbrenner 1971). Nonetheless, Lorenz curves remain the accepted standard for a first approximation of distributions of resources across a population.

Since transport facilities and services are inherently spatial, a metric of vertical equity could be the distribution of access or mobility. There could be, for example, a Lorenz curve mapping total travel time to and from work; or, for more detailed network analyses a network, matrix showing relative differences in travel time between specific origins and destinations (Levinson 2002). Gordon and Peters (2011) calculated Lorenz curves and Gini coefficients to obtain an initial approximation of the relative burden of road tolls across the population of greater New York. Other metrics, such as who bears external environmental costs are also possible, the latter being specially important in the environmental justice literature (Di Ciommo & Shiftan 2017). While conceptually the potential applications of distributional analysis to transport services are large, there is relatively little implementation mainly because of data limitations as opposed to the (relatively) data-rich arenas of tax burden, income, and wealth disparities, where pure distributional analysis is well established.

14.6 SOCIAL EXCLUSION AND TRANSPORT DISADVANTAGE

This is not to say that transport equity is not a well-developed field in and of itself. Transport policy has long been concerned with achieving outcomes such as improved mobility, reduced travel times, and increased access, and the effects, such as regional economic development across a whole area or population, that these deliver. Social exclusion is a concept that has been developed which refers to the relationship between a potential user's initial circumstances (such as socioeconomic and demographic profile) and the accessibility and mobility levels they possess. Poor and older people, for example, often have limited access to transport and/or live far away from work and social and other amenities. Hence these groups can be said to be socially excluded in many places. The phrase entered the European social science literature in the 1980s after which it became a benchmark of policy in the UK Labour government of Prime Minister Tony Blair (Kenyon et al. 2002).

The concept of social exclusion makes a direct link between socioeconomic status and transport, with the link being causally two-way: poor transport can make for poor individuals and vice-versa. Equity here refers to equality of actual social and economic outcomes rather than opportunity. Reports by the UK's Social Exclusion Unit (SEU) make this point by referring to evidence showing that poor transport yields, or is associated with, poor social metrics in areas such as employment, education, and health (UKSEU 2003).

Accessibility generally refers to the relative location of opportunities, which is a function of spatial form and transportation supply. Mobility generally refers to how much a person is able to travel, and how much travel they actually undertake. Transport disadvantage refers to the degree of limitations in accessibility and mobility specific individuals and groups have to contend with. Access to transport is closely intertwined with social exclusion and affected by proximity to essential services, social connections, and amenity. In areas with (a) many transport alternatives, (b) dense locations containing many diverse work, home, and diversion opportunities, and (c) relative equality of access across all groups to both, there can be said to be relatively little transport disadvantage. But where one or more of these conditions is violated, some transport disadvantage occurs in which some people have less mobility and/or accessibility than others (Guiliano 2001, 15871–15872).

Thus, poor people generally have less access to private cars because they cannot afford them; but the relative transport disadvantage that flows from this will vary according to the locational accessibility they face in getting to work, services, and amenities. Poor people in rural areas without cars will generally have more reduced transport access to opportunities than similar populations in dense urban areas with good public transit. But even within the latter category, the elderly poor may be more disadvantaged than the young because of disability. And urban poor generally often have to live in peripheral locations far from services and employment and poorly served by transit. Some therefore refer to "transport poverty", defining it as a condition of reduced access to employment and services due to inadequate or costly transport facilities (Gunn 2018, 24). Others have spoken of a "mobility gap" or "accessibility deficit" for low-income, mobility-impaired, very elderly, ethnic minority, and female populations (Knowles 2006, 422).

Transport disadvantage does not necessarily just affect the poor. Deregulated airline service has increased accessibility in some hub markets of hub-and-spoke networks, but decimated it in many locations that have been bypassed as a result, creating localised "pockets of pain" (Knowles 2006, 419). Rural communities more generally have seen closures of schools, shops, and essential services, leaving those who remain cut off from easy access to even the basics, much less more discretionary activity. In the UK, for example, between 1965 and 1990, approximately 15% of rural communities lost their last general store or food shop and around 200 post offices closed each year between 1980 and 2000. Rural schools also closed at increasing rates in the 1970s and early 1980s, the rate of closure slowing after that but still on-going up to around 1997. These kinds of spatial eviscerations can deeply affect even relatively affluent communities (Davoudi & Stead 2002, 270–272).

14.7 TRANSPORT JUSTICE AND RIGHTS

Khisty (1996) distinguishes between: principles of justice, which allow one to determine whether a state of affairs is just or unjust; and theories of justice that allow one to apply the principles to specific situations. Three types of principles are specified: rights (what a society defines to be acceptable or unacceptable), deserts (what is due a person depending upon their abilities, virtue, etc.), and needs (what a person requires to exist in society).

A right generally can be broadly defined as a legitimate claim to protect specific personal interests such as freedom of movement. A civil right is more specific in that it refers to the rights that individual members of an organised political community have by virtue of that membership. A negative right is the right to say "no" to harm or some undesired or unwanted demand or circumstance. A positive right is the right to some social benefit that must be granted if one asserts their right (Dworkin 1977).

Justice can be defined as a situation where no one's rights are being infringed and all are being honoured. In a transport justice framework, negatively disadvantaged groups are not to bear disproportionate burdens or costs of transport investment decisions and service provisions. If such burdens are unavoidable, all groups must be adequately and equally compensated for the burden they bear. For example, if housing is provided to people displaced by a highway project, it must be provided to all affected parties and be of the same quality for all (Sanchez et al. 2004). On the other side of the coin, if all members of a community have a right to equal transport service, then the provision of a transport network in that area should deliver at least minimum equal levels of service to all at a given price.

Since a positive right is the right to demand a social benefit, all individuals must have access to equal and adequate transport services with similar accessibility to services and relevant employment. For example, US Urban Mass Transit Administration (UMTA) regulations, still in effect, state that

> No person or group of persons shall be discriminated against with regard to the routing, scheduling, or quality of service of transportation service furnished as a part of the project on the basis of race, colour, or national origin. Frequency of service, age and quality of vehicles assigned to routes, quality of stations serving different routes, and location of routes may not be determined on the basis of race, color, or national origin.
>
> (NCHRP 2003, 5)

In the US, transport equity policy concern is very closely tied to civil rights law. In 1968, Martin Luther King argued that adequate transport was a fundamental right of American citizenship, noting that

> Urban transit systems...have become a genuine civil rights issue – and a valid one – because the layout of rapid-transit systems determines the accessibility of jobs to the African-American community. If transportation systems in American cities could be laid out so

> as to provide an opportunity for poor people to get meaningful employment, then they could begin to move into the mainstream of American life.
>
> (quoted in Sanchez et al. 2004, 3)

The US Civil Rights Act of 1964, which guarantees protection against discrimination in all public services on the basis of arbitrary classifications, was born out of the struggle that King and others fought in and has heavily influenced and shaped US transport justice and equity policy. These protections are not consistently enforced but are heavily influenced by the American concept of transport as a basic civil right (Sanchez et al. 2004, 35).

14.8 SOCIAL EXCLUSION VERSUS RIGHTS AND JUSTICE

Rights are intrinsic and generally drawn from deontological ethics rather than instrumental consequentialist theories. Thus, social exclusion and other equity policies potentially thus differ from a rights approach in important ways. The exclusion approach does not explicitly aver a "right" to transport but instead defines and measures the problem across a community in order to change those measures for the better. In this sense social exclusion is narrower. The rights view considers the individual as a unit of planning while the exclusion view downplays or ignores the individual; and by definition a right is more fundamental and secure than a social policy since a social policy can be changed but a right, barring epochal shifts, is generally inviolable, or at least not easy to alter (Gordon 2015).

However, social exclusion is in some ways broader and more robust than civil rights. Equity refers to actual equality of social and economic outcomes rather than just the opportunity or baseline requirements implicit in a right. Exclusion makes a direct link between socioeconomic status and transport, with a two-way causality: poor transportation can make for poor individuals and vice-versa. Because of this holistic linkage, policies designed to address transport inequity can be more full-bodied, especially against the sort of indirect discrimination which Martin Luther King and other civil rights leader were focused on after achieving *de jure* desegregation (Gordon 2015).

Thus, justice and equity, while related, are clearly not the same thing in a transport context. Transport justice emphasises equal standing under legal and policy processes to ensure that no one group is disadvantaged (or, conversely, advantaged) when those processes are carried out. Of course in the end one group may well win while another loses. For example, voting rights legislation is designed to provide everyone equal opportunity to vote and have that vote count equally. It is not designed to ensure a "just" outcome on election day. Equity, on the other hand, has more to do with actual outcomes than process. A judgement is made about which groups get what, perhaps setting floors on minimally acceptable outcomes. But, unlike a justice/rights approach, these are not entitlements *per se* and can be reversed (or expanded) depending upon the policy environment of the time.

14.9 MEASURING TRANSPORT EQUITY

Much attention has been paid to measurement of transport equity and justice. Lorenz curves have already been mentioned as a canonical but underutilised metric. But there are many others available to operationalise equity assessments, ranging from aiming for equal shares of expenditure or service provision for all, down to criteria such as maximising average net benefit with a minimum floor benefit for all users.

The earliest phases of transport justice and equity measurement focused on direct outcomes, both in normative and positive terms (see Chapter 13). A meta-review of toll road equity analysis in Texas and California concluded that low-income users were as often as likely to drive on toll roads as high-income users and that they often see benefit from the existence of such roads; the study did not assess actual relative toll burden (Ungemah 2007). A later study of California roads drilled down deeper and examined total user tax burdens and distribution of broad time saving across different income quintiles (Agrawal et al. 2023).

This earlier work has been expanded on greatly in a number of ways. The equity dimensions of all modes, not just roads, have been studied extensively, with the links between modal accessibility disparities and social exclusion being teased out and specified in more detail than ever before. The impacts of social exclusion and transport disadvantage have been measured not just in objective terms but increasingly in subjective terms as well, capturing the "disutility" aspects that economists include in their generalised transport cost models. A burgeoning array of survey research has documented transport disadvantage and exclusion impacts such as deficiencies in reported levels of personal well-being, sense of community, strength of close relationships, and strength of wider networks. These deficiencies have sometimes been combined into social exclusion risk ratings for different groups, with their spatial incidence mapped. These "welfare" costs have often been monetised, to better allow for incorporation into economic evaluation methods and to be weighed against the broader societal and government costs of amelioration programmes (see Chapter 15) (Weisbrod & Hensher 2023, Section 3.2).

REFERENCES

Agrawal, A. W., Speroni, S., Manville, M., & Taylor, B. D. (2023). *Pay-as-you-go driving: Examining possible road-user charge rate structures for California.* Mineta Transportation Institute.

Arrow, K. J. (1950). A difficulty in the concept of social welfare. *Journal of Political Economy*, 58, 328–346.

Atkinson, A. B. (1971). *On economic inequality*. Oxford University Press.

Becker, G. (1971). *The economics of discrimination* (2nd edition). University of Chicago Press.

Bronfenbrenner, M. (1971). *Income distribution theory*. Alstom-Atherton.

Davoudi, S., & Stead, D. (2002). Urban-rural relationships: an introduction and brief history. *Built Environment Journal*, 28(4), 269–277.

Di Ciommo, F., & Shiftan, Y. (2017). Transport equity analysis. *Transport Reviews*, 37(2), 139–151.

Dworkin, R. (1977). *Taking rights seriously*. Harvard University Press.

Gordon, C. (2015). Varieties of transportation justice: US transportation equity policy and the civil rights movement. *Transportation Research Record*, 2531(1), 180–186.

Gordon, C., & Peters, J. (2011). Measuring toll burdens: applying Lorenz curves to a detailed dataset of users of MTA Bridges in New York City. *Transportation Research Record*, 2221, 96–103.

Gordon, C., & Zimmerman, A. (2009). Fair shares: A preliminary framework and case analyzing the ethics of offshoring. *Science and Engineering Ethics*, 16(2), 325–353.

Guiliano, G. (2001).Transportation geography. In Smelser Neil J. & Baltes, Paul B. (eds). *International encyclopedia of the social & behavioral sciences*. Pergamon, 15866–15873.

Gunn, S. (2018).The history of transport systems in the UK. In *Future of mobility: evidence review foresight*, Government Office for Science, Centre for Urban History, University of Leicester.

Jaspers, E. (2016). Values. *Oxford Bibliographies*. www.oxfordbibliographies.com/display/document/obo-9780199756384/obo-9780199756384-0182.xml

Karner, A., Pereira, R. H., & Farber, S. (2024). *Advances and pitfalls in measuring transportation equity*. Transportation, 1–29.

Kenyon, S., Lyons, G., & Rafferty, J. (2002). Transport and social exclusion: Investigating the possibility of promoting inclusion through virtual mobility. *Journal of Transport Geography*, 10(3), 207–219.

Khisty, C.J. (1996). Operationalizing concepts of equity for public project investments. *Transportation Research Record*, 1559, 94–99.

King, B. H, & McCusker, B. (2007). Environment and development in the former South African bantustans. *The Geographical Journal*, 173(1), 6–12.

Knowles, R. D. (2006). Transport shaping space: Differential collapse in time–space. *Journal of Transport Geography*, 14, 407–425.

Levinson, D. (2002). Identifying winners and losers in transportation. *Transportation Research Record*, 1812, 179–185.

Matthias, M. (2024). Pass Law. www.britannica.com/topic/pass-law. Last Updated: July 25, 2024.

Musgrave, R. A. (1969). Provision for social goods. *Public Economics*, 124–144.

NCHRP (2003) *Legal research digest 48: Civil rights in transportation projects.* National Cooperative Highway Research Program. http://onlinepubs.trb.org/onlinepubs/nchrp/nchrp_lrd_48.pdf

Sanchez, T. W. et al. (2004). *Moving to equity: Addressing inequitable effects of transportation policies on minorities.* The Civil Rights Project at Harvard University.

UKSEU (2003). *Making the connections: Final report on transportation and social exclusion.* United Kingdom Social Exclusion Unit.

Ungemah, D. (2007). This land is your land, this land is my land: Addressing equity and fairness in tolling and pricing. *Transportation Research Record*, 2013(1), 13–20.

Weisbrod, G., & Hensher, D. A. (2023). Improving transportation project evaluation by recognizing the role of spatial scale and context in measuring non-user economic benefits. *Transport Policy*, 144, 80–89.

CHAPTER 15

Economic evaluation of transport

15.1 INTRODUCTION: EVALUATING POLICY AND PROGRAMME OUTCOMES

A key issue for assessing any action (policy, programme, intervention, investment, etc.) is to determine its effect on a situation. Monitoring and evaluation (M&E) lies at the heart of much programme management, its main purpose being to observe and record changes as they arise after a policy action is effected. The technical terms for these changes are impacts. More formally, impact can be defined as the difference between outcomes with the programme and without it. M&E cannot get at causality, i.e. how programme effects flow through to final results. The main concern is to properly observe and record all changes in a relevant situation. Impact Evaluation (IE) has the broader goal of measuring these differences in a way that can attribute these changes to the programme, separated out from other influences.

Formally, an IE compares a state of the world with and without a given programme (intervention is the term of art in the health field) at a given point in time after the programme has fully taken effect. This is known as the "counterfactual" and is akin to a controlled comparison in an experimental setting. This change can be modelled as follows:

$$\alpha = (Y \mid P=1) - (Y \mid P = 0)$$

in which α refers to the difference between the state of the world (Y) with an intervention (P = 1) and without one (P = 0).

DOI: 10.4324/9781003350866-19

BOX 15.1 INTRODUCTORY CASE: ENCOURAGING WALKING AND CYCLING TO SCHOOL

The Industrial Revolution brought many, many changes to society. One was the institution of compulsory mass public education for children. Prior to this, children were generally socialised and educated within households that were largely self-sufficient, with little need for formal education. Industrialisation, however, created an increasingly interdependent economy based on technical skills of one sort or another and with adult work separated from the home. Public schooling was designed to care for children while their parents worked, and also to train and prepare them for adult work and functioning in a modernised society.

This created a new transport problem of handling mass movements of children to and from school. Prior to World War II this was not generally a major societal issue since most families tended to work within walking distance of their homes and schools were generally located nearby (with exceptions, of course, not least when official racial segregation policies were involved, as with South African apartheid or the Segregated South in the US – see Chapter 14 opening section). Thus, most children could walk to and from school unaided.

However, with the rise of car travel and suburbanisation, walking became less of an option for many families. Government school buses, or cars driven by parents, became the logistical solution for moving large numbers of children in a synchronised fashion to and from primary and secondary education centres. This came at the cost of less walking which, combined with other social changes, has led to what public health experts refer to as an "epidemic" of physical inactivity in children. This has major health implications engendering substantial costs over the long-run in the form of increased illness and death from conditions such as obesity and diabetes.

For this reason there has been a sustained focus on policies encouraging children to walk to school. In a public health setting, these policies are referred to as interventions and there is no one-size-fits-all shape these have to be effective. One set of programmes encourage children to cycle or walk to school while convincing their parents of the safety and benefit of letting them do so. These include "walking school buses" where adult volunteers walk groups of children to and from school; school travel plans and "Safe Routes to School" which identify barriers to active travel to school (such as busy crossings) and correct these barriers through either public information or modifications to the infrastructure, like building designated paths; and public education, ranging from cycling/walking promotion programmes to training children in cycling competency, and providing tailored independent mobility plans for particular individuals.

There have been numerous evaluations of these types of programmes and the general findings are that they do result in reductions in morbidity (incidence of illness) and mortality (incidence of death and change in lifespan). Indeed the life-cycle impacts are arguably greater for children than for adults since the physical inactivity in childhood accumulates into worse health in adulthood. Some interventions in some contexts are more effective than others, however, so intervention design is a critical element to consider.

In general well-designed walking/cycling to school programmes do improve child health. But are the health benefits obtained worth it? This may seem like an inappropriate question, but if the costs of delivering positive health changes are greater than the benefits obtained, then from a pure net resources gain position, society is going backwards. This is where economic evaluation comes in. There are various methods, all having the primary aim of measuring the full resource costs of interventions and comparing these with the full resource benefits they incur, to see whether society is better or worse off in material terms.

This is not an easy task. Intervention costs are relatively straightforward as these are generally well captured in programme budgets. But measuring benefits are much more fraught. Even if there is a high level of confidence that an intervention does deliver a specific set of health impacts, their economic valuation is difficult. How much is a month of life extended, or the avoidance of diabetes, actually worth in monetary terms? This is one of the many issues that economic evaluation must grapple with.

Despite these difficulties there does need to be comparative analysis, both between types of interventions with a specific purpose and between programmes with entirely different objectives. Walking and cycling to school is indubitably valuable. But so is the health of the aged and the alleviation of poverty. How should policy-makers allocate their resources across these different areas? These are inherently political questions that economics cannot fully address. But economic evaluation can help determine the relative economic efficiency of different alternatives, which is a good starting point.

(The discussion in this section is drawn from Gordon 2018)

M&E aims at the factual, i.e., what is happening on the ground without disentangling what are causes, what are effects, and how the two relate to one another. IE aims at the counterfactual question of "what would the world look like if the program being analysed didn't exist"? As an example, M&E of a walk-to-school incentives programme might show strong health gains occurring in tandem with a public information programme promoting healthy weight and exercise (a factual gain). By contrast an IE would aim to disentangle the separate effects of the two interventions from each other, and from general background changes, like income growth, to reveal how much gain came from the interventions versus broader factors unrelated to the programme (a counterfactual gain).

The number and types of counterfactual policy questions are myriad. How much does a driver education programme improve road safety? What is the impact of a new road on regional traffic flow? How do lowered transit fares affect transit usage? One has to precisely construct these questions, though. Thus, the first question above focuses on an outcome, a substantive change in a societal variable of genuine interest, namely road safety. The last two focus however on what are referred to as outputs: intermediate variables that are of interest only because of the wider outcomes they may contribute to. Traffic flow and transit usage are means towards broader ends such as lowered congestion across a transport system or reduction of transport disadvantage and social exclusion. It is these outcomes that are of ultimate interest from a policy perspective, and comparisons should be made that clarify how specific interventions change them. Intermediate output questions may be needed to get at this (and agencies and other service delivery entities may legitimately focus on their more narrow purviews). But the analysis should go beyond this if the interest is to get at genuine impact on final outcomes.

The defining characteristics of an IE are thus the use of some sort of counterfactual analysis, hopefully well-defined and feasible, with a focus on ultimate outcomes, using a well-constructed comparison. The information gained through an IE should identify the actual impacts of the programme as separate from other influences, how much better off the beneficiaries are because of the programme/policy, and how outcomes would change if programme design were changed.

IE can be done *ex post* (after the fact) of a project or intervention. In this case one is examining what happened. It can also be *ex ante* (before the fact) of a proposed intervention, in which case the analyst is aiming to predict potential effects. Obviously the two are not mutually exclusive and it may be a good idea to do both. In all cases the intervention should be precisely defined whether it be a project (typically referring to a narrower focus action, such as the building of road bypass) or programme (which broadly refers to a package of projects, like the upgrading of a road combined with public information campaigns about safe driving).

(The discussion above draws heavily on Gertler et al. 2016).

15.2 ECONOMIC EVALUATION

IE is a generic term. Economic evaluation is a specific sort of IE referring to any method of determining and measuring economic impacts, and/or putting all impacts, economic and otherwise, in economic terms (usually a monetised value). The most full-bodied method according to economists is cost–benefit analysis (CBA) (synonymously also referred to as benefit–cost analysis (BCA)). CBA is meant to capture real net resource gains or losses to society that result from specific actions that are the subject of analysis. Generally, if society has a net resource gain from an action (such as a project like a new cycling path), then the action is one that should be undertaken by society. If society has a net loss, then that action should not be taken. CBA is the major focus of this chapter.

A more limited method is a financial analysis. In this case, only monetary flows are considered, and not larger real resource flows such as non-monetary and intangible benefits and costs (see Chapter 10). Often entities undertaking a project are primarily concerned with its effect on the entity's net financial position. For example, an agency may want to invest in projects that make the agency money regardless of whether society as a whole benefits or loses. A road toll authority may set tolls, for example, to maximise its own revenues rather than optimising network traffic flow. In this case, the analysis takes the perspective of the net financial position of the agency undertaking the project rather than society as a whole. This is not an illegitimate exercise, and sometimes necessary in its own right (if, for example, an agency is legally required to be financially self-sufficient). But it is not CBA.

A related but somewhat simpler economic evaluation method is cost-effectiveness analysis (CEA). Here one is not trying to estimate an overall gain or loss but just the cost of achieving a particular gain in a desired objective as delivered by a particular intervention. For example, one might compare the cost of saving an individual life by different road safety interventions, e.g. a traffic signal versus a roundabout. In this case, the lowest-cost intervention per life-saved would be preferred. CEA requires less data than CBA but it takes the value of the stated goal and its benefits as a given, assessing the least-cost method of attaining it rather than measuring costs against measured benefits of the outcome.

15.3 COST–BENEFIT ANALYSIS (CBA)

CBA is based on the core theory which collapses all causes and effects into the realm of material production and consumption. Every cause and effect can be reduced to materially based metrics: net profit or income on the production side and net utility derived from consumption of activities and goods and services on the consumption side. This is done for individual agents and the total well-being position of society at any given time is simply the sum of the net profit/utility positions of the agents. This is what economists refer to as social welfare, with changes being referred to as welfare gains or losses. Net benefit in a CBA therefore equals the total of individual utility/profit (economic benefits) minus the total of individual utility/profit losses (economic costs), all valued in market (i.e. monetary) terms. The appropriate valuation standard is said to be derived from individual willingness to pay (WTP) for the goods and services provided (Mishan & Quah 2020).

In the core model, social welfare is maximised by the workings of the market in equilibrium delivering a "social" optimum. But this ideal is rarely met and some kind of nonmarket intervention is often required to correct market failure or to meet non-economic objectives such as merit wants (see Chapter 13). CBA economically evaluates the intervention. If society is judged to have a net gain (as defined above) from an action, then the action will improve welfare, and the action should be undertaken. If there is a net welfare loss making society worse off, the action should be shelved. If society is neither worse off nor better off, it will be "indifferent" to taking the action or not.

The concept of counterfactual welfare comparison is conceptually diagrammed in Figure 15.1. The current state of affairs without the action is referred to as the "without" case, and welfare in this state is compared to a notional state of the world and its social welfare with the action undertaken, i.e. the "with" case. Thus, the world's social welfare as it exists now is compared with another possible world which is identical to it except for one thing: the alternative world contains an action (such as a project) of interest to the analyst. CBA compares the two worlds to see whether, in the alternative world, there is a greater total social welfare or not and how much of this can be ascribed to the action specifically. In CBA this is collapsed into the total welfare across agents in a world without the action and the total welfare of agents across the world with it, subtracting the one from the other to get the net gain or loss of total social welfare that the project results in.

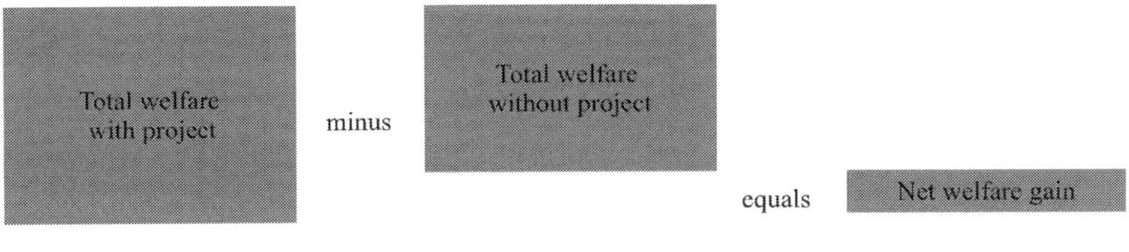

FIGURE 15.1
The concept of a CBA counterfactual welfare comparison.

15.4 NET GAINS VERSUS TRANSFERS

In general, an economic analysis will adopt the perspective of the whole society. It is important therefore to distinguish between overall (net) gains and losses and transfers. Net gains/losses refer to increases/decreases in the total resources available to society. Transfers refer to movements of resources from one group to another. A project will typically result in both transfers and gains/losses. The analyst needs to avoid the possibility of counting transfers as net gains/losses. Even if the concern is with distributional equity, and transfers are of primary interest, they still must be carefully distinguished from net changes.

Figure 15.2 provides a conceptual example of the difference between transfers and net gains or losses in a supply and demand analysis based on all the usual assumptions (perfect competition etc.).

Suppose the government is considering building a new High Speed Rail (HSR) corridor. This corridor will increase travel speeds and reduce supplier costs, thus shifting the S curve of suppliers from S_1 to S_2. Assuming for simplicity that this is the only impact of the project, the initial supply-demand equilibrium in the "without" baseline delivers a quantity Q_1, at a price of P_1.

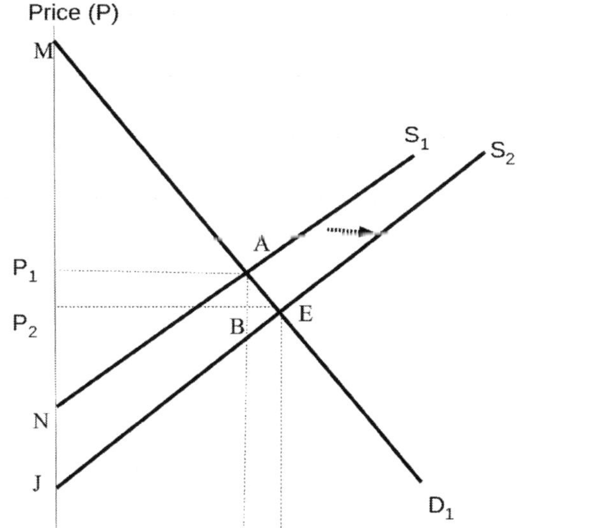

FIGURE 15.2
Net changes versus transfer in CBA.

The new equilibrium delivers a lower price and quantity at P_2 and Q_2, due to the new HSR line increasing supply while lowering costs.

In equilibrium, consumers pay the market price for all the units they consume. But with a downward sloping demand curve, consumers would pay a lot more for the first unit consumed than they actually do, though with diminishing utility from additional units of the good: imagine, for example, the difference between the first milkshake and the tenth. In a perfectly competitive market, however, they pay the same price for all units, that being for the last (marginal) unit consumed. This un-priced gain in satisfaction is referred to as consumer surplus (CS) and represents a net welfare gain for consumers. The HSR corridor creates a new equilibrium where CS is captured by the triangle of MEP_2, which is larger than the initial triangle of MAP_1.

Supply is roughly analogous to demand. Suppliers have an opportunity cost corresponding to each unit that they produce. However, like consumers, they sell each unit at the marginal price determined by market equilibrium. But given a typical supply curve, the price received for each unit sold is the same for all units even though the producer is willing to accept a much lower price for the first unit than units sold after it. Thus, suppliers receive a producer surplus (PS) analogous to CS, though this is based on net profit rather than utility. In this example here too there is an increase, from the inverted triangle area P_1AN without the HSR corridor as compared to the larger triangle of P_2EJ with it.

CS and PS are both net gains. But there are various other changes amounting to transfers from one group to another, such as the rectangle P_1ABP_2 which is a consumer welfare gain at the expense of producers. These transfers are distinct from net changes, and in CBA it is only this net gain or loss that matters, although policy-makers are generally also interested in distribution of gains. The distinction between the two is easy to make looking at textbook diagrams, but often unclear in practice, where the mistake of "double-counting" of transfers as net gains or losses is easy to make. In this case there are net gains from the project, but no information about costs is provided here and these must be subtracted from gains to make a go/no-go decision.

15.5 TRANSPORT BENEFIT VALUATION AND MONETISATION: VTTS

Some transport project costs, such as direct costs of infrastructure expansion, can be drawn from market information, which can be assumed to have accurately done the valuing and monetising already. However, for goods and services provided outside markets, or through markets with serious imperfections, such as externality or imperfect competition, this should not be taken for granted even if there are market prices to draw upon.

Transport project benefits are more subtle. Because consumers do not desire transport in and of itself, the primary benefit of a transport improvement comes from the utility gains (lowered disutility) coming from lowered transport times. Unit travel time value is determined according to the corresponding WTP each consumer has for this savings to arrive at VOTT (see Chapter 7). VOTT is then multiplied by travel time savings delivered by a transport project to calculate the value of travel time saved (VTTS). VTSS is the standard benefit measure used in almost all economic evaluations of transport interventions, typically monetised (i.e. expressed in units of a particular currency) so that all gains and losses can be compared.

Strand (1999) argues that the evaluation of time savings should be evaluated in three stages: (1) measurement of time and time savings; (2) aggregation; (3) monetisation. Problems encountered in stages (1) and (2) are generally glossed over by many analysts, often managed through monetisation adjustments in stage (3). But this approach amounts to a guess and a tweak, not a genuine solution. VOTT usually varies even over a single trip, between the first minute of travel and the last. It will also vary contextually according to a traveller's preferences, income, time of day, and trip purpose, among other things. In practice one cannot calculate and apply all of these values, and so broad averages are used, such as the value of leisure and work travel, or peak and off-peak journeys. For VTTS there is a difference at the aggregate level between the value of, for example, 60 people saving 1 minute of travel time, as opposed to 1 person saving 60 minutes, even though formally they are assumed to add up to the same thing. Approximations for these various issues will often be "near enough", but not always. Travel time savings constitute 75%–80% of the total benefits of most projects, so getting the VTTS as accurately as possible is critical (Strand 1999, 47).

Finally, VTTS is not a complete picture of transport benefit. There are many amenities, agglomeration, and other benefits that must be considered as well and they often interact with one another. Some of these issues have been considered in Chapters 4 and 13. But consider an example of the WTP for travel time saved on a train trip shortened by tunnels. Suppose that this is achieved by losing views of beautiful scenery along the route (Strand 1999, 48–49). Should this loss be counted as a cost? Theoretically, yes, since it is a loss of consumer utility, and it might be very important in some contexts. But impacts such as these are often not even conceived of by analysts and thus ignored. They may or may not be significant enough to change the ultimate result of a CBA. But they should be considered more fully where they might be relevant.

15.6 TIME VALUE AND DISCOUNTING

The core model by default ignores time. Temporal processes may be admitted but they are typically glossed over, with the focus being on a "final" static equilibrium. For most projects this is clearly an inadequate simplification, since their resource flows and impacts generally unfold slowly. Intertemporal flows between present and future (i.e. flows across time periods) have different time values from each other. Resource flows received or paid in the future are worth less than current flows received or paid today because there is an opportunity cost differentiating the two. Resources tomorrow cannot be spent today and that lack of use for them has a real cost in that one cannot follow up opportunities that having those resources in hand now would offer, such as putting money in the bank and earning interest. On the other side of the coin (so to speak), sacrifices that must be made later are not obviously as onerous as those made presently (Heilmann 2017, 1334–1335).

This is why discounting is used to adjust flows across time to account for their relative opportunity cost in present value (PV) terms. Arithmetically, this is a fairly simple operation. If the rate of interest is 7% annually, the current PV of \$100 in one year is equal to \$100/(1 + 0.07) = \$93.46 (where 7% is expressed in decimal terms as 0.07). More generally, to calculate the PV of a series of cash flows over time, one adds up the series:

$$PV = C_1/(1 + r_1) + C_2/(1 + r_2)^2 + \ldots C_n/(1 + r_n)^n$$

where n refers to time period n. The higher the discount rate, the lower the PV of flows further out in time; the lower the discount rate, the higher the PV. Flows in the present are discounted by 0% because they do not need any temporal adjustment. Flows further out will almost always have positive discount rates.

An important issue in discounting is the choice of discount rate since these will markedly affect the PV. For most private projects, the market rate of interest, as determined by the supply and demand for loanable funds, will prevail, adjusted for different levels of risk present in both projects and entities undertaking the investment. Economic theory assumes that if financial markets are functioning well, the market rate of interest should thus represent the true opportunity cost of capital. However, if they are not, this may not be the case. But this complication is beyond the scope of this discussion.

For government projects there is an additional possible choice of discount rate: the social discount rate. Government potentially can draw not just from private investors, but from all agents in society, both savers and spenders. That means that not only is the government diverting investment funds to public use; it is also diverting funds which could otherwise be used for consumption to that use, and that generally is presumed to have a lower social opportunity cost (and hence discount rate) because it is an activity with no financial yield. One proxy for the social discount rate is the rate charged on government bonds, which is typically lower than private rates, at least for creditworthy governments. However, there are cases where there is an argument for using a discount rate even lower than this. The basic idea is that lower social discount rates value the welfare of future generations more relative to present ones as compared to (higher) private rates and are therefore more appropriate for government spending, which is at least partly meant to be stewarding funds in such a way as to maximise the welfare of all generations (Paulden 2014). The specific discount rate that should be used however will vary according to actual context. In practice, discount rate choices can be gamed to make a project look better (or worse) than it actually is. This is a real risk but does not therefore imply that lower-than-market rates should be ruled out as a matter of course.

15.7 DECISION RULES: NPV AND PROJECT INDEPENDENCE

A decision rule is a criterion which a decision-maker uses to make a decision. An example from political theory would be majority rule: do something only if 50% plus one or more of the voters say to do it; otherwise don't do it. In CBA the decision rule is to go with any project that has a positive net welfare gain for society. When discounting is involved, this rule is expressed in terms of net PV (NPV). NPV takes the value of present and future discounted resource inflows from an investment (which represent the gross benefits) and subtracts the discounted resource outflows required to make the investment (which represent the gross costs). That is, $NPV = PV_{benefits} - PV_{costs}$. If NPV is positive, this indicates that a project returns a net resource gain to society over all flows over time; if negative, then the value of money being put into the project over time is worth more than the money being returned by the project.

Most standard discussions of CBA make two implicit assumptions: that projects are independent of one another; and that there is an unconstrained resource budget for projects. This is what the NPV decision rule just outlined is based on. However, finance theory indicates that there is actually more than one decision rule for project selection, depending upon the conditions in which projects are considered. The negative NPV rule is essentially a first-best rule. But there are many second-best cases where modified decision rules are required (see Chapter 13).

The first-best case, as already mentioned, is of independent projects and no budget constraint. The first condition refers to a situation where there is absolutely no interdependence of any kind between one proposed action or another. The second refers to a situation where there are unlimited resources available to invest. Neither of these conditions generally holds in practice, especially in transport, where there is often a great deal of interrelationship between different project alternatives, almost always undertaken with constrained budgets.

If a budget constraint is present, and projects are independent, then a society should pick the portfolio of projects that has the highest total NPV. Obviously, this rule still excludes negative NPV projects. But it also rules out doing every available positive NPV project, leaving some potential net gains unrealised. As an example, suppose a maritime shipping firm has only $160 million to spend in a current budget period and has three projects it could undertake: (A) buying some new ships; (B) upgrading its intermodal terminal; (C) upgrading its scheduling software. The NPV of A is $150 million; of B $50 million; and of C $10 million. These projects are independent of one another in that doing one does not in any way preclude doing the others.

To undertake all three projects would cost $210 million, which is above its $160 million budget, so a choice has to be made. Project A has the highest NPV at $150 million. But choosing this one leaves the firm with $10 million unspent and idle. This is better than a portfolio consisting of B and C, which has a joint NPV of $60 million, while leaving $100 million in idle funds. The best choice that the firm can afford is a portfolio of Projects A and C. This has the highest NPV of all the portfolios, of $160 million, and is within the firm's budget (and in fact exhausts it). Granted, this is a contrived example since all available funds are invested, and this may not always be the case. But the rule is clear: the portfolio of projects with the highest NPV within the budget constraint should be undertaken, even if there are funds left over.

Another second-best rule comes in the case where there are unlimited funds, but mutually exclusive projects. Suppose the maritime firm is now faced with three different projects: (A) building an entirely new terminal in place of its existing one on its existing site which yields an NPV of $150 million; (B) expanding its existing cargo handling terminal, with

TABLE 15.1

Mutually exclusive project NPV rankings (see text)

Project	NPV	Rank
Project A	$150 million	1
Project B	$50 million	2
Project C	$10 million	3

an NPV of $50 million; or (C) knocking down its terminal and using the emptied dock space to allow for more efficient movement of vehicles, with an NPV of $10 million. Only one of these options is possible because there is interdependence between the options. In this case the decision rule is to do the project with the highest ranking NPV. The options are laid out in Table 15.1. (This is an extreme case; sometimes projects are not completely exclusive of one another and not completely independent either, as with, for example, a suite of partial facility refurbishment and rebuild options. The mechanics there are more complex. But the basic principle is the same.)

With independent projects and an unlimited budget, the firm would do all of these projects because they all have positive NPV. However, since in this case it is physically impossible to do all of these projects because they are mutually exclusive, the firm will pick the one which adds the most NPV, and that is Project A. If there is a budget constraint, the same rule applies except the firm will pick the highest NPV project that it can afford.

The core idea underneath all these scenarios is to maximise *feasible* NPV, feasibility varying with operating conditions.

15.8 PROJECT RISK AND CBA

Projects are inherently risky. Risk is a term with varying meanings but in essence it refers to a distribution of possible outcomes with known probabilities. Uncertainty, by contrast, refers to possible outcomes with unknown probabilities and/or entirely unknown possibilities. There are various types of risk, but of concern here is project-specific risk, which refers to the possibility that the project will not generate the returns that the entity undertaking it was planning on.

CBA can incorporate risk in various ways. The simplest method is to use risk-adjusted discount rates (RADRs). The appropriate discount rate which captures true cost of capital is used, with either a premium added to that rate to account for additional risk or a discount subtracted to account for lower risk. Leaving the discount rate without such adjustments typically indicates that the project-specific risk is at some sort of average of other projects of a similar type.

For example, a private firm with a project with an NPV of $100 million and a market rate of 10% for its cost of capital based on the market rates for similar projects can use 10% as its discount rate if the firm managers think that this project has a risk which is in accord with the risk on similar projects in general. But if managers have reason to believe that the project is riskier than average – that it has a greater chance of exceeding or falling short of expected resource flows over time – then the discount rate should, at a minimum, have a risk premium added to it. If the project is thought to be less risky than average, then a risk discount should be added. In the former case the project's NPV will fall *ceteris paribus*; in the latter case it will rise. This is an appropriate risk-adjusted signal for managers to use as they pick projects.

RADRs are a very crude way of incorporating project risk into a CBA. A somewhat more sophisticated method is to calculate expected values. The basic method of doing this is to assign probability weights to the array of potential returns to come up with a single risk-weighted return which is referred to as the expected return. The formula for doing this for an array of "n" returns is as follows:

$$\text{Expected return} = (\text{Return A} \times \text{probability A}) + (\text{Return B} \times \text{probability B}) \ldots + (\text{Return n} \times \text{probability n}).$$

Of course the probability weights must sum to 1, because the probability of all possible returns added together is 100%.

As an example, if a project has a 50% chance of a net gain of 20% and a 50% chance of a net loss of 10%, the expected rate of return would be 5% (50% × 20% + 50% × −10% = 5%).

As to what projects should be picked, the decision rule of maximising NPV still holds. But now risk appetite needs to be considered as well. This refers to how much risk is acceptable to the managers of the entity investing the funds. A risk-averse entity manager will tend to prefer lower risk projects over higher-risk ones, all other things being equal. A risk-seeking entity will tend to prefer higher-risk projects. A risk-neutral entity will be indifferent to risk. Thus, a risk-seeking manager may well pick a higher-risk project over a lower risk one between two having equal expected values of NPVs, because the manager's risk appetite leads to a preference for projects that have a chance of higher-than-expected potential returns, even though this involves the risk of possibly lower ones. Risk appetite is pertinent in project selection. But it should not be accounted for in CBA, this being a strategic consideration imposed by management.

There are other more sophisticated methods for incorporating risk into project evaluations, such as real options. These are not discussed here. Note also that this chapter is looking only at some basics of incorporating risk into a CBA. The more complex task of actually managing project risk operationally is a different issue, some aspects of which are considered elsewhere in the book.

15.9 MEASURING INTANGIBLES AND EXTERNAL BENEFITS

The discussion thus far has been implicitly focused on tangible user benefits and costs, especially VTTS and other related flow-on effects. Many transport projects, however, involve intangible benefits, as well as external impacts on groups other than transport users, such as the value of recreation, or environmental quality. Tangible and user costs and benefits are hard enough to assess. Intangible and non-user impacts present even greater challenges.

There are a variety of techniques used to measure and value intangibles. The simplest is the direct survey, i.e. to ask people how much a particular intangible is worth to them. The loss of views from moving a train underground, referenced earlier, is an example. People could be surveyed as to how much they value those views and their answers could then be used as a basis for including a monetised project cost of lost views. However, direct surveys are notoriously inaccurate, because people often are not actually sure of what many things are really worth to themselves, and because there can be an incentive to misreport values if those being surveyed surmise that their inputs might affect a project decision, possibly leading them to consciously distort their views with an aim of bending project decisions towards their own interests (Mishan & Quah 2020, Chapter 41).

Nonetheless, stated preferences can still be useful, constituting the core of a whole set of stated preference methods. These tend to take the form of more general attitudinal research which aims to discover general propensities that underlie behaviour and which can thus be used to predict that behaviour. Individuals are asked their opinions about their own actions and from this information more formal decision models can be derived from which values can be inferred. These are not perfect to be sure, but they do get around some of the limitations of using direct survey information (Mishan & Quah 2020, Chapter 41).

More robust approaches use direct observation of agent behaviour where possible, at least of a proxy activity. For example, to continue with the lost views example, analysts might see what travellers are willing to pay on similar train routes with views similar to those that will be lost to impute (i.e. estimate) a more generalised value of those views. But such observations are not always possible. Even if they are, generalising from one case to others is not easy. Valuation of intangibles is thus knotty. Which does not mean that it should not be attempted.

External benefits (and costs) present other problems, some similar and some different. Take valuation of a highway project. One could limit oneself to analysing the costs of construction and maintenance as compared to the value of time saved to commuters due to reduced travel times. However, increased traffic may lead to increased environmental damage, a social cost that is not generally directly captured with market or engineering data. Here too estimates are not straightforward (Mishan & Quah 2020, Chapter 16).

There has been significant progress made in indirect valuation techniques, both in scale and in scope, with more impacts being covered than ever before. CBA practitioners have recognised that transport policy objectives are expanding, with growing emphasis on equity, access, and climate change issues, leading them to enhance CBA in various ways. Equity concerns are sometimes addressed by incorporating distributional weights to different groups, rather in the manner of a notional SWF (see Chapter 14). A precursor to, and sometimes replacement for, this weighting is a disaggregated assessment by income, gender, location, or other group characteristics. Weighting in particular is challenging. But at least CBA is including these aspects more often. Climate change is a particular policy imperative that CBA is increasingly incorporating. The use of shadow carbon prices (a hypothetical surcharge added to reflect carbon emission changes due to a programme) is becoming widespread, as are supplementary analyses focusing on climate change impacts (OECD/ITF 2020).

The single bottom-line measure of positive NPV is also being broadened. Multi-criteria analysis (MCA) is not new but is being resorted to more often to calculate, highlight, and weight performance across multiple aims beyond just economic welfare (OECD/ITF 2020). Triple bottom line (TBL) accounting is a related framework that reports along three dimensions of performance: social, environmental, and financial (Slaper & Hall 2011). In both cases, a single score or index number across these multiple dimensions can be calculated, though the weighting to use in this scoring can be controversial, and with the final number usually very sensitive to weight changes. Of course the separate dimensional scores are available, though these too can offer conflicting messages and don't always provide analytical confidence or clarity for the decision-maker (OECD/ITF 2020). Still, the multiple measures remain available to consider separately.

15.10 COMPLEX CAUSALITY, CO-BENEFITS, AND A PORTFOLIO APPROACH TO ECONOMIC EVALUATION

This discussion concludes with the fact that many transport interventions have very complex causal effects and relationships. CBA assumes that a conceptual controlled comparison can be made within a single theoretical paradigm. However, this framing is often inapplicable. Consider, for example, the relationship between health and transport, a particularly multi-causal phenomenon with backwards, forwards, and cross causal chains. The idea of "co-benefits" arose with the formulation of health impact analysis (HIA), a separate analytical framework designed to capture the fact that in the health arena multiple effects can be yielded by a single cause and multiple causes are often parents to a particular effect. The phrase co-benefit has a somewhat variable definition depending upon the context, but a standard usage defines them as the unplanned positive side effects of a policy occurring in parallel to their intended effects (Zusman et al. 2021). Giles-Corti et al. (2010) define co-benefits as those arising when multiple policy areas and aims are considered concurrently, providing the example of the City of London's initial congestion charge reducing both traffic – its intended effect – and carbon and particulate emissions – its initially unintended but ancillary effect (124). Co-benefit is still a concept mostly confined to the health field. But there is increasing cross-fertilisation between health and transport evaluations in the economic sphere and others.

Another area of complex causality that is grappled with by CBA is the often controversial measurement of "Wider Economic Benefits" (WEB) which refer to the many spatial effects and agglomeration economies that result from transport infrastructure investment, as discussed in Chapter 4. Economic analysts understand the reality of such things. But CBA can still struggle to properly capture, model, or estimate such effects. The fact that they must often be approached in highly politicised settings where methodological manipulation is incentivised doesn't make them any easier. But there is also much attention paid to this area and much modification of CBA to properly capture these impacts as accurately as possible, including sophisticated spatial modelling.

A definitive "fix" for these issues – and others like them – is not likely or even necessarily desirable. CBA remains a very useful economic evaluation tool for transport and it is adapting to changing complexities. But arguably

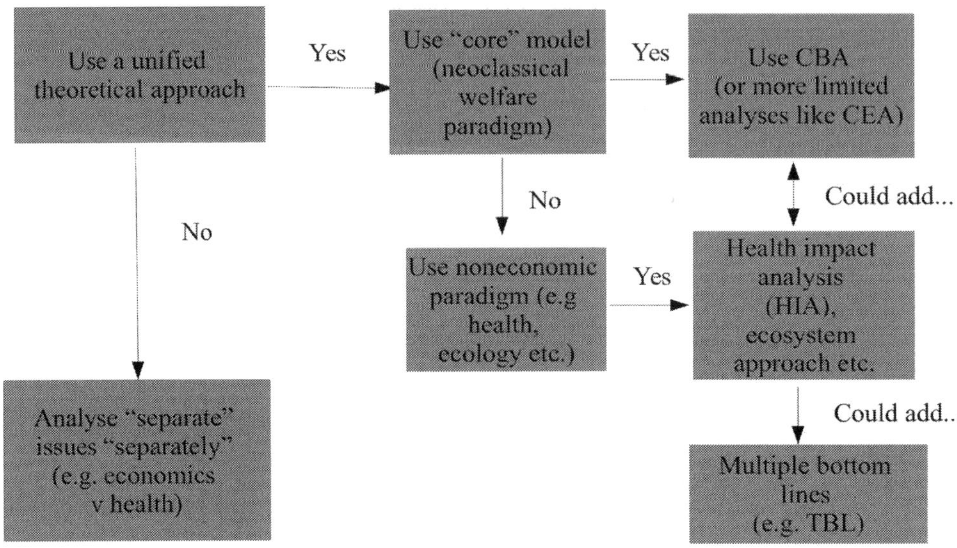

FIGURE 15.3
A decision tree of evaluation approaches.

CBA should not be the only method, or always the default standard, when evaluating interdisciplinary complex causality in particular. There already exists a wide portfolio of methods that can be used for intersecting areas, and these should be drawn on. Figure 15.3 provides a decision tree that can be used as a starting point to assess target effects of transport programmes in health, WEBs, and other areas.

This decision tree presents an analytical ecosystem rather than a single framework that is meant to encompass all phenomenon. The first branch of the tree asks whether to use a unified analytical approach, such as CBA. The advantage of a single paradigm is, of course, consistency: all impacts, causal chains, processes, valuations, and so forth are looked at through a single lens, making comparisons and judgements easier to make. CBA also has the important advantage that all dimensions of society – health, environment, resources, etc. – can be viewed uniformly and consistently in economic terms. It is, as already noted, very adaptable. Even if one does not like its premises, and all that it includes and excludes, one can add categories of benefits and costs, provide auxiliary reports, weigh different outcomes, and so forth, to account for special circumstances. And results need not stop at net benefit measures alone. Other metrics can be estimated, including distributional impacts, financial costs, benefits to specific entities, and multiple bottom lines. And it is possible to modify some of the neoclassical assumptions behind CBA, such as adding "bounded rationality" to agent behaviour.

This does not mean, therefore, that CBA is best for all transport analyses even if one wants to opt for a singular framework. If economics is a minor concern, an HIA (for example) based in broader health models may be more fit-for-purpose. Moving away from economics in this case may actually lead to a stronger and clearer assessment of health issues. One could start with HIA as the fundamental analysis and then add various economic measures and metrics afterwards, perhaps yielding more realistic and accurate results in the domains where it fits best. This could also be true of other areas too, such as environmental and social issues.

The other extreme is to not use a unified approach at all but employ a variety of methods and theoretical bases in a multi-pronged analysis. The disadvantage of such an approach is incomparability across categories, greater amounts of analytical effort, and less clarity for decision-makers. But this may be the better option when dimensions are quite incomparable, such as with merit wants and merit goods; or where there is complex and subtle causality that requires a cross-disciplinary approach for fuller understanding. CBA generally is a good jumping off point for transport economic evaluation, but not always to be relied upon exclusively.

REFERENCES

Gertler, P. J., Martinez, S., Premand, P., Rawlings, L. B., & Vermeersch, C. M. (2016). *Impact evaluation in practice*. World Bank Publications.

Giles-Corti, B., Foster, S., Shilton, T., & Falconer, R. (2010). The co-benefits for health of investing in active transportation. *New South Wales Public Health Bulletin*, 21(6), 122–127.

Gordon, C. (2018). Economic benefits of active transportation. In *Children's active transportation, editor Richard Larouche*. Elsevier, 39–52.

Heilmann, C. (2017). Values in time discounting. *Science and Engineering Ethics*, 23, 1333–1349.

Mishan, E. J., & Quah, E. (2020). *Cost-benefit analysis*. Routledge.

OECD/ITF (2020). *Broadening transport appraisal: Summary and conclusions, roundtable 188*. Organisation for Economic Coordination and Development/ International Transport Forum.

Paulden, M. (2014). Time preference and discounting. In Culyer, Antony J. (ed). *Encyclopedia of health economics*. Elsevier, 395–403.

Slaper, T. F., & Hall, T. J. (2011). The triple bottom line: What is it and how does it work. *Indiana Business Review*, 86(1), 4–8.

Strand, S. (1999). Bottlenecks in transportation research: Understanding behavior, the alpha and omega for the applicability of applied research. *Transportation Research Record*, 1659(1), 46–50.

Zusman, E., Chae, Y., Kim, H., & Farzaneh, H. (2021). An introduction to co-benefits: Core concepts and applications. In Farzaneh, Hooman, Zusman, E Eric, and Chae, Yeora (eds). *Aligning climate change and sustainable development policies in Asia*. Springer. https://doi.org/10.1007/978-981-16-0135-4_1

CHAPTER 16

Logistics, freight, and supply and value chains

16.1 INTRODUCTION: THE FREIGHT ECONOMY OVER THE LONG TERM

The major – though not sole – focus of this book has been on passenger movements. This is appropriate in the sense that these are the larger domain in terms of sheer volume. The P&O case indicates, though, how interrelated and permeable the boundary between passenger and freight transport is (Box 16.1). The company began primarily as a mail carrier, morphed into a passenger liner business with significant freight operations, and ended up back largely in freight but significantly intermodal in its activity. Over its 186 years of operation, the company's organisational form, technology, scope, and scale transformed dramatically, reflecting broader changes in the global transport system.

The P&O experience is a small modern example of change processes in freight movements going back thousands of years. The rise of cities, states, empires, and international trade all depended upon the ability to move supplies internally and externally, near and far. Even small principalities needed to move "stuff" around. The small seafaring nation of Phoenicia of around 1200 BC and the ancient Greek city-states during the same era lived off of trade between locations around the Aegean and Mediterranean seas. In Greece especially, soil productivity was poor and long-distance trade was the means towards economic sustenance, with cities specialising

DOI: 10.4324/9781003350866-20

BOX 16.1 INTRODUCTORY CASE: THE EVOLUTION OF THE P&O SHIPPING COMPANY

One of the most iconic shipping companies in modern transport history is the "P&O", a shortening of the original name of The Peninsular and Oriental Steam Navigation Company. The enterprise's exact origins are slightly murky, with prospectuses issued and some irregular steamship service offered by the company between the UK and Portugal and Spain as early as 1835; but regular service with a small fleet of steamers with auxiliary sail did not begin until 1837 (13). (The discussion in this section is mostly drawn from, and page references are to, Howarth & Howarth (1994), unless otherwise noted.)

From these humble origins, P&O grew to be a major international freight and passenger business, closely aligned with the waxing and waning of the British Empire. What is most interesting about the company's historical arc is the shifting role that freight versus passenger operations played in its growth. Like most early steamship companies, the securing of a mail delivery contract, in this case with the British Post Office to carry parcels to and from Spain and Portugal, was vital to a regular cash flow, essential for a steam operation because of its extra expense relative to sail due to the need to pay for and carry coal and have facilities and staff for both steam and sail, the latter being a back-up for the former. Steam did have the advantage of consistency: it could run whatever the prevailing winds might be. When winds were good, sailing was faster and cheaper. But when they were not, nothing moved, and this irregularity was costly to customers.

P&O was better managed than its relatively few competitors and this allowed it to secure routes to India employing an overland segment through Egypt. The more direct all-sea route was the official monopoly of the British East India Company, which plied it with its famous "East Indiamen" ships. But the company agreed to let P&O try its hand at the longer route from Suez (before the canal was in existence). Perhaps the Company thought that P&O would fail. Instead the firm gambled by building its biggest ships to date for the route, paddlers with 60 cabins and 150 berths. This move yielded economies of scale (EOS) because steam, unlike sail, could increase capacity without sacrificing speed or reliability. P&O had always carried some passengers but greater commitment to this business was the main money-spinner since there was a large cadre of British Empire civil servants who needed to move back and forth between India and London regularly (28–35).

The company came to its greatest prominence in the latter part of the 19th and early part of the 20th centuries, becoming primarily a tightly managed, high quality, passenger ship service that carried cargo, a turnaround from its earliest origins in which the reverse was true. P&O was not a technical innovator, although it did quickly adopt all the major steamship innovations between the 1850s and the 1870s: iron replacing wood, screw propellers replacing paddles, and steam engines going from simple to compound and then triple expansion. This allowed its ships to grow larger, its engines to become more efficient, and the miles travelled per tonne of coal to rise (73).

Where P&O was a real innovator instead was in service and marketing. In its earliest days, the company focused on profitable first-class passengers, selling roughly two such tickets for every lower margin second-class fare. Until 1874, wine, beer and spirits, and mineral water were included in fares, starting with claret for breakfast (which the company was famous for), and ending with brandy and gin at bedtime. Champagne was free on celebration days, such as entering or leaving port (56–61). As the decades progressed, P&O became focused more and more on the growing "tourist" market, a neologism invented to capture the phenomenon of the masses being able to afford "tours" due to rising incomes and falling fares. Tourist class became the new name for the old second class and it was a consistently full and profitable berth (135). All this meant that, along with its iconic travel posters, the name "P&O" became synonymous with ocean travel, for both upper and middle classes (see Figure 16.1).

P&O's activity had always been closely tied up with the British Empire, beginning with its very first mail contract and continuing with the company providing its ships for government service during the two world wars. The decline and fall of this Empire therefore was a negative development for the company, as newly independent nations, starting with India, began to move away from their reliance on both the shipping and shipbuilding that P&O had provided (153). The P&O cruise business continued, using, as in the rest of the industry, ever bigger ships (160–161). But the firm also shifted back more and more to its origins as a freight business. Over the course of five post-war decades, the company went into (and in some cases back out of) oil tankers (156–157); small airlines that carried autos and passengers across the English Channel (162–163); roll-on–roll-off (ro-ro) ferries; and increasingly non-transport activities, especially real estate investment, based at first on selling its large stock of centrally located terminals and ticket operations into other uses (201–207). But as the 20th century ended, all these, including cruise ship operations, were increasingly sold or spun off. The P&O brand is still used under licence to other cruise ship companies. But the remaining business itself was sold to a private firm in 2006, ending it as a continuously operated enterprise after 186 years (BBC 2006).

FIGURE 16.1
A P&O travel poster circa 1928.

Source: Scanned image from personal collection. Artist unknown. Posted in Wikimedia. https://commons.wikimedia.org/wiki/File:P_%26_O_Poster.jpg

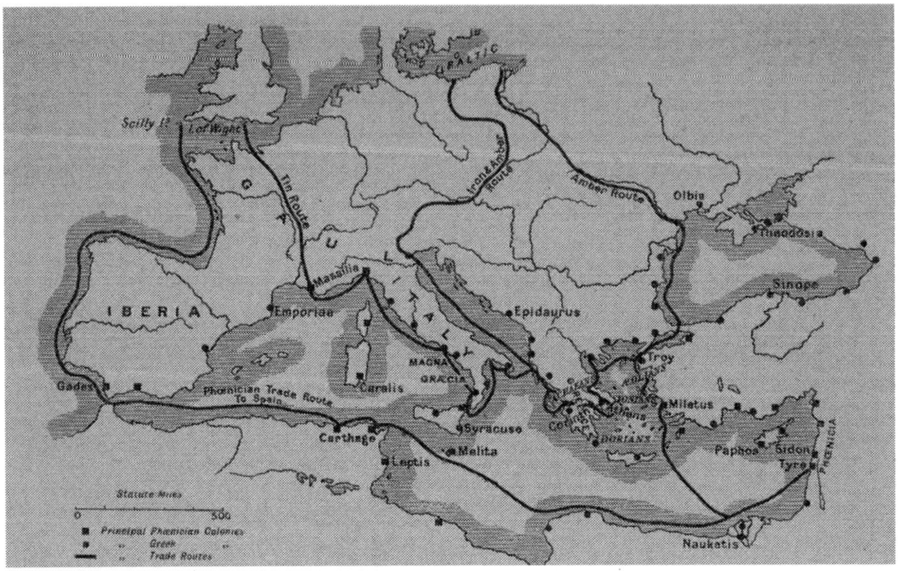

FIGURE 16.2

Ancient Phoenician and Greek colonies, with principal trade routes.

Source: Image from Griffiths (1919, 15). Image and book are in the public domain.

in different goods and activities. Phoenicia's specialisation, meanwhile, was in shipbuilding and providing good sailors (Griffiths 1919, 10–20) (see Figure 16.2).

Urbanisation and trade went together as centres of specialised stages of production and distribution emerged, starting with raw material extraction and export and moving on to intermediate processing and wholesale and retail distribution. Many places tended to be relatively self-sufficient in agriculture on an average basis but needed to trade to meet periodic domestic shortfalls or to export unneeded bounties (Egypt was archetypal in this regard), also to meet growing urban demands for luxuries and specialised products not available at home. Various long-range trade land routes emerged between China, India, and the Middle East, expanding later to Europe and Africa, and these became more and more permanent, establishing specialised cities of their own. Ancient caravan routes, especially the Silk Road, Spice Route, and Gold and Salt Route, were already well-established multimodal paths for carrying goods across all production stages backwards and forwards in ancient times (Griffiths 1919, 31–39) (see Figure 16.3).

By the Common Era (CE), these were becoming genuine long-range distribution chains with highly elaborated value-add processes, and numerous transfer links along the way. The relative strength of nodes and links of

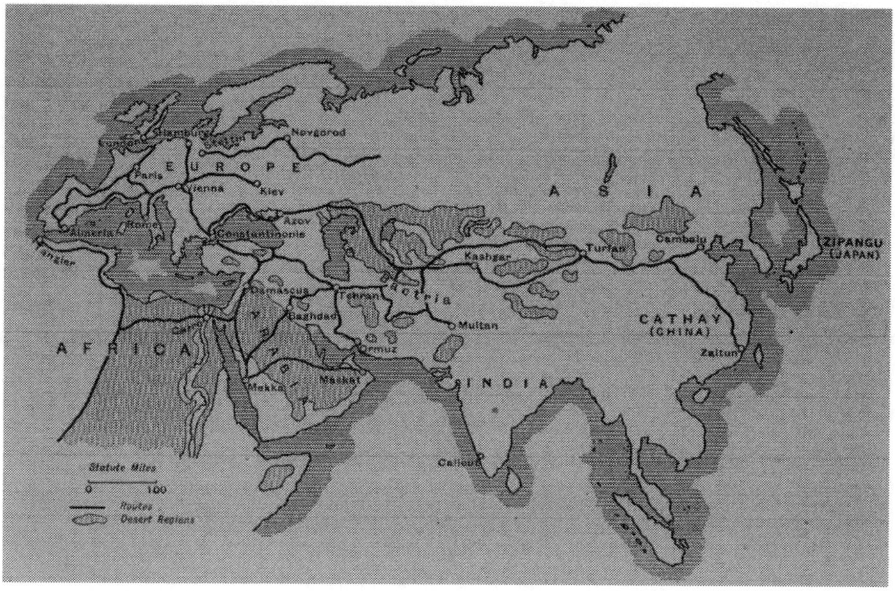

FIGURE 16.3
Ancient caravan routes.

Source: Image from Griffiths (1919, 33). Image and book are in the public domain.

these networks ebbed, flowed, and shifted depending upon various political, social, and economic changes in the world around them. The vast Roman road network of 50,000 mi of paved roads within an integrated and relatively secure internal trade area enhanced the importance of the Middle East and Mediterranean for goods supply and transshipment in the ancient world, a pattern that would fade with the Roman Empire's decline, but which would revive in a different form with the emergence of the Italian trading cities in the 1400s and 1500s. This shipping interdependence remains today.

Historians argue about whether the pre-industrial economy was more or less globally integrated than the modern one. But there is no doubt that the intensity and extensiveness of freight transport in the 21st century is unprecedented in scale and scope. Total freight activity volume equalled 145,229 billion tonne-km in 2019. Organisation for Economic Co-operation and Development (OECD) projections are that this level will more than double by 2050. This is down from prior predictions of a tripling over the same period, with the Covid-19 pandemic and lowered GDP growth projections being the major dampening factors. But this still amounts to an annual compound growth rate in freight activity between 2015 and 2050 of 2.7%, instead of the pre-pandemic projection of 3.4% (ITF 2021, Section 5).

16.2 SOME BASIC CONCEPTS

The movements of goods and services – freight flows – thus have tremendous relevance to the world economy. Some firms are specialists in carrying these flows. These are called carriers. Their customers are somewhat confusingly called shippers to denote that they initiate demand for the journey. Both rely on freight flows to get goods and services from one location to another.

The core theory presents a bifurcated economy consisting of consumption and production, i.e. supply and demand. The production side can be represented via the production function in which output = f (inputs) in which inputs are processed through technology to create outputs. A typical notation might be Y = f (K, L, T), where K refers to capital, L to labour, and T to transport (see Chapter 2). T would include all the freight activities referred to thus far.

This is, however, a very disembodied model. Production involves a great deal of movement of actual things for making a product or service, adding value to it, and improving it. The most basic level of operation is logistics, a term that refers to the transmission of physical materials through a production process, from procurement through production and distribution. Production and logistics are closely linked since a firm's ability to perform its production activities relies on the efficient procurement of inputs and distribution of outputs.

Logistics is obviously not an end in and of itself. Efficient and least-cost logistics are a foundation of market competitiveness but by itself doesn't guarantee successful market outcomes. Logistics is just a part of an overall supply chain. While logistics focuses mostly on moving materials, the supply chain goes beyond this to encompass the entire process of making and distributing a saleable product or service, from raw materials to final sales. Supply chain management (SCM) refers to the oversight and coordination of this system of connecting supply with demand (McKinsey & Company 2022).

The supply chain is part of a larger value chain (VC). A well-managed supply chain leads to the outcome of an efficiently produced and distributed product. But it does not guarantee maximum value in the marketplace. Achieving this also requires effective selling to customers, efficacious relationships with suppliers, and other market engagement that results in maximum profit. The VC thus focuses on delivering market value across the supply chain, while the supply chain focuses on delivering efficiency in the movement of materials manufacturing from initial to final output and sales (UNCTAD 2006). A global VC (GVC) consists of a VC in which at least two stages are in different countries (World Bank 2020). This distinction can be applied to supply chains as well. In both cases the designations refer to geographic scale. The more international borders crossed, the more global the chain.

Sourcing is a related concept, referring to a firm's selection of suppliers for its various supply chain stages. Outsourcing refers to the purchase of goods and services from an outside supplier, while in-sourcing refers to performing these functions within the producing entity, usually a firm. Single sourcing is an arrangement in which a company purchases goods and services from only one supplier. International business scholars refer to the "make-or-buy decision" in referring to whether a producer chooses to make VC components in-house or buy (source) them from outside. The make–buy trade-off includes decisions about differentials between internally versus externally sourced production costs, efficiencies, core competencies, administrative control, transaction costs, legal compliance, tax advantage, and so on (Friedrich et al. 2022). A central concern is how freight flows and transport costs interact with sourcing to increase efficiencies across all dimensions of the VC.

16.3 SUPPLY CHAIN INTEGRATION

SCM involves working with varying numbers of suppliers, manufacturers, distributors, wholesalers, warehousing operations, retailers, and shippers. Fragmentation can easily occur between these parties, leading to raised transaction and coordination costs. Supply chain integration involves improving information sharing across supply chain members, early problem detection, rapid response, collaborative planning, and "whole picture" forecasting. Supply chains have generally become more fragmented as markets have globalised, although this trend has reversed somewhat in the past decade. This means that more parties are involved, but it does not necessarily mean that they have become less integrated. Indeed, supply chain managers have become adept at wringing maximum efficiency from highly complex global supplier arrangements through the use of real-time information management and processing, and the use of dynamic incentives captured through formal and informal contracting. This involves sourcing from the lowest-cost, highest-value-add suppliers all along the production process, moving material rapidly and efficiently across far-flung locations, and economising on inventory, minimising storage costs and spoilage and obsolescence of stock.

Supply chain integration creates the potential for higher capacity utilisation throughout the production process using various strategies, such as just-in-time (JIT) production in which suppliers produce just what is required rather than accumulating stocks. There is, however, no "magic bullet". JIT was once the default for supply chain managers and its benefits remain, when effectively managed. But JIT is very sensitive to supply chain disruptions, both endogenous (as when there is a spike in demand that outstrips existing production capacity) and exogenous (such as wars). The Covid-19 pandemic demonstrated that there is a role for redundancy and supply back-ups, which are costly, but often critical in a crisis. Even under normal operating circumstances, the rise of mega-warehousing and cheap digital storage has lowered inventory holding costs on average, making JIT less cost saving than it once was.

Integration has both demand and supply side implications. On the supply side, integration allows for coordinated workflow, production, operations, and procurement, and the ability to more easily adopt new business models and technologies. On the demand side, integration allows for greater penetration of new markets, creation of new products, and greater ability to effect mass customisation (which, as the term implies, involves large batch production tailored to meet particular demand segments). Levinson et al. (2016) thus break down supply chain decisions into strategic and operational categories. Location, sourcing, inventory, logistics, and other dimensions of the supply chain must operate efficiently. But this is only a prerequisite for the more strategic goal of maximising net profits (whether by increasing total sales, unit margins, or both) based on an effective flow and storage of raw materials, in-process inventory, finished goods, and information between point-of-origin and point-of-consumption (120–121).

16.4 GLOBAL VALUE CHAIN MANAGEMENT (GVCM)

GVC management (GVCM) refers to the oversight of a GVC. A particular challenge for GVCM is dealing with cross-border flows along that chain, i.e. moving product and value-add across international borders, with all the variance in trade rules, local costs and culture, etc., that this entails. This can involve multiple movements of value-add back and forth across the same border. Figure 16.4 provides a simple conceptual mapping of GVCM.

A prosaic transport example of how this comes together is the production of a bicycle. Whatever the particular brand name, most bicycles are assembled with parts and components from across the world. Asia and Europe are especially key regions for the Bianchi brand, with its maker conducting all of its design, prototyping, and conception work in Italy, assembly mostly in Taiwan (China), and parts and components sourced from mainland China, Italy, Japan, Malaysia, and other global locations (see Figure 16.5).

Interestingly, the widespread use of international sourcing means that the value of international trade in components is often calculated to be much

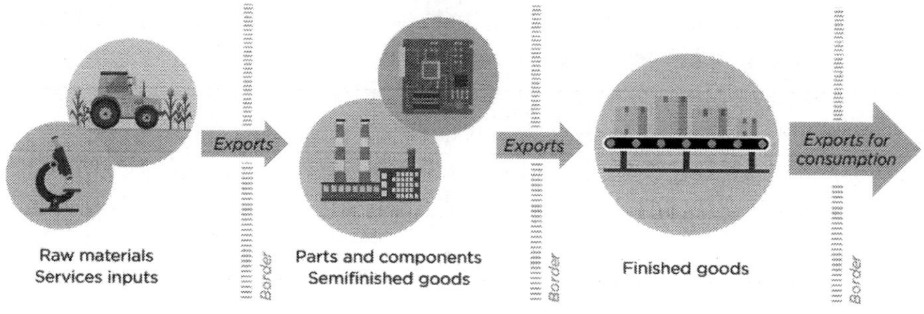

FIGURE 16.4
Global value chain management (GVCM).

Source: World Bank (2020). "World Development Report (2020): Trading for Development in the Age of Global Value Chains." Overview booklet. World Bank, Washington, DC. Licence: Creative Commons Attribution CC BY 3.0 IGO.

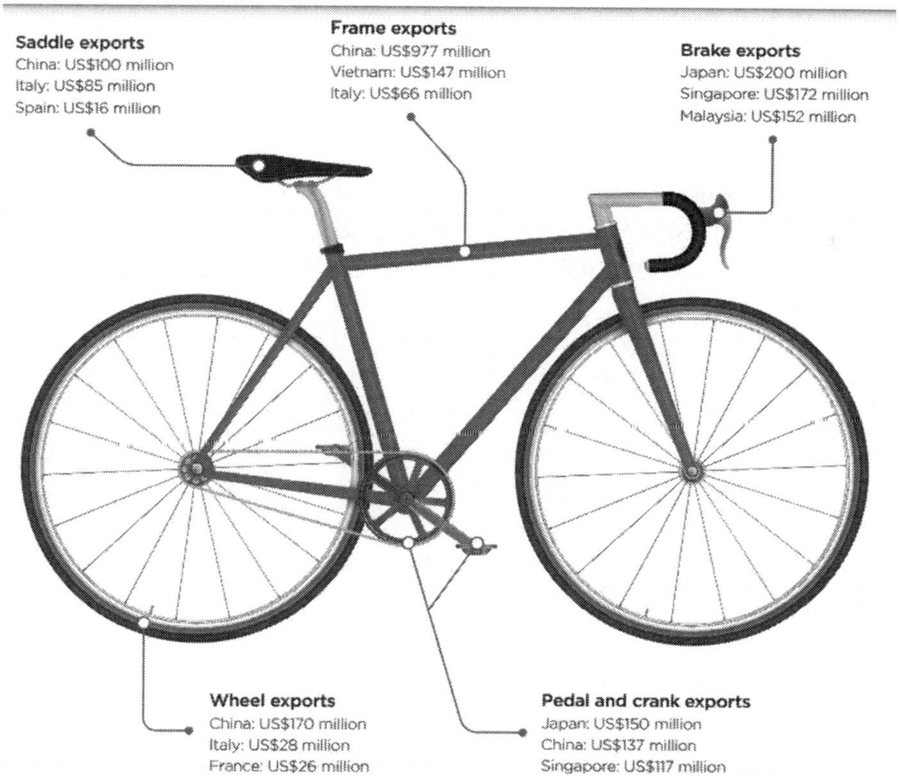

FIGURE 16.5
The GVC of the Bianchi bicycle in 2020.

Source: World Bank (2020, Figure 1.1., 16). "World Development Report (2020): Trading for Development in the Age of Global Value Chains." Chapter 1. World Bank, Washington, DC. Licence: Creative Commons Attribution CC BY 3.0 IGO.

higher than the value of trade in the final product itself. The trade in bicycle parts has outstripped the trade in bicycles by 15%–25% in recent years. In Finland, for example, 33% of bicycle value-add is from outside the country, in this case largely from the European Union (EU), Asia, and North America (World Bank 2020, 17). This indicates a very fragmented GVC, but as the prior section indicated, not necessarily a less integrated one as bicycle production is typically very efficient.

16.5 FREIGHT MODES VERSUS PASSENGER MODES

Freight is carried on modes parallel to those for passengers in that they move by surface, water, and air, and by similar means. For surface movements, there is heavy utilisation of rail and road. On the water, sea movements from the late 20th century through to the present are dominated by freight, with passenger movements reduced to small fractions largely concentrated on the leisure travel cruise ships once pioneered by P&O and now run by a whole variety of specialised operators (Banomyong 2000).

What differs the most between passenger and freight modes, besides purpose, are the nature of the vehicles used. While there are small freight movements within cities that are mostly carried by passenger vehicles such as cars and light lorries, most cargo is carried in specially designed vehicles. This is most clear in sea travel where there have been major innovations in shipbuilding technology leading to mega-size bulk carriers and container ships, loaded and unloaded at almost fully mechanised port handling facilities, and reaping large economies of scale (EOS) that have sharply reduced maritime freight costs. Containerisation is a major part of this process, replacing old labour-intensive break-bulk methods, in which sacks and boxes of items had to be carefully and slowly loaded into ships and then slowly and carefully unloaded by stevedores, often with significant breakage and wastage along the way (Figure 16.6). With containers, this process has been greatly streamlined, lowering costs, and enabling a vast increase in vessel sizes. These innovations have allowed global sourcing to explode (Knowles 2009, 443).

Maritime trade is now overall dominated by very large ships known as bulk carriers, which accounted for around 60% of total TKM in 2015. Oil alone had a 25% share of this carriage, down from its 60% share in 1970. Mineral ores, grain, and coal make up the rest. Bulk carriers are the largest vessels currently in operation, with the largest oil tankers reaching up to 500,000 deadweight tonnes (DWT) (Noussan et al. 2020).

The ocean itself is not, however, one open space as far as shaping operations are concerned. Maritime circulation takes place in relatively

FIGURE 16.6
Stevedores on a New York dock loading barrels of corn syrup onto a barge on the Hudson River in 1912.

Source: Image from National Archives of the United States. NAID: 518287. Local ID: 69-R-1K-35. https://catalog.archives.gov/id/518287. Image is in the public domain.

small parts of the sea, partly because of the asymmetric location of economic activities and high-value-adds that need to be served. These are particularly concentrated in the North Atlantic and the North Pacific, and thus much shipping activity takes place there, into and out of large ports. But other factors play a role in where freight ships go, such as circulating currents and regular weather systems, with some areas being avoided some times of the years, while utilised more heavily in others (Rodrigue 2020, Section 5.1) (see Figure 16.7).

Technology plays a key role in ocean accessibility. As already alluded to shipbuilding innovations increased the largest size of operating ship more than 12-fold over the space of a few decades, from 3,800 Gross Registered Tonnes (GRT) in 1871 to 47,000 GRT in 1914. This change, combined with the adoption and refinement of steam power, increased the amount of spatial patterns of shipping. Steamships originally needed refuelling on

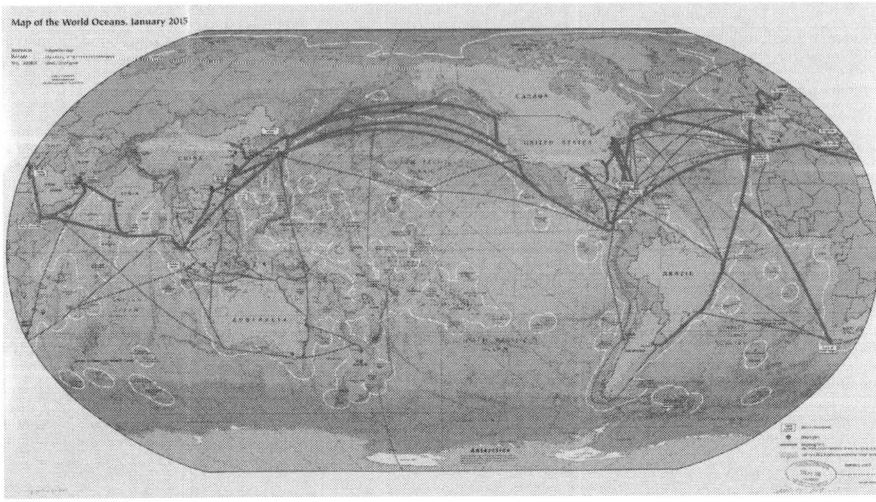

FIGURE 16.7
World oceans 2015.

Source: United States Central Intelligence Agency (2015). [Map] retrieved from the Library of Congress, www.loc.gov/item/2015588704/

inter-continental routes, requiring a series of intermediate coal bunkering ports such as Gibraltar, Malta, Port Said, Aden, Colombo, Singapore, and Darwin on the Great Britain to Australia route. These all fell into disuse when diesel-powered motor ships allowed long passages without refuelling (Knowles 2006, 410).

Meanwhile a global canal building boom during the 1800s and early 1900s created whole new shipping channels and greater interconnection between regions. With the opening of the Suez Canal in 1869, London to Bombay (Mumbai) now became 6,274 nautical miles long, suddenly 47% shorter than the pre-canal route via the Cape of Good Hope in South Africa. The opening of the Panama Canal made New York to San Francisco into a 5,262 nautical mile trip, 60% shorter than via the Straits of Magellan near Cape Horn. The Kiel Canal in Germany opened in 1895 and linked the North and Baltic Seas, cutting a day off journey times from Baltic countries. This was not just true on the oceans. The St. Lawrence Seaway between Montreal and Lake Ontario opened in 1959 allowing for much larger ocean-going ships to continue their journey inland on the Great Lakes (Knowles 2006, 410) (see Figure 16.8).

Ship sizes shape canal sizes and vice-versa. By the end of the 20th century, oil and natural gas tankers had reached sizes of 100,000–250,000 GRT, in addition to the aforementioned ultra large oil tankers. But the biggest

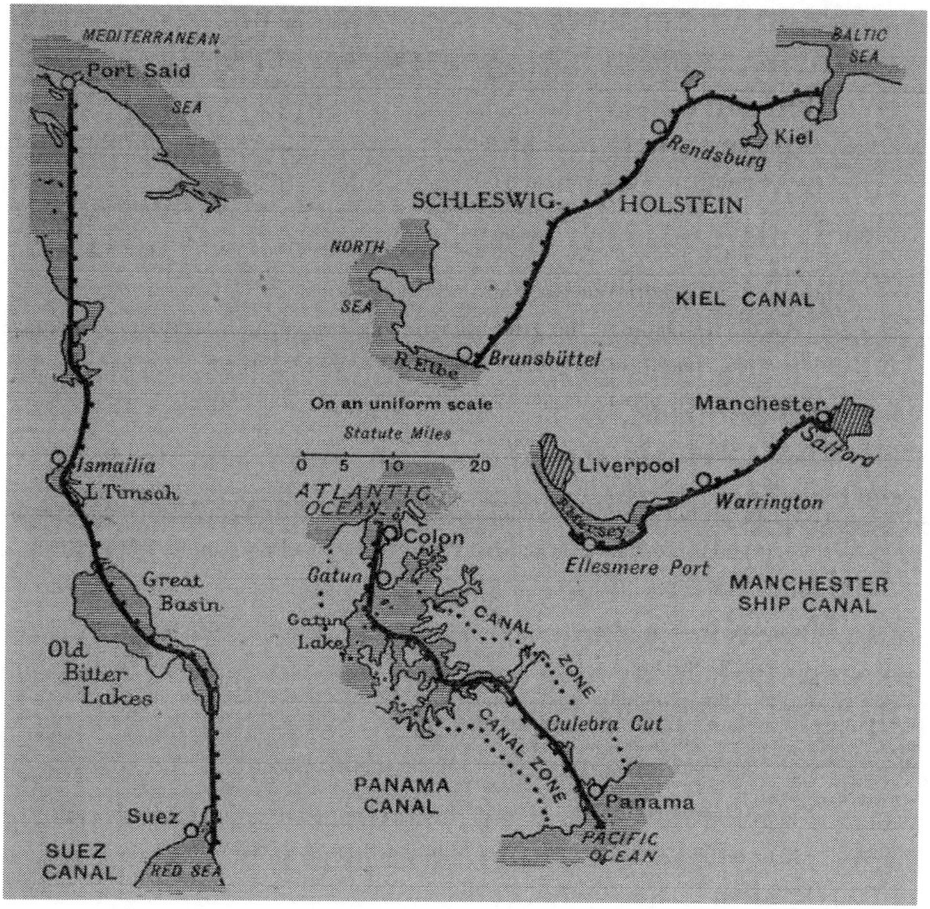

FIGURE 16.8
Some major ship canals circa 1919.

Source: Image from Griffiths (1919, 59). Image and book are in the public domain.

ships were now too large for the Suez and Panama Canals, and their reduced tonne–mile shipping costs were somewhat offset by the longer alternative routes these large ships had to take. Still, shipping costs for all manner of wet and dry bulk carriers fell dramatically, even for those vessels unable to use canals. Both smaller and larger ships have their niches, however, with the former being more suitable for serving multi-origin and destination cargo runs, the latter being best for long point-to-point journeys. Shallow draughts in many local ports also require vessels with relatively little displacement. In 1992, for example, 48% of world trade in grain was transported in ships of under 40,000 DWT and only 6% in ships over 80,000 DWT (Knowles 2006, 412).

16.6 PIPELINES

One mode of transport is unique to freight: pipelines. A pipeline is pretty much what the word suggests, namely a long pipe for conveying liquids over long distances. Pipelines can be laid underground or underwater. Occasionally they must be laid above ground for reasons of surface conditions and topography, as was the case with Trans Alaskan oil pipeline in the US due to Alaska's permafrost (i.e. perennially frozen ground) that required its 1,300 km to be placed mainly on the surface. The longest gas pipeline is between Alberta and Sarnia in Canada at 2,911 km in length; while the longest oil pipeline is the Trans-Siberian going across more than 9,344 km from the Russian Arctic oilfields to Western Europe. Pipelines move liquids very efficiently and cost-effectively over long distances once constructed. They are especially important in the oil and gas industry, where they provide the main conduits between extraction fields and terminals. At these latter points, refining often takes place, for further value-add before shipping product on to final consumption points (Rodrigue 2020, Section 5.1).

There can be many social, political, and geopolitical constraints to pipeline placement and operation. Some pipelines have been the subject of controversy, with projects blocked because of local community resistance and fears about environmental disruption and the potential hazard of leaks or explosion. Populated areas can thus engender resistance to pipeline placement. Oil and gas fields are often located in geopolitically volatile areas with pipelines transiting through similarly fraught locations. Pipelines in the Middle East have often been caught up in war and conflict, and the 2023 destruction, during the Russia–Ukraine War, of the Nord Stream 1 gas pipeline from Russia through Ukraine and into Germany shows that this is a worldwide problem.

Pipelines are not cheap to build, their construction costs varying with diameter and increasing proportionally with length and viscosity of fluids (gas being low-viscosity, oil, high-viscosity). A 2023 estimate is of $US 10.7 million cost per mile, including the purchase of right-of-way (ROW), labour, and other materials (Smith 2023). Obviously there will be a wide range around this mean.

There is an interesting parallel between these physical pipelines and the cables that carry electronic information. As Box 16.2 discusses, these are critical adjuncts to freight of all kinds but are surprisingly resource-intensive in their own right.

BOX 16.2 THE UNBEARABLE HEAVINESS OF INFORMATION

Information has always been central to freight movements and there is a whole history of changes in cargo manifests, customs documentation, ship logs, and the like that parallels the changes in freight carriage technology. In the present "digital age", information has become even more integral to real-time tracking, adjustment, and delivery. Information is paperless, up on the "cloud", and instantly available from any point on the globe and in the supply chain.

There is a strong parallel between falling transport and communication costs, as shown in Figure 16.9. Sea freight rates and airfares both fell dramatically between 1920 and 1950, accompanied by advances in telegraphy and telephony that enabled better coordination across physical trips, leading to dramatic falls in the unit costs of both. This trend deepened and continued with the rise of computers, mobile phones, and the internet.

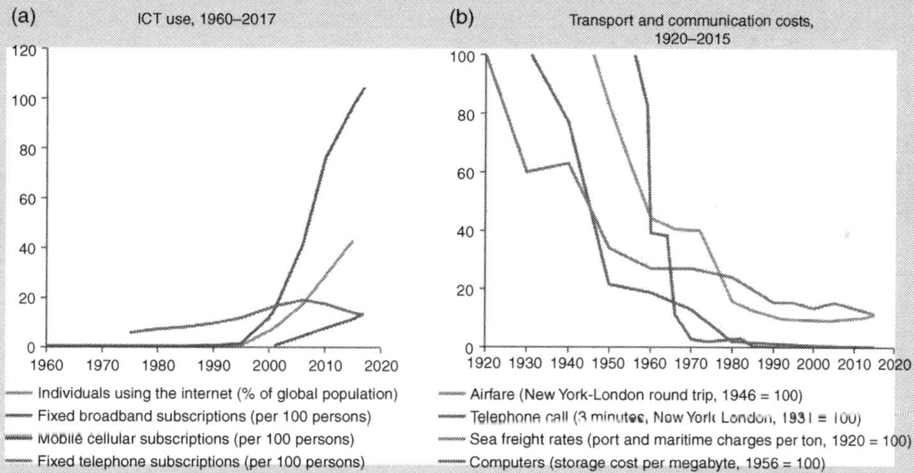

Sources: WDR 2020 team,using data from ITU's World telecommunication/ICT indicators database for panel a and based on Rodrigue, Comtois, and Slack (2017) for panel b.

Note: In panel a, data are available for over 200 countries. Mobile cellular subscriptions per 100 persons may be over 100 as some people may have several mobile phones. In panel b, for each indicator the cost is reported as 100 for the first year with data. ICT = information and communication technology.

FIGURE 16.9

Trends in transport and communication costs and ICT use.

Source: World Bank (2020, Figure 1.3, 20). Used under a Creative Commons Attribution 3.0 IGO licence (CC BY 3.0 IGO).

Two panels are shown. The first labelled "a. ICT use, 1960-2017", shows a rapid rise of internet use between 1990 and 2017 from 0% of the global population using the internet to almost 100%, with corresponding increases of fixed broadband subscriptions rising from 0 to around 15 per 100 persons, mobile cellular subscriptions going from 0 to over 100 per 100 persons, and fixed telephone subscriptions rising from roughly 4 per 100 persons, peaking at around 20 between 2000 and 2010 and then declining slowly from there. The second panel labelled "b. Transport and communication costs" shows exponential falls of varying amounts between 1920 and 2020 in the unit costs of airfares, telephone calls, sea freight rates, and computer storage.

Contrary to popular belief, however, information has not gotten less resource-intensive with these advances. Granted, physical archives of files and the associated clerks and archivists needed to manage them are largely a thing of the past, as are telephone switchboards, exchanges, and operators. But data centres and networks consume between 2% and 3% of the world's electricity. Upgrades in those networks will likely only increase that share since the latest 5G systems use three times more energy than 4G. In the six years between 2020 and 2026, electronic network energy requirements are estimated to increase by over 150%. Similarly, the pervasiveness of wireless transfer and increases in bandwidth makes downloading and sending ever bigger data amounts more and more prodigious, but wired networks are more efficient by a factor of ten (Cobb 2023).

AI is the latest trend in all things, including transport (though not as new – or quite as promising – as its enthusiasts often make out – see Chapter 19). But these require more energy and resources than traditional systems. Granted, they may economise on skilled technical labour and the facilities needed to serve it. But net impact on energy and other resource use is yet to be determined.

In a strange sense, then, the "virtual" delivery of information is more weighty, literally, than one might think, having its own "actual" physical supply chains to manage.

16.7 MULTIMODALISM, INTERMODALISM, AND CONTAINERISATION

Changing between modes is present in almost all travel, in which case it is called intermodal. Freight trips are intermodal in most instances, for most things heavier than a takeaway meal (food deliveries to individuals are typically conducted by individuals on foot, on a bicycle, motorised cycle, or by car). With heavier and larger packages, intermodal transport is the norm. When individuals order a product from an online store, to them it appears as if the store is simply sending them a product. But behind the scenes, a series of shippers and carriers, often using a series of modes, is actually arranging and executing the delivery. This may consist of a trucking firm carrying a truckload from a factory door to a wholesale warehouse, with another local trucking firm carrying smaller shipments to retail outlets, with these outlets then hiring cycle messengers to carry the order to the final customer. Freight intermodalism refers to the movement of cargo from a shipper to consignee via two modes or more under a single rate, bill, and liability cover, though not necessarily a single carrier. A variant on this theme is multimodal transport, in which there is intermodalism, but a single carrier takes responsibility for an entire shipment door-to-door (Banomyong 2000).

Containerisation transformed multimodal transport and pushed intermodalism to new heights. Most general cargo is now unitised (a term meaning separate elements bundled together in a single package) by means of an international standardised transport unit like a container. Only particularly large and heavy cargoes cannot be containerised, having to be handled directly. For most other freight, containers are loaded and sealed by the shipper, with the carrier picking them up intact. The contents are not touched until delivered to the end recipient. This process has not just transformed unloading and loading of ships but has enabled much deeper linkages between rail, road, and maritime modes since transfers are so efficient and low cost (Banomyong 2000).

Containerisation and unitisation are not new concepts. There is evidence that primitive containers were used in Roman times and ro-ro containers were used for coal shipments by the Liverpool and Manchester Railway as early as 1830, with an intermodal use of them by the Birmingham and Derby Railway moving similar containers to and from rail cars on to horse carriages beginning in 1839. By the early 20th century, rail containerisation had become more systematised, leading to the first containerisation wave. New York Central Railroad established the first dedicated container service from Cleveland and Chicago on March 19, 1921. Containerisation was conceived of and sold as "door-to-door" transport, enhanced by "Piggy Back" systems where trailers themselves were carried aboard specialised "flat cars". This rail–road interface, technologically updated, has now become universal (Banomyong 2000).

Cargo ship companies were also long familiar with intermodalism. Ro-ro ferries had been developed in Denmark in the late 19th century to allow integration of its national railway network across the Danish archipelago. Rather than embarking and disembarking multiple times, ro-ro train ferries simply moved entire from water to rail and back again, going beyond Danish islands to the Jutland Peninsula, Sweden, and Germany (Knowles, 2006, 415).

But modern maritime intermodalism exploded with the rise of container usage during the 1960s, generally attributed to M. McLean, founder of Sea-Land Inc., who was a trucking company executive who found himself head of a maritime shipping company. He simply adapted road/rail combination operations to sea operations (Banomyong 2000). The original port-to-port perspective of ocean shipping was replaced by a door-to-door perspective. P&O was one of many other companies that moved in this direction, as the opening case showed.

This innovation appealed to freight customers (shippers), but for carriers it was driven by a focus on achieving minimum total distribution costs whatever their source. EOS were achieved by concentrating only on very big ports for long-haul runs. The economic geography of these ports has evolved. In North America the tendency has been for a few mega-ports, supported by a few secondary regional ports, to become ever more dominant. In Europe, with its more complex and more densely populated topography, a hub-and-spoke port pattern has emerged, with large transit container ports receiving international shipments carried on to secondary ports and terminals closer to final markets, by water, rail, or road. Thus, Gioia Tauro in Italy was the fifth largest in Europe and number 20 in the world in 2006, and Algeciras (Spain) and Marsaxlokk (Malta) were among the top 15 European ports, even though they are not near any particular important economic agglomerations. This system has been helped along by seamless transfers to inland and overland routes referred to as landbridge services, allowing for double stack container trains to maximise capacity and lower unit overland transport costs. This is what the feeder transit ports are designed to integrate with, functioning as pure logistic hubs located on round-the-world shipping routes (Knowles 2006, 412–415). Such patterns can be seen more nationally as well, as with British ports, Felixstowe and Southampton emerging as the leading ports for the new containers, while Immingham overtook the old ports of London and Liverpool in carrying coal (Gunn 2018, 10).

As the GVC evolves, the hierarchy of ports shifts with it. In 1975, 7 of the top 20 container ports were in the US, with 5 in Europe, 5 in Southeast/East Asia, and 2 in Australia, handling a total of 10.6 million (20-foot equivalent unit) (TEU). New York and Rotterdam were once the world's largest ports. A few decades later the 20 largest container ports handled 144.8 million TEU and Hong Kong and Singapore were the largest ports, with China claiming three of the world's top four (Knowles 2006, 443). By 2023, China (including Taiwan) claimed 9 of the top 10 ports by TEU, Rotterdam being the 10th; 12 of the top 20 ports were Chinese (World Shipping Council 2023). The shift of manufacturing activity from global North to South has been a major driver of this development.

Indeed, there are agglomeration economies for freight, just as there are for transport and location density more broadly (see Chapter 4). There is increasing recognition that user benefits of freight improvements are not just the time and cost savings for trucks and their drivers (a parallel with passenger vehicles), but also broader logistics and supply chain benefits to freight shippers, carriers, and receivers achieved through density. There is a growing literature on the wider scale of freight agglomeration benefits both over compact and broad scales (Weisbrod & Goldberg 2023).

These effects are manifested in a number of ways. For example, transport hubs, such as motorway junctions, discount malls, and even airports, have sometimes become economic activity generators in their own right. Heathrow Airport for example employed 76,000 people in 2018, a community the size of Guildford in the UK (Gunn 2018, 20). There are cost and access threshold effects for supply chains to be sure, as there are for commuting. In other words, agglomerations have costs as well as benefits and returns to density are not unlimited in scale. But they do exist and have powerful effects (Weisbrod & Goldberg 2023).

16.8 SHORT HAULS, "THE LAST MILE (KILOMETRE)", AND CITY LOGISTICS

The discussion thus far has been focused on long-haul freight movement, ranging from "arterial" movements from origin port to destination port, from terminal to distant terminal, or through intermediate movements, such as moving from a transit terminal to a set of receiving terminals for further distribution to final customers. The journey lengths here range from many thousands of kilometres down to around 100 or so.

Short hauls are an in a different category. These generally cover distances of under 100 km. They are a critical part of most long-haul journeys since they get product to their ultimate intended consumer. But these short-haul trips, referred to as drayage, are a particularly challenging part of the supply chain because EOS and density economies are not typically realisable over these shorter runs. Vehicle sizes are limited because most trips take place on smaller capacity local roads, and sometimes rails and waterways, that are not nearly as large as arterials, and which carry fewer vehicles at any one time, usually at lower speeds. Loads are often relatively small and break-bulk and thus less economical to handle.

Many final consumers are located in dense urban cores and metropolitan areas and further problems arise there. Trucking is the primary mode in this case, often having to operate in conditions of ageing or inadequate infrastructure, with high congestion most times of the day, weight limits on bridges and underpasses, clearance restrictions, tight curves and turning radii, limited access to facilities and parking, and noise and idling restrictions in many residential neighbourhoods. Thus, there is a whole set of "city logistics" issues to deal with. Getting to the final customer is often especially difficult, something referred to as "the last mile (or kilometre) problem" (King et al. 2014).

Economical solutions to these problems are not easy. Infrastructure improvements in dense urban environments can be expensive and often infeasible. The main choice carriers have is in vehicle capacity. The trucking industry is segmented into many different fleet sizes with different vehicle sizes, ranging from large fleet operators down to small individual owner-operators (King et al. 2014). Much drayage relies on individual subcontractors using their own vehicles, mainly cars and vans, to take a package from an urban distribution point, such as a post office or local terminal, to the customer door in a residential neighbourhood. All major carriers, including government postal authorities, rely on this strategy to one degree or another.

From an economic point of view, however, these make a profit mainly by paying the subcontractors poorly and offloading operational risk onto them, rather than being true efficiencies. Customers want cheap shipping rates. But these can come at a great cost to those involved in last kilometre end of the business.

16.9 REVERSE LOGISTICS

The primary aim of supply chains is to move product forward, from producer to customer. But there also needs to be a reverse channel for waste, discarded packaging material, and defective or obsolete products to be brought back down the chain for final disposal and processing. "Reverse logistics" thus refers to flows back through the "forward" chain that goes from producer to consumer, in a "reverse" direction to deal with various detritus (Hesse & Rodrigue 2009). These return points can be varied. A defective product, for example, may be taken back by distributors. These, in turn, often hand it off to a specialised segment of the industry that dismantles and disposes, or, in some cases, refurbishes, products for recycling for re-use. Some items, such as packaging, can be collected and re-used or recycled, with many of these tasks relegated to the consumer. But this is not always the case, especially when the defect or waste occurs along the way before reaching the customer, or is part of an intermediate supply chain that does not include the final user or involves toxic or other difficult waste.

There is now an increasing demand by government on firms to manage and minimise their reverse logistics cycles, especially through waste reduction and re-use at the producer level. Existing consumer inducements for re-use and recycling, such as "soft" requirements to put things into recycle bins, and incentives to buy re-usable bags, are long-standing but have had relatively little impact on a growing waste stream. These, in any case, do not address the fact that much of the excess product sits within industry itself, without ever reaching a consumer. Now policies are designed to "internalise" this waste "externality" (see Chapter 13) to make firms more cognisant of the

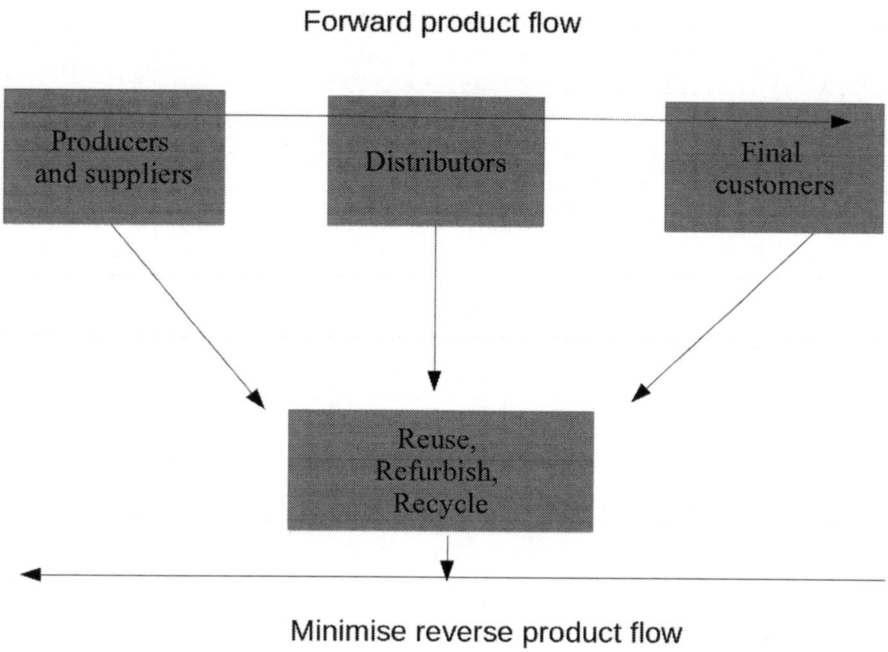

FIGURE 16.10
The cooperative circular consumer–producer reverse logistics recycle model.

social costs of their waste, and to make reverse logistics more of a cooperative flow with less waste and less reverse logistics. This change is conceptually represented in Figure 16.10.

There has been some success in this move, partly generated by internal cost-savings incentives of the freight industry itself, in making these reverse flows less environmentally costly. But the overall demand for product has generally outweighed these gains.

Reverse logistics is part of a more general push on making transport systems more sustainable. These issues are covered in the next chapter.

REFERENCES

Banomyong, R. (2000). *Multimodal transport in South East Asia: A case study approach*. Ph.D. Thesis.

BBC (2006). P&O shareholders back Dubai bid. British Broadcasting Corporation, Monday 13 February.

Carter Jr., W. H., & Dodge, R. E. (1939). *Economic geography*. Doubleday, Doran & Company.

Cobb, K. (2023). AI: The information economy becomes ever more energy and resource intensive. *Resource Insights* (November 23). https://resourceinsights.blogspot.com/2023/11/ai-information-economy-becomes-ever.html?m=1

Friedrich, A., Lange, A., & Elbert, R. (2022). Make-or-buy decisions for industrial additive manufacturing. *Journal of Business Logistics*, 43(4), 623–653.

Griffiths, J. P. (1919). *Transport: The magic carpet of industry, briefly describing the history and development of transport by sea, road, canal and railway*. George Philip & Son.

Gunn, S. (2018). The history of transport systems in the UK. In *Future of mobility: Evidence review foresight*. Government Office for Science, Centre for Urban History, University of Leicester.

Hesse, M., & Rodrigue, J. P. (2009). *Logistics*. Elsevier.

Howarth, D., & Howarth, S. (1994). *The story of P&O* (Revised edition). Weidenfeld & Nicolson.

ITF (2021). *ITF transport outlook 2021*. OECD Publishing. https://doi.org/10.1787/16826a30-en

Kim, S. (2008). Urbanization. In Durlauf Steven N. and Blume Lawrence E. (eds). *New Palgrave dictionary of economics* (2nd edition). Palgrave Macmillan, 6917–6921.

King, D. A., Gordon, C. E., & Peters, J. R. (2014). Does road pricing affect port freight activity: Recent evidence from the port of New York and New Jersey. *Research in Transportation Economics*, 44, 2–11.

Knowles, R. D. (2006). Transport shaping space: Differential collapse in time – Space. *Journal of Transport Geography*, 14, 407–425.

Knowles, R. D. (2009). Transport geography. In Kitchin Rob and Thrift Nigel (eds). *International encyclopedia of human geography*. Elsevier, 441–451.

Levinson, D., Gillen, D., et al. (2016). *Transportation economics*. en.wikibooks.org July 9, 2016. Print (pdf) version.

McKinsey & Company (2022). What is a supply chain? McKinsey & Company Featured Insights (August 17). www.mckinsey.com/featured-insights/mckinsey-explainers/what-is-supply-chain#/

Noussan, M., Hafner, M., & Tagliapietra, S. (2020). The evolution of transport across world regions. In *The Future of transport between digitalization and decarbonization*. SpringerBriefs in Energy. Springer.

Rodrigue, J.-P. (2020). *The geography of transport systems* (6th edition). Routledge.

Smith, C. E. (2023). Land pipeline construction costs hit $10.7 million/mile. *Oil and Gas Journal*. October 2, 2023. www.ogj.com/pipelines-transportation/pipelines/article/14299952/land-pipeline-construction-costs-hit-record-107-million-mile

UNCTAD (2006). *Global Value Chains for building national productive capacities*. UNCTAD – TD/B/COM.3/79.

United States Central Intelligence Agency (2015). *Map of the world oceans*, January. Washington, DC: Central Intelligence Agency.

Weisbrod, G., & Goldberg, J. (2023). Relationship of regional, freight, and intermodal market access to industry location and productivity. *Transportation Research Record*, 2677(5), 403–419. https://doi.org/10.1177/03611981221131306

World Bank (2020). *World development report 2020: Trading for development in the age of global value chains*. World Bank.

World Shipping Council (2023). The top 50 container ports. www.worldshipping.org/top-50-ports, accessed 10 December 2024.

CHAPTER 17

Resilience and sustainability

17.1 INTRODUCTION: CLIMATE CHANGE IMPACTS ON TRANSPORT SYSTEMS

The likely impacts of climate change on global transport systems fall into two broad categories of impact across two transport system dimensions: changes in (a) temperature and (b) water levels, impacting on (c) transport infrastructure and (d) transport users. The New York Academy of Sciences (NYAS 2010, Chapter 4) breaks impact types down as follows:

1. Temperature-related infrastructure and material stresses, such as greater freeze-thaw cycles, buckling of road and rail beds due to intense heat, etc.
2. Temperature-related stresses on users, requiring more use of ventilation, air-conditioning, etc.
3. Water-related infrastructure and vehicle stresses such as flooding, salt-water intrusion, moisture damage from humidity, bank erosion due to heavy rainfalls, etc.

The specific manifestations of these impacts are manifold and vary by local conditions. In Australia, for example, where roughly 95% of the population lives in cities along the ocean coast, or along rivers feeding into the oceans, sea level rise, and increased storm surges, will significantly affect coastal transport infrastructure, with tunnels and culverts particularly prone to damage from increased tidal and salt gradients. Bridges will be stressed

DOI: 10.4324/9781003350866-21

BOX 17.1 INTRODUCTORY CASE: TRANSPORT, CLIMATE CHANGE, AND THE MODERN WORLD

Transport activity has always presented environmental challenges. London was legendary for its coal-fed smog as far back as the late Middle Ages, during a period when the English were busy cutting down and burning the country's many forests to near extinction, including the Sherwood Forest of the Robin Hood legend. The same phenomenon of ecosystem stress and degradation was taking place to varying degrees in the rest of Europe and in other highly structured states and societies like China, well before the First Industrial Revolution began (Pomeranz 2000).

What has changed since then is the sheer scale, scope, and complexity of burden placed on ecosystems by human activity. Climate scientists refer to what is taking place as the Anthropocene, i.e. a new earth systems era in which humans are one of the main agents of change. The designation has not been officially accepted yet by geologists, but there is near-consensus among scientists about human climate impacts and their species-threatening nature. Table 17.1 summarises some of the long-term trends.

As the table shows, a major anthropogenic impact has been the production of emissions, particularly CO_2 and methane, which have been shown to have a major impact on the average surface temperature of the earth. This change appears small to the layperson, but they disrupt ecosystems, lead to more volatile weather events, melt polar ice caps, raise sea levels, and in general are threatening most living species, most notably *homo sapiens* itself. Moreover, the rate of change in temperatures has been increasing. A 1.5 degrees Celsius increase is considered "locked in" at this point and a 2 degree

TABLE 17.1

Changes in selected earth system trends, 1800–2000

	Year			
Earth system trends	1800	1900	2000	Units of measurement
Carbon dioxide (CO_2)	282.58	296.10	366.82	Carbon dioxide. Parts per million (ppm)
Methane	735.50	875.58	1724.18	Methane. Parts per billion (ppb)
Surface temperature	–0.3	–0.34	0.4	Temperature anomaly, degree Celsius (1850 data for 1800)

Source: Source of data: IGBP (2014).

Note: Global surface temperature anomaly (measured as combined land and ocean observations, relative to 1961–1990, 20 year Gaussian smoothed).

increase seems highly likely. Small as these may sound, these changes are wreaking increasing levels of damage. It is argued that these levels must not be gone beyond if the possibility of human extinction is to be avoided, although significant destruction of other species must now be accepted as irreversible (IPPC 2023).

The transport sector is a major contributor to this situation, accounting for close to 30% of the world's final energy consumption in 2015 (32,494 TWh or (2,794 Mtoe), a 43% increase from 2000. Transport energy consumption almost tripled between 1971 and 2015. By comparison industry consumption rose by around 80% and residential consumption by roughly 90% over the same period (Noussan et al. 2020, 4).

Transport directly accounted for 23% of the world's energy-related CO_2 emissions as of 2023. Indirectly, transport infrastructure construction, vehicle manufacturing, and fuel production contribute significant amounts of additional greenhouse gas (GHG) emissions. Transport has the highest reliance on carbon-intensive fossil fuels of any sector. And there are many other significant environmental costs as well, e.g. transport tailpipe emissions being responsible for around 385,000 premature deaths in 2015 (ITF 2023, Section 2).

Not all transport activities are equally dirty, however. In 2018, road travel accounted for 74.5% of transport emissions, the larger share coming from passenger vehicles, namely cars and coaches (45.1 percentage points of the

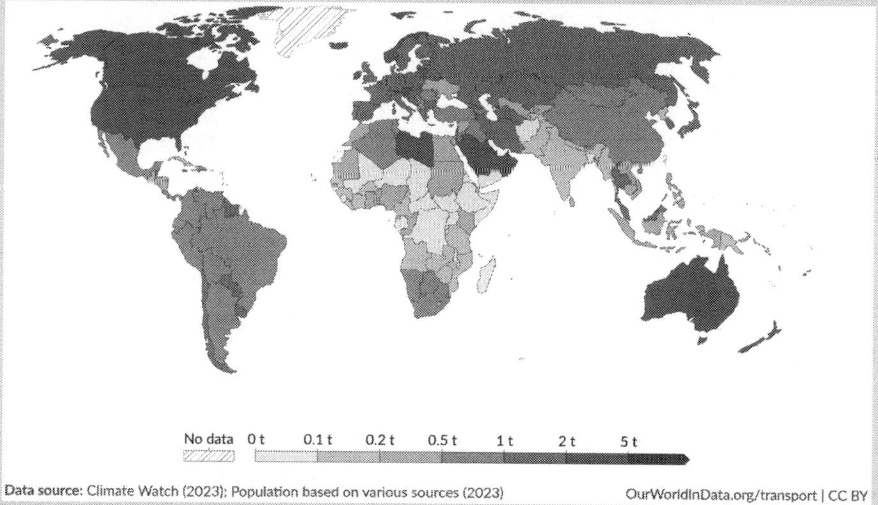

FIGURE 17.1
Per capita CO_2 emissions from transport in 2020.

Note: Emissions measured in tonnes. International aviation and shipping emissions excluded. (Source: as embedded in Figure).

total) and the rest from freight lorries (29.4 percentage points). Aviation accounted for 11.6% of transport emissions (just under 1 billion tonnes of CO_2 each year); global maritime shipping contributed 10.6%; pipelines contributed 2.2%; and passenger and freight rail collectively emitted 1% (Ritchie & Roser 2021).

Transport activity and emissions are also unequally distributed geographically. Figure 17.1 indicates per capita CO_2 emissions by country in 2020 (including road, train, bus, and domestic air travel but not international aviation and shipping). The richer countries are disproportionately responsible for per capita emissions, though rapidly industrialising middle income countries such as China are quickly catching up.

further by predicted increases in coastal winds as will infrastructure more generally, which at a minimum will need to be designed to higher standards than currently apply. Temperature extremes will increase expansion stress and movement on bridges and rail tracks (Taylor & Philp 2010). Severe heat waves will swell rails beyond the historical temperatures that they were built for, causing a visible waviness in their layout that is referred to as a "sun kink", causing misaligned tracks interfering with operations. Rails heat up faster than the air temperature so speed slow-downs are often required by rail operators even in relatively "moderate" heat waves (Simon 2024).

Users and vehicles will also be heavily affected; in Alaska for example 35 years ago frozen tundra supported the driving of heavy equipment on roads 225 days a year. By 2012 it was safe to do so only 75 days a year (Venner & Zamurs 2012, 21). In more moderate climates, cars and trucks will break down more due to overheating and be rendered inoperable by increasing incidences of facility malfunctions.

Related to all this is the link between global warming and increases in the number and severity of extreme weather events. In the US in 2012, weather accounted for 25% of all non-recurring delays and was involved in 25% of all vehicle crashes, disrupting 1.5 million people annually. Dust storms caused by erosion and water depletion are cropping up more often. One notable instance was a dust storm, 50 mi wide in spots and a mile high, that descended on Phoenix, Arizona, in July 2011, grounding flights and closing roads. The American Southwest overall is getting hotter and drier, reducing perennial vegetation cover and resulting in increased dust storm activity. At the other extreme, ice and snow removal alone cost American transport agencies more than $US 2 billion per year on average. Warming reduces this particular expense of course, but the increases in severe snowstorms and periodic hyper-cold winters adds to it (Venner & Zamurs 2012, 20–22).

From an earth system's perspective, climate change is not the only threatening aspect of anthropogenesis (i.e. human-caused environmental change). To continue the focus on transport, vehicle operations produce toxic chemical runoffs that weaken habitats, create sparks that sometimes lead to fires, produce noise and vibration levels detrimental to human and animal health, and, of course, lead to substantial numbers of regular, and occasionally catastrophic, accidents. Transport infrastructure like roads can destroy the ecosystems they pass through, degrade surrounding aesthetics, and create hazards for wildlife interacting with them, of which "road-kill" is but one obvious manifestation. Of course, the metals and other minerals required for production of both infrastructure and vehicles comes from mining which itself carries a very high environmental burden (Spellerberg 1998). (The impact of "everyday" weather on transport operations is considered in Chapter 12).

17.2 CLIMATE CHANGE ADAPTATION, RESILIENCE, AND SUSTAINABILITY

For a long time, climate change policy was concerned with prevention of serious global warming, seeking to reduce emissions and warming enough to return to homeostatic levels and human "business-as-usual". Now policy has shifted to adaptation to serious warming that is now considered unavoidable. Prevention is still an element, with continuing calls to stop GHG emissions from rising into what scientists consider to be a catastrophic tipping point. But climate change itself is not reversible at this point, as was once hoped. The requirement now is to rein in deterioration while accommodating the negative changes that are coming already.

Resilience is the lowest order of adaptation which in its simplest form refers to the ability of a system to maintain homeostasis and return to its initial state of dynamic equilibrium after disturbance. Many now speak of the need for transport systems (and human/infrastructure systems more generally) to be designed to have a faster and more nimble speed of return to functional equilibrium, the speed and closeness between initial and return state being key elements (Holling 1973; Walker et al. 2004).

This can be a purely mechanical and infrastructural concept and often transport engineers and planners interpret it this way. If, for example, extreme weather events occur more frequently, system managers will want to make sure that services are offline as little as possible, returning to "normal" service levels as quickly as possible. This can be as simple as, for example, having extra vehicles in safe storage for ready deployment to replace disabled vehicles, maintaining system redundancies such as relief rail tracks that can take the place of damaged infrastructure, and expedited contracting procedures in the event of emergencies. For longer-term changes such as sea level rise, relocation of key facilities like terminals and airports to higher ground might be recommended (Rowan et al. 2012; Venner & Zamurs 2012).

There is a human social dimension to this too, of course. Physical systems might be restored relatively easily but users might be traumatised and loathe to return to their normal usage patterns. Employees might be too physically uncomfortable to work, or work productively. Thus, social psychologists look at the human ability to cope with, and adapt to, disaster and other disruption (Reich 2006). Both infrastructural and social senses can be used when speaking of transport system resilience, with the most resilient system designs obviously accounting for both.

Resilience focuses typically only on restoring a prior state rather than attaining a superior state to the status quo. Improvement is not excluded but maintenance of existing function is the emphasis. This is fine for some scenarios. But clearly resilience is inadequate as an end goal if the equilibrium being restored is no longer well adapted to changed conditions. Mere resilience may thus be maladaptive rather than adaptive if societies and systems revert back to a state that no longer suits an altered environment (Lin & Petersen, 2013).

A useful alternative concept is antifragility (Taleb 2012). The idea here is that stress often improves rather than breaks down entities, living and non-living, and that the strongest systems should be designed so as to thrive off of perturbation. An antifragile state goes beyond resilient or robust ones in that a resilient entity resists shocks to stay the same, while the antifragile gets better as a result. Taleb provides the example of a city-state whose compactness renders it antifragile as compared to a nation-state, which might be resilient but which is also more likely to come apart under stress. A transport provider that would be able to actually increase operations during and after a disaster might be termed antifragile, and a general claim could be made that decentralised network providers, like Uber, are an example of this. This is the idea, anyway; generalities like these are best taken as exploratory, not definitive.

Denyer (2017) provides a quadrant to frame thinking about "organisational resilience", with a notion similar to antifragility that organisations should not just "bounce back" but "bounce forward". This template dichotomises between behaviours that are defensive (stopping bad things from happening) and those that are progressive (making good things happen) along one axis; and between behaviours that are consistent and those that

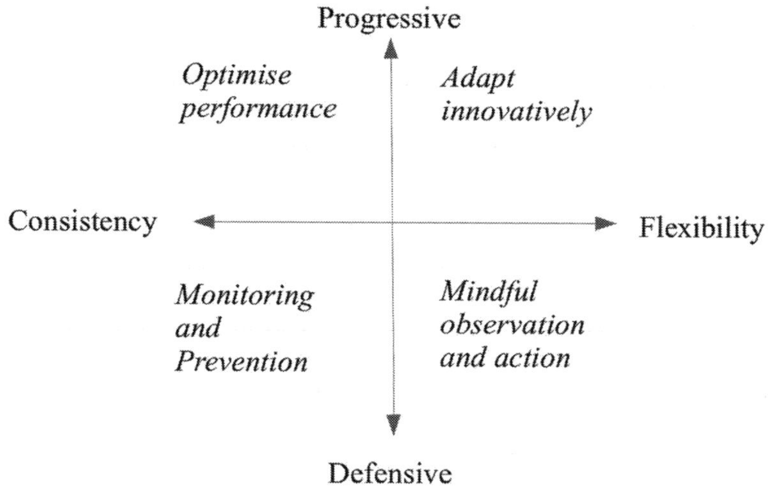

FIGURE 17.2
Organisational resilience template.

Source: Based on Denyer (2017, figure 2, 10).

are flexible, along the other axis. These four possibilities are part of what is termed a "tension quadrant", noting that these forces aren't necessarily bad or good but indicative of choices that transport (and other) entities have when determining whether their structures are adaptable in a robust way (Figure 17.2).

Sustainability is a concept which encompasses resilience but goes beyond it to consider how a system can evolve towards benevolent states rather than just surviving as a status quo, or even "bouncing forward" to an improved, but still diseased, condition. A useful definition relevant for transport systems is an approach "relating to the holistic consideration of environmental, economic, and social concerns, with a long-term perspective… with respect to future generations' needs, i.e., preserving the earth's natural life support systems into the future" (Ramani et al. 2011, 9).

Resilience is arguably most useful from a short-term perspective and for smaller scale domains, where choices are more constrained, as with existing land use patterns and existing infrastructure investment that take time to evolve and direct, but which must nonetheless functionally cope with immediate and unexpected events. Sustainability is much more applicable for the longer-term and at a systemic level because the level of disruption is expected to be greater over time but, on the other hand, with more time more fundamental change may be possible.

17.3 ECONOMIC EFFICIENCY VERSUS SUSTAINABILITY AND RESILIENCE

There are obvious conflicts between efficiency, sustainability, and resilience. At the core of economic efficiency is "consumer sovereignty", which is the notion that individual consumer utility maximisation is sacrosanct and its preservation is the preferred ethical standard by which to judge collective action. The economic efficiency concept also assumes that markets yield the best solutions for optimal resource allocations, except when there is a market failure. Sustainability frameworks in general do not sit well with these ethical and empirical premises, seeing individuals are just a part of a larger holism, and in more robust definitions, seeing individual human preference as subordinate to higher values such as protection of nature and the earth. Many sustainability theorists are also sceptical of the market's efficacy in dealing with systemic earth system challenges, particularly given the state of earth systems at present. Resilience is more neutral in this regard, being compatible with multiple ethical benchmarks.

Having said all this, economists have incorporated sustainability into their models in their own particular ways. One approach is to focus on renewability of natural resources along some "optimal" economic growth path. The results are highly sensitive to underlying assumptions, but the economically "sustainable" equilibrium is one where an economy invests in reproducible capital at exactly the same amount (value) at which the non-renewable capital stock is being diminished. If this is done then a society will be able to maintain a constant stream of consumption into the infinite future without running out of resources (Bromley 2008).

This, of course, is just about resource extraction rather than preservation of things such as a pristine ecosystems or the health of the planet and its species. Thus, this baseline is referred to as "weak" sustainability because it is theoretically possible to meet it and have an "efficient" economy, but still degrade the planet in the process or at least destroy a lot of what makes it worth living on. Strong sustainability extends the model to define "resources" more broadly to include bundles of attributes regarded as valuable in their own right and beyond just their use value. The "strong" paradigm is like the "weak" one in that both examine trade-offs between consumption and production across time (referred to as intertemporal trade-offs). But the strong version is more inclusive of non-economic values (Bromley 2008).

Use-based benchmarks like these, especially economic efficiency, are anathema to many environmentalists because of their primary emphasis on putting resources in the service of human consumption, in which used-up natural capital is simply replaced with constructed capital to allow for on-going human material gratification. Even if the human economy survives, many unethical, immoral, and fundamentally ineffective choices are supported. As Bromley (2008) notes, the economist's version of sustainability is akin to an alcoholic person who drinks all they want but makes sure they have lined up replacement liver or kidneys when their own eventually fail.

A related but intermediate paradigm that at least partly gets around some of these issues is public value (Moore 1997). Economists and many policy analysts see government as a kind of neutral referee that orders relationships and regulates societal conflict rather than being a creator of substantive value in an of itself. Public value encapsulates the idea that government managers can create real but more encompassing material value for their stakeholders in society in much the same way as private firm managers add value for their shareholders. Ecological integrity and preservation could be added as one such value that the state can actively provide and protect.

Frameworks like these that aim for achievement of optimality of any sort require an implicit or explicit ethical standard. To avoid this knotty choice, economists, and many climate scientists, turn to minimum safeguard conditions. This offers a way of sidestepping ethical dilemmas, and also the uncertainty and complexity that abounds in environmental issues. One widely used schema is the precautionary principle which argues for limiting potentially problematic activity, even if uncertain about its harmful effects, to safeguard options for future generations and to preserve system predictability. This amounts to a "do no harm" principle involving refraining from engaging in something whose effects are unpredictable until one knows more about the risks (Gollier & Treich 2013).

Various policy standards can be formulated around the precautionary principle. One is the safe minimum standard (SMS) of conservation which asks policy-makers to ask the question: "Are you really sure you want to do that?" when any tampering with critical eco-resources and capabilities is proposed. Alternatively, future generations could be assigned rights that present generations must honour and take into account. Much climate change policy discourse already employs this type of rhetoric. But economists offer their own versions of how they can be codified more explicitly. Bromley (2008) posits one potential rights assignment in which future persons hold inalienable rights, and members of all prior generations, including the present one, thus bear a duty towards those future right holders. The complete protection of wilderness areas from development or encroachment, or absolute protections of species from extinction, are examples of policies based on such a schema. An alternative is a liability rule which commits present generations to pay future persons some form of offsetting compensation. This could be literal, in the sense of establishing an annuity now to make payments to future persons; or it could be in the form of current actions to limit future obligations, by, for example, setting aside additional areas of wilderness (see Chapter 18 for more on property rights).

17.4 THE EFFICIENCY OF MANAGING VULNERABILITY

Transport managers need to take practical actions to build resilience and sustainability. Denyer's (2017) quadrants are useful here as a guide towards action. Preventative control focuses on risk management, physical barriers, redundancy (spare capacity), back-ups, and procedures to protect against threats and allow for "bounce back" from disruptions. "Mindful action" in this setting refers to an organisational capacity to notice and respond effectively to threats, familiar and unfamiliar. Performance optimisation is the process of continually improving, refining, and extending existing competencies. "Adaptive innovation" is the ability to explore the unknown and create novel responses to it as it arises (akin to Taleb's antifragility) (8–9).

Transport system resilience and sustainability relies on institutional capabilities (the general ability to respond and adapt to changes) and capacity (the overall ability to deliver a certain volume and quality of service). A widely used theory of corporate strategy is the resources-based theory of the firm which essentially holds that a company's ability to exist, accumulate, maintain position, and grow rests on its stock of internal resources that allow it an edge in the marketplace for goods and services. These resources include core capabilities underlying the competitive advantage of a firm that must adapt to a fast-changing marketplace (Grant 1991). Moore's public value notion can be seen as an extension of this model to government operations. One critical organisational resource is superior planning and execution abilities. Adaptive capacities can be seen in this light, requiring short-term sacrifices while generating long-term returns and a adaptive edge of real-time strategic flexibility to make necessary adjustments to existential change.

A resilient transport organisation should thus be more adaptable and nimble and thus potentially more competitive and efficient, all at the same time. For example, building system redundancy, such as spare capacity, is often seen as economically inefficient because it takes resources that could be productive and puts them into "unproductive" reserve. But resilience (and sustainability) require proactive capacity and not just reactive capacity to heighten adaptability to deal with potentially catastrophic uncertainties (Rice & Caniato 2003). Even private firms in normal business conditions, especially those in transport, require some spare capacity to make sure customer service is sufficient across the network to meet relevant demand. If there is not sufficient spare capacity for peak periods, customers, and profits, will

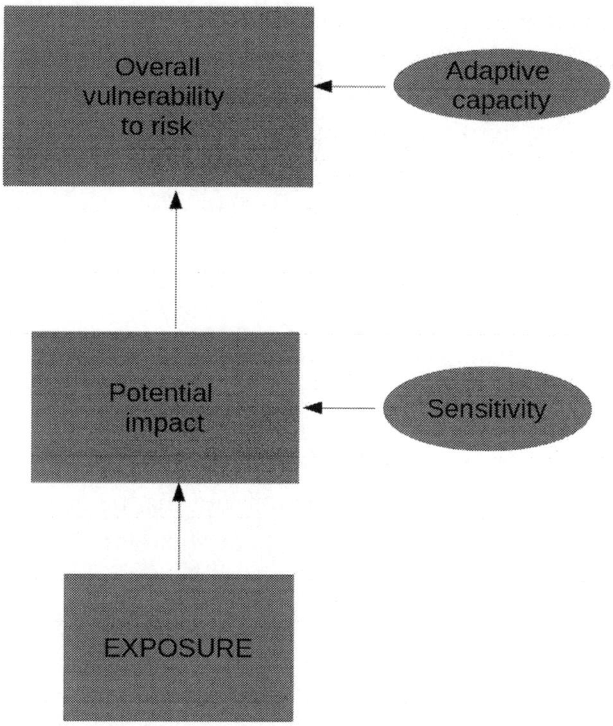

FIGURE 17.3
Vulnerability components.

Source: Adapted from Garnaut (2008, chapter 6).

have to be turned away. The key task of any strategic manager is to strike the balance between supporting mainline operations and maintaining redundancy in the face of uncertainty (Gordon 2016).

Vulnerability to uncertainty arises from exposure and sensitivity to risks, both of which flow into potential risk impact and an entity's adaptive capacity to absorb it. Figure 17.3 maps out these relationships.

As one can see there are two lines of causality that determine overall vulnerability. An entity can face varying degrees of exposure to adverse events which in turn will have differing degrees of potential impact depending upon the entity and its circumstances. For example, transport facilities located along coastlines are especially vulnerable to sea level rise, while those away from water are not; the sensitivity to risk increases with the amount of fixed capital employed because of its relative inability to adjust to flooding due to immovability and the high cost of replacement and repair when damaged. Given this, a system manager can assess potential impact scenarios to determine how much and what kind of adaptive capacity is needed. This would include proactive, (i.e. forward-looking), measures such as relocation of fixed assets inland; and reactive (i.e. more immediate) measures allowing for real-time response, such as the use of temporary structures like pontoon bridges in the event of flooding of main facilities. The result of a such strategic process is an appropriately reduced vulnerability to climate change impacts. But one can easily see that other objectives, including more efficient normal operations, could and should also be part of this exercise. In the ideal this might result in even more efficient outcomes than a single-minded economics approach (Gordon 2016).

The examples here suggest linear causality. One should always keep in mind that risk and vulnerability are not linear, and as complexity theory suggests, cascading effects are common, leading to unpredictable net results (Pescaroli et al. 2021). For example, climate change is increasing snowmelt in cold areas. Roads located in these areas will not just be exposed to increasing water runoff, but also ancillary effects such as slush flows that block culverts, erode structures more quickly, and lead to washouts that can destroy an entire road section. In assessing vulnerability and responses to it, these "multiplicative" impacts need to be understood and planned for as much as possible.

There are, of course, inefficient ways to prepare for and adapt transport systems to climate change. Measures such as hardening of facilities or building spare capacity that sits idle most of the time are examples of what economists would call generators of deadweight losses which tie up resources completely unproductively. Some of this is certainly necessary, as discussed above. But more emphasis could be placed on building of spare capacity that can be useful in non-emergency situations, such as interoperability for spare capacity, e.g. a back-up rail line that can be used as in emergencies, but also for periodic carriage movements from yard to yard in normal circumstances, without interfering with regular operations (Gordon 2016).

Some resilience and adaptation measures can be even "cost neutral", such as painting surfaces of transport facilities white rather than a darker colour, to reflect rather than absorb heat. Other measures, such as urban agriculture and greening around transport lines, may have immediate "co-benefits" (see Chapter 15) that outweigh their costs regardless of how much adaptive capacity they might provide. Energy efficiency is an example of a policy that has definite and immediate co-benefits, making their undertaking a "no regrets" affair. Clear and identified short-term benefits can make resilience projects pay off even if the worst case does not eventuate (GAO 2009).

Even for large engineering works that have little use beyond being needed insurance against catastrophe, a phasing and staging of works might be possible that both minimises costs and hedges bets by building reactive capacity in increasing increments, adding stages only if future predictions at each stage of completion seem to justify it. (Though it must be noted that such phasing can sacrifice economies of scale (EOS) and thus cost more rather than less depending on the project and the context.) This is the approach being taken with the floodgates for the Thames of London which are not all one mega-project, but a series of interlocking projects being added to in a modular fashion. This allows for the possibility of adding or subtracting facilities as risks become clearer over time (UK Government Environment Agency 2015). Resilience and sustainability concerns can thus be a way of forcing transport planners to take project programming into account much earlier in the policy formulation than they may do currently.

Finally, one should not take the economic efficiency concept, as conceived of in welfare economics, without qualification. There is reason to question the efficiency of the status quo *ex ante* in this narrow sense. Even in private markets, uncertainty and risk management and biases in human judgement arguably often lead to "suboptimal" outcomes. Satisficing, in which companies follow routines that may be more adaptive than more purely rational strategies because they are known to be effective under a wider variety of scenarios, are often observed in the field. As noted above this so-called inefficient behaviour may be a good response to unforeseen events and disasters and a general unknowing about the future which the core model ignores. A "pure" efficiency standard would judge such actions as non-optimal (Gordon 2016).

Resilient and sustainable design requires sensible questioning of the existing economic order and whether it is a desirable default for what should be restored in the event of disruption (resilience) or a model for an ideal "efficient" homeostasis (sustainability). Resilience and sustainability planning offer an opportunity to examine the possibility that environmental adjustments now might in fact improve efficiency overall, in addition to achieving the non-efficiency goals they are designed to address.

17.5 BROADER SOLUTIONS – THE IPAT CONSTRUCT

A simplified mechanical summation to describe the links between impacts on planetary systems and human activity is contained in the formula:

$$I = P + A + T$$

I = impact of human activity on the global environment;
P = population, i.e. how many people in total the earth is supporting at a given time;

A = affluence, which broadly refers to how much consumption is being undertaken, crudely measured by Gross Domestic Product (GDP) per capita in output value/person/year;
T = technology, which conceptually refers to state of technical sophistication at a particular point in time but which usually is boiled down to economic intensity of a particular resource or pollutant, such as energy joules per unit value of GDP (Ward et al. 2016).

The IPAT model is less an explanatory device than an illustrative one. It is an accounting identity, i.e. a relationship said to be true by definition, rather than a causal theory. And it is based on static averages. For this last reason, another widely used version of IPAT is multiplicative ($I = P \times A \times T$) rather than additive as above to roughly capture the nonlinearity and dynamic variability that earth system behaviour is subject to. But for simplicity the additive version is presented here.

Either way the IPAT model heuristic lays out three main levers for reducing anthropogenetic climate change: (a) reduce population growth (P); (b) reduce consumption and production (A); and/or (c) come up with technological solutions (T). Environmentalists focus on all three to differing degrees, with some calling for large changes in human consumption and production patterns (to reduce A); others emphasising population control and reduction through birth control and other methods (to lower P); and others calling for green technology and other technical changes to change the way that T impacts the environment, especially by reducing the intensity of resource use and waste outputs (Hawken 2017). Most analysts all agree that all three elements are important. The big policy debate is over which variables to focus on, and how to do so.

17.6 SUSTAINABILITY, DECARBONISATION, AND THE ENERGY TRANSITION

An area of relative agreement seems to be around T. If technical change can support continual increases in A and P but do so in way that nonetheless keeps the cumulative I stable or reducing, then perhaps the human species can have its cake and eat it too, so to speak. Most economists are in this camp implicitly, as mentioned above. But so are some environmentalists, as are others, such as executives in the high technology sector whose business model is all about selling innovations as the solution to all problems.

A leading policy being implemented for reducing GHG is to move from "dirty" fossil fuels, to "clean" renewable ones. In 2017 oil accounted for close to 97% of the transport energy mix, decreasing only slightly to 92% over the following three years. The current global climate change policy agenda is to make an "energy transition" away from oil and gas to energy sources that have reduced or no emissions. Decarbonising transport networks in this way is intended to reduce their contribution to GHG emissions, while still allowing for high levels of transport activity (Noussan et al. 2020, 16).

Decarbonisation of transport can be effected in three ways: (a) by changing the energy powering transport vehicles and infrastructure; (b) by shifting to modes that already use low- or no-emission energy; (c) by making transport more fuel-efficient, regardless of its energy source. These options are obviously not mutually exclusive.

The energy transition is presently focused on electrification, and indeed many of the gains thus far have come through that strategy. The earliest benefits were obtained from an increased penetration of electricity into rail services, which already has a significant portion of service powered that way. But the bigger gains need to come from the road sector, both passenger and freight. Road freight transport is still heavily reliant on diesel because of the greater efficiency of diesel engines, especially at constant speed over long distances, a typical scenario for most long-haul trucking journeys. Road freight thus far has accounted for around 70% of energy consumption but only 20% of global tonne kilometres (TKM), most of which comes from medium and heavy trucks. Light commercial vehicles account for only a marginal share of freight movements and are far less efficient. These smaller vehicles are the ones most amenable to electrification but they are not particularly important in terms of freight transport volumes. Thus, in freight the focus has been not so much on electrification but on alternative fuels such as biodiesel (Noussan et al. 2020, 16).

The bigger action on electrification has been on passenger electric vehicles using batteries – hence the moniker BEV for battery electric vehicle. These are now coming in for their second-generation uptake after their false start at the turn of the 20th century (see Chapter 9). In 2018, China was the primary market for BEVs worldwide, then the US, and then Europe. The market share of BEVs worldwide was only around 3% in 2018 but it is growing substantially, with large absolute numbers even in these early stages. The US sold 360,000 units, 17% of EV global sales (Noussan et al. 2020, 21–23). Since then sales have increased and China is now a leading producer of electric vehicles (although very recently demand has been slowing).

Aviation has been one of the *bête noirs* of GHG, accounting for 12% of transport sector CO_2 emissions in 2016. Alternatives to jet fuels are still far off so the aviation sector has instead focused on fuel-efficiency, as much for economic reasons as for environmental ones given the tight margins in that industry. Between 2000 and 2016, efficiency improved by 2.9% per year due to better aircraft utilisation and fleet renewal with more efficient engines: the average fuel burn of new aircraft models has dropped by 45% between 1968 and 2014 (Noussan et al. 2020, 11–12).

Rail and maritime offer the most promise for GHG reductions. A single rail wagon can carry around three times the weight of a truck, and railways typically carry multiple wagons reaping EOS in both fuel consumption and unit operating costs. Rail freight transport runs on diesel or electricity, electricity-powered trains carrying 48% of the total worldwide TKM in 2016, though much of this is concentrated in Japan, Russia, and Europe. North America and South America are more diesel-reliant. But electric trains are more efficient as well as cleaner so there is scope for more electrification there (Noussan et al. 2020, 18).

Maritime shipping is already highly efficient because of the huge EOS in that sector, and the ability of vessels to maintain high and steady cruising speeds. The specific energy consumption of ships is 5–20 times lower than trucks depending on the country (Noussan et al. 2020, 19). Still there is work on-going to come up with clean fuels for the maritime sector. And while much progress has been made on GHG, maritime activity is still very dirty as far as particulates and other emissions are concerned (Jonson et al. 2020).

The next step in the energy transition is hydrogen, particular FCEV (fuel-cell electric vehicles). Hydrogen FCEVs would be truly revolutionary in terms of GHG and other emissions, and highly efficient as well. The BEV transition is, however, not yet complete, and even now many electric vehicles are hybrid, rather than solely electric. The reason for this is limits on battery life and charging infrastructure. A transition to pure battery electric vehicles (BEVs) will require a substantial collective investment in a new charging network to allow for the full replacement of petrol-powered cars. Improvements in battery life, allowing for a greater range of travel on a single charge, and shorter charging times (recharging time for BEVs presently takes at least five times longer than filling up with petrol) will reduce the number of charging stations along a network and hence the total cost. But even so, up-front costs will be substantial. One cost estimate of building an adequate charging network for a 10% transition of the current fleet of petrol automobiles in the US State of New Jersey alone to BEVs using current battery technology is $US 2.3 billion (Peters et al. 2021). Scaling this up across 100% of the fleet across all 50 US States suggests an investment in the hundreds of billions or even trillions of dollars. The petrol fuel network was built up over many decades and gradually so its substantial network costs are now obscured. With BEVs and other technologies, these network costs must be more front-loaded, especially if the aim is rapid change in energy source.

There are other issues as well. With BEVs, one must consider the capacity of the electric grid to provide the power needed to charge vehicles on-demand during peak loading periods. With FCEVs, an entirely new power grid must be built. And in both cases the shift to a different fuel source also requires a shift in public tax and revenue structures, e.g. the replacement of petrol and diesel excises with new revenue sources. There are also substantial equity issues as costs of new technology vehicles generally tends to be very high in the beginning and many low-income households will not be able to afford them initially – or afford the cost of maintenance, which is also generally higher than traditional petrol or diesel machines.

Finally, the generation of electricity itself requires energy, both in the embodied form of building the grid, generators, chargers, etc.; and in the direct form of the power source for the electricity itself. The idea, of course, is that electrification allows for more efficiency and greater ability to use clean fuels. But this is not necessarily a given, especially during a transition period that could be quite long. Also there are some, especially in the passenger transport arena, who argue that too much use of cars for trips is the fundamental problem, not the energy source they use. Electrification also is not currently applicable to the maritime and aviation sectors and likely not to be in the foreseeable future.

17.7 "SMART" CITIES AND TRANSPORT SYSTEMS

Another "T" solution is "smart" systems, referring to the use of computerisation, digitalisation, AI, and "Big Data" to wring efficiencies out of operations and thus lower carbon and other footprints. One of the original transport conceptions was intelligent transportation systems (ITS) which aimed to apply advances in both software and hardware to vehicles and infrastructure in an integrated manner. ITS and its subsequent "smart" progeny are designed to improve safety, reduce congestion, enhance mobility, minimise environmental impact, save energy, and promote economic productivity. An ultimate goal is to make an entire network technologically cognisant of all the vehicles using it and coordinating their movements to achieve optimal capacity usage. For example, a smart highway could have cars following each other very closely at high constant cruising speeds with seamless entry and exit from the road. The energy savings from both vehicle operations and infrastructure building are obvious.

A broader concept is the smart city. This is essentially an extension of ITS to entire cities. This includes the use of artificial intelligence (AI)-led sensors and software to monitor all urban movements, functions, and service provisions for maximum efficiency. Given that 9.2 billion people are projected by 2040 to be living in cities, with 43 megacities of more than 10 million people expected by 2030, mainly in Asia and Africa, this is an area of great importance (Noussan et al. 2020, 7). Still, it must be said that there is an environmental cost to all of these solutions, ranging from the energy required to run them, the rare earth minerals necessary for their electronics and sensors, and so on. Technology overall is thus not magical but has definite costs and benefits to be weighed against one another.

17.8 INCENTIVE SCHEMES TO REDUCE GHG

Economists offer a classic solution to pollution with the imposition of a "Pigovian Tax" to cover the externality of transport activity (see Chapter 13). This measure internalises the external costs of transport activity *ceteris paribus* and so reduces the activity by making it more expensive for the perpetrator of it. The tax also raises revenue that can be used to achieve environmental or other purposes. One such solution to climate change is a tax on CO_2, otherwise referred to as a carbon tax.

Related to this is carbon emissions trading and permitting, a "mimicking the market" policy in which carbon caps are imposed but emitters can trade flexibly underneath these caps. Thus, a large emitter emitting above the caps can buy carbon credits from a smaller emitter emitting below them, potentially allowing for greater efficiency in compliance, with the transactions conducted determining a market price for carbon that is variable with changing supply and demand conditions. This is supposed to be more efficient than older "command-and-control" regulations that forced all regulated creators of environmental externalities to meet government-set targets regardless of circumstances. The exchange-based "price" for carbon also sets a price signal that flows throughout the economy to cause more extensive and faster "decarbonisation" than could be achieved by older methods.

In 2021, there were 64 carbon pricing instruments (CPIs) in operation, as compared to 58 the prior year. Overall, 21.5% of global GHG emissions were covered by CPIs in 2021, as compared to 15.1% in 2020. China launched its national scheme in February 2021, becoming the world's largest carbon market (World Bank 2021) (see Figure 17.4).

17.9 THE (POSSIBLE) FUTURE

As should be clear by now, the major thrust of climate change adaptation in transport is presently focused on technology, especially for GHG reduction and maximal capacity utilisation. However, there is reason to doubt that this

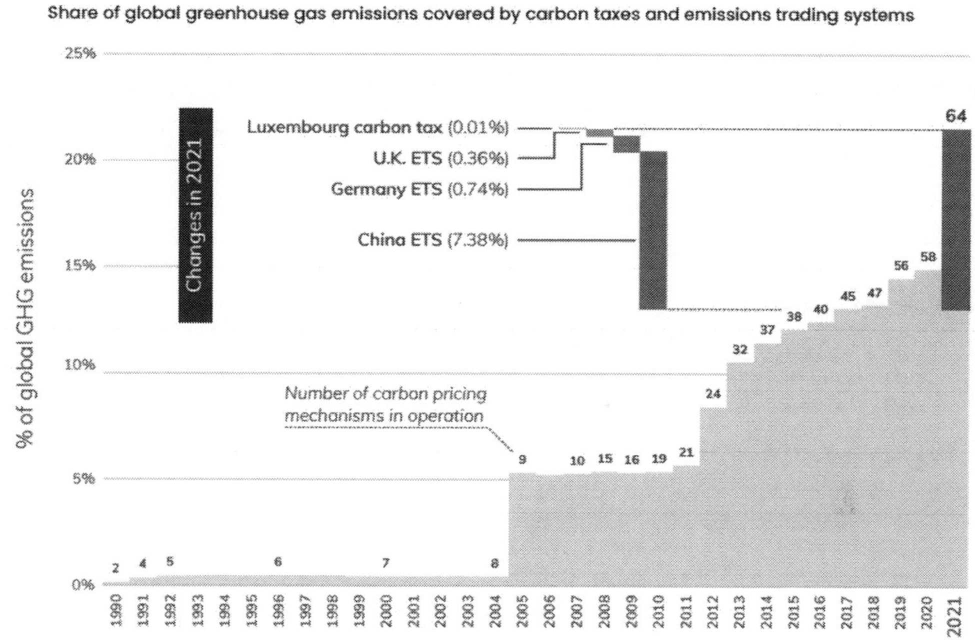

FIGURE 17.4
Carbon pricing instruments worldwide.

Source: World Bank (2021), used under a License: CC BY 3.0 IGO.

approach will be sufficient to meet the task at hand. Economic growth since the First Industrial Revolution has seen tremendous increases in efficiency – but also proportionately even greater increases in consumption and production, with the anthropogenic impact these entail. If past is prologue, we are likely to come up with basically the same result.

The solutions discussed in this chapter, such as decarbonisation, carbon trading, and the energy transition, are still in varying degrees of rollout and their ultimate impacts are not yet clear. None of them seek to reduce affluence – A – in the IPAT construct, which some believe is the major causal factor for climate change, a form of living well beyond our earth system means. There are some other measures being experimented with around A, such as resource re-use and use reduction (discussed in Chapter 16). Related to this is local sourcing, in which supply chains rely on inputs sourced from compact geographical areas into which outputs are also sold. In this way freight movements are reduced and so are GHG and other climate change emissions. Encouraging local tourism has a similar intent on the passenger side, with reduction in distances travelled sometimes referred to as "green miles".

The uptake and success of all these initiatives is relatively marginal thus far. Each has it benefits, but also its costs, with the net result over the long-term not always clear. In short, there is no easy way out of climate change and, in this context, lessening the contribution that transport makes to it in a truly transformative way. Changes are happening, to be sure. But it is not clear that they will have the desired effect, in time.

REFERENCES

Bromley, D. W. (2008). Sustainability. In Durlauf, Steven N. and Blume, Lawrence E. (eds). *New Palgrave dictionary of economics* (2nd edition). Palgrave Macmillan, 6469–6472.

Denyer, D. (2017). *Organizational resilience: A summary of academic evidence, business insights and new thinking*. BSI and Cranfield School of Management.

GAO (2009). *Climate change: Future federal adaptation efforts could better support local infrastructure decision makers*. US General Accountability Office (GAO-13-242).

Garnaut, R. (2008). *Garnaut climate change review: Interim report to the Commonwealth, State and Territory Governments of Australia*.

Gollier, C., & Treich, N. (2013). The precautionary principle. In Shogren, J. F. (ed). *Encyclopedia of energy, natural resource, and environmental economics*. Elsevier.

Gordon, C. (2016). Can transport system resilience and sustainability be economically efficient? (Paper # 16-1319). In *95th Transportation Research Board Annual Meeting Proceedings*. Washington, DC.

Grant, R. (1991). The resource-based theory of competitive advantage: Implications for strategy formulation. *Knowledge and Strategy*, 33(3), 3–23.

Hawken, P. (2017). *Drawdown: The most comprehensive plan ever proposed to reverse global warming*. Penguin.

Holling, C.S. (1973). Resilience and stability of ecological systems. *Annual Review of Ecology and Systematics*, 4, 1–23.

IGBP (2014). The Great Acceleration data (October 2014). *International Geosphere-Biosphere Programme* (spreadsheet). www.igbp.net/download/18.950c2fa1495db7081ebc7/1421334707878/IGBPGreatAccelerationdatacollection.xlsx

IPPC (2023). *AR6 Synthesis Report: Climate Change 2023*. The Intergovernmental Panel on Climate Change. www.ipcc.ch/report/sixth-assessment-report-cycle/

ITF (2023), *Transport Outlook 2023*. OECD Publishing. https://doi.org/10.1787/b6cc9ad5-en

Jonson, J. E., Gauss, M., Schulz, M., Jalkanen, J. P., & Fagerli, H. (2020). Effects of global ship emissions on European air pollution levels. *Atmospheric Chemistry and Physics*, 20(19), 11399–11422.

Lin, B. B., & Petersen, B. (2013). Resilience, regime shifts, and guided transition under climate change: Examining the practical difficulties of managing continually changing systems. *Ecology and Society*, 18(1), 28.

Moore, M. H. (1997). *Creating public value: Strategic management in government*. Harvard University Press.

Noussan, M., Hafner, M., & Tagliapietra, S. (2020). The evolution of transport across world regions. In Noussan, Michel; Hafner, Manfred; Tagliapietra, Simone (Eds). *The future of transport between digitalization and decarbonization*. Springer Briefs in Energy. Springer Nature. https://doi.org/10.1007/978-3-030-37966-7_1

NYAS (2010). *Climate Change Adaptation in New York City: Building a Risk Management Response*. New York Academy of Sciences, New York City

Panel on Climate Change 2010 Report, 1196, (May). https://nyaspubs.onlinelibrary.wiley.com/doi/10.1111/j.1749-6632.2009.05415.x

Pescaroli, G., Guida, K., & Kelman, I. (2021). Promoting societal resilience to cascading risk and concurrencies. In Brears, R. C. (ed). *The Palgrave handbook of climate resilient societies*. Palgrave Macmillan. https://doi.org/10.1007/978-3-030-32811-5_125-1

Peters, J, Gordon, C., & Flanagan, R. (2021). *The cost of driving in New Jersey: Putting the pedal to the metal – New Jersey's public funding burden on vehicle users*. The Garden State Initiative.

Pomeranz, K. (2000). *The great divergence: China, Europe, and the making of the modern world economy*. Princeton University Press.

Ramani, T., Zietsman, J., Gudmundsson, H., Hall, R., & Marsden, G. (2011). Framework for sustainability assessment by transportation agencies. *Transportation Research Record*, 2242, 9–18.

Reich, J. W. (2006). Three psychological principles of resilience in natural disasters. *Disaster Prevention and Management: An International Journal*, 15(5), 793–798.

Rice, J., & Caniato, F. (2003). Building a secure and resilient supply network. *Supply Chain Management Review*, 7(5), 22–30.

Ritchie, H., & Roser, M. (2021). *Transport*. Our World in Data.org. Retrieved from: https://ourworldindata.org/transport

Rowan, E., Evans, C., Riley-Gilbert, M., Hyman, R., Kafalenos, R., Beucler, B., Rodehorst, A., & Schultz, P. (2012). Evaluation of resiliency of transportation networks after disasters. *Transportation Research Record*, 2284, 109–116.

Simon, M. (2024). Taking a train during a heat wave? Watch out for 'sun kinks.' *Grist* (July 9). https://grist.org/transportation/taking-a-train-during-a-heat-wave-watch-out-for-sun-kinks/

Spellerberg, I. A. N. (1998). Ecological effects of roads and traffic: A literature review. *Global Ecology & Biogeography Letters*, 7(5), 317–333.

Taleb, N. N. (2012). *Antifragile: How to live in a world we don't understand*. Allen Lane.

Taylor, M., & Philp, M. (2010). Adapting to climate change – implications for transport infrastructure, transport systems and travel behaviour. In *Australasian Transport Research Forum Proceedings*. Adelaide, Australia.

UK Government Environment Agency (2015). *Environmental guidance: The Thames Barrier*. www.gov.uk/the-thames-barrier /

Venner, M., & Zamurs, J. (2012). Increased maintenance costs of extreme weather events: Preparing for climate change adaptation. *Transportation Research Record*, 2292, 20–28.

Walker, B., Holling, C. S., Carpenter, S. R., & Kinzig, A. (2004). Resilience, adaptability and transformability in social–ecological systems. *Ecology and Society*, 9(2), 5.

Ward, J. D., Sutton, P. C., Werner, A. D., Costanza, R., Mohr, S. H., & Simmons, C. T. (2016). Is Decoupling GDP growth from environmental impact possible? *PLOS One*, 11(10), e0164733. https://doi.org/10.1371/journal.pone.0164733

World Bank (2021). *State and Trends of Carbon Pricing 2021*. Santikarn,Marissa; Churie Kallhauge,Angela Naneu; Bozcaga,Mustafa Ozgur; Sattler,Leyla; Mccormick,Michael Stephen; Ferran Torres,Ana; Conway, Darragh; Mongendre, Leo; Inclan, Carolina; Mikolajczyk, Szymon; Gilde, Lieke 't; Long, Imogen; Bravo, Felipe; Lorenzo, Federico; Korthuis, Adriaan.

State and Trends of Carbon Pricing 2021 (English). World Bank Group. http://documents.worldbank.org/curated/en/771941622009013802

CHAPTER 18

Political economy

18.1 INTRODUCTION: POLITICAL ECONOMY AND ITS DISCONTENTS

Economic theory models decisions involving politics via a construct known as political economy, which examines the relationships between individuals, governments, and policy-makers by treating them all as rational maximisers and positing political decisions as bargains in which there is an exchange of gains and losses until "mutual gains from trade" (to paraphrase Adam Smith) leave enough people better off to seal the deal, or not.

The notion of political decisions as consisting of a series of exchanges between agents over losses and gains does seem to fit the politics of road pricing pretty well, especially in the area of congestion pricing where motorists, long used to free or low-cost rides on public roads, are loath to give up that present privilege for the promise of faster travel times for everyone, especially when some of these do not pay a toll at all (such as transit users) (Box 18.1). Benefit from lowered congestion will also come in the future, not now, when decisions are being made and implemented. Thus, when it comes time for a vote on a congestion charge the result may well be "no" as those who will bear the cost are strongly motivated to vote against as opposed to those benefiting being only weakly motivated to vote "yes".

Political economists have proposed a number of policy fixes for this problem, based on the assumption that all politics is about distribution of resources across individual constituents or groups of like-minded constituents. Even on these narrow terms, however, actual construction of a revenue formula that will yield the winning coalition is elusive. Goodwin (1989) for

DOI: 10.4324/9781003350866-22

BOX 18.1 INTRODUCTORY CASE: NEW YORK CITY'S FIRST (FAILED) ATTEMPT AT CONGESTION PRICING

In 2007, New York City's Mayor Michael Bloomberg announced a plan for a congestion pricing scheme for Manhattan, south of 86th Street. This cordon price in its initial incarnation was modelled on London's scheme and would have imposed an $US 8 dollar a day charge for passenger cars (and a $US 21 dollar a day charge for trucks) to travel into Manhattan south of 86th street, with the zone charge operative between Monday and Friday, from 6:00 AM until 6:00 PM. A $US 4 reduced charge was imposed for passenger cars ($US 5.50 for trucks) driving solely within the zone. Adoption of the plan had a sweetener attached: a possible award of a $US 354 million grant from the US Federal Highway Administration under its Urban Partnerships Program (Peters & Gordon 2009).

If considered solely along winner–loser coalition lines this proposal should have been a "slam-dunk" to use American slang. The congestion price could have significantly lowered traffic in Manhattan and raised significant amounts of revenue for the city, possibly supplemented by a significant federal grant. However, the plan died, without even a vote in the New York State Legislature.

One reason for the failure was that although the congestion charge might have yielded a net benefit to society in social welfare terms, there were quite a few losers from the proposal that would have lost quite a lot, while the gains were more diffused throughout the population. Indeed, the bridges across the East River in New York were (and still are) un-priced, and the drivers in the two most populous boroughs in the City that used those crossings, Queens and Brooklyn, would have been quite hurt by having that situation changed. New Yorkers in general would each benefit a bit from lowered congestion, with the total net gain likely being large. But the Queens and Brooklyn residents who would see sharp losses up front organised vociferous opposition to congestion charging (Gordon & Flanagan 2012). Thus, King et al. (2007) argue that congestion and other road pricing is generally politically difficult because "what pricing lacks is a constituency who will derive concentrated benefits that exceed their costs" (111).

However, economic gains and losses, important as those are, were only part of the picture. New York also suffered from both a deleterious institutional environment and a political leadership that was arguably complacent and not strongly committed enough to the proposal to overcome the obstacles to its passage.

London's successful imposition of congestion charging provides an interesting contrast to New York City's defeat. Both the London and New York governments are creatures of higher levels of government. During the time of the congestion charge, London had been granted extremely broad powers of transport within its domain, able to regulate that sector as it saw fit and to use any tolling revenues as it desired (Peters & Gordon 2009). London could have these powers because in England all grants of political sovereignty flow from one unitary central government (as explained in Chapter 13).

But in the US there is shared sovereignty between a national government and 50 US States. New York City is a creature of the sovereign US State of New York. But that State does not have nearly the powers of the English national government. Moreover, the New York City metropolitan area transport region covers three sovereign States – New York, New Jersey, and Connecticut – in contrast to London whose large area was made sovereign unto itself. Thus, there is a much lower level of political autonomy within New York City as compared to London. And, for various historical reasons, New York City's municipal government has limited and fragmented authority over transport (and other) issues (Gordon & Flanagan 2012).

London's substantial local powers allowed it to create a central agency, Transport for London (TfL), which could design, build, and control the charging mechanism and use of all the revenues raised by it as deemed appropriate. These revenues were, in turn, used to support the running of the cordon charge (making it self-financing) and to invest in a major expansion of transit. New York City's proposal, by contrast, would have created a "Smart Authority" that would have been responsible for administering the congestion charge. But this authority did not have unlimited control over the revenues raised. The NY Metropolitan Transportation Authority (MTA), a special public authority of NY State, would continue to run the city's transit system and also some of the tolled bridges, thus controlling new revenues raised on those facilities, including the East River bridges. The New York–New Jersey Port Authority, a bi-state entity, also controlled some bridges and crossings and it too would have kept control of its own revenues. This decentralisation created various political and administrative problems for the proposed charge in New York since the disposition of toll revenues back into the transport system could not be reliably predicted or managed by the city government (Gordon & Flnagan 2012).

The political leadership also was quite different in the two cities. London's Mayor Ken Livingstone became a fierce champion of cordon pricing despite its intense unpopularity in the beginning. His unwavering political commitment, combined with the strong powers of the London government, allowed for the proposal to be implemented with little friction. Its quick success in reducing congestion combined with robust investments in new transit soon made the scheme popular. New York City mayor Michael Bloomberg also faced early opposition. But, by contrast, Bloomberg had to negotiate with many groups to even move the proposal forward, in a way that Livingstone did not need to, and he proved to be unequal to the task. Bloomberg, a self-made billionaire, had been CEO of a company he named after himself, and his somewhat distant and arrogant management style proved to be a hindrance when sensitive negotiations were required, as was the case here. Bloomberg's political party affiliation of a Republican turned Independent in a city and State where Democrats controlled the State legislature that had to pass any and all of the elements of the charge scheme before it could begin at all was a further handicap (Gordon & Flanagan 2012).

In the end, nothing came of the whole thing, not even a vote on an enabling law. The details of this collapse are a labyrinthine story, as most New York political transactions are. But Bloomberg's management and political style were one key factor, as was his being outside the dominant political party establishment. In this case, it was not just the distribution of gains and losses, but also leader personality, governmental arrangements, and political institutions that were collectively responsible for a political failure.

There is a post-script to this story, however, which reinforces the points made above. As this book was going into production (in early 2025) New York City finally did establish a congestion price cordon. In 2017, New York State governor Andrew Cuomo put forward a new proposal for congestion pricing in the city, a significant move because it came from the State government which had ultimate authority to pass and implement such an initiative. The entire idea was waylaid by the Covid-19 pandemic and then the election of US President Donald Trump who was hostile to the notion. The election of a Democratic Party president, Joe Biden, in 2020, and the end of the pandemic shortly afterwards, reinvigorated congestion pricing and a new governor, Kathy Hochul, managed to gain approval for the charge in early 2023, only to halt its implementation suddenly because she was concerned about its potential political effect for her (Democratic) party in upcoming national in November. This caution did not prevent Donald Trump from winning a second term or from Republicans gaining control of Congress, after which Hochul felt she might as well go ahead after all, though with a lowered $9 charge for a zone below 60th street in Manhattan, as opposed to the $15 originally planned. Already, however, the governor of the neighbouring state of New Jersey has sued New York State to reverse the decision, and Trump may well try to reverse federal government support given by Biden (Reisman & Rivard 2024). The contrast between American federalist complexity with the relatively simplicity of English unitary government in this case couldn't be clearer.

example proposes a "rule of three" in which thirds of toll revenues are respectively spent on road improvements, mass transit, and general revenue, a template that is supposed to buy off different interests and thus neutralise opposition by any one of them. Small (1992), however, says this proposed solution is inefficient in that it spends too much on roads; he would shift to one-third to drivers as a group to cover their operating expenses, such as licences, rather than infrastructure. Meanwhile King et al. (2007) say that cities should get the greater share of revenues from any congestion pricing. They argue that this concentration of money will cause politically powerful urban governments to organise on behalf of congested pricing, with the added benefit that this group has a defensible claim to the revenue.

Thus, much political economy analysis of congestion pricing shares a basic logic: the winners from road charging are the many drivers who save more time than they pay in tolls but whose gains individually are either small, as compared to the typically numerous losers whose losses are fairly large and more than the value of travel time saved (VTTS) they gain. These losers will thus will be vociferous in opposing new tolling; while the winners will have more diffuse and notional gains and thus tend to be fragmented and haphazard in their support. The revenue-sharing schemes discussed above, and many others like them, are purportedly design to create coalitions supportive of congestion charges enabling them to be supported and implemented. The reasoning is similar to a parallel and standard political economy formulation of constituencies for "free" trade, i.e. that gains from liberalised trade are widely distributed, but losses are concentrated, and hence protectionism has the initial advantage when trade restrictions come up for consideration.

As the opening case describes, reality often deviates from the elegance of theory. Importantly, while beneficiaries and cost-bearers may seem to be natural groupings of affected individuals, constituents and voters often do not act as mere coalitions of atomised agents or even internally negotiated blocs as theory seems to suggest. Groups like "road users" and "transit users" are, in fact, often very heterogeneous, and do not necessarily make up natural political blocs even if suitably compensated. For example, drivers who pay tolls are rich, poor, and everything in between, with differing value of travel time (VOTT) and hence different senses of gain from VOTT reductions brought by a congestion charge. Depending upon this internal valuation, some notional beneficiaries may in fact consider themselves losers from a congestion charge, even one that actually reduces congestion. Similarly, drivers live in different locations, travel to and from different origin-destination pairs, identify with different social groupings, and so forth (Gordon & Flanagan 2012).

Granted, there are "central tendencies" across groups and to this degree revenue redistribution schemes between agents might work on an "average" basis. But there is often a difference between groupings of individuals, such as road users, who have broad commonalities in individual interest, and more organised pressure groups, which are something different. Indeed, in political settings agents often work through political and economic institutions and organisations such as political parties and State structures. The London and New York cases illustrate this vividly. These two cities are not simple entities institutionally and it is the institutional detail that often blows apart even a well-designed pricing scheme. The personal aspects of political and community leaders, ideas and ideologies, and historical "path dependency" are further complicating factors.

This is not to say that the fundamental calculus of resource transfers across different groups is not a valid frame. Particularly where material issues are the primary focus, as in road charging and many other transport policies and investments, a net gains and losses approach is very useful. And even where institutional and personal issues play a role, the core theory can accommodate these as well.

18.2 PUBLIC CHOICE THEORY

The economic justification for the existence of government is based on the necessity of providing public goods that the private market will not provide, and to correct market failures such as externality (see Chapter 13). The government also exists to provide "rules of the game", such as property rights, which allow Pareto-optimal market exchanges to occur in the first place. But while the core model offers reasons and criteria for state action, it does not offer a theory of how the state will actually behave. Welfare and public economics effectively assume that government is a cipher that mechanically fills in the gaps that the market leaves unfilled.

Transaction costs economics (TCE) is one theoretical extension that begins to fill this gap, positing the government as being an agent to the principal of the general public (at least in the case of notional democracies), with the agency problem arising as an issue (see Chapter 11). Public choice theory extends on this by explicitly assuming that the state is composed of actors like any other economic actor, and thus with their own agenda. Its assumptions include the following:

- Agents of the state are rational, maximising, and self-interested, just like private actors.
- The political "market" can be described in the same way that the economic market can be, i.e. through examination of its equilibrium positions, stability, efficiency, etc.
- There is exchange between agents in the political market to set "prices" and "quantities" of public and other governmentally provided goods and services, analogous to what happens between agents trading private goods and services within private markets.

- In democracies, individual agents' preferences are expressed through voting: a vote, like a private purchase or sale, both reveals preferences and collectively "buys" a public good.
- Government, being an agent of the general voting public, but one that has ulterior private motives, will aim to provide as little as possible to its principal, while maximising its own gains.

A major focus of public choice theory is on how government institutions detect collective preferences and formulate policies based on them. In the case of one-person, one-vote democracy, the most relevant theory is that of the "median voter". If there is a majority-rule electoral procedure to pick representatives to run the government (and assuming away additional rules such as preference voting, plurality rules, and so forth), individuals running for office will appeal to the preferences of the "median" voter, i.e. that voter that sits in the middle of a normal bell-curve distribution of voter preferences (see Figure 18.1).

The analytical logic is exactly analogous to the Hotelling theorem considered in Chapter 4. Just as in that model, in which merchants aim to locate a spot along a boardwalk that gives them spatial access to the most customers as compared to their competitors, politicians will position themselves along a political spectrum to ensure that they get the 50% plus one of voters they need to win election. To use a simple example, assume there are

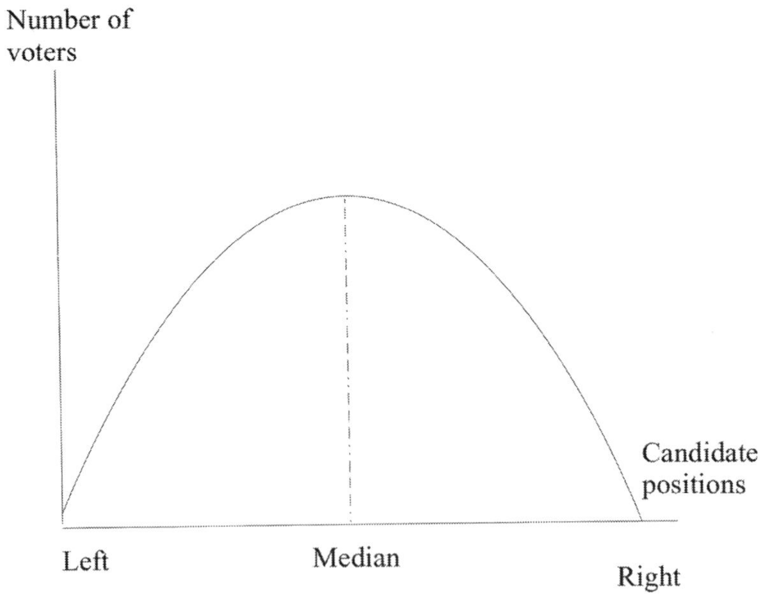

FIGURE 18.1
The median voter theorem.

several candidates for election. Applying the conventional political terms of "left" and "right", and assuming a two candidate race a "left" candidate taking a position on the spectrum will capture voters to his/her left, while a "right" candidate will have all voters to the right on his/her side. But by itself this is not enough to ensure a majority vote at the polls. Candidates have an incentive to position themselves as close to the centre to capture a majority. The "right" candidates will tend to move leftward, while the "left" candidates will move rightward. Ultimately, a majority is claimed by that candidate which successfully stakes out the position of the median voter (Rowley 1984).

In transport policy-making especially, this theory would suggest that even with an interest-group winning resource redistribution for a project or policy that improves economic welfare, it may be stymied at times by the need of elected representatives to get elected. Taking a median position will meet the politician's objective, but not necessarily the preferences of the greater public. There is also an incentive for politicians to put forward only agendas that ensure their own majority result, rather than one that might progress the greater good, even, possibly, one that might itself have majority support but perhaps not behind a particular politician. This process is referred to as "agenda setting" (i.e. the manipulation of a choice menu offered to voters to favour some proposals over others). In some ways the contrasting cases of New York and London congestion pricing give some credence for this view, with electoral politics intruding much more in the former case than the latter one.

As with other aspects of core theory, though, the median voter theorem is highly simplistic. On its own terms, the median voter outcome requires modification if the distribution of voter preferences is other than normal and/or if the voting rules used are other than majority rule. These modifications are feasible and there are many public choice models that accommodate plurality voting (the largest number of votes wins, whether it is a majority or not) and other variants, as well as polarised and other voter preference distributions. Indeed a very useful applied field of public choice is the design of "optimal" voting rules to capture voter preferences as closely as possible (Congleton 2004).

But once voter preference enters the realm of not being fully "rational" or "maximising", great volatility can be introduced that cannot be captured by even a sophisticated model. Voters are social animals, prone to herd and other social dynamics that do not match the requirement of atomism in choice and preference. They also can have ideas, beliefs, and values that do not collapse so easily into purely material gains and losses. The role of "charismatic" or "strong" leadership, so essential in much transport policy change for good and for ill, does not fit easily in these constructs either, as the opening case hinted at. Also much power is exercised outside the ballot box, as Box 18.2 presents.

BOX 18.2 THE RISE AND FALL OF ROBERT MOSES

Robert Moses was a New York State and City planner who never held an elected office nor particularly high official plenipotentiary authority. Yet during a 44-year reign in various, relatively minor offices, mostly in New York City, he built nearly 700 mi of roads, including major highways, 20,000 acres of parkland and public beaches, 658 playgrounds, 7 new major bridges, the UN headquarters, the Central Park Zoo, and the Lincoln Center arts complex, at a total cost of $US 27 billion in nominal dollars over the years, equivalent to hundreds of billions in current dollars (Caro 1974).

Moses began his career in highway building, being a proponent of recreational automobile travel, and he was the father of the Long Island parkway system. He ended his career as the man responsible for some of the most infamous urban freeway projects in the US, including the Cross-Bronx Expressway and Gowanus Parkway which cut through stable neighbourhoods in New York City, and as a leading champion of a stillborn plan to build interstate freeways through the heart of Manhattan (Caro 1974).

What was exceptional about this achievement, beyond its sheer scale, was that Moses acted largely independently of established planning departments and authorities and of the electoral democracy which they were accountable to. Indeed, he disparaged professional planners, sometimes referring to them as "municipal smart alecks" and generally building his projects without reference to larger official city plans, designing them first as stand-alone facilities, and only after that in relation to other parts of larger highway networks that he spearheaded (Brown 2005, 19).

Moses began his highway-building career presiding over the construction of parkways which delivered roads having throughput dressed with extensive landscaping and aesthetic beauty. As urban congestion increased, however, he emphasised roadways that increased speed of travel using functional facilities with less adornment. During the 1940s, he started building modern freeways in New York City. He then increasingly transitioned to building freeways around and through neighbourhoods in the boroughs of Queens, Brooklyn, and the Bronx. Moses accomplished all this largely by creating his own institutions to leverage state and federal grants to pay large proportions of the cost of his projects and to control the toll income from his various roads to build yet more roads (Brown 2005, 22). Moses was generally able to almost literally steam-roll the gathering opposition to his projects, though he finally met his match when residents of Greenwich Village in New York successfully opposed his plan to put an expressway straight through lower Manhattan. This failure began a quick fall from grace that ultimately deposed him from public office and influence.

> Moses's career is an example of the power of individual agency, ideology, and charisma that is hard to capture, either as cause or effect, in standard political economy or public choice models. Such cases are relatively rare, to be sure. But they are frequent enough in transport, and, sometimes quite consequential, to require moving beyond the purely economic paradigm of collective decision-making at times.

18.3 THE AGENCY PROBLEM IN EXTREME: LEVIATHAN

This discussion above still assumes that government agents are at least attempting to approximate public tastes. The public choice-based theory of *Leviathan*, named after the 18th-century English philosopher Thomas Hobbes's book of the same name, questions even this premise. This theory sees public bureaucrats as self-maximising just like all other agents in the economy. And at the extreme, the agency problem gets turned on its head, with government becoming the principal, with voters turned into chattels.

At a macro-political scale, politicians are the agents to the voters. But politicians are also principals to the agents who carry out their directions. These are the bureaucrats, and they are not as constrained as the politicians. Granted they require "their" politicians to remain in office in order to exercise their power (though Robert Moses seems to be a contrary case). But they are often only weakly and indirectly tied to the rigours of electoral democracy and, worst of all, have the power of the law and the threat of government force behind them.

What this means, according to public choice logic, is that public servants will accrue as many resources as they can rather than do what they are tasked to do, which is to serve the public and follow the directions of the elected representatives of the people. This leads at best to wasted and misdirected resources, such as the building of bureaucratic fiefdoms. There is also the possibility of government failure, a term economists use to refer to situations in which state entities create problems of their own, making problems worse, and in the extreme, consuming more and more private resources, while limiting individual freedom, creating the monster "Leviathan" within the theory's name. This is particularly problematic in non-democratic systems, but a threat in all political arrangements (McGuire 2019).

The Leviathan idea is quite anti-state, enshrining the belief that the government which governs best governs least. Public choice more generally is somewhat more agnostic on this point, but there too the general tenor is one of scepticism about government action. The basis for this conclusion is the premise that while the state is meant to be an agent for social good, it is difficult to control and monitor and its intervention in markets tends to screw things up.

Is this a fair representation of the public policy apparatus? Certainly, there have been numerous examples of government failure and other problems in the transport arena, the example of Robert Moses being indicative. But there have also been notable, and very public-minded, successes as well, the London congestion scheme being a good example, and inconsistent with the notion that public servants are *always* power hungry and selfishly motivated and politicians limited seekers of median voters. The preferences of public functionaries are definitely not as uniform as Leviathan and its underlying core theory precepts hold, with many transport professionals, public and private, being inclined to care about outcomes that serve the greater good.

18.4 LAW AND ECONOMICS AND PROPERTY RIGHTS

A related theoretical building block of political economy is the discipline known as law and economics, which encompasses various theories about the economics of property rights. Indeed, a basic economic claim for the existence of government is that it exists to establish well-defined and well-functioning property rights, without which markets would be unable to function. A property right entitles a party to use a specified resource in a specified way under specified circumstances. A property right is often called an entitlement for this reason.

For example, if an agent owns a car, property rights in most countries allow that agent to do with that car whatever the agent desires, so long as it does not infringe upon anyone else's property rights or inflict a societal harm. Thus, the car owner can drive the car when and where they please except when going against on-going traffic, violating speed limits, etc. (Cole & Grossman 2002).

There are two major categories of property rights (or rules, to use legal parlance). Property rules refer to an arrangement where one party has an entitlement that cannot be taken away except by voluntary agreement (typically, though not exclusively, in exchange for a payment). This is the case just described. Liability rules are those in which one party can take away the entitlement of another so long as the taker compensates the loser for this taking. With a property rule, no one can infringe upon the holder's right without that holder's permission. With a liability rule, anyone can infringe upon the holder's right without permission so long as compensation for any damages is paid by the person doing the infringing. With property rules, the value of the right is generally assessed by the market since rights are only traded as a result of mutual agreement. With liability rules, the value of the right (as measured by the cost of damages) is usually assessed by a third party such as a judge during legal proceedings that arise out of conflicts between rights holders. They also may be codified within regulations or other formalised documents (Barzel & Allen 2023).

Property rights are fairly straightforward with purely private goods. Public and quasi-public goods, however, make the definition, assignment, and enforcement of either property or liability rules problematic because they can potentially be jointly consumed. Thus, agent A may have clear rights to a pure public good X, but since agent B can consume X at will without A's permission and without compensation to A, that property right is largely meaningless. Property rights allow for economic efficiency by allowing for internalising all costs and benefits. But in cases involving publicness and externality, the setting of a legal entitlement likely cannot achieve this.

The assignment and design of implicit and explicit property rights are quite important in many transport arenas. With urban public transit (UPT), informal competitors to formal transit systems, such as independent vans and jitneys, are present in many lower-income countries, and quite a few large urban areas everywhere. These services, which typically operate with smaller vehicles on relatively fixed routes, and not always on fixed schedules, often feed off established official routes served by regular, fixed-schedule formal services, though they also often fills gaps in those services as well. In this case, formal rights to operate and offer services conflict with informal operations outside official purview (Cervero 2001). Here rights assignment and specification is not so much the problem as enforcement of existing rights to operate.

A related issue is "curb rights", i.e. who has the right to pick up passengers along various points along the street. In US cities during the 1910s, for example, private jitney operators arose to pick up passengers along the routes of streetcars in US cities, sometimes running ahead of the scheduled streetcar arrivals and poaching streetcar customers. At first there was a rather chaotic situation in which there were no rights assigned to pick up (or drop off) passengers at particular locations or during particular time periods. An assignment needed to be made, and in this case the streetcar operators got local governments to enforce their exclusive franchise rights (the usual local monopoly arrangement made between governments and operators) to drive out the jitneys. This was not necessarily an economically efficient solution since it eliminated a valuable adjunct to official service and reduced overall competition for the traveller's trip (Levinson et al. 2016, 45). Here rights were assigned and enforced, but perhaps not at an "efficient" level.

More recently, there has been talk of leveraging the value of real estate contained in street parking places to potentially raise new revenues and more efficiently allocate use of such spaces. Of course much street parking is already priced. But the right to this space is generally allocated on a first-come, first-served basis that does not necessarily lead to efficient outcomes. Urban commercial deliveries value such spaces in dense urban areas typically much more highly than individual drivers, and they would also prefer to have more predictability in securing such spaces. One idea is to lease some prime public street parking and commercial delivery zones to private freight carriers. This would allow freight companies a set of reliable parking spaces that they could use when desired, cutting the amount of time spent searching for parking, or parking illegally and incurring infringement fines. This latter item is a source of much revenue for localities, but one that imposes unpredictable costs on businesses with little benefit to them; a public lease would allow localities to capture these same revenues, while easing the business conditions of carriers and also potentially reducing traffic congestion somewhat since commercial vehicles would spend less time hunting for a place to set down. This method redesigns the typical assignment of rights to street parking to attain a hopefully more economically efficient outcome (Gordon & Peters 2013).

18.5 THE COASE THEOREM

An economist named Ronald Coase, a figure also influential in TCE, developed a landmark hypothesis known as the Coase theorem which claims that if a property right is extended to an externality, then the economically efficient outcome will result simply because of this initial assignment (with the usual simplifying assumptions of perfect competition, perfect information, and costless transactions). The theorem works on the basis that rational maximising agents will negotiate with each other after a right is assigned to maximise their own interests and, as in all market transactions, achieve a social optimum. Who gets that right will not affect the efficiency of the final outcome though it will affect its equity (i.e. who gets what in the final redistribution of resources that the rights assignment leads to). The policy recommendation that flows out of the Coase theorem is that government should create and assign property rights wherever feasible when externality exists (the case of public goods is not so clear) to resolve market failures that might otherwise result, and design them to be economically efficient.

A transport-related example of the Coase theorem is auto insurance as a policy solution for road accidents. Most jurisdictions around the world require drivers to insure their cars before they can legally drive. Usually the basic requirement is for liability insurance providing payments for financial and other losses incurred when an accident occurs. This can be seen as a standard liability rule, namely that a driver has a "right" to cause an accident but must compensate those injured bodily and financially by that accident (Wriggins 2010). In Coasean terms, a right has been assigned in the form of a liability, rather than an entitlement assignment. In the pure world of theory, this assignment should lead to an "efficient" level of auto accidents. That is, drivers will internalise the cost of accidents that their driving might cause and adjust the care they take in driving to get these costs down to a level that they deem acceptable to them as individuals. In a world of perfect markets and rational, maximising, selfish, atomistic agents, constrained by competition, this will result in a total quantity and quality of accidents that maximises social welfare losses. The trade-off between gains from faster travel time and losses from accidents will be equalised at an efficient level.

Governments in this case have deemed that the assignment of a right in the form of a liability rule is not, however, sufficient to reach this optimum. Mandated insurance is called for as well. One reason for this is that the Coase theorem implicitly does not account for the effects of resource distribution. Not everyone can afford to cover the cost of damages from accidents they cause out of their own pockets. Hence a third-party insurer is brought in to make sure that all payments that need to be made will be made. The imposition of insurance requirements, and the insurance markets they create, are also a means of collecting complete data on accident costs and risks across drivers, meeting the requirements of the Coase theorem for complete information.

Like the core model, the Coase theorem is highly simplified and there are many reasons to doubt that the full reliance of property rights assignment and negotiations between parties based on those rights will alone be sufficient to deal completely with the economic inefficiencies caused by externality and publicness, and even many other private good situations. With insurance, an institution Coase does not consider, moral hazard arises, a term that refers to a situation where agents have an incentive to engage in risky behaviour because they do not bear the full costs of the risks they take, in this case because of insurance coverage. And, despite Coase's own use of a homespun example of sparks from a railway causing fire damage to crops, Coasean logic is implicitly disembodied. Damages and benefits are treated as entirely abstract, with liability calculations and negotiations able to be done without reference to any real physical world, a condition that makes the theory generalisable but also less applicable. Property rights require some sort of contract, formal and informal. But these cannot possibly capture all relevant details for all relevant situations, not least because of the defects and limitations of natural language, both oral and written, and because embodied phenomena cannot be completely captured by such language. Transactions are assumed to be costless – and yet contracts and negotiations often entail large costs. This and many other limitations mean that Coasean logic, influential and useful though it is, is also limited by practicalities.

18.6 POLICY TRANSFER

At a more granular level, political processes result in formulation and execution of policies. The world of policy specialists and technicians can be considered as one group within the constellation of an overall political economy. Public choice theorists consider such functionaries as just like any other economic agents, not so much interested in policy but in themselves.

As noted earlier, this is likely often much too limiting an assumption. Assuming that policy-makers actually do at least try to develop means to achieve public ends, scholars have asked how policy plans and ideas get formed, disseminated, sorted through, and ultimately implemented. What institutions play roles in these various stages and how do they play those roles? How is the public represented – or misrepresented – in this process? These are the basic questions of the policy transfer literature.

The term itself is relatively fluid, referring generally to the way in which knowledge of policies, ideas, implementation, and institutions in one governmental jurisdiction flow to and are translated into the development of similar policies in other political systems. Emulation and learning are simple encapsulations of the concept (Dolowitz & Marsh 1996, 2000). But transfer of policy contains a complex set of ends and means. Regarding ends, theorists distinguish between policy diffusion, in which a particular concept becomes more widely disseminated; imitation, whereby the concept is copied in some manner from an external source; and learning, in which the concept is more deeply internalised and adapted (Dobbins et al. 2007).

A key element of any policy transfer is the social network. Policy transfer scholarship initially focused on government-to-government networks but has broadened out to consider the role of nongovernmental organisations (NGOs), international institutions, think tanks, and advocacy and professional groups amongst others, in formulating and spreading policies and their adoption (Shipan & Volden 2008). One outcome of a policy network can be the creation of "social capital", which refers to actual or potential resources generated by a durable network of fairly institutionalised relationships of mutual acquaintance. The returns to social capital might be purely private (i.e. limited to the members of a particular network); but they also might result in a social externality in which the overall society gains in some way from a capital base which was invested in by only some members of that society (Lin 1999).

The transport arena contains many examples of policy diffusion and policy transfer. Indeed, cordon pricing for cities, which London pioneered and succeeded at, became an example which other cities have copied or at least attempted to (New York initially failing in this regard). There has been significant policy transfer in the areas of rail market reform, smart card adoption for transit agencies, and urban transport adaptation to climate change, to name just a few instances (Marsden & Stead 2011). It is not just government policy that is subject to diffusion and transfer. Freight and logistics professionals also share ideas, information, and experiences regularly through various professional and informal networks, for example.

18.7 INTERNATIONAL POLITICAL ECONOMY (IPE) AND TRANSPORT

The discussion of political economy in this chapter focuses on domestic politics within ountries. International political economy (IPE) by contrast looks at the interaction of politics and economics at a global level. Particular emphasis is put on the power of different actors, especially nation-states.

Transport investments turn out to be a critical component of the inter national balance of power. This has been true for as long as there have been empires, whose power internally and externally heavily relied in dominance in trade, which, of course, required reliable movements of goods and people. By CE 610 China had completed and was using its Grand Canal to integrate its northern wheat and southern rice regions into a single territorial economy and empire, ensuring its regional hegemony in the process. This canal operated for centuries afterwards. The Roman Empire had similarly knitted much of Europe together through an extensive road and sea network, commanded by a formidable military machine. It took another 1,000 years after Rome's fall before Europe began to become re-integrated via various trade/transport political-economic system building with formations such as the self-defending trading cities of the Hanseatic League of the relatively independent feudal cities of the North Sea and the Baltic, and the rise of the Spanish and English territorial empires, and Portuguese trading empires between the 15th and 18th centuries, both based on dominance of maritime trading routes (Hugill 2009, 339). There are numerous other similar examples.

Nations and empires compete and conflict with one another, sometimes over wide geographical scales. It took the rise of industrialisation, European imperialism, and technical change to have this play out on a truly worldwide, rather than merely regional, stage. In the 19th century the new transport technologies of steamships and railroads hyper-charged political-economic developments already underway, adding scale and scope to the movement of bulk goods and people through continental interiors and across wide oceans. This was the era when the field of geopolitics arose, its new practitioners proposing that there were now several competing state models jostling for supremacy: the British Empire, based on the knitting together of scattered land colonies through command of the seas; more traditional internal land-based polities such as the fast-rising German Empire on the European continent; and hybrid empires with large internal landmasses that also had significant coastlines and the potential for projection of naval power from a strong land base, such as Russia and the rapidly growing US. Some theorists thus believed that the sea was central to worldwide political and economic hegemony, most notably Admiral Alfred Thayer Mahan. Others, especially Halford Mackinder, looked back to more ancient times to conclude that control of internal landmasses through military and economic domination, now based on railroads and telegraphs, was the wave of the future. Mackinder went so far as to posit that powers that controlled the Eurasian landmass between Russia's European and China's Pacific borders could effectively control the world because this was a critical crossroads of global movements of all sorts (Hugill 2009, 338–339).

The Great Power competition of European empires ultimately exploded in World War I and its even more destructive second act 20 years later. The rise of the US, referred to as a "European offshoot" by economic historians, seemed to invalidate the Mackinder hypothesis, seemingly side-lining a once dominant region of the world. The rise of air power in the 20th century further cemented the importance of having both a critical landmass and a network of air and sea bases that could serve both military and economic-political purposes, allowing the US to become one of two superpowers during the Cold War and then a sole "hyperpower" after the fall of the Soviet Union in 1991 (Cohen 2004).

But history doesn't stand still and the world is becoming more multipolar in political, military, and economic terms. "Eurasia" once more is increasingly at the centre of world affairs, as shown by the growing proportions of world's gross domestic product (GDP) taken up by China, Russia, and India. These countries, and others in the global "South", are becoming increasingly assertive about what they see as their proper roles in the world political and economic system. And once again, transport infrastructure, technology, and investment are a critical part of this rebalancing. China's Belt-and-Road Initiative is but one of many examples of non-Western countries financing and building new trade corridors to reshape economic geographies in their strategic interests. The process has been fraught to say the least. But it is just the latest development of a long evolution of trade, transport, and geopolitical links.

REFERENCES

Barzel, Y., & Allen, D. W. (2023). *Economic analysis of property rights*. Cambridge University Press.

Brown, J. (2005). A tale of two visions: Harland Bartholomew, Robert Moses, and the development of the American freeway. *Journal of Planning History*, 4(1), 3–32.

Caro, R. A. (1974). *The power broker: Robert Moses and the fall of New York*. Knopf.

Cervero, R. (2001). Informal transit: Learning from the developing world. *Access Magazine*, 1(18), 15–22.

Cohen, E. A. (2004). History and the hyperpower. *Foreign affairs*, 83(4), 49–63.

Cole, D. H., & Grossman, P. Z. (2002). The meaning of property rights: Law versus economics?. *Land Economics*, 78(3), 317–330.

Congleton, R. D. (2004). The median voter model. In *The encyclopedia of public choice*. Springer, 707–712.

Dobbins, F., Simmons, B., & Garrett, G. (2007). The global diffusion of public policies: Social construction, coercion, competition, or learning? *Annual Review of Sociology*, 33, 449–72.

Dolowitz, D., & Marsh, D. (1996). Who learns what from whom? A review of the policy transfer literature. *Political Studies*, 44, 343–357.

Dolowitz, D., & Marsh, D. (2000). Learning from abroad: The role of policy transfer in contemporary policy-making. *Governance*, 13(1), 5–24.

Goodwin, P. (1989). The rule of three: A possible solution to the political problem of competing objectives for road pricing. *Traffic Engineering and Control*, 30(10), 495–497.

Gordon, C., & Flanagan, R. (2012). Politics of urban congestion pricing: Cautionary tales from New York City. (Paper # 12-0443). In *91st Transportation Research Board Annual Meeting Proceedings*, Washington, DC.

Gordon, C. & Peters, J. (2013). Funding urban transport in New York: Revenue potential of VMT and carbon taxes in New York State. In *92nd Transportation Research Board Annual Meeting Proceedings* (Paper # 13-0443). Washington, DC.

Hugill, P. J. (2009). Trade, transport and communications, historical geographies of. In *International encyclopedia of human geography*. Elsevier, 338–344.

King, D., Manville, M., & Shoup, D. (2007). The political calculus of congestion pricing. *Transport Policy*, 14(2), 111–123.

Levinson, D., Gillen, D., & Iacono, M. (2016). *Transportation economics*. en.wikibooks.org July 9, 2016. https://en.wikibooks.org/wiki/Transportation_Economics/Print_version

Lin, N. (1999). Building a network theory of social capital. *Connections*, 22, 28–51.

Marsden, G., & Stead, D. (2011). Policy transfer and learning in the field of transport: A review of concepts and evidence. *Transport Policy*, 18(3), 492–500.

McGuire, M. C. (2019). Leviathan, taxation, and public goods. In Congleton, R. D., Grofman, B., and Voigt, S. (eds). *The Oxford handbook of public choice, volume 2*. Oxford University Press, 239–262.

Peters, J., & Gordon, C. (2009). Results not guaranteed: A tale of road pricing in New York and London. *Journal of Urban Technology*, 19, 113–131.

Polinsky, A. M. (1983). *An introduction to law and economics*. Little Brown.

Reisman, N., & Rivard, R. (2024). First congestion toll plan in US facing serious hurdles under Trump. *Politico.com*. www.politico.com/news/2025/01/05/hochul-manhattan-toll-plan-trump-00196489

Ritter, B. (2024). Congestion pricing in NYC timeline: How we got here. *Eyewitness News ABC 7 New York City*. https://abc7ny.com/post/congestion-pricing-nyc-timeline-toll-starts-stop/14895566/

Rowley, C. K. (1984). The relevance of the median voter theorem. *Zeitschrift für die gesamte Staatswissenschaft/Journal of Institutional and Theoretical Economics* (H. 1), 140, 104–126.

Shipan, C. R., & Volden, C. (2008). The mechanisms of policy diffusion. *American Journal of Political Science*, 52(4), 840–857.

Small, K. (1992). Using the revenues from congestion pricing. *Transportation*, 19(4), 359–382.

Wriggins, J. B. (2010). Automobile injuries as injuries with remedies: Driving, insurance, torts, and changing the choice architecture of auto insurance pricing. *Loyola of Los Angeles Law Review*, 44, 69–90.

CHAPTER 19

Human factors

19.1 INTRODUCTION: SUPPLY, DEMAND, AND MODAL EVOLUTION

The bicycle industry cameo presented in Box 19.1 shows that while a general desire to be able to travel at fast speeds had been long-standing, it took inventors and innovators to come up with workable machines suited for human use delivering such speed in a long process of trail and error. The initial contraptions were aimed towards where the money was, at first the very wealthy, and they were little more than toys. But with time bicycles became faster, lighter, easier to operate, and safer. As economies of scale (EOS) in production were realised, bicycles became cheap enough to become a truly mass phenomenon.

This growth of demand was arguably not merely utilitarian and atomistic. Social forces and institutions played an important role in overcoming social biases against cycling, with technical changes dealing with genuine human safety issues, and design and marketing fostering attachment and interest in riding this new machine. Cycling became associated not just with mobility but with social status, freedom, and independence, something that grew as cycle models became easier and safer to ride. Capturing the spirit of the age, HG Wells wrote an 1896 novel entitled, *The Wheels of Chance*, in which a vagabond cyclist finds a new liberation in a footloose lifestyle of cycle-powered movement across wide areas. Rootlessness had traditionally been seen as a negative thing, and speed was traditionally not needed in most ordinary contexts. But the bicycle whetted a modern appetite for ever faster and easier travel brought about by human ingenuity.

DOI: 10.4324/9781003350866-23

BOX 19.1 INTRODUCTORY CASE: MODERNISING THE BICYCLE

The earliest prototypes of the bicycle can be seen in European drawings and plans as early as the Renaissance. However it took until the late 1700s before machines resembling the modern cycle came into being. These were referred to generally as celeripedes, though they came in many forms, and consisted of two-wheeled contraptions propelled by the feet of the rider sitting on it. Originating in France, the English versions became known as "hobby horses" (15–21) (the discussion in this box, and page references, is drawn from Ritchie (1975)).

By the early 1800s, these machines were still relatively expensive but cheap enough to be within the reach of the gentry, and capable of reaching up to 16 km per hour or more on level, good-quality roads. This was a pace well beyond walking, and a good margin above horse travel (22–24). These earliest models were superseded by ones that amplified foot power with gears and other mechanical contrivances. These became known as velocipedes, initially either three- or four-wheeled, and had forms that would be recognisable to the modern-day cyclist. Production techniques improved, manufacturing costs fell, and the machines became increasingly affordable and more widely adopted (39–42).

Technical improvements and cyclist achievements expanded together at a rapid rate over the course of the 19th century. In 1858, inventor Henry Hill Hodgson rode a velocipede from Dover to London and back in two days, a distance of 70 mi. In the prior year he completed a round trip between London and Salisbury, 130 mi each way, 62.5 mi in one day. Others undertook shorter but still remarkable trips, such as one 16-mi journey taking 2.75 hours, including walking up hills for a good portion (44–45).

The term "bicycle" emerged in the late 1860s to distinguish two-wheelers from three- and four-wheelers but soon became a generic signifier (53). Britain, France, and America became major centres of design, innovation, manufacture, and ridership in the last three decades of the 1800s (54–62). Riding schools emerged in all countries to train riders and build demand, with schools variously providing celebrity launches, free entertainment, and competitive races. Cycling "manuals" were printed in abundance. The American industry even suffered from a "patent troll", with Calvin Whittey buying up a patent for $2,000 allowing him to send infringement notices to all manufacturers in the country, forcing them into litigation or settlement. He prospered by collecting a royalty of $10 on every machine made in the US (62–65).

This first bicycle "craze" of the 1860s fizzled out after a few years, but the cycling industry would nonetheless continue to grow. The UK industry was not as subject to fads as America, but in both places, and in France, innovations continued and a trade press, advertising industry, and range of booster groups emerged along with them. Popular songs about bicycles were written and would proliferate into century's end. "Velocipedomania" became an aspect of popular culture and along with it came a whole series of new manufacturers, many of them set up by inventors themselves on a small scale. These developments caused many to predict the demise of the horse (71–73, 79). This would ultimately come to pass but due much more to the combustion engine rather than the bicycle (see Chapter 7).

Two-wheelers slowly became dominant but co-existed with versions with more wheels until the early 20th century. In the 1880s and 1890s the "ordinary" – also called the "Penny-farthing" – with its huge front wheel and tiny back wheel was the cycle of choice for those seeking peak performance (80–81) (see Figure 19.1). That enormous front wheel allowed for great leverage of foot-power into speed, though speed was variable because bicycle chains and gears were still quite imperfect and the pneumatic tire had not yet been invented. Numerous clubs of "ordinary" users emerged (84–86).

Of course the "ordinary" was not for everyone, especially the leisure rider, the elderly, those less physically fit, and women, for whom such vehicles were seen as improper and indecent. This is where tricycles had a niche, being much less efficient but also much safer and ride-able in ordinary clothing. "Sociable" two-seaters also emerged, in which two riders could pedal side-by-side, seen as especially good for chaperoned women. Bicycles for two with one rider in front and the other in the back, rather than besides each other, also were produced and were more popular with men (108–111, 116–117).

Cycle prices eventually fell enough that cycling became a solid middle-class pursuit. New cycles were still mostly out of reach of the working class in the 1880s and 1890s, though a used cycle from an expanding second-hand market was sometimes within reach for lower income people. But enthusiasm spread throughout all classes (89–90). Bicycle manufacturing centres soon became established – Coventry was it epicentre in England – along with a few leading celebrity innovators, such as the Englishman James Starky. Bicycles were seen as a source of speed, individual freedom, and mobility. Competitive cycling events reinforced this notion as riders continued to smash speed records. In 1882, for example, a cyclist broke new ground by covering more than 36 km in an hour. Such speeds inspired enthusiasm by promoters who organised various races. But they also raised concerns about disruption on the roads, accidents, and social disorder (98–99). Thus there was a growing amount of government regulation in the US and UK prohibiting riding on footpaths, requiring lights after dark, and mandating bells at all times (84–86).

With the emergence of the "safety", cycle came the earliest version of the two-wheeler we all are familiar with now. The "safety" combined the speed and velocity of the "ordinary" with the stability of the three-wheeler (121–123). The most popular and best designed version was the

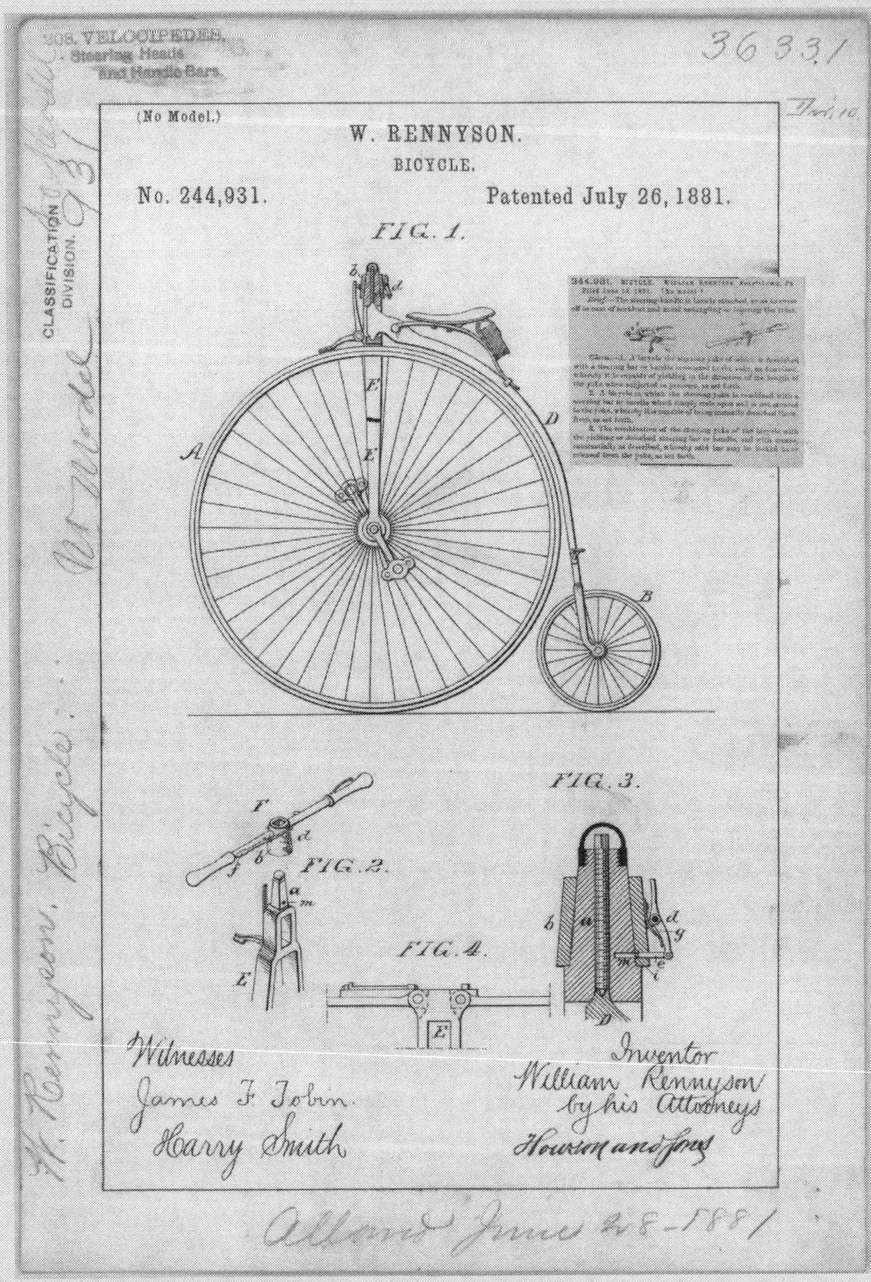

FIGURE 19.1

The "Ordinary" bicycle. No known restrictions on publication.

Source: W. Rennyson Bicycle Patent. Records of the Patent and Trademark Office. US Record Group 241: Series: Utility Patent Drawings. US National Archives. NAID: 362230144. Local ID: 244931. Produced: July 26, 1881. https://catalog.archives.gov/id/362230144. No copyright restrictions.

Rover which looks very much like a modern cycle with the chain running on the back wheel, rather than the front like most other models up to that time. Riders broke new speed and distance records on the "safety", most notably an 1886 ride of 475 km in 24 hours and an 1889 ride of 521 km. With the invention of the pneumatic tire in 1889 driving out solid tyres, the present version of the cycle was established (130–132).

The last decade of the 19th century and the first few decades of the 20th century were a time of mass production and mass consumption of bicycles. In 1882 there were 200,000 cyclists in England; in 1893, 500,000; in 1903, over a million; and by 1926, 6 million. Bicycle manufacture became a large-scale and highly capitalised industry. Gone were the days of the inventor–builder boutique firm. Supply often outran demand, with 800,000 cycles being produced in the UK in 1895, 300,000 more than existing supply. This would initially cause a boom in cycling company share prices. But a correction came in both supply and share values in 1897, though this only temporarily interrupted an established growth trend (136).

Meanwhile, speed and distance records continued to fall. In 1898 161 km was ridden by one intrepid cyclist in 4 hours, 16 minutes, and 35 seconds, with 689 km covered in 24 hours. One group of enthusiasts set out together to ride 30,959 km around the world in 774 days (142). The bicycle was here to stay, and humans would now adapt themselves to yet another new machine in myriad and unpredictable ways, before new ones, like the automobile, would succeed it.

The bicycle industry also set the stage for the following automobile revolution. Many of the first English car manufacturers were originally bicycle makers, like Humber, Morris, Singer, Austin, and Hillman. And many centres of cycle manufacturing, like the aforementioned Coventry, later became car-making centres. Many technological innovations developed for bicycles were adapted to the new auto, as were many marketing and publicity campaigns for whipping up consumer demand (Ritchie 1975, 143). Finance techniques and institutions raising the needed sums for new factories had also been well established in the bicycle realm as had intellectual property regimes, including, as noted earlier, one of the earliest patent trolls.

It is also no accident that Orville and Wilbur Wright, the pioneers of American aviation, had been skilled bicycle mechanics, where they learned many useful things which they brought to their early prototypes. (There were also parallel developments in other countries so there are multiple national claimants for the honour of inventing the airplane.) History thus indicates that technical and institutional cross-fertilisation between different transport modes has been a widespread feature of modern transport supply.

19.2 MACHINE VERSUS HUMAN: THE CAR

Transport modernisation, even in the 19th century, was highly focused initially on invention and production which, after initial periods of entrepreneurial and small-scale innovation, became relatively centralised affairs. The human being and the human form were dealt with along the way, incrementally as needed for functionality, saleability, and performance enhancements supporting the basics for human operation. The machine came first, the human second.

This emphasis carried over into automobile design. As with bicycles, carmakers were primarily interested in vehicle speed and performance, making adaptations to humans in a piecemeal way. The earliest vehicles simply applied mechanisms that had long been used in horse carriages, e.g. brakes for the first motorised vehicles using a wooden block pressed against one of the wheels via a hand-operated lever. Analogising from the operation of small boats, a tiller was connected to the front wheels for steering (Akamatsu et al. 2013, Section 2.1).

As cars became heavier and faster, these simple borrowings were no longer sufficient. Thus the first seatbelt was employed in late 19th-century cars simply to keep passengers in their seats when going fast, and a foot-operated pedal was first used in 1894 because it could exert greater force than a hand brake and freed up both hands to manage what were then clunky steering wheels which had replaced the tiller because it no longer worked as vehicles got heavier and more rapid. (The steering wheel became standard beginning in 1895.) Early cars had no gauges. But manufacturers soon realised that reliable operation required drivers to have real-time information about various mechanical functions. Oil-pump and water pressure gauges were introduced around 1900, and the speedometer soon after that. These gauges and others (including a thermometer for measuring engine heat) were soon moved from the outside of the passenger cab to the inside where the driver could easily and regularly monitor them (Akamatsu et al. 2013, Section 2.1).

This primary focus on mechanics and vehicle performance continued well into the 1930s. Speed was the major focus, with the 1934 Chrysler *Airflow* having a rounded car body, smaller passenger cab, and better visibility of the road to allow for faster travel. It was this imperative, not an inherent interest in the human being, that paradoxically caused more design centred on that being. A smaller cab and seats required specifications more suited to the actual human body to make a good and functional fit, while higher speeds in higher traffic environments required more readable and accessible driver controls. Thus switches and knobs were labelled in the 1930s, in contrast to the 1920s where drivers had to memorise their functions. All the instruments, including speedometers, were consolidated in a central panel clearly visible and adjustable by the vehicle operator. Seat-sliding mechanisms, introduced in the 1920s, now became increasingly common. Exterior signals became mechanical in the 1930s (then electrical in the 1950s), with turn signal levers installed in the steering column (horn buttons had been put there in the late 1920s). By the 1940s all these features were standard and the car of those times is broadly similar to current ones (Akamatsu et al. 2013, Section 2.2).

Humans were thus accommodated in automobile design, but slowly, and mostly because of vehicle operational factors, and not the other way around. Granted, consumer preferences were being met in a sense because manufacturers continually added features that would hopefully increase sales. But these manufacturers also played a tremendous role in shaping those desires and production necessities drove much design. Slowly manufacturers could batch-produce different model lines and tailor some features to provide different packages for individuals. But for the most part supply literally created and shaped consumer demand from very early on.

19.3 THE BIRTH OF HUMAN FACTORS AS A TECHNICAL DISCIPLINE

All these alterations in car manufacture and design decisions were initially unsystematic and largely based on heuristics drawn from engineering experience and field observation. Safety was becoming an increasing concern as cars became speedier and traffic more widespread. There was reference in the late 1930s automotive industry to "human factors" as an issue in traffic crashes. The Society of Automotive Engineers (SAE) had been established in 1905 in the US, and work on standardisation had started in 1910 with issuance of the first SAE Handbook (Akamatsu et al. 2013, Sections 2.1 and 2.2).

Professional forums that facilitated discussion and development of concepts and knowledge within the automotive design and engineering community proliferated during the first half of the 20th century. This broadened out to include other disciplines and non-transport activities, enough so that, in 1957, the Human Factors Society was established as the primary organisation for human factors and practitioners in the US (Shaver & Braun 2008). In Europe, the field became known as Ergonomics, and in England, the Ergonomics Research Society was formed in 1949 (and the US association thus later changed to the Human Factors and Ergonomics Society in 1992) (Maddox 1998, Chapter 1).

The big shift in turning a largely experience-based field (not completely a bad thing, it must be said) into a highly technical endeavour (conversely, not an entirely good thing) was World War II. The need to quickly select and train pilots to fly the newly invented airplane in combat during World War I laid the groundwork in establishing basic methods to rapidly screen and upskill individuals for the job. Aviation psychology and aeromedical research were born out of this need, solidified by the establishment of US laboratories at Brooks Air Force Base in Texas and Wright Field in Ohio. But World War II brought a critical mass to human factors research because of the need to mobilise and employ huge numbers of people in a unified global fighting effort. It was now impossible to fill positions according to individual attributes based on individualised recruiting. Instead, functions were now designed for the capabilities and limitations of categories of people. Also, technological advances were outpacing the ability of people to adapt to poor designs in novel configurations in highly stressful wartime conditions that required quick decisions by operators. Early in the war, radar operators were having trouble maintaining focus and, more catastrophically, highly-trained pilots were crashing frequently because of poor control configurations and instrument displays (Shaver & Braun 2008).

In these crisis times trial-and-error adjustment and experiential intuition had to be replaced by systematisation and technical specification. In one sense this was a more human-focused approach in that machines were constructed to flow from "typical" aspects of the human body and mind, in contrast to the way in which automobiles (and, prior to that, bicycles) had evolved. But the machines and the systems they operated in were becoming bigger than ever before with humans fit in increasingly as cogs, even if more functional and, perhaps, comfortable ones. Here the modern field of human factors and ergonomics really came into its own (see Box 19.2).

19.4 ANTHROPOMETRICS AND PSYCHOMETRICS

The study and measurement of human body dimensions is known as anthropometry. The study and measurement of human psychological functions and aspects is known as psychometrics. These two fields, especially anthropometrics, came out of, and fed back into, the human factors discipline. Many of the key initial studies and data measurements were taken by the military (Jones & Thissen 2006).

In anthropometrics, measurement and standardisation are thorough, with detailed databases available on selected body dimensions across many individuals which are then reported according to gender and percentiles within each gender. Thus a value for the dimension "seated eye height" for a 75th percentile male is posited to mean that 75% of all males in the population

BOX 19.2 FLIGHT DURING WARTIME

The human factors developments of World War II were varied, with both psychological and physiological aspects. Experiments, using the first airborne polygraph, were conducted in 1939 to measure pilot performance as correlated with physiological responses in flight. That same year the US National Research Council Committee on Aviation Psychology was established, morphing later into the US Army Air Forces Aviation Psychology Program. Founding of a large US Army aviation psychology programme followed in 1940. Across the Atlantic, the new Applied Psychology Unit of Cambridge University in England began work on problems in the design of aviation and armoured force equipment.

Of particular interest in both countries were the effects of system design on manual control performance, including direction-of-motion relationships between controls and displays. What became known as "pilot error" started cropping up in training and combat accident reports. Further study showed that pilots and co-pilots frequently retracted the wheels instead of the flaps after landing and the reason was bad cockpit design, not pilot errors *per se*. The controls for the two actions looked similar and as an *ad hoc* fix, a small, rubber-tired wheel was fixed to the wheel control and a small wedge-shaped end to the flap control, drastically reducing accidents. These mnemonically shape-coded controls were standardised worldwide after the war, soon moved from being side-by-side to more set apart from one another. Psychoacoustics, i.e. the intelligibility of speech transmitted over noisy aircraft interphones, was another area of research. Intelligibility was improved by clipping the peaks of vowel sounds in transmission of human speech while amplifying the remaining mixture of vowels and consonants.

A huge American military-academic human factors research complex blossomed after the war. The US Navy and the Air Force led the charge in founding new (and competing) service-based labs such as the Air Force Personnel and Training Research Center (commonly referred to as "Af- patrick") and the Naval Research Laboratory in Washington, DC; though the Air Force managed to have its naval counterpart dismantled in 1958. Out of these initiatives and others came the first complex manned system simulation study, experimental study of flight display and control design principles, and transfer of pilot training to simulators.

In the nuclear age, command-and-control systems became bigger and more complex, with potential consequences of errors and malfunctions having potentially global catastrophic impact. New and complex electronics in both ground and airborne weapon systems sometimes behaved in unpredictable ways and they were so complicated that they were often inoperable and unfixable by human technicians. This led to a large coordinated research effort in the late 1950s and early 1960s spearheaded by military and academic entities and the newly established, and initially purely military, offshoot known as the RAND Corporation. It was found that technicians needed better training and simulation facilities for practising diagnoses, joined with on-going and objective performance evaluation. This would be the first of many efforts to better understand the interaction between human beings and complex machine systems to redesign them to minimise adverse events. (The discussion in this box is drawn from Roscoe (1997).)

have a seated eye height lower than this value. In transport design, the aim is to accommodate the 5th through 95th percentiles for human occupants and operators (and the same can be said for other settings such as workplaces attempting to adapt to workers). This sounds like it would capture most of the population, but individuals tend not to fall into the same percentile across multiple body dimensions. For example, a person with an "average" hand size often has above or below average leg size. Although an element designed for the 5th through 95th percentiles would be expected on average to exclude only 10% of the population, one study using 13 body dimensions found that 52% of the population ended up being excluded in one way or another. Thus anthropometrics-based design, while clearly useful, can fall into the "myth of the average person" (Maddox 1998, Chapter 1). Having said that, anthropometrics remains a foundation for much transport vehicle and support system design. Published data now typically provide 5th through 95th percentile values for use in vehicle cab layout (see Figure 19.2).

Collection of such data by auto manufacturers goes back to the 1940s. The focus on laying out the cab for the large majority of drivers made good business sense since this maximised marketability. Basic functionality, to ensure that the driver could see the external environment and effectively interact with it by being able to easily identify, reach, and manipulate controls and displays inside the cab, was the primary goal. Studies on vehicle vibration and comfort also were conducted. The two are related since vibration can cause lower back pain and interfere with operations. Additionally, bumps and shocks can disrupt driver performance and create various types of discomfort and even injury. Vehicle suspension systems and seats began to be steadily improved due to these investigations (Akamatsu et al. 2013, Sections 3.2–3.4).

At first automotive research was mostly physiological in its basis. The study and application of physical mechanics to human movement, known as biomechanics, blossomed. But soon a distinction emerged between engineering psychologists, focusing on cognitive and perceptual factors of the

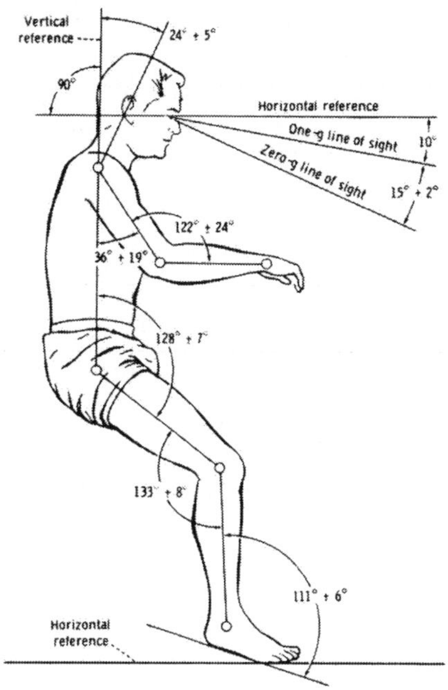

Figure 16.- The segment angles of the weightless neutral body position.

Figure 17.- The body position of the SL-3 PLT while loading film illustrates the relaxed posture in an unposed work situation.

FIGURE 19.2

Anthropometrical measurement in the US space programme.

Source: Figures taken from NASA (1978, I-24). Figures and book are in the public domain.

human operator, working "above the neck", and those biomechanical experts focusing on the rest of the body "below the neck" (Durso et al. 2014). There are still specialities like these and others, but human factors and ergonomics are now very much interdisciplinary efforts (Maddox 1998, Chapter 1).

Advances in methods allowed for more sophisticated anthropometric, psychometric, and biomechanical measurement and analysis. Standardised metrics of the perception of discomfort were issued in the form of International Organisation for Standardization standard, ISO 2631, in 1974. Eye trackers to measure eye-gaze location arrived for vehicle and simulator use in the 1970s. A whole new set of measurements of glance time to mirrors, radio, and the road for novice and experienced drivers were thus compiled and fed back into future designs (Akamatsu et al. 2013, Section 3.4).

Human thermal comfort was another area of research in the 1970s, examining the roles played by air temperature, radiant temperature, air velocity, humidity, and clothing. As these were very difficult to assess in a real vehicle cab, the automotive industry borrowed techniques developed in the US space programme for evaluating space-suit thermal comfort, the leading one being the thermal manikin. This became widely adopted and adapted by the industry to estimate thermal comfort in vehicle cabs by the end of the 1970s (Akamatsu et al. 2013, Section 3.5).

19.5 SAFETY

Interestingly enough, safety as a formal concern came relatively late to the transport arena. As has been seen it took World War II to bring a systematic review of the causes of aviation accidents, and even then the concern was more on mission performance and preservation of scarce trained personnel rather than an innate desire for lowered fatalities and injuries in and of themselves.

Safety can be broken down into two parts: (a) the avoidance of accidents and (b) the minimisation of accident impacts. Laypersons usually think of the former. But in a human factors setting, the latter is equally important. Thus while getting car collisions to as a low a level as possible is desirable, much attention in transport human factors is also paid to injury prevention, an example of which is the addition of air bags and other design features to prevent the transfer of injury-inducing energy if an accident occurs (Lorimer & Guarneri 1996, 101). In this sort of approach it is expected that accidents will happen, but overall the aim is to limit injuries and property damage when they do (Lorimer & Guarneri 1996, 106).

There is another dimension to this, however, which is the nature of the system itself. The term "accidents" implies a natural hazard. But modern technical systems actually manufacture risk, even as those same systems apply technical methods to reduce their impacts (Sovacool 2009, 412). Transport accidents indeed can be seen as large statistical regularities that allow for relatively precise calculation and prediction of their occurrence (Gunn 2018, 22).

To take an example from rail history, the early steam engines of trains were extremely dangerous. Over 100 people were killed in boiler explosions during the first decades of the English railway. Technical improvements in steam power and, later, the switch to diesel and electric made train operations much safer (Lowson 1998, 16). But train crashes and derailments and collisions with people and vehicles at grade crossings and on tracks continued and continue still. If one takes the railways as pre-existing natural features, then it makes sense to consider these as "random" events. But as railways are not natural features of the human environment, these incidents are really more appropriately considered to be regular operating features.

The same is true, of course, for more modern transport modes like cars and planes. The immediate decades after World War II saw construction of special-purpose, high-speed roads in the US (the Interstate Highway system), France (Autoroutes), the UK (Motorways), Italy (Autostrada), and in many other countries. This changed the frequency, impacts, and nature of risk and accidents. Trips on such roads tended to be long and fast, and driver fatigue became an increasing concern (Akamatsu et al. 2013, Section 3.3).

Still, automotive safety features were rolled out relatively slowly at first, lagging behind their airplane compatriots with its head-start driven by wartime exigency. Nash Motors in the US was the first to provide seatbelts in 1949, with others following in the 1950s. In 1952 Daimler Benz invented the non-deformable passenger cell, followed by the crumple zone and collapsible steering column. In 1959, Volvo was the first to provide three-point seatbelts, while American Motors equipped their automobiles with head restraints protecting against neck injury in rear-end collisions. In Europe, some carmakers introduced symbols rather than words for controls, to eliminate the need for re-labelling across multiple language markets, but also to allow for quicker recognition and response by drivers. The position of gauges was also moved into a "normal" line of sight for easier reading (Akamatsu et al. 2013, Section 3.2).

These were all ameliorations primarily to reduce injury and death in the event of an accident, secondarily to reduce driver errors that might cause them. But in the US in 1965 alone, more than 50,000 Americans died in road accidents and the car had become the leading cause of death in the population below age 44 (Mashaw & Harfst 1990). In that country, car safety became a major area of news reporting and, for around two decades, a major impetus for regulatory and manufacturer safety reform (see Box 19.3).

Impact-reducing safety modifications to vehicles at first continued to be the main line of improvement. In 1967 General Motors created collapsible steering columns designed to reduce chest impact injuries, for example. With the development of control theory, studies were conducted to apply this theory to steering manoeuvres. This was associated with improvement of understanding of what happened in crashes, with crash dummies developed by several different organizations and integrated into the *Hybrid I* in 1971, *Hybrid II* in 1974, and *Hybrid III* in 1976. This last model had 10 sensors located in the head, neck, upper body, femur, knee, and leg, sites where most crash injuries might occur. Correlations between acceleration and injury severity resulted in the development of Head Injury Criteria (HIC) to assess the severity of head injury as indicated by experiments with the dummy. The Abbreviated Injury Scales (AIS-1971 and AIS-1976) were developed for

BOX 19.3 THE AMERICAN MEDIA AND AUTOMOBILE CRASH SAFETY

The Chevrolet *Corvair*, produced by General Motors, was an unusual rear-engine vehicle. It turned out that in a sharp turn, it had a tendency to spin and roll over. Accidents involving the *Corvair* attracted considerable news coverage and the car served as an opening case study in consumer advocate Ralph Nader's 1965 book, *Unsafe at Any Speed*, which was a wide-ranging indictment of the various ways in which US auto manufacturers degraded safety in exchange for flashy adornments, some of which actually caused hazard themselves, such as pointy grill elements. US Congressional hearings on auto safety were held, leading to the passage of the National Traffic and Motor Vehicle Safety Act in 1966 which created a new federal agency responsible for overseeing automobile safety, the National Highway Traffic Safety Administration (NHTSA). The *Corvair* was withdrawn from production and General Motors' reputation was considerably tarnished, not least because it came out that the firm had hired private investigators to smear Nader personally (Mashaw & Harfst 1990).

Auto safety now became a regular "beat" for American news reporters. The Ford *Pinto* garnered much negative publicity in the 1970s when it was shown that, when struck from the rear under certain circumstances, the car would dramatically catch fire. Coverage of this fact caused a sharp sales decline and its ultimate withdrawal from the marketplace. The 1980s would be an especially fecund period for reporting of car defects. The American Motors Corporation *Jeep CJ-5* had a rollover propensity that was the subject of a December 21, 1980, broadcast by *60 Minutes*, the most-watched investigative news programme on US television, showing the vehicle rolling over when making sharp turns. Later, the Suzuki *Samurai*, a four-wheel drive utility vehicle with a short wheel base, was also found to have a propensity to roll over by the then influential *Consumers Union* and its monthly magazine full of product reviews, *Consumer Reports*. Suzuki later sued *Consumers Union* unsuccessfully (Akamatsu et. al. 2013, Sections 3.4–3.5).

Allegations of unintended acceleration of the Audi *5000* were aired on *60 Minutes* on November 23, 1986, after which sales of the vehicle fell from 74,000 in 1984 to 12,000 in 1991. However the US Department of Transportation judged that despite some flaws, the car's design aspects did not merit a defect notification, the first time that media investigations were not supported by official ones. Still, *Consumer Reports* rated the vehicle as "not acceptable" and sales dropped to 1,400 over the next year. Again Suzuki sued the *Consumers Union* but lost, and the company pulled the Samurai out of production (Akamatsu et al. 2013, Section 3.5).

The worm began to turn, however, with an investigation of General Motor's *CK* pickup truck in a presentation on the very popular show *Dateline* on the NBC network in 1993. A *CK* was shown being struck in the side and bursting into flames, allegedly because the fuel tanks, mounted outside the frame rails, were vulnerable to fires if struck. In this case, though, General Motors showed that the crashes had been staged, ignited with rocket igniters. NBC retracted the story, paying General Motors for their investigative costs (Akamatsu et al. 2013, Section 4.1).

This was not the end of crash reporting, however, with the 2000s bringing stories about Ford passenger van rollovers and rear-end crashes, and fires involving the 2005–7 Ford *Crown Victoria* car (commonly used as police cars), as well as rollovers of the 1998–2001 Ford *Explorer* (Akamatsu et al. 2013, Section 4.2). However, this decade proved to be the high water mark of US media coverage of, and influence on, crash safety and such stories are relatively little covered now, not least because of liability concerns by media organisations.

determining the level of injury produced by actual accidents (Akamatsu et al. 2013, Sections 3.3–3.4).

A shift was also made towards examining operator behaviour, especially cognitive characteristics, with studies to measure mental workload beginning in the 1960s, and driving simulators, first used in the 1950s, becoming more widely used in the 1960s and beyond. This trend was greatly accelerated by digital computers and software in the 1980s allowing for sophisticated and economical simulation models for designing cabins, and video systems for measuring drowsiness and operator attentiveness (Akamatsu et al. 2013, Section 3.3–3.5).

19.6 HUMAN–MACHINE SYSTEMS

Modifications of vehicles to incorporate driver behaviour so as to reduce impact and frequency of incidents are fine so far as they go. But transport systems have become so big and all-encompassing that human factors research has had to focus more and more on modifying, rather than just incorporating, human behaviour to improve safety and overall system performance.

The sociologist Wolfgang Sachs (1983) noted that traffic is a system of conflicting behaviour tendencies in which technical precautions and legal force are required to synchronise individual human behaviour, despite cars being put forward as agents of individual mobility, speed, and power. The car produces enormous effects with minimal effort by the driver, giving rise to feelings of heightened personal authority that is both exhilarating and comforting, and in this sense potentially regressive, giving a false sense of security (352). Because of this, mass motoring, he argued, has made this external and internal conflict ever greater (359–360).

Norbert Elias, another sociologist, has studied the way in which automobiles and the systems they rely on have upended organic human growth and self-regulation. His earlier studies showed how social forces, i.e. the links between individuals and across human beings collectively, internalised and changed standards of behaviour at a personal, psychological level. He argued that the car was at least partially de-humanising this process as far as human movement was concerned. Elias refers to this as "technisation". Which is not to say that it is not a necessary adjustment in part. Human beings in cars are moving at far faster speeds and with the potential for much more deadly force than if they were on foot or horse or even bicycle. Mechanical aids of all sorts, ranging from traffic lights, to signage, to automatic barriers, are needed to minimise casualties and properly manage system traffic flow and people need to adjust accordingly. But the cost is a sort of inner alienation from both oneself, one's mode of movement, and potentially from the human embodied and intuitive pathways of human society. Clearly the modern message is that people must adapt to the car, not the other way around (Elias 1995).

The subjective experience of the user has had to be given second place to overall functionality and efficiency. The car, which has been the subject of much study in this regard, has been seen to engender a wide range of individual feelings and sensations, while also producing some collective effects that are of particular interest to advertisers and marketers. Individual car drivers and passengers (and people often have very different experiences when shifting from one role to the other) have varying "impressions" and affective dispositions towards car motion, including feelings of happiness, excitement, fear, anxiety, and sometimes motion sickness. Some have argued that such feelings cannot be identified solely with the person or the vehicle but are a synthesis of effects on and between both in a wider social setting (Sheller 2004, 227). These effects, as noted above, can be contradictory.

In this sense, then, a human factors approach treats humans as an element in mechanised systems, with "human-machine" the term used in referring to that relationship. The simplest example of a human–machine unit is of an individual operating a single machine. The human operator senses the "machine display", a term referring to the signal(s) the machine is providing about its functioning and conditions. The operator then interprets this display, perhaps doing some analysis or computation before reaching and then enacting a decision. Systems are designed for specific kinds of operators, e.g. pilots for planes, astronauts for spacecraft, and drivers for cars; and system design will take into account the general human psychological and bodily abilities and the particular abilities of classes of operators (Chapanis & Holstein 2018).

Human factors engineering applies this knowledge about physical and psychological characteristics to the design of devices and systems for human use. The body of knowledge drawn upon is a collection of data and principles about human characteristics, capabilities, and limitations in relation to machines, jobs, and environments, using knowledge of anatomy, anthropometry, applied physiology, environmental medicine, psychology, sociology, toxicology, industrial design, and operations research (Chapanis & Holstein 2018).

19.7 AUTOMATION, ADAPTATION, AND HUMAN–MACHINE SYSTEMS

The technical requirements and performance of the transport system are paramount in the present environment. The human operator has obviously and necessarily to be taken into account. But their humanity is necessarily reduced to abstract data as inputs into system design and their actions, feelings, and thoughts are reduced to technical inputs and outputs, to be standardised, where possible, in service to technical prerogatives.

There continues to be research into improving the performance of individual operators, or at least containing the effects of their human propensity towards imperfect perception, cognition, and action. But increasing attention is being paid to automation which, in the extreme, eliminates the human from the equation entirely, supposedly eliminating a primary source of error. In this way the auto and other transport modes are following the path of the aviation industry in attempting to remove human operators as much as possible from operations except in exceptional circumstances. Flight decks are, for the most part, fully automated, with operations mostly invisible, and sometimes inaccessible to, the human pilot (Hoogendoorn et al. 2014, 117).

With car driving, at least four hierarchical levels of automation have been distinguished: Driver assistance, partial automation, high automation, and full automation. Driver assistance is a state where a human being retains permanent control, with some form of automated assistance accessed for things like level of speed choice or keeping in lane. Partial automation entails some of these functions being taken over by an automated system but with continuous driver monitoring and preparation for humans to take over control at any time. With high automation, the system takes over most driving functions, and the driver is no longer required to continuously monitor the system but still must be prepared to respond to a takeover request by the system. With full automation the system has full control, and can request assistance from the driver as needed, but will still operate the vehicle at a "minimal risk condition" even if there is no driver response (Hoogendoorn et al. 2014, 113).

Flight cockpits have largely attained full automation. But a plane flies within a tightly controlled, regulated, and monitored ground and air control system, piercing through a "trackless" sky. Automobiles travel on roads that are much less regulated and that cannot be easily deviated from. Full and high automation have still largely not yet been achieved with cars. But there has been substantial headway made into partial automation and driver assistance.

In-vehicle navigation systems became widespread after GPS became available in 1990 (and as a standard feature beginning in 1993). Lane-keeping and cruise-control soon followed and are now standard and sophisticated. However, these assistance systems come at the cost of excessive task demands leading to increased mental workload, putting strains on human cognitive activity, and what is now known as "driver distraction". This has been met by more automation, such as antilock braking systems (ABS), first introduced in 1970; electronic stability control (ESC) and vehicle stability control (VSC) after that; and then adaptive cruise control (ACC) systems, which allow a vehicle to follow the preceding vehicle automatically by maintaining a pre-set time gap (Akamatsu et al. 2013, Section 4.1–4.2).

There is a tension between automation adding to safety and performance on the one hand while deprecating it on the other. Automatic systems are designed around what is known about the average operator at the time it is installed. But the operator will then adapt to the automation in ways that are both intended and unintended. These latter effects are particularly troublesome for those designing automation systems. For example, driving performance can deteriorate when ACC is used because drivers may over-rely on it and lower their attention to the driving task in potentially dangerous ways (Hoogendoorn et al. 2014, 116). Drivers may also not properly comprehend the system's behaviour, especially when it behaves "unexpectedly" in response to an unusual circumstance. The system may be performing as intended but "automation surprise" occurs for the user, who may take an undesirable action as a result (Akamatsu et al. 2013, Section 4.2).

Driving is a highly habituated activity, the more so for the experienced than inexperienced driver. This allows for performance in relatively unthinking and effortless ways, with often disengaged, distracted, or un-reflexive modes of attention. This can be quite useful and effective, as illustrated by the tale of the centipede that forgets how to crawl because it suddenly thinks about the whole process too much. But habit obviously also lowers cognition, vigilance, and responsiveness, bad qualities when circumstances change by surprise (Merriman 2009, 141). Automation is meant to get around this, but it is possible that the more advanced the system, there is actually a greater need for human monitoring, especially to counter over-trust and complacency (Hoogendoorn et al. 2014, 117). As a result of this conundrum, it is now generally thought that automation should both take away routine calculation and control from human operators, while protecting them against impulsive decisions and mistakes. The logical conclusion is that machines should monitor people, rather than the converse, because machines, it is said, are better watch-keepers and have better memories and judgements than people (Roscoe 1997).

This is largely the state of affairs in aviation where the old joke goes: Why does the pilot travel with a huge gorilla? Answer: Because the gorilla keeps the pilot from ever touching the controls. But this approach, even when feasible, is far from fool-proof.

19.8 HUMAN VERSUS MACHINE ERROR

Systems engineers consider human beings as part of an integrated whole that is often summarised by the acronym SHEL: software, hardware, environment, and liveware. Software consists of rules, procedures, and other elements determining system operation, while hardware refers to any physical entity other than people such as buildings and vehicles. Liveware consists of people. All three of these operate within a physical, political, organisational, and economic environment (Maddox 1998, Chapter 1).

The presumption is that the system will run more safely and efficiently in the active role if the "liveware" is taken out. Is this true? Certainly human limitations are well-known. In workplace settings, for example, 60%–80% of accidents have been estimated to be caused by human mistakes, not including design problems (Maddox 1998, Chapter 1). Humans are emotional, impulsive, limited in their perceptual and cognitive abilities, and can get confused or overwrought in a crisis – or even just in what is perceived to be a crisis.

However, the lines between human error and limitations are not always entirely clear. The SHEL designation and other representations of human–machine complexes suggest sharply delineated components with clearly identifiable and separable causal chains. But in fact these lines are not so clear and things might look differently if the development of our current transport systems had proceeded from the human being first to the machines second, rather than the other way around. This is a counterfactual question with no immediate answer but it does point to the potential pitfalls of too much confidence about human versus machine capabilities.

Even if one accepts current thinking about components, is it obviously true that machines are more free error and limitation than humans? The current (as of this writing) artificial intelligence (AI) craze would suggest so, but there are many reasons to doubt it. For one thing machines are human-created and by definition will always contain in some ways features of human thinking and ways of seeing and navigating the world. Machines certainly aid and augment human ability. But they have yet to transcend them entirely and pure logic alone cannot prove that it will be possible eventually. The answer to the question is ultimately empirical. But the results of the current major focus of intelligent systems – driverless cars – give some reason to doubt the predictions of enthusiastic tech advocates. Autonomous vehicles have been the focus of research and development for around 40 years so far. And yet outside of closed-loop systems, they are still not reliable enough for real-world use.

Of course it is possible that the breakthrough is "right around the corner", and there are many discussions of how to deliver the critical "missing piece" technically that is hard, but not insurmountable and which will ultimately deliver the holy grail. But purely autonomous vehicles are still not road-ready after decades of effort. The big debate there continues to be why. Machine advocates claim that investigation shows human error to be the root cause in almost all cases. Others claim that machine software and/or hardware is often to blame. But what seems clear from the numerous and many recent failures and accidents in this arena is that if there is human error it very often is embedded in human instructions contained in the complex software that autonomous vehicles rely on. And these errors cannot always be reliably found by checking the software because the code is too unwieldy for humans to check and one cannot be totally confident in machine-checking alone. Beyond that, many errors clearly issue from the machine, with no obvious human involvement anywhere, and not always with clear causes. Because of the complexity of the software, these errors are not entirely predictable or clear in their logic or origin (Cummings 2023). Additionally, all built systems break down and malfunction sometimes, and this is as true of "intelligent" software and hardware as its "dumb" versions. Even a "perfect" machine will suffer from the laws of physics.

This is not to make a definitive judgement on these matters. Opinions can be strong on all sides. However the issue of human error is not as simple as it seems. Human factors in transport has thus far followed a trajectory from focusing first on more purely mechanical problems, and then on to physical and cognitive limits of human operators. The earliest developments were focused on the physical structure of the vehicle and the skills of the mechanical engineer. With early autos, the driver just got the vehicle started and steered the vehicle and controlled its speed. In human–machine system terms this was just a single operator in a single vehicle. Now the system is much more complex, made so to protect and guide the human being, but meanwhile creating new problems of its own along the way, such as driver distraction and overload in an increasingly complicated larger environment. Could the current situation be akin to the Sorcerer's Apprentice tale where the magician conjures up more and more entities to exert power over the world only to be ultimately swamped by them? That is rhetorical question, with answers less clear than many suggest.

REFERENCES

Akamatsu, M., Green, P., & Bengler, K. (2013) Automotive technology and human factors research: Past, present, and future. *International Journal of Vehicular Technology*, 2013, 526180, 27 pages, 2013. https://doi.org/10.1155/2013/526180

Chapanis, A., & Holstein, W. K. (2018). Human-factors engineering. *Encyclopaedia Britannica*. 11 May 2018. britannica.com/print/article/275693

Cummings, M. (2023). What self-driving cars tell us about AI risks. 5 conclusions from an automation expert fresh off a stint with the U.S. highway safety agency. *IEEE Spectrum*. May 30. https://spectrum.ieee.org/self-driving-cars-2662494269

Durso, F. T., Margulieux, L. E., & Blickensderfer, E. L. (2014). *Human factors*. Oxford University Press.

Elias, N. (1995). Technization and civilization. *Theory, Culture & Society*, 12(3), 7–42.

Gunn, S. (2018).The history of transport systems in the UK. *Future of mobility: Evidence review foresight*. Government Office for Science, Centre for Urban History, University of Leicester.

Hoogendoorn, R., van Arerm, B., & Hoogendoom, S. (2014). Automated driving, traffic flow efficiency, and human factors: Literature review. *Transportation Research Record*, 2422(1), 113–120.

Jones, L. V., & Thissen, D. (2006). A history and overview of psychometrics. In Rao, C.R. & Sinharay, S. (eds). *Handbook of statistics* . Elsevier, volume 26, 1–27.

Lorimer, H., & Guarnieri, M. (1996). Accidents and acts of God: A history of the terms. *American Journal of Public Health*, 86(1), 101–107.

Lowson, M. V. (1998). Surface transport history in the UK: Analysis and projections. *Proceedings of the Institution of Civil Engineers-Transport*, 129(1), 14–19.

Maddox, M. (1998). Chapter 1: Human factors. *Human factors guide for aviation maintenance and inspection*. Office of Aviation Medicine Federal Aviation Administration, 1–23.

Mashaw, J. L., & Harfst, D. L. (1990). *The struggle for auto safety*. Harvard University Press.

Merriman, P. (2009). Mobility. In Kitchin, Rob & Thrift, Nigel (eds). *International encyclopedia of human geography*. Elsevier, 134–143.

NASA (1978). Anthropometric source book. Volume 1: Anthropometry for designers. US National Aeronautics and Space Administration. https://archive.org/details/nasa_techdoc_19790003563/mode/1up

Ritchie, A. (1975). *King of the road: An illustrated history of cycling*. Wildwood House London/Ten Speed Press Berkeley.

Roscoe, S. N. (1997). *The adolescence of engineering psychology*. Human Factors and Ergonomics Society.

Sachs, W. (1983). Are energy-intensive life-images fading? The cultural meaning of the automobile in transition. *Journal of Economic Psychology*, 3(3–4), 347–365.

Shaver, E. F., & Braun, C. C. (2008). *What is human factors and ergonomics*. Benchmark Research & Safety, Inc.

Sheller, M. (2004). Automotive emotions: Feeling the car. *Theory, Culture & Society*, 21(4–5), 221–242.

Sovacool, B. K. (2009). Early modes of transport in the United States: Lessons for modern energy policymakers. *Policy and Society*, 27(4), 411–427.

Wells, H. G. (1896). *The wheels of chance: A holiday adventure*. J. M. Dent.

CHAPTER 20

Micro-mobility versus large networks and mobility as a service (MaaS)

20.1 INTRODUCTION: A MOBILITY SPECTRUM

Box 20.1 points to the fact that everyday mobility is not so clearly distinct and separate from longer and more permanent moves such as residential migration. Rather, personal mobility is on a continuum ranging from short-distance daily moves to international migration and virtual motion (Pooley 2009, 144). This mobility spectrum is depicted in Table 20.1 (freight movements are rather different and this template is not meant to be applied there) (see Chapter 16).

The individual travelling "agent" has a whole series of mobility needs across spatial and temporal scales, large and small. Mobility needs, desires, and movements within the time–space of a day, such as an hour, can be referred to as everyday mobility. This can be as tiny as movements between rooms within a home, but the usual focus of transport analysis is movements outside internal spaces, such as between home and nearby locations like a local park or store. These movements will generally be accomplished using walking, cycling, transit, or driving modes. (A few very rich people will have

DOI: 10.4324/9781003350866-24

BOX 20.1 INTRODUCTORY CASE: THE MOBILITY TRANSITION

A traditional view of historians has been that pre-modern societies were generally stable and self-sufficient entities that had little need or means of movement over any but the smallest spatial areas. There was obviously plenty of long-range movement, to be sure, across the seas and large landmasses. But while significant, these were specialised categories concentrated in specialised groups such as traders, raiders, and religious missionaries. The great mass of people were born, lived, and died mainly within very small geographical radii.

Industrialisation and modernisation in the 19th century changed all this, it was once argued. The pattern of more footloose activity and frequent relocation, already emerging in Europe in the prior two centuries, now accelerated as modern production technologies took hold and international trade took off. People started to move both within and between countries, no longer bound to particular places and much less motivated, or able, to do so, in any case. Thus, as societies "modernised", "everyday mobility", i.e. levels of both residential migration and population circulation, rose. The result was a dramatic increase in internal and external migration accompanying modern economic change and growth (Lucassen & Lucassen 2009, 348–349). This hypothesis that human society has become increasingly mobile as it has become increasingly modern has been termed the "mobility transition" (Zelinsky 1971).

Certainly movements of people and goods rose dramatically in the 1800s. There was a sharp jump in the level of migration after 1850 as the rate of economic and social change in Europe and its "offshoots" (i.e. Australia, Canada, New Zealand, and the US) appeared to radically unsettle individual and collective lifestyles and locations. Even if one didn't move across international borders, increases in downward and upward economic mobility now led to many moves within neighbourhoods or between cities out of choice and necessity in the course of a single lifetime.

The social images of the time reflected this restlessness. Both Americans and Europeans were pushing outwards in internal and external empire building, with various "frontier" myths emerging. This was especially strong in America where rapid economic growth rapidly expanded White settlement westward across the continent, accompanied by the building of extensive rail and road networks, and waves of migrants from home and overseas seeking fortune in both cities and remote areas (from the settler perspective; obviously many long-established indigenous populations were ruthlessly pushed out or exterminated). The rails in particular carried increasing numbers not just of migrants but of displaced and homeless "vagrants", an 1875 source claiming that as many as 10,000 "tramps" rode the boxcars every day. A popular panic was whipped up about these "hoboes", being seen with a mix of scorn, fear, and admiration of their independence and free-spiritedness – though they remained at the bottom either way, Charlie Chaplin capturing this sort of fragile nobility in his famous "Tramp" character in his silent films (Merriman 2009, 136).

Historically though, there is a question of how unprecedented this change in mobility actually was. Vagrancy and homelessness are certainly nothing new and were a constant of many European (and non-European) societies for centuries, England having panics about vagrants as early as the late 15th century (Merriman 2009, 137). The ancient world was the scene of much wandering and roaming, sometimes motivated by religion, St. Paul's evangelising being but one of the most prominent examples. And one could argue that trade itself was much less specialised than it is today, requiring the active participation of ordinary individuals on multiple levels often across surprisingly long distances at times for a whole range of movements of goods.

Even at the height of the First and Second Industrial Revolutions, personal mobilities were still thin and fragmented. Railroad networks expanded unevenly, steamships were still relatively slow, and the fastest modes were expensive and out of reach for most individuals for a long time. Telegraphy moved information at the speed of light but its final transmission to human beings still required slow repeater stations staffed with human operators re-keying messages, sometimes introducing errors along the way (Hugill 2009, 341). There has also been criticism of the particularities of Zelinsky's model, which posited "stages" of growth in which mobility progressed along with economic and social modernisation, a template very much in vogue at the time he wrote. Economic and social change is now seen as a much more disorderly and unpredictable process that is not so easily generalised into pre-cut slices (Pooley 2009, 145).

Nonetheless, the idea of a mobility transition has caught the scholarly imagination with some justification. Although the earlier stages of industrialised transport were characterised by choppy diffusion, they became more seamless with time and eventually were adopted on a mass scale. More recently there has been a de-localising of activity combined with an increase in its pace, scope, scale, and speed. Many people now effectively live and/or work in multiple places, increasingly virtually, with the various journeys from home to work becoming more indistinct (Pooley 2009, 144). The period of the later 20th and early 21st centuries has thus been referred to as an era of "hypermobility" in which individuals take more frequent trips, over great distances, and for multiple purposes. Since the 1960s, in the UK, for example, travel has increased faster than economic growth, seemingly independently of other major economic and political shifts, with only occasional interruptions such as the first and second oil price shocks of the 1970s, the global financial crisis (GFC) of 2008 (Gunn 2018, 24); and of course, the Covid-19 pandemic of 2020–23. These sharp breaks nonetheless seem to quickly return to longer trends of rapid travel growth. One can thus argue that a "new mobility paradigm" has become embedded in which travel and mobility often become significant activities in and of themselves (Pooley 2009, 146). Whether this is a positive development is another question.

TABLE 20.1

The mobility spectrum

Agent requirements	Network services
"Everyday" ← → "Long-range"	"Micro-" ← → "Macro"

access to private jets or helicopters for shorter jaunts, but these are obviously exceptional.)

On the other end of the spectrum are "long-range" movements which take place generally over more than a day, and distances that typically cannot be returned from within a day. These can range up to hundreds or thousands of kilometres. The modes available for these trips now include an aeroplane trip as a possibility for most people. The trip purposes can vary. From a pure mobility perspective, the main differentiation is scale and scope of motion.

The network services dimension refers to the agent's choice of, and interaction with, the means of mobility and the network it travels on. "Micro-mobility" typically refers to individualised modes such as cycling, walking, and e-scooters, for a one-off trip or multiple ones. These can be done on surface routes dedicated to the exclusive use of these modes, such as bicycle paths. Or they can take place on mixed-mode routes, like roads shared between cars and bicycles. Either way the focus is on means that are oriented towards individual trips making small demands on, and having little need for, extensive networks designed for larger purposes. (Incidentally, the term is often contracted into one word, "micromobility", but is hyphenated here to highlight that this is a specific type of a more generalised mobility continuum.)

Macro-mobility is used here meanwhile, to indicate large movements of large numbers across large networks. The individual agent is not as important a focus here as is mass motion. Topics pertinent to this category are covered in more detail in Chapter 9 on vehicles and infrastructure.

20.2 MOBILITY AS A SERVICE (MAAS)

A key factor in mobility outcomes is the interaction between agent requirements and available network services. The trend of the past two decades has been to detach mobility from transport modes and networks and to consider it as a bundle of movement services to be "consumed" by agents via as-needed transactions. Approaching things in this way, planners, network managers, and agents can theoretically more efficiently match transport demand with available supply, while demanders and suppliers can more effectively coordinate with one another by breaking down their movements into discrete and adjustable parts.

This sort of thinking has led to the formulation and implementation of mobility as a service (MaaS). MaaS is typically offered as a model for solving urban mobility problems, the bulk of such movements being on the everyday mobility. It can also, however, be applied to larger mobility tasks including intercity trips. Rather than have to rely on personally owned modes, such as cars or bicycles, or on central mass transit and other networks, a MaaS provider can be consulted for a "one-stop shop" for all transport needs, mixing and matching various modes to deliver a desired trip at a desired time. The chosen modes range from traditional fixed public transport services to "shared" modes such as ridesharing, peer-to-peer rentals, and e-bikes or scooters (Mapbox 2024).

The functional pivot of this model is digital, i.e. the use of an online trip planner or of a mobile phone trip service app. A user will be provided with a given platform to input their desired origins and destinations and in return will get a selection of routes, times, and costs that are supposed to match their desires as closely and as cost-effectively as possible. Thus, MaaS can be broken down into three components: (a) services, which refer to the digital elements; (b) mobility solutions, which refer to the portfolio of specific modes available for a given journey; and (c) integration, which refers to the ways and degree to which the first two components are linked to one another. Ideally, a single application can be used to schedule and obtain a trip, rather than having to use multiple ones (Mapbox 2024).

The basic premise of MaaS is that personal ownership of vehicles and collective provision of transit services are both economically inefficient because they lead to waste in the form of unused capacity and an inability to offer a full range of services for each and every trip. Car-owners only use their cars part of the time, letting them sit idle and inaccessible otherwise. Similarly, transit networks are overused in peak times and underused at other times and generally cannot get people door-to-door. MaaS supposedly gets past both of these problems by allowing users to use a shared vehicle whenever they wish and integrate this with public transit to obtain a seamless point-to-point journey on-demand and with less carrying cost to themselves.

20.3 MAAS ECONOMICS

Certainly digital technologies have deeply penetrated transport. The US, for example, has seen the rise of ridesharing companies Uber and Lyft delivering 5 billion and 620 million passenger trips in 2018, respectively (Noussan et al.

2020, 21). Trip planning apps are ubiquitous, and their integration into the pervasive Google Maps app has made them extremely widely used. Freight movement has also been altered by MaaS, especially "last-mile" deliveries that are especially well suited to integrated micro-mobility electricity-based services, such as scooter sharing and electric bikes (see Chapter 16). In some Asian countries, two- and three-wheelers are already the most diffused road transport mode (94% in Vietnam, 73% in India, 54% in Thailand) and thus easily integrated into digital platforms (Noussan et al. 2020, 8).

But there is reason to question how much of a mobility solution MaaS really is. For one thing, its effectiveness ultimately rests on a totally devolved car fleet and a transit network with extensive market penetration rates. Both of these conditions are far from realised in most places. The vast majority of the global car fleet, even in dense urban areas, is still privately owned and, for the most part, privately deployed for private purposes, though a portion of these are operated for rideshare. The global MaaS market size in 2021 has been estimated at 126 billion euros, expected to grow prodigiously to 500 billion euros by 2030. But this still is expected to deliver only a 19% share of urban trips by on-demand transport by 2030 (Statista 2024). This represents a rapid rate of expansion but full penetration of the market appears to be decades off.

Transit, meanwhile, is deficient in many urban peripheries, and sometimes not well scheduled even in urban cores. Figures 20.1 and 20.2 provide some illustrative data.

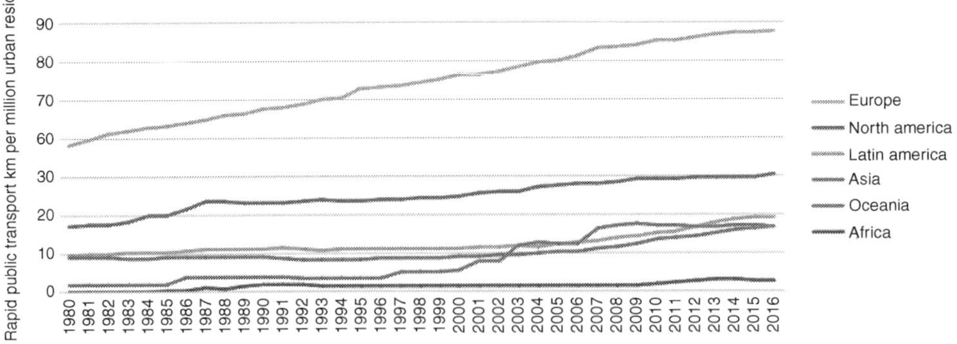

FIGURE 20.1

Supply of rapid transit relative to urban population.

Source: World Bank (2017, Figure 2.5, 48). Reproduced under a CC.BY.3.0 licence.

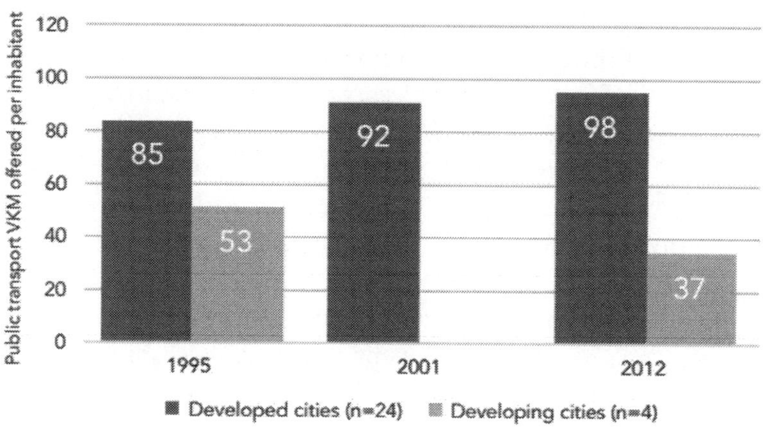

FIGURE 20.2
Average level of public transport supply, in vehicles per kilometre, in 24 developed cities and 4 developing cities.

Source: World Bank (2017, Figure 2.4, 47). Reproduced under a CC.BY 3.0 licence.

Although this information is somewhat fragmented and dated, it illustrates the uneven penetration of transit networks globally and their relatively slow growth over time. Europe is the most well-endowed transit region in the world, but even here transit supply relative to population went from just under 60% to just under 80% over the 36 years between 1980 and 2016 (World Bank (2017) 47). Other regions had much lower rates over the same period. And while developing world cities, especially in Latin America, have built a number of new systems and extensions, population growth there has often caused demand to outpace supply considerably. Where transit is already extensive, such as in Europe and in certain North American and other transit-dense cities like New York or Shanghai, MaaS has made the greatest inroads and contributions since it fills in relatively small system gaps in timing, spatial access, and user requirements. Here MaaS can lower user trip cost with both user and network providers potentially benefiting from economic synergies. But this is not the case in many other parts of the globe, in both rich and poor countries. And even in those places most amenable to MaaS, it is likely to remain an important but nonetheless "niche" solution for global mobility needs.

Road capacity is also problematic in many cities. Roads and streets are expensive to build and maintain, and in dense environments road space is often literally tapped out. Cars sit in traffic whether they are rideshared or private. By itself MaaS cannot solve this particular problem. And to the extent that car-based MaaS solutions divert trips from transit or walking and cycling, they may add traffic to already burdened roads, as discussed more below.

In fact, an unstated element of MaaS is its necessary reliance on costly collective provision of infrastructure. Timms et al. (2014) note that a transport system can be defined as being made up of three elements: (a) the mobility of people and goods; (b) the physical aspects (including transport infrastructure, the built environment, vehicles, and technology) that facilitate or inhibit such mobility; and (c) the system of governance with respect to formulating and implementing transport policy (85). MaaS focuses mainly on (a) and the purely digital aspects of (b) but leaves out everything else for the most part, especially the hard elements of (b) and almost everything out of (c). This does not invalidate MaaS as a useful concept. But it does call into question some of the utopian rhetoric sometimes offered by analysts and providers.

A true mass MaaS (to pardon the wordplay) is therefore still in the relatively distant future. The digital platforms are well developed, but the hardware supported by this software is far less advanced and is likely to progress only slowly. This does not deny any genuine benefits and conveniences that MaaS is delivering in certain places now. But it also indicates that MaaS is not a panacea for urban mobility.

One could argue that this is nonetheless just a transition problem and that, like any technological evolution, considerable time is required between fruition to optimality. The data above indicate that this transition is taking quite a while and may still be incomplete within the next decade or two. Also the historical reality is that an optimal equilibrium does not automatically emerge from technological change alone, with the resources required to attain it considerable, and not always arising purely from market dynamics.

Some have therefore noted that MaaS is not as technologically neutral as its proponents suggest. Sheller and Urry (2000) propose that there is a predominant global form of "quasi-private mobility" that subordinates other "public" mobilities of walking, cycling, travelling by rail, etc. with MaaS as its latest extension (739–740). This can also be posited in more traditional economic theory terms as a mode-shift versus mode-share dynamic. The MaaS ideal is one of complementary mode use, in which modes complement and augment one another, e.g. ridesharing stimulating transit usage and vice-versa. But there is considerable evidence that ridesharing and other transport network company (TNC) enterprises like Uber often replace and substitute for other modes. An Uber ride may replace a transit or cycle ride as easily as it may complement it. This need not be a problem *per se*. But it does undermine somewhat the premise that MaaS is a global mobility solution, rather than just a private business model, and that the unbundling of mobility services is always positive-sum rather than zero-sum game, in which every mode wins and no mode loses. To the extent that ridesharing undermines transit, for example, this will weaken the general model of modal connectivity MaaS is based upon (Wong et al. 2020).

The particular sharing and peer-to-peer elements of MaaS also have had teething pains. E-scooters, for example, have emerged as a significant part of urban mobility as of this writing. They do appear to be more popular in many cases than personal auto trips. But they also can be substitutes for shared or private bicycles and often nudge out transit and walking options for some types of journeys (Wang et al. 2023). There are also safety issues in scooter operation, especially in crowded spaces shared with pedestrians, with occasionally unfortunate interactions between the two. Perceived safety of operation can be as significant as real safety in affecting the uptake and use of scooters as well (Hardt & Bogenberger 2019). Introduction of e-scooters, like most every mode in the past, has largely started with little policy guidance or any sort of general interest oversight or coordination. These have been dribbling in after the fact, but it cannot be assumed that an optimum will naturally emerge.

The economics of the large ridesharing companies are complex. Uber is a good case in point, alternating between idol and *bête noire* depending on perspective. The company started modestly in 2009 and today has a major brand name and is one of the leading rideshare and food delivery companies in the world. It also has a growing freight business. Uber describes itself as a transport company and, like many tech companies, hails itself as a "disruptor" bringing new efficiencies and innovation in its wake. Traditional taxi fleets have been hard pressed by the emergence of a sector that the company invented. The firm initially ran big losses for years. It is now becoming increasingly and steadily profitable. But is this because of its genuine value-adding delivered by its transport function? In fact, Uber can as easily be seen more as a distribution network for others rather than its self-designated moniker of transport provider. This is a genuine service in its own right, but much of its profitability may possibly be traced to its quasi-monopolistic dominance as a platform, helped along by the demise of competing taxi fleets which the company had some role in bringing about. Uber drivers are not paid particularly well, generally treated as independent contractors with no fixed benefits, and paid on what could be described as a piece-work basis. Operators must provide their own vehicles and pay all the upkeep on them. The company's market power over consumers has meanwhile been demonstrated by its controversial "surge" pricing policy in which ride prices can shoot up to extraordinary levels immediately, supposedly only for unusual spikes in demand, but often in seemingly ordinary times as well (Sengupta et al. 2021).

No transport innovation is perfect, of course, and many people rely on Uber and other ridesharing platforms, both passengers and drivers, with great benefit. But in general, the economics of these companies, and of MaaS in general, is still a work-in-progress. Some important advances have been made and the rethinking of mobility has opened some new vistas. But whether overall economic welfare, or even general mobility, has been increased still remains to be seen.

20.4 MOBILITY AND SUSTAINABILITY

MaaS and other mobility transformations are sometimes touted for their potential contributions to sustainability and resilience. There has been much discussion, once more, about the automobile, which MaaS supposedly reinvents into a shared device that seamlessly plugs into all other modes for efficient mobility outcomes. Rather than being the bane of Earth systems, it is claimed that a reinvented automobile can become a powerful part of the solution of global ecological ills. The car has always been a means towards more personal mobility. Suitably redesigned and integrated through MaaS and other innovations, the car may be able to maintain and even enhance current levels of urban personal mobility at lower unit cost and greater system efficiency. Energy and materials requirements of overall mobility systems can decline, along with tailpipe emissions and other external dis-amenities (Mitchell et al. 2010, 1–2).

Automobiles are already widely accepted and even embraced, partly through the magic of mass marketing, as not just utilitarian, but as fun, fashionable, and adventurous. But they do entail a significant up-front purchase outlay and on-going operating expense. They must be housed and parked at additional cost. And as currently deployed, they still offer mainly private, rather than public, benefit. Some argue that the automobile therefore is in a good position to be repurposed into delivering sustainable personal and collective mobility through ridesharing since the mode is already ubiquitous but can be leveraged to get full social benefit from the embodied transport capacity it represents (Mitchell et al. 2010, 3). The fact that many current vested interests, such as car manufacturers and energy companies, are amongst some of the advocates does not necessarily invalidate this logic.

An alternative but related vision is that MaaS and ridesharing could be used as a way of easing the car out of its current dominance to deliver even greater sustainability improvements than auto repurposing. Carsharing could potentially reduce the size of the total car fleet while delivering more desired trips than the status quo, and privileging cleaner and more active modes, like cycling and transit. To the extent that the MaaS transition seems to be mostly repurposing the car rather than replacing it suggests that some significant gains in system sustainability and resilience may be being left on the table. This is an empirical question and depends much on the relative contributions of different modes to climate change in the form of embodied and direct emissions and energy use, amongst other things. The main point here is that a more resilient and sustainable transport outcome is not guaranteed by improved mobility delivery alone without explicitly designing this in. How much this is being done presently is debatable.

20.5 MOBILITY, SPATIAL DEVELOPMENT, AND CAR-DEPENDENCY

Transport advances have sped up travel time and expanded individual traveller spatial ambits (Sachs 1983, 355). From a collective perspective, transport has compressed time and space, enabling increases in output through a reorganisation of activities temporally and spatially (Banister 2011, 957). Thus, mobility improvement has caused location shifts that potentially maximise both economic product and consumer utility and satisfaction. Mobility innovation potentially promises more of this. But will it deliver?

Much attention has been paid to the relation between density and mobility, with the greatest amount of attention paid to whether or not low-density sprawl is associated with car use and, if so, whether this has actually reduced mobility for many people by putting them in a state of car-dependency. Spread out residential and employment patterns are by definition easiest to travel around with a decentralised mode like the auto, and once these patterns have become widespread, the built environment, it is argued, essentially forces its use (exacerbated by transit service cuts in some places that were partly caused by these same reductions in density). One proposition is that spatial location therefore needs to be re-densified to reduce car-dependence and allow greater mode choice and hence greater mobility (Ewing et al. 2018).

The debate on this proposition has been robust. Some have made methodological challenges, arguing that many studies showing an inverse relationship between density and car usage do not adequately control for confounding effects such as fuel prices, technology, and income. Others have found that the intensity of automobile usage varies across individuals, and over time, with causation being both social and personal, interacting in complex and subtle ways. Lifestyle and parental influence are especially important determining factors at some critical stages of life. And automobile ownership itself drives car usage somewhat independently of spatial form, people often buying autos for convenience but then coming to rely on them exclusively, even if alternative and superior modes are available (Zhang 2005, 55–56). Earlier findings of strong associations between urban density and car-dependency have not always been replicated by later studies or have been found to vary much more according to other underlying variables, particularly spatial accessibility of desired locations (Ewing et al. 2018).

Bruegmann (2008) thus challenges the label of automobile dependency entirely, provocatively claiming that we do not use the term "refrigerator dependency", even though we all certainly rely on that machine even more than we do the car. In his view the car is just a very useful facilitator of movement just as the refrigerator is a very useful facilitator of keeping things cold. This last is a fair rhetorical point, in that labels can stifle empiricism. But this also may be carrying the point too far. Even Bruegmann admits that newer and more efficient transport modes have tended to spread urban activity into generally declining densities. He claims that this was largely a matter of personal preference, with a desire for lower-density living being enabled by the car, rather than the other way around. He and others also note that earlier modes like rail led both to the dense industrial city of the 19th century, while also contributing to its later decentralisation through the "streetcar suburb" (referring to the ways cities expanded outwards with the advent of that technology).

Yet this sort of development was in the context of accessible and cheap land that enabled and encouraged more space devoted to housing and front gardens while maintaining local walkability for many daily tasks to and from the nearby streetcar stop. So the streetcar simultaneously expanded accessibility across space (e.g. in Boston, where the area of urban settlement expanded from 2 mi beyond the city core during the horsecar era to 4 mi during the first decade of its streetcar service) while also maintaining dense and compact urban concentrations as compared to the automobile-centric suburbs that came later and which created more time–space convergence on a wider scale but created divergence on a local scale (Young 2015). The car is a more centrifugal mode in comparison to rail with its common carriage and fixed tracks. Infrastructure and land developer choices have also been critical levers in this process, making the argument that urban sprawl and car-dependency is simply an outgrowth of personal preference *en masse* debatable.

20.6 MOBILITY AND ACCESSIBILITY

This issue of mobility's relationship to accessibility is very important for transport choice. Mobility refers to an ability to move, while accessibility refers to an ability to get to desired locations and desired activities in a meaningful way. Many have remarked on how technological change has affected accessibility, especially those changes that enable faster travel. For example, an auto with an average speed of 35 km/h could potentially afford a maximum daily accessibility (with return trip) to a territory of about 1,000 km^2, 50 times more than the 20 km^2 of a purely pedestrian city. And people are, as noted earlier, travelling much more than before. For example, between 1800 and 2000, American mobility has been estimated to have grown an average of 2.7% per year, a doubling every 25 years (Ausubel & Marchetti 2001, 23–24). But there is evidence that desired locations and activities are becoming more spread out. If all an increase in mobility does is expand the space across which people must travel, then net accessibility has not necessarily increased (Banister 2011, 254).

Indeed, technical improvements may have arguably led to increases in average distance travelled, and a decrease in use of slower modes, including walking, with more travel required to get to the same activities as before. Universal statements are not entirely possible though. The core model of space is a featureless plain. But this does not encompass the workings of real space, built or natural. Access to jobs and markets for suppliers, labour, customers, goods, and services is important for both producer and consumer decisions which are, in turn, very much, affected by collective landscape, built environment, and natural topography (Weisbrod & Hensher 2023, Sections 3.1, 3.2).

What does seem clear is that mode choice and development affects mobility, which affects and is affected by the existing spatial environment and level of density. It's also clear that "choice" is a relative term as well. Agents are constrained both by the modal alternatives offered and the terrain they have to cover. In theory, the separation of mobility from modes may loosen some of these relationships, since MaaS purports to move beyond modes and infrastructure to more flexible mobility choices. But as already discussed, while MaaS makes many trips more modally heterogeneous, trips still must rely on existing mode portfolios and supporting infrastructure within a broader physical, social, and economic context. At present it is not clear how much this particular development in mobility may change the transport-development-accessibility-mobility nexus in future.

20.7 MOBILITY AND CONGESTION

The implications of all this for congestion reduction remain rather ambiguous. This is because traffic outcomes flow from collective travel decisions involving decisions to make a trip or not, along with distance, frequency, travel mode choice, departure time, and route choice. Changes in the overall built environment and specific features of it obviously influence various aspects of travel in countervailing directions causally. MaaS and other mobility innovations change the availability and performance of modes, but the net effect on traffic, even when isolating just this impact, seems to depend on the situation at hand. The final outcomes of all these combined changes on traffic and capacity have to be determined empirically (Zhang 2010).

The way in which mobility changes are manifested and the context in which they are made is highly intertwined with the level of congestion on the facilities travelled on. This includes local provision of public transit systems, topography, and the availability of a car. Thus, MaaS in German cities with relatively good public transport options and high active travel (in 2007, 54% of all trips there were made on foot, and cars used for only about 32% of all trips) will deliver mobility in a different shape than in the American cities where the same statistics were, and are, much lower (Mollenkopf 2007, 201). This means that its effects on road and transit congestion (and other dimensions such as sustainability) will be quite different as well. Changes in the mobility array will have ambiguous and contextual effects on congestion and only time and experience will clarify how positive or negative these changes will be.

An interesting wrinkle here is that time and space are as much subjective and objective. The mental image of a terrain, including perceptions of activity locations, and availability and preferability of travel paths are likely shaped in part by how a traveller typically gets around, whether by foot, bicycle, bus, train, driver or auto passenger. Subjective differences in mobility experience are often stark and quite at variance with "objective" metrics. These mental maps and spatial learning patterns interact with objective factors to change perceived accessibility and mobility and travel choices along with it (Mondschein et al. 2007). How MaaS and other innovations will change this, and how this further flows into traffic levels, especially by car, is still an open question.

20.8 MOBILITY CULTURES

Cultural and social factors can be very important to the various aspects of mobility outcomes, sometimes as much as economic and material factors. Many environmentalists have argued for a paradigmatic shift in "mobility cultures" away from fossil-fuelled mobility baselines and towards post-fossil ones. These can vary widely both in concept and in practice. The current focus on a transition towards decarbonisation of energy source retains much more automobility than other "post-car society" visions which look to deliver mobility via means other than the car. "Mobility cultures" can be defined as consisting of shared meanings underpinning the production and consumption of mobility-related goods and services and the practices and beliefs associated with them (Mögele & Rau 2020, 16–17). Economic theory generally side-lines or dismisses this dimension. Sociology and social theory emphasises them. The mobility transition discussion that opened this chapter demonstrates the close links between the economic and non-economic spheres. MaaS itself could be argued to be a reframing of mobility culture as much as anything else.

Analysts of the history of science and technology tend to focus on the emergence of new technologies as distinct episodes. Examination of the survival and maintenance of older preceding technologies across periods of change is generally neglected. Yet old technologies typically prevail for much longer than such an episodic framing intimates, and there is often a long interregnum in which old and new survive and meld together (Margócsy & Brazelton 2023, 2–3). While MaaS in particular is presented as something "new", it is quite clearly a hybrid of largely existing modes, with on-going modifications, on existing networks, coordinated by purpose-built digital platforms which themselves are by now not particularly novel except, perhaps, for their software configurations, and the experience gleaned by climbing up the learning curve with significant aid from large amounts of data generation analysed through the use of artificial intelligence (AI) algorithms. Arguably the biggest innovation is actually organisational and managerial, with various commercial entities applying electronic distribution methods to the mobility decision-making of individuals and the scheduling and delivery of transport operations. Even this concept is not entirely unprecedented, since network products like transport have long been perfecting their distribution abilities with an aim towards greater efficiency and market power.

Nonetheless, the impact of the MaaS paradigm and its related decentralised mobility concepts has been significant. Thinking about such things has been heavily altered and many traditional urban transport markets have indeed been disrupted and reshaped. Whether this has resulted in a true mobility revolution, or will result in one any time soon, is debatable. The future is not as obvious as either booster or naysayer suggests.

REFERENCES

Ausubel, J. H., & Marchetti, C. M. (2001). The evolution of transport. *Industrial Physicist* (April/May), 20–24.

Banister, D. (2011). The trilogy of distance, speed and time. *Journal of Transport Geography*, 19(4), 950–959.

Bruegmann, R. (2008). Point: Sprawl and accessibility. *Journal of Transport and Land Use*, 1(1), 5–11.

Ewing, R., Hamidi, S., Tian, G., Proffitt, D., Tonin, S., & Fregolent, L. (2018). Testing Newman and Kenworthy's theory of density and automobile dependence. *Journal of Planning Education and Research*, 38(2), 167–182.

Gunn, S. (2018). *The history of transport systems in the UK future of mobility: Evidence review foresight.* Centre for Urban History, University of Leicester. Provided for UK Government Office for Science.

Hardt, C., & Bogenberger, K. (2019). Usage of e-scooters in urban environments. *Transportation Research Procedia*, 37, 155–162.

Hugill, P. J. (2009). Trade, transport and communications, historical geographies of. In *International encyclopedia of human geography*. Elsevier, 338–344.

Lucassen, J., & Lucassen, L. (2009). The mobility transition revisited, 1500–1900: what the case of Europe can offer to global history. *Journal of Global History*, 4(3), 347–377.

Mapbox (2024). The future of transportation: Mobility as a service (MaaS). Mapbox Inc. www.mapbox.com/insights/mobility-as-a-service-maas

Margócsy, D., & Brazelton, M. A. (2023). Techniques of repair, the circulation of knowledge, and environmental transformation: Towards a new history of transportation. *History of Science*, 61(1), 3–18.

Merriman, P. (2009). Mobility. In Kitchin, Rob and Thrift, Nigel (eds). *International encyclopedia of human geography*. Elsevier, 134–143.

Mitchell, W. J., Borroni-Bird, C. E., & Burns, L. D. (2010). *Reinventing the automobile: Personal urban mobility for the 21st century*. MIT Press.

Mögele, M., & Rau, H. (2020). Cultivating the "car state": A culturally sensitive analysis of car-centric discourses and mobility cultures in Southern Germany. *Sustainability: Science, Practice and Policy*, 16(1), 15–28.

Mollenkopf, H. (2007). Mobility and flexibility. In Birren, James E. (ed). *Encyclopedia of gerontology* (2nd edition). Elsevier, 196–204.

Mondschein, A., Blumenberg, E., & Taylor, B. D. (2007). Accessibility and cognition: The effect of transportation mode on spatial knowledge. *87th Annual Transportation Research Board Meetings*.

Noussan, M., Hafner, M., Tagliapietra, S. (2020). The evolution of transport across world regions. In *The future of transport between digitalization and decarbonization*. Springer Briefs in Energy. Springer.

Pooley, C. G. (2009). Mobility, history of everyday. In Kitchin, Rob and Thrift, Nigel (eds). *International encyclopedia of human geography*. Elsevier, 144–149.

Sachs, W. (1983). Are energy-intensive life-images fading? The cultural meaning of the automobile in transition. *Journal of Economic Psychology*, 3(3–4), 347–365.

Sengupta, A., He, S., & Li, X. (2021). Book-or-drive: The impact of ridesharing on the automobile industry. SSRN Working Paper 3810178.

Sheller, M., & Urry, J. (2000). The city and the car. *International Journal of Urban and Regional Research*, 24(4), 737–757.

Statista (2024). Forecast: MaaS market size worldwide 2021 and 2030. *Statista Research Department*, February 23, 2024. www.statista.com/statistics/1180559/global-mobility-as-a-service-market-size/

Timms, P., Tight, M., & Watling, D. (2014). Imagineering mobility: Constructing utopias for future urban transport. *Environment and Planning A*, 46(1), 78–93.

Wang, K., Qian, X., Fitch, D. T., Lee, Y., Malik, J., & Circella, G. (2023). What travel modes do shared e-scooters displace? A review of recent research findings. *Transport Reviews*, 43(1), 5–31.

Weisbrod, G., & Hensher, D. A. (2023). Improving transportation project evaluation by recognizing the role of spatial scale and context in measuring non-user economic benefits. *Transport Policy*, 144, 80–89.

Wong, Y. Z., Hensher, D. A., & Mulley, C. (2020). Mobility as a service (MaaS): Charting a future context.

Transportation Research Part A: Policy and Practice, 131, 5–19.
World Bank (2017). *Global mobility report 2017*. World Bank.
Young, J. (2015). Infrastructure: Mass transit in 19th-and 20th-century urban America. In *Oxford Research Encyclopedia of American History*. Oxford University Press.
Zhang, M. (2005). Intercity variations in the relationship between urban form and automobile dependence: Disaggregate analyses of Boston, Massachusetts; Portland, Oregon; and Houston, Texas. *Transportation Research Record*, 1902(1), 55–62.
Zhang, M. (2010). Can transit-oriented development reduce peak-hour congestion? *Transportation Research Record*, 2174, 148–155.
Zelinsky, W. (1971). The hypothesis of the mobility transition. *Geographical Review*, 61(2), 219–249.

CHAPTER 21

Some conclusions above the past, present, and future

21.1 OUR INDUSTRIAL PAST

The transport system as it exists today is very much a product of the First and Second Industrial Revolutions that roughly spanned the period between the late 1700s and the 1930s. During this time there was a vast increase in the ability to intensively and extensively exploit inputs to produce ever greater amounts of output. Historians sometimes refer to this era as "machine age", and the label is apt since industrialisation worked along lines of mechanisation powered by industrially produced energy sources such as coal and oil. Efficiencies were obtained by breaking down as many processes as possible as minutely as possible into standardised chunks that could be then be run through machines, assisted by human labour that itself was standardised and regimented. It turned out this way of doing things increased in efficiency as it was scaled up and intensified; so factories, cities, and networks got larger and larger, simultaneous with getting denser and denser.

Throughput – a term referring to the volume and speed with which things pass through a process – was a core metric of the industrial enterprise. The faster things moved from raw materials to final sale, the cheaper everything got, including mass movements of goods and people. Automation, in which human labour and decision-making were increasingly taken out of the system

DOI: 10.4324/9781003350866-25

BOX 21.1 INTRODUCTORY CASE: THE FUTURE AS SEEN THROUGH 1930S WORLD'S FAIRS

As industrialisation spread and expanded, a series of "world's fairs" were held that were designed to showcase the marvels of science and industry. The first of these was held in London in 1851 with successor events held through Europe and North America through the rest of the 19th century and well into the 20th century – though they began to wane somewhat after the 1960s (Encyclopedia.com 2024). A popular feature of these fairs were exhibits purporting to show what a future society would look like in a few decades time. Such predictions were made with a notion that human beings were living in a technological age in which ever-expanding material progress was inevitable and that current problems such as poverty, hunger, and human hardship all had technical solutions that human ingenuity would solve sooner or later.

The fairs held during the 1930s are interesting in that they took place in the depths of a worldwide Great Depression that ended in World War II, both seemingly products of the very technological progress being celebrated. This didn't stop organisers of the 1933–34 Chicago world's fair from using the title *Century of Progress Exposition*, whose guidebook offered the slogan: "Science Finds – Industry Applies – Man Conforms". This particular event hosted two new 628-ft (191-m) high towers, the tallest in the city at the time, set 1,850 ft (546 m) apart, supporting a "rocket car" that travelled on cables between the two structures. The most popular exhibit was built by the Ford Motor Company at a cost of $US 5 million (roughly $US 122 million in 2024 dollars), a statement in and of itself that the firm was doing well despite that fact that it was struggling financially, like every other carmaker during the prolonged economic slump of the 1930s. The 900-ft (274-m) long building displayed an assembly plant, a globe depicting the company's international plants, and models of historic highways (Encyclopedia.com 2024).

The 1939 New York World's Fair similarly promised to show visitors "the world of tomorrow". Here the most popular feature was again built by a car company, in this case General Motors, which hosted an entire pavilion, inside of which was a ride called "Futurama". Participants were strapped into moving armchairs and passed over a large diorama showing the (American) world as it was to be in 1960, in this case a country dotted with straight superhighways speeding traffic through cities and rural areas alike, more efficiently than ever before. This particular exhibit was based on applications of existing technologies and thus proved to be fairly accurate in its projections about car-based sprawl – although this term was not used and the tone was upbeat not cautionary. Other exhibits depicted cities and societies of tomorrow, touting urban landscapes consisting of high-rise buildings containing apartments full of labour-saving appliances.

There were also various futuristic devices, including a robot (Auer et al. 2016, 1–2).

The world did survive the upheavals of the 1930s, and the prosperity of the post-war decades of the 1950s and 1960s seemed especially promising. True, threats of environmental and nuclear catastrophe loomed, but the optimism about future technology was stronger than ever. Times might be hard but transport, at least could be made faster and easier, whatever else was going on in the world. At least this was the comforting belief in a modern, but earlier time.

because these were judged to slow things down too much and introduce too much error and caprice, was increasingly employed. Automation was implicit in mechanisation, since the latter involved arrogating tasks to machines. For example, Ford's assembly line essentially made human beings automatons in a chain of standardised parts and jobs run by a great mechanical chain. This was intense and mind-numbing work, with one worker's wife complaining that her husband was so tired upon coming home from the job that he laid down in bed and couldn't eat his supper. But the assembly line was so efficient that cars became an affordably priced household item that could nonetheless be steadily improved and adapted with every new production year. Ford was quite open about his processes and other industries quickly adopted them, from home appliances to furniture, eventually spreading even to basic services such as the fast food sector that emerged in the 1950s. The assembly-line model with human beings as cogs in machine processing became known as Fordism (Rees 2020).

Fordism however soon reached a number of limits. One was the need for mass consumption, namely a constant appetite for all the products that exponentially churned out of factories. The Great Depression brought this problem into sharp relief as highly technically efficient producers, like Ford, struggled, and sometimes failed, in the face of demand drought. The centralisation of mass production was another issue, since a lot of capital was tied up in any given production line and major product changes required massive expenses to retool production processes. Ford's 1927 Model A was a case in point, requiring plants to be shut down for months, only to sell poorly (after strong initial sales) when the global economy tanked (Rees 2020).

Once more, automation seemed to provide an answer to both problems. It just had to be applied completely, replacing human beings entirely. The basic goal was full and total managerial control over production. At a basic level, machines never got sick (though they could and did sometimes break), made no mistakes (theoretically, at least), and could be pushed to their limits without complaints or demand for more pay. Automation could also be used for process redesign and retooling itself, with more sophisticated machines doing the work, under human oversight and direction, and much more quickly and cheaply than the semi-automation of the assembly line. Technological change, first with computerisation and then digitalisation, accelerated this trend and made production more economical, leaner, more flexible, and more adaptable, especially with the ability for "batch" production of smaller specialised product runs that allowed for "mass customisation" to appeal to smaller groups of consumers rather than just a generalised mass. For this reason automation appeared to solve some of the mass consumption problem as well, in that demand management could go beyond creating new mass appetites – though this remained extremely important – but meet and shape-changing demand segments in a dynamic and focused fashion as well.

21.2 THE PRESENT AS PAST'S PROLOGUE

The cliché about history is that those who forget it are doomed to repeat it. But perhaps the more accurate credo is to recognise how much of the past remains in the present. Techno-utopianism is currently the rage and much of mainstream discourse offers prognostications about brave new worlds powered by advanced science and smart tech that will eliminate all the limitations and inconveniences of the present techno-social-economic order. On the transport front, emissions-free, hyper-efficient, hydrogen-powered, and fully autonomous vehicles will provide unlimited point-to-point travel for individuals anywhere they wish to go, at any time, and without congestion, because smart networks will fully optimise traffic flow while eliminating accidents. Drones will effortlessly accomplish drayage on the freight side, while "space" – at least travel above the earth's atmosphere – will be the medium for all manner of mass – and ultimately possibly personalised – space modes. All this will emerge within a fully networked "smart" system consisting of smart cities, smart neighbourhoods, and smart devices, all managed through artificial intelligence (AI).

Future projections such as this are unassailable in the sense that they are about what might happen, and might-haves are always arguably possible at some point, however unlikely they might seem today. But the continuities between today and yesterday can be analysed and critiqued as to what they suggest about what tomorrow might plausibly look like. This exercise suggests a much less "innovative" future. The modes responsible for most of the movements in 2024 are essentially modifications of inventions that have been with us since 1924 and before – the automobile, the ship, the jet plane, and the train. The major technical advances in that time have been around safety, capacity, and, following from the first two, operating efficiency, with gains in maritime and aviation being the most notable. Average speed has not increased much, and in aviation, it has actually gone backwards, especially with the lapse of commercially available supersonic travel in the 1980s. Rocketry and space travel have definitely advanced, particularly in military applications, such as missiles and drones, with some of these innovations bleeding into civilian applications. But rocket travel into space for anyone but the very rich seems decades away.

Granted, the way modes operate has rather dramatically changed, with automation, smart technology, and robotics penetrating rather deeply. This has been especially true in freight, where ships are loaded and unloaded with just a few humans in charge, and literal auto-pilot doing most of the driving for both planes and ships. Automobile operating has also been substantially altered, with adaptive cruise control and other levels of semi-automation being adopted effectively. But a driver of a century ago would still draw on roughly the same skills as required today, though with considerably more safety, comfort, and speed.

Moving from the vehicle technology to the system level, the picture looks a bit less advanced, especially if the time-frame is cut in half, to 1974–2024, still a long time in technology cycles. New surface roads have been built since then, with improved materials, electronic guidance and tolling systems, and better design principles. But much of the road system of 50 years ago is actually still largely in place in most rich countries, not always in better condition, with new roads substantively built and managed along the same lines. Air traffic control is better and there are new and improved airports. But congestion is arguably worse (the same can be said for roads) and the biggest changes in airports have come with commercial and intermodal development. Airports are now big centres of economic value-add in their own right. Maritime ports actually have improved their transport and commercial performance the most, becoming highly specialised and yet interconnected and capable of efficiently handling huge amounts of cargo. Railways have also seen substantial improvement in some regions, with major HSR construction in China especially, but also in many other places, like Spain. Transit too has seen innovation, though not especially high-tech, bus rapid transit (BRT) being a major improvement of capacity delivered cost-effectively with enhanced versions of the coach. All of this is impressive, but it is hardly transformative from a travel perspective.

21.3 FUTURE PROJECTIONS

So the present of transport looks different as compared to how it looked 50 or 100 years ago, but not unrecognisably so. This doesn't mean that the next 50 or 100 years will not offer dramatic change. But at the dawn of the 20th century, when the doctrine of scientific progress was at its height, and new fundamental fields of science and technology, ranging from aviation, mechanised transport, electrification, pharmaceuticals, synthetic materials, and many others, were all born within just a few decades before, radical projections seemed well justified. The technical shifts witnessed in over the two and half decades after the dawn of the 21st century are far less awe-inspiring, impressive as some of them have been.

The Fordism of the assembly-line economy was replaced with a series of progressive phases referred to collectively with various labels such as post-Fordism, knowledge economy, and post-industrialism. These terms are somewhat misleading in suggesting that industrial production has somehow been replaced or supplanted, eliminating all the dirtiness, dislocation, and centralisation that this came with. In fact, mass production and mass consumption are both still operative, though now geographically more dispersed and with system control exercised digitally and virtually in greater proportion to the mechanical analogue direction that was so dominant earlier. Production is much cleaner, probably the major advance of the times, though not nearly clean enough from a climate change perspective. As noted above, production systems can produce much more variegated output across a whole range of batch sizes, with real-time information management allowing for less physical co-location and more decentralisation across spatially widely dispersed contractors. But throughput and unit-output per unit-input maximisation delivered through returns to scale (RTS) and economies of scale (EOS) remain the motive forces of operation. Standardisation and control has become more subtle but it still required on a maximal scale.

How might the future of several decades out plausibly look given development along technical and social lines already well laid down? This is a more narrow but more tractable and perhaps relevant question than the blue-sky musing of much futurism, however useful that may be.

Although the rhetoric of "smart" technology is individualistic and decentralised, the promised gains rely almost exclusively on tightly controlled top-down systems. One of the cutting-edges here is in the Gulf States of the Middle East, such as Saudi Arabia, Dubai, and the United Arab Emirates. These countries have grown rapidly on unplanned trajectories leading to more populous cities with more cars – seemingly the default scenario of most places on the globe without policy shaping of some sort. Autonomous driverless personal vehicles and similarly guided transit vehicles are being implemented in some places such as Doha and Kuwait City. But upon closer inspection, their safe and reliable operation requires substantial investments in street-level guidance systems that effectively automate the streets. And in some cases, such as Doha's metro system, automation is accomplished by driverless vehicles in entirely closed systems moving within loops akin to airport people-movers (Alamoudi et al. 2024). In other words central control via an entirely new or heavily augmented existing infrastructure is required. Arguably this is Fordism, updated for the digital age, rather than a new technical or scientific paradigm. Such updating offers efficiency advantages, but also the same challenges as arose during the First Industrial Revolution.

21.4 RESOURCE LIMITS

Human beings have always been environmental disruptors. Even their primate ancestors have historically taken heavy tolls on their local ecosystems, perhaps an outgrowth of the imaginative "monkey mind" we humans have inherited. Industrialisation has merely vastly increased the scale and scope of that impact on both the existing "natural" environment, and the human-made "environments" that people are now completely dependent on. The interactions between the two are perhaps as important as what is going on in either separate realm.

The sustainability and resilience of both earth and human sociotechnical systems has been discussed at length in Chapter 13. The solutions to earth system macro-stresses being proposed and implemented are almost entirely technological in nature. As noted already these proposed adaptations work mostly within existing social and economic patterns of consumption, production, and activity, with the main changes being to energy sources for existing modes of travel, and with the use of information technology to make the infrastructure within which they move more efficient and less dirty.

The likelihood of these solutions affecting the required transformation is debatable on both earth system and human system terms. On the former, they imitate the many tweaks and innovations that kept environmental crisis at bay during the intensifying negative externalities and imbalances of industrialisation. There was then a policy-forcing component and a technical change component, as there are now. The UK, for example, imposed public health laws, industrial emissions regulations, and land use requirements in the 19th century, though rather tepidly at first, and these became more widely adopted and expanded by various developed nations, peaking with the environmental movement of the 1970s. These policy limits arguably had the greater impact on ecological damage, more so than technical improvements, most of which were focused on productivity rather than cleanliness, though things like fuel-efficiency enhancements that came out of efficiency drives did have salutary ecological benefits. Policy changes were largely national in scope until the 1970s when some problems, including climate change, were recognised as requiring international action.

Now, in a sense, the pendulum has reversed. Policy forcing has waned, replaced with market-mimicking trading and carbon charging schemes, and subsidies for "clean" fuels and "smart" technologies. These are judged to be more efficient and effective than the old blunt regulatory instruments of the past. There is also now a large international policy apparatus studying global impacts and effecting global agreements on transnational action; though much implementation, and even much of the strongest policies are still being exercised through national governments at national levels.

Putting aside the tactical questions of how well this approach is actually working, one does have to interrogate whether there is enough earth system left, so to speak, to wring efficiencies out of. Even before the Industrial Revolution, societies around the planet were constantly suffering and then escaping eco-crisis by adopting new food crops and technologies, shifting trade relations, and sometimes taking resources from elsewhere by force through war and colonialism. These solutions "worked" because there was plenty of "slack" in the global ecology which governments and individuals could exploit to offload their own environmental costs. But the whole world, and individual nations, probably cannot rely on such slack any more, even with technologies and markets delivering some partial gains. Even when measuring single resource bases, modern human consumption has been prodigious. By one estimate, humans now directly consume 18% of the total available freshwater runoff of the globe, while appropriating 54% of it (Simeonov 2019).

Additionally, even if one could stop every environmental degrading activity tomorrow – obviously impossible – the on-going effects of what has already been done are long-lived. This is well-recognised for greenhouse gases (GHG). But the stopping of production and use of ozone-layer-depleting chlorofluorocarbons (CFCs) by international agreement in 1989, one of the few truly successful global environmental pacts thus far, has left much of this very stable compound in the atmosphere contributing to what has been called the "ultraviolet century" of 1970–2070, as the ozone "hole" only gradually reduces. And at a very coarse level, the amount of "space junk" orbiting at speeds of around 30,000 kph, is still being added to and cannot be easily reduced even if it were not constantly augmented (Simeonov 2019). Many other examples could be cited.

Finally, technology creates its own problems which more technology often only adds to. In the transport arena, a 1992 World Bank estimated that particulates alone in the world's cities killed between 300,000 and 700,000 people a year, and other research speculated that air pollution killed about 20–30 million between 1950 and 1997, and perhaps 25–40 million deaths across the whole 20th century (Simeonov 2019). Safety is a prime transport policy concern and yet it seems that only local remediation is possible, especially given the nature of modern transport itself with its emphasis on speed. The Covid-19 pandemic showed that even with the widespread use of environmental disease control with its methods of vaccines, antibiotics, and public health systems, microbial resistance has led to the comeback of microbial infections. Technical systems, in other words, offer the prospect of total control, but this control is not only elusive but perhaps ultimately self-defeating in the broadest sense.

21.5 THE FUTURE HUMAN BEING IN A FUTURE SOCIETY

In fact, the ultimate control would be gained, according to technologists, by merging human and machine completely. Ray Kurzweil, a former director of engineering at Google, has argued that this merger, which he refers to as "Singularity", will have taken place by the middle of this current century, powered by massively powerful computers equipped with massively sophisticated AI which will have scanners able to map brains neuron by neuron, and enough computing power and storage have a complete database of all 8 or more billion minds in the world to run decision-guiding programmes that individuals can use in real time. These machine-based minds will be fully networked, constantly sharing information with one another. The apotheosis will be carbon- and silicon-based intelligence coming together in a single global consciousness (Kurzweil 2005). A world like this will look rather close to that of the "core" model – disembodied, optimising, maximising, effectively transcending time and space, and it is only several decades away, if one believes Kurzweil.

This triumphalist prediction is bold, and almost certainly wrong, at least in the time-frame given. Even AI, despite the massive (tech industry-funded) hype that is all around as of this writing, is still basically hyper-charged data processing paired with rapid and massive iterative algorithmic calculation – impressive on its own terms, but probably not "intelligence" in the full sense of that word (see Chapter 8). But it does point to a widespread mind-set in some circles which fully accepts the necessity and desirability of transforming human beings into machines, the latter said to be superior in every respect.

Is this vision a beautiful dream or a nightmare? The motto of the 1933–34 Chicago World's Fair can be usefully repeated here: "Science Finds – Industry Applies – Man Conforms". Even if one assumes the beneficence of the first two terms (a rather questionable proposition), the last imperative of "conformity" should give one pause. The human need to adapt to technology – technisation using Elias's parlance (see Chapter 19) – is required to make any technological advance work. But there can be too much a "good" thing.

Modern transport supposedly gets people where they want to go when they want to get there as fast and as cheaply as possibly. But the social reality does not always seem to match this ideal. For example, many people now effectively live and work in multiple places, with the concept of home and workplace, and journeys between them, becoming indistinct (Pooley 2009, 144). Places and locations have, in some ways, become more indistinct from one another, more functional, and less rooted, leading to what some social theorists refer to "placelessness". Modern infrastructure like highways, rail corridors, and airports often look like one another, passing through locations that are identified only by signage. These "in-between" transport facilities are designed to make transport smoother and faster, but they also can be experienced as "non-places" of excess information, mediated social relations, and insulation from the "real" world which itself becomes just a collection of objectives to reach in particular nondescript locations. Economic activity is done in many such non-places such as hotel lobbies, shopping centres, office parks, and suburban strip malls (Merriman 2009, 138–140).

Of course one should not overstate or romanticise social and "meaning" elements of transport systems, nor deny the positive aspects of modern transport. But social sustainability is as important as the environmental sustainability of engineered systems and technology. A lack of social sustainability can easily undermine environmental sustainability, as with the car, which is now being branded as part of the solution to climate change even though some of the impetus for this is no doubt being shaped by the significant social status that driving and cars has in society already, as well as the motives of strong vested interests. And even "mere" technological solutions require significant changes to social institutions, structures, beliefs, and meanings to be implemented, with a good technical idea possibly un-implementable if the precise social means of achieving of ends are not clearly understood and planned for (Timms et al. 2014, 80).

21.6 UPDATING OUR MODELS

Economic theory posits a short-run and long-run, the former being a time when relatively little can be changed. In the long-run supposedly most everything is changeable. But the biggest door to true transformation is a change in the way the world is thought about and seen by both ordinary human beings and specialists.

Transport economics as currently practised is quite powerful and elucidating, but also quite limiting. The omission of human sociality, the still relatively short-shrift given to non-rational behaviour, and the focus on optimisation and maximisation of material consumption and production through a decentralised process of bargaining between atomistic agents working through minimally articulated markets: all these depart from facts on the ground rather extremely. Indeed, economic reality began to move away from these features even before the First Industrial Revolution was over, as large-scale producers and mass economies began to become more fully formed. No model is meant to be "realistic" of course, and practitioners of the core model have augmented it to include many useful explanations of things like property rights, institutions, behavioural quirks, and other unique facets of the human animal. A primary purpose of this book is, in fact, to show all that economic theory can accomplish and how adaptable it is in explaining and predicting transport function and execution.

But theory should also evolve appropriately with the times and the core model is not always sufficient to the tasks at hand. These gaps can be filled in no small order by models and approaches from other disciplines such as planning, engineering, sociology, psychology, philosophy, health, and political science, to name a few that have been considered in this volume. The field of transport broadly defined is already highly polyglot and collaborative so there is already a good foundation of interdisciplinarity to work with.

Still, close and critical reflection on one's own field, as well as of others, is required to change thinking purposefully and usefully. This book has taken the approach of breaking down transport economics into its first principles and working up from there. This investigation indicates at a minimum that institutions and their "internal" markets are much more relevant to present and future transport systems than a model based on perfectly competitive markets; that earth system resource limits need to be put in the foreground rather than the background; and that the methodological benchmark of consumer sovereignty is both ethically and theoretically debatable. These and other issues have been plumbed in this book and readers can draw their own conclusions. The opinion of this author is that some major revision of transport economic theory is required and that some existing constructs often serve as obstacles rather than aids to clarity and understanding.

Timms et al. (2014) offer the concept of exploratory futures as a device not so much of prediction, but of conceiving of and comparing different "visions", defined as images of desirable and undesirable scenarios (80–81). This ideally should be a conscious process that highlights strengths and limits of current thinking and explores unknowns, uncertainties, and hidden biases in that thinking.

Indeed, "modernism" and "modernity" could be argued to have been a sort of visioning that was actually somewhat unconscious, embedded with an assumption that human problems were primarily material and technical in nature and that all solutions were thus material and technical also. In effect technical innovation would not only technically optimise, but would socially optimise as well, a circular conclusion that follows from the implicit assumption of thoroughgoing materialism in all dimensions. The competing modernist transport paradigms of the 20th century all focused on optimising the distance-location-travel time choice bundle in three different possible ways: the great metropolis – using mass transit and active travel in the city and "rapid" expressways cutting through the city to go to other cities and places; moderate decentralisation, in which different precincts were designed for living and working, lowering the costs and dis-amenities of density in exchange for having to travel more distance served by multiple modes of medium speed; and extreme decentralisation in which the car served every travel need while giving individuals maximum choice of designing their own personal environment (Timms et al. 2014, 85).

In many ways our current society has manifested a changing mix of all three visions, though now with increasing density everywhere combined with a primary reliance on auto travel in most places. The modernist vision has its pros and cons but one thing it lacked was any interrogation of how the flywheel of the entire vision, the automobile, should be deployed and developed in the broader natural environment in a way compatible with human social, ethical, and cultural development. To put this another way, the interaction between the car (or any transport mode) and human "civilisation" (in the sense of a long-standing macro-culture and leaving aside normative judgements) were taken for granted as being positive because the technical change was judged as a forward move.

But technology is never neutral with respect to society, as modern history shows. Now, especially, any theory of transport economics must centrally incorporate the contribution of a transport change, negative and positive, to civilisation in the broad sense given above. The models used should consider how introduction of a technical change into the wild (so to speak) also ensures that human society is advanced along with technical progress. This author has argued elsewhere that this was not done with the car and that much "carbarism" (a play on the word "barbarism" as defined as anything going against norms and behaviour central to humaneness) has resulted – though, of course the net results are subtle and complex (Gordon 2017).

Laying out a "reformed" or more fully revised theory of transport economics is obviously well beyond the scope of this book, which has focused on critically laying out what current thinking is, rather than what it should be. But such a revision is a critical collaborative project to effectively and humanely respond to the changes already upon us, which require much more than technical attention and effort. It is needed to better understand present challenges and likely future scenarios, rather than uncritically accepting any prediction as definite.

REFERENCES

Alamoudi, M., Imam, A., Majrashi, A., Osra, O., & Hegazy, I. (2024). Integrating intelligent and sustainable transportation systems in Jeddah: A multidimensional approach for urban mobility enhancement. *International Journal of Low-Carbon Technologies*, 19, 1301–1314. https://doi.org/10.1093/ijlct/ctae078

Auer, A., Feese, S., & Lockwood, S. (2016). *History of intelligent transportation systems*. US Department of Transportation Intelligent Transportation Systems Joint Program Office, Publication Number: FHWA-JPO-16-329.

Encyclopedia.com (2024). World's fairs 1933–1939. *Historic Events for Students: The Great Depression*. www.encyclopedia.com/education/news-and-education-magazines/worlds-fairs-1933-1939, Retrieved September 11, 2024.

Gordon, C. (2017). Carbarism: Civilising the automobile. *World Transport Policy and Practice*, 23(1), 27–39.

Kurzweil, R. (2005). *The singularity is near: When humans transcend biology*. Viking.

Merriman, P. (2009). Mobility. In Kitchin, Rob and Thrift, Nigel (eds). *International encyclopedia of human geography*. Elsevier, 134–143.

Pooley, C. G. (2009). Mobility, history of everyday. In Kitchin, Rob and Thrift, Nigel (eds). *International encyclopedia of human geography*. Elsevier, 144–149.

Rees, J. (2020). Industrialization and urbanization in the United States. In *Oxford research encyclopedia, American history*. Oxford University Press.

Simeonov, V. (2019). Environmental history of the twentieth century. An introductory didactic course. *Chemistry-Didactics-Ecology-Metrology*, 24(1–2), 7–21.

Timms, P., Tight, M., & Watling, D. (2014). Imagineering mobility: Constructing utopias for future urban transport. *Environment and Planning A*, 46(1), 78–93.

INDEX

Note: Figures are indicated by *italics*. Tables are indicated by **bold**.